'To portray the Holocaust, one has to create a work of art', says Claude Lanzmann, the director of *Shoah*. But can the Holocaust be turned into theatre? Is it possible to portray on stage events that by their monstrosity defy human comprehension? These are the questions addressed by the playwrights and the scholars featured in this book. Their chapters present and analyse plays performed in Israel, America, France, Italy, Poland and, of course, Germany. The style of presentation ranges from docudramas to avant-garde performances, from realistic impersonation of historical figures to provocative and nightmarish spectacles. The book is illustrated with original production photographs and some rare drawings and documents; it also contains an important descriptive bibliography of over 200 Holocaust plays.

Staging the Holocaust

CAMBRIDGE STUDIES IN MODERN THEATRE

Series editor

Professor David Bradby, *Royal Holloway, University of London*

Advisory board

Martin Banham, *University of Leeds*
Jacky Bratton, *Royal Holloway, University of London*
Tracy Davis, *Northwestern University*
Richard Eyre
Michael Robinson, *University of East Anglia*
Sheila Stowell, *University of Birmingham*

Volumes for Cambridge Studies in Modern Theatre explore the political, social and cultural functions of theatre while also paying careful attention to detailed performance analysis. The focus of the series is on political approaches to the modern theatre, with attention also being paid to theatres of earlier periods and their influence on contemporary drama. Topics in the series are chosen to investigate this relationship and include both playwrights (their aims and intentions set against the effects of their work) and process (with emphasis on rehearsal and production methods, the political structure within theatre companies, and their choice of audiences or performance venues). Further topics will include devised theatre, agitprop, community theatre, para-theatre and performance art. In all cases the series will be alive to the special cultural and political factors operating in the theatres they examine.

Books published

Brian Crow with Chris Banfield, *An introduction to post-colonial theatre*
Maria DiCenzo, *The politics of alternative theatre in Britain, 1968–1990: 7:84 (Scotland)*
Jonathan Kalb, *The theatre of Heiner Müller*
Jo Riley, *Chinese theatre and the actor in performance*
Claude Schumacher, ed., *Staging the Holocaust, The Shoah in drama and performance*

Staging the Holocaust

The Shoah in drama and performance

edited by
Claude Schumacher

CAMBRIDGE
UNIVERSITY PRESS

PUBLISHED BY THE PRESS SYNDICATE OF THE UNIVERSITY OF CAMBRIDGE
The Pitt Building, Trumpington Street, Cambridge CB2 1RP, United Kingdom

CAMBRIDGE UNIVERSITY PRESS
The Edinburgh Building, Cambridge CB2 2RU, United Kingdom
http://www.cup.cam.ac.uk
40 West 20th Street, New York, NY 10011–4211, USA
http://www.cup.org
10 Stamford Road, Oakleigh, Melbourne 3166, Australia

First published 1998

Printed in the United Kingdom at the University Press, Cambridge

Typeset in Trump Mediaeval and Schadow BT, in QuarkXPress™ GC

A catalogue record for this book is available from the British Library

Library of Congress cataloguing in publication data

Staging the Holocaust: the Shoah in drama and performance / edited by
Claude Schumacher.
        p. cm. (Cambridge Studies in Modern Theatre)
Includes bibliographical references and index.
ISBN 0 521 62415 0 (hardback)
1. Drama – 20th century – History and criticism.   2. Holocaust.
Jewish (1939–45), in literature.   3. Jews in literature.
1. Series.
PN1879.H65S72   1998
809.2'9358–dc21   97–28656   CIP

ISBN 0 521 62415 0 hardback

Contents

Contents

Illustrations

FIGURES

Figures 1–7 are in the chapter 'Representation and Unrepresentability:
Primo Levi's Stage Version of *Se questo è un uomo* at Turin's Teatro
Stabile', by Helga Finter, on pp. 239–49. Drawings by Helga Finter of the
reconstruction of the scenery, after the production photographs, 1997.

Contributors

ATAY CITRON heads the School of Visual Theatre in Jerusalem. He also
teaches the subjects of ritual, carnival and the avant-garde at the
Department of Theatre Arts, Tel Aviv University.

ANAT FEINBERG studied at Tel Aviv and London Universities and now
teaches at the Hochschule für jüdische Studien in Heidelberg.
She has published *Wiedergutmachung im Programm: Jüdisches
Schicksal im deutschen Nachkriegsdrama* (Cologne, 1988), articles
on Jacobean, modern German, Austrian and Hebrew drama and
literature. She has edited two anthologies on Israeli literature and
culture in German, and she is the author of three novels (written
in Hebrew). She is currently writing a book on Tabori's theatre.

HELGA FINTER is Professor and Director of the Institute of Theatre
Studies at the Justus-Liebig University in Giessen. She has
written extensively on modern theatre and literature (futurism,
Mallarmé, Jarry, Roussel, Bataille . . .). Her current work focuses
on avant-garde theatre and performance art in Europe and the
United States. She also works as dramaturge in Frankfurt (Theater
am Turm) and Strasbourg (Opéra du Rhin).

ALVIN GOLDFARB is Dean of the College of Fine Arts and Professor of
Theatre at Illinois State University. He has published articles,
notes and reviews in many journals and scholarly anthologies,
including *Theatre Journal, Performing Arts Journal* and *Journal of
American Drama and Theatre.* He is the co-author with Edwin
Wilson of *Theater: The Lively Art, Living Theater* and *Anthology
of Living Theater.*

HANK GREENSPAN is a psychologist, playwright and lecturer at the
University of Michigan. He is the author of *Recounting the*

xiii

Holocaust: Survivors and their Listeners, and numerous articles about survivors' recounting. Among his plays, *That Again* and *No Survivors* have been staged at the University of Michigan. *Slideshow* and *Call Forwarding* have been finalists in the Playwrights Studio Theatre Festival: they were presented in Milwaukee in 1994 and 1996 respectively.

JOHN IRELAND, Assistant Professor of French at the University of Illinois, Chicago, is the author of *Sartre, un art déloyal. Théâtralité et engagement* (Paris: Place, 1994) and a number of articles on contemporary French literature and theatre. He is currently working with a CNRS team on the first complete edition of Sartre's theatre to be published in the Pléiade collection.

GAD KAYNAR lectures at the Department of Theatre Arts, Tel Aviv University. He writes on dramatic and theatrical reception theory, performance analysis, intertextuality, German expressionism, contemporary German drama, Israeli performance art, and Holocaust theatre. He has translated some thirty plays into Hebrew, including works by Strindberg, Dürrenmatt, Kipphardt, Kroetz, Süsskind, Tabori and Ingmar Bergman. He is currently dramaturge and head of the education department at Habima, Tel Aviv. He also pursues an active career as stage, screen and television actor. Has published two books of poetry.

ROY KIFT is an English dramatist who has lived in Germany since 1981. His play, *Stronger than Superman* (GRIPS Theatre, Berlin, 1981), ran for 214 performances and has been staged in over twenty countries. His translations of Molière, Goldoni, Süsskind, Kipphardt and Volker Ludwig have been performed on stage and radio in Great Britain. He has published articles and reviews in *Theatre Quarterly, New Theatre Quarterly, Theatre Research International* and *Western European Stages,* directs professionally and in drama schools. He is author of two Holocaust plays, both set in Theresienstadt: *Dreams of Beating Time* (1987) and *Camp Comedy* (1996).

DOROTHY KNOWLES, Docteur d'Etat en Sorbonne, Honorary Research Fellow of Royal Holloway College, London University, was Professor of French at Liverpool University. There she directed over twenty productions, most memorably Gatti's *La Vie imaginaire de l'éboueur Auguste Geai*. She published *The Censor, the Drama and the Film, 1900–1934* in 1934, followed by *French Drama of the Inter-War Years, 1918–1939, La Réaction idéaliste au théâtre depuis 1890* and more recently *Armand Gatti in the Theatre: Wild Duck Against the Wind* (1989). She has written extensively on all aspects of French culture, theatre and literature.

DAN LAOR is Professor of Modern Hebrew Literature and Head of the Department of Hebrew Literature at Tel Aviv University. He is the author of many books and articles on modern Hebrew literature and culture, including several works related to Holocaust literature. In 1992 he won the Yad Vashem Buchmann Prize for his contribution to the teaching and research of Holocaust literature. He has recently completed the biography of S. Y. Agnon, to be published by Schocken Books in Israel in 1997.

JEANETTE R. MALKIN is Senior Lecturer and Chair of the Theatre Studies Department at the Hebrew University, Jerusalem. She is the author of *Verbal Violence in Contemporary Drama: From Handke to Shepard* (Cambridge University Press, 1992), and *Memory Theater and Postmodern Drama* (University of Michigan Press). Her articles on German/Austrian drama, and on Postmodernism, have appeared in academic journals such as *Modern Drama, Theatre Journal*, and *Journal of Dramatic Theory and Criticism*.

YEHUDA MORALY is Professor at the Theatre Department of the Hebrew University, Jerusalem. His main fields of research are Genet's theoretical texts and Claudel's directing experiments (*Jean Genet, la vie écrite*, 1988; 'Claudel and Vitez Direct Molière' in *The Play Out of Context*, Cambridge University Press, 1989). He is also a director (*The Beauty and the Beast; The Dispute of Barcelona*) and a playwright striving towards the creation of a new Jewish theatre (*Le Tombeau des poupées*, Palais de Chaillot, 1983; *La Musique*, France-Culture, 1993).

FREDDIE ROKEM is Professor at the Department of Theatre Arts at Tel Aviv University. He has published books on the history of the Swedish theatre and on theatrical space in Ibsen, Chekhov and

Strindberg, articles in scholarly journals on the theory of acting, performance theory, and the theatre of Strindberg, as well as Israeli theatre. He is associate editor of *Assaph: Studies in the Theatre* and *Theatre Journal*, translates Hebrew literature, mainly drama, into Swedish and works as a dramaturge.

CLAUDE SCHUMACHER teaches French theatre, directs for the stage and edits *Theatre Research International*. He has published on Marivaux, Musset, Jarry, Apollinaire, Artaud, Arrabal and Gatti. He is editor of *Naturalism and Symbolism in European Theatre, 1850–1918* (Cambridge University Press, 1996).

ROBERT SKLOOT is a stage director and Professor of Theatre and Drama and Jewish Studies at the University of Wisconsin, Madison. He has written extensively about the theatre and the Holocaust, including *The Darkness We Carry: The Drama of the Holocaust* (1988).

ALEXANDER STILLMARK was born in 1941. From 1964 to 1970 he directed at the Berliner Ensemble. From 1971 to 1986 he was director at the Deutsches Theater, Berlin. From 1987 to 1989 he taught at the 'Ernst Busch' School for Acting, Berlin. From 1989 to 1991 he was director at the Staatstheater, Schwerin. He is now a freelance director in Berlin. He has directed plays in Hanoi, Dacca and Helsinki, and on radio and television.

SETH WOLITZ is the Gale Professor of Jewish Studies and Professor of French, Slavic and Cultural Studies at the University of Texas at Austin. He has published many interdisciplinary studies, particularly *The Proustian Community*, and has written many articles on Jewish art and theatre in Israel and the United States.

Introduction

CLAUDE SCHUMACHER

However this war may end, we have won the war against you;
none of you will be left to bear witness, but even if someone
were to survive, the world would not believe him. There will
perhaps be suspicions, discussions, research by historians,
but there will be no certainties, because we will destroy the
evidence together with you. And even if some proof should
remain and some of you survive, people will say that the events
you describe are too monstrous to be believed; they will say that
they are the exaggerations of Allied propaganda and will believe
us, who will deny everything, and not you. We will be the ones
to dictate the history of the Lagers.

So spake some of Hitler's henchmen, 'cynically admonishing the prisoners' of the death camps.[1] Hitler, in the end, did not win. A few of his
victims were spared annihilation and they came back to bear witness. A
few returned, fewer testified, fewer still were listened to.

In his last book, completed weeks before his suicide, Primo Levi
– who had been one of the very first to confront the nightmare of
l'univers concentrationnaire, from which he had been delivered at the
end of the war – declares that he, as a survivor, cannot claim to be a true
witness to the Nazi hell:

---

[1] Quoted in Primo Levi, *The Drowned and the Saved* trans. Raymond
Rosenthal, introduced by Paul Bailey (London: Abacus, 1989; originally
published, New York: Summit Books, 1988), p. 1, from Simon
Wiesenthal, *The Murderers Are Among Us*.

> I must repeat – we, the survivors, are not the true witnesses. This is an uncomfortable notion, of which I have become conscious little by little, reading the memoirs of others and reading mine at a distance of years. We survivors are not only an exiguous but also an anomalous minority: we are those . . . who did not touch bottom. Those who did so, those who saw the Gorgon, have not returned to tell about it or have returned mute, but they are the 'Muselmen', the submerged, the complete witness, the ones whose deposition would have a general significance. They are the rule, we are the exception.[2]

Some of the 'exception', exceptional men and women who through 'good luck' (Levi's expression) survived, chose on their return to speak, not just hoping, but convinced that the world would be eager to listen sympathetically to the victims of an unheard-of evil. Robert Antelme, in the foreword to L'Espèce humaine, reflects on the verbal delirium to which survivors succumbed: at last they could speak (speak again); at last they would be heard. But the world (their families, their friends) refused to listen – they were told that their ghostly physical appearance was eloquent enough – and the survivors came up against an unexpected and insurmountable obstacle. Soon, to the survivors themselves, to the victims who still bore all the scars of months and years of torture, what they had suffered took on an air of unreality, what had happened to them became unimaginable; the monstrously unimaginable became unimaginable even to those who had endured the unimaginable: 'A nous-mêmes, ce que nous avions à dire commençait alors à nous paraître *inimaginable*.'[3] If the experience of the Nazi atrocities, so deeply inscribed in their minds and bodies, proved so intractably difficult to communicate by the victims themselves, what hope is there for others to speak or to understand the *univers concentrationnaire* in a deep, meaningful way? These questions have haunted, are haunting every human being who desperately wants to grasp that which is beyond understanding. 'The Nazi slaughter', says Primo Levi, is 'dreadfully

---

[2] Ibid., pp. 63–4.
[3] Robert Antelme, L'Espèce humaine (Paris: Gallimard, 1996), p. 9. Written in 1946–7, L'Espèce humaine was first published in 1957.

"exemplary" and, if nothing worse happens in the coming years, it will be remembered as the central event, the scourge of this century.'[4]

As I write this introduction (May 1997) new facts and fresh revelations are being uncovered. Yesterday (Tuesday, 20 May 1997) the British media announced that documents, dated September 1941 and now released by the Public Record Office, reveal that the slaughter of hundreds of thousands of Jews started in occupied Russia a year before the Nazis 'officially' launched their Final Solution. More facts will come out as the secret archives dealing with World War Two are gradually opened. But, at a distance of more than fifty years, are new facts going to help the world towards a deeper understanding?

'To portray the Holocaust', Claude Lanzmann once said to Raul Hilberg, 'one has to create a work of art.' And Hilberg to comment: 'such recreation is an act of creation in and of itself'.[5] Raul Hilberg is, of course, the author of the most comprehensive, meticulously documented, closely argued analysis of the Nazi destruction of the European Jews. Without his courageous and painstaking historical work our understanding of the mechanism and the process of the Nazi genocide would be greatly impaired. Yet, despite his devotion to academic precision and intellectual clarity, he recognizes that, to bring us (those of us who were lucky enough to be spared the horrors of the war) anywhere near a grasp of what the Holocaust could have been, a daring imaginative leap is required.

Can theatre provide the artefact that will help the spectator towards a better 'grasp' of the Holocaust? Is such a theatrical 'recreation' justified? And if it is, how can an actor hope to portray either the perpetrator or the victim, without glamorizing or demonizing the former and belittling or sanctifying the latter? Such questions are not simply legitimate, they are so fundamental that the contributors to this volume address them over and over again; they are most cogently raised in Robert Skloot's opening chapter.

---

[4] Levi, *The Drowned and the Saved*, p. 8.

[5] Raul Hilberg, *The Politics of Memory: The Journey of a Holocaust Historian* (Chicago: Ivan R. Dee, 1996), p. 83.

That an artistic creation or re-creation has a positive impact on its beholder is self-evident. The reason why the question is raised here is because the Holocaust is an event of such magnitude[6] that no play text or theatrical performance can hope to get anywhere near the truth. And, whatever Theodor Adorno said, or meant to say, about the barbaric impossibility of writing music after Auschwitz, his remark touched a nerve and it cannot be dismissed lightly.

Charlotte Delbo, in one of the rare plays that is set *inside* an extermination camp, *Qui rapportera ces paroles?*, ends her prologue by asking, provocatively: 'pourquoi dire'. Why speak, indeed, 'puisque ces choses que je pourrais dire / ne vous serviront / A rien . . .', since what she says will be of no use to us because the meaning of the words are not the same to her and to her audience. Her answer is the play itself. Deported in 1943 to Auschwitz, she came back in 1945, and she survived because she was determined to let the world know. Delbo's prologue is echoed by Elie Wiesel in his dialogue with Jorge Semprun: 'Se taire est interdit, parler est impossible' ('Forbidden to keep quiet, impossible to speak').[7]

To bear witness is one thing, but to 'perform' the testimony is another. The staging of a theatrical text requires the physical presence of the actor, that 'other', that 'impostor' who was not in Auschwitz. How can that actor, who lives in the same world as us, who performs in the same space which, we, the audience, inhabit, how can that actor effectively convince us that he is a camp inmate, a Nazi officer, or even a survivor from those days? My answer is that theatre – theatre which has true integrity and the highest artistic standards – does not try to create an illusion of reality (that cheap kind of mimetism found in cinema or television), and it is precisely in the absence of mimetic *trompe-l'œil* that the real strength of the theatrical performance lies. True theatre affords the spectator a heightened experience 'liberated from the lie of being the truth'.

---

[6] 'The destruction of the Jews was an unprecedented occurrence, a primordial act that had not been imagined before it burst forth.' Ibid., p. 84.

[7] Jorge Semprun and Elie Wiesel, *Se taire est impossible* (Paris: Arte, 1995). Transcript of a television programme, *Entretien*, broadcast on Arte, 1 March 1995.

Theatre, by the very presence of the actor on the stage, under-lines the absence of the character. Antony Sher on stage proclaims the absence of Arturo Ui. As far as we are concerned, dealing with plays about the Shoah, the actor on stage clearly signifies the absence, from the here-and-now, of the character he is presenting. His being there pro-claims the absence of the 'other' and the spectator must, in order to make sense of what is presented, reconstruct in his mind the missing reality and lend his own being, thoughts and emotions, to the character evoked by the actor.

But can theatre raise the spectator's awareness of the Holocaust? In the first chapter of this collection, Robert Skloot argues that, diffi-cult as the task may be, the theatre remains perhaps the only place 'to advance – with decreasing credibility or efficacy – images and explana-tions for events that leave only the irreparable and the opaque as their legacy', the only art form that will convey 'the reality of an unreality whose aim was genocide'.

At a recent Holocaust conference, Alvin Rosenfeld has argued that 'the public at large remains readily drawn by the spectre of the Holocaust' and that there 'is a receptive audience for stories and images of the Third Reich'; he then went on to investigate the nature of the stor-ies and images that are being proposed by some storytellers and image makers.[8] Rosenfeld's perceptive analysis of the reception of Spielberg's *Schindler's List* concludes that the film has 'the effect of dislodging earlier and more difficult feelings of shame and guilt that typically accompany reactions of the persecution and mass slaughter of Europe's Jews'. The reason for the dislodging of difficult feelings is located by Rosenfeld in a characteristic American urge to find a redemptive mean-ing in every event and a longing for the 'happy end'. This is not the place to undertake a radical critique of Spielberg's film which, in my estima-tion, is trivializing, sensationalizing and, above all, sentimentalizing the catastrophe. This is a clear instance of 'the lie of truth' and, because so many people will have seen it, *Schindler's List* will affect the reading of the Holocaust in ways that Alain Resnais' *Nuit et brouillard* or Claude

---

[8] Alvin H. Rosenfeld, 'Holocaust, Popular Culture, and Memory', paper given at the Olocausto: La Sho'ah tra interpretazione e memoria conference, Naples, May 1997.

Lanzmann's *Shoah* never will, because these profound and unique works are too austere and too demanding to achieve popular success.

The great majority of playwrights discussed in this book have written harsh and challenging plays that ask difficult questions and refuse the comforting closure of popular narrative. Against the 'characteristic American urge' to reach a happy ending, Hank Greenspan's survivors confront the spectator with impossible questions, the most intractable being, 'How would I have behaved if . . .' Freddie Rokem and Gad Kaynar explore the limits of representability which contemporary Israeli playwrights and performers try to extend in order to elicit emotional and intellectual responses which elude more traditional plays. The same limits have been tested less recently in the staging of Primo Levi's *If This Is A Man*, an Italian production which, as Helga Finter reports, had to find a compromise between the high literary values of the text and the pitfalls of realism by eschewing a mimetic or documentary style of representation, thanks to a dramaturgy that created a secular oratorio.

What we might call 'the politics of remembrance' are examined by several authors. Seth Wolitz discusses a curious commemorative play which turns history on its ear in order to celebrate Communist resistance in Poland; Dan Laor charts the change of attitude towards the Holocaust which has taken place in Israel, as reflected in public discourse and in the treatment of two major historical figures, Hannah Szenes and Israel Kasztner. Alvin Goldfarb's crop of American playwrights, to some extent, justifies Rosenfeld's harsh judgement quoted above: the plays of the four playwrights discussed here do not stage the nightmare of concentration camp internees, but offer comforting reassurances to their spectators. That judgement is partly upheld and partly contradicted by Atay Citron's investigation of the events surrounding the staging and performance of an extraordinary propaganda pageant, *A Flag Is Born*, which galvanized many American Jews, immediately after the war, to bring their active support to the displaced persons in European refugee camps and to campaign even more actively for the creation of an independent homeland. As a stage director, Alexander Stillmark had to contend with many conflicting political issues when he directed Heinar Kipphardt's *Brother Eichmann*, first in 1984 in East

Berlin, and then in (West) Berlin in 1992, as part of an exhibition entitled 'Jewish Spheres of Life', the main issue, in both instances, being of course the impersonation of the main perpetrator of the Final Solution in front of German audiences.

Of the three French playwrights, Charlotte Delbo and Armand Gatti are camp survivors and they speak with incredulity of the events through which they lived. Their aim is to testify, with lucidity and directness, creating new and appropriate dramaturgies with which to confront their audience. John Ireland and Dorothy Knowles map Gatti's theatrical involvement with the Holocaust over more than thirty years. Gatti denies any possibility of representing history, and insists that our only meaningful access to history is creative endeavour, which needs to be renewed again and again. Although Liliane Atlan was not deported, the tragedy of her childhood prompted her to invent a ritual based on the Passover Seder: her *Un opéra pour Terezin* tells of the destruction of the Jewish people through the ritual that rekindles each year the memory of their salvation when they successfully completed the Exodus from Egypt. Another, most unexpected, aspect of Theresienstadt is highlighted by Roy Kift, namely the varied and boisterous cabaret performances staged by and for the inmates of the ghetto/concentration camp who, in the face of death, found the courage to laugh at their own predicament and to poke some well-disguised fun at their tormentors.

No trace of fun, no concession to popular taste, no letting up of the tension in George Tabori's *Jubiläum* and Thomas Bernhard's *Heldenplatz*, and yet both plays are filled with venomous irony and bitter resentment. For Tabori, as Anat Feinberg demonstrates, the theatrical experience of remembrance must involve actors and spectators physically, intellectually and emotionally, obliterating the division between theatre and life. Finally Jeanette Malkin deals with the most unforgiving playwright and harshest play of them all. For Bernhard there can be no forgiving: he speaks in the name of concrete memory itself, as one who refuses to accept historical amnesia and erasure – on principle. In Bernhard's position, in a world bent on compromise, in a society where 'understanding' and 'flexibility' are extolled as supreme virtues, such an uncompromising attitude is nothing short of heroic – and it is fitting that he should have the last word in our collection.

There is no model, there can be no model of representation of the Holocaust. As the variety of approaches mapped out in the following pages clearly show, each playwright must solve the problem of representing the unrepresentable, of offering staging suggestions for the unstageable which will stimulate the imagination of directors and actors and challenge the spectator. Is it possible to judge the success of the various attempts, inasmuch as one can offer a judgement on plays divorced from performances? I shall venture to argue that the successful Shoah drama or performance is one that disturbs, offers no comfort, advances no solution; it is a play that leaves the reader or spectator perplexed, wanting to know more although convinced that no knowledge can ever cure him of his perplexity. It must be a play that generates stunned silence.

Françoise and Denise, the only two survivors of Charlotte Delbo's *Qui rapportera ces paroles?*, speak alternately the play's epilogue:

Nous sommes revenues	So we got back
Nous sommes revenues pour vous dire et nous voilà devant vous tout empruntées.	We got back to tell you and here we stand before you tongue-tied.
Que dire . . .	What can we tell you . . .
Comment dire . . .	How can we tell you . . .
C'est que là d'où nous revenons Les mots ne voulaient pas dire la même chose.	You see, where we come from Words had other meanings.
Les mots qui disent les choses simples:	Words for simple things
avoir froid	cold
avoir soif	thirst
avoir faim	hunger
être fatigué	tiredness
avoir sommeil, avoir peur,	fatigue and fear
vivre, mourir.	life and death.
Si vous ne voyez pas la différence c'est que nous ne savons plus les prononcer avec le sens que là-bas ils avaient.	If you can't see the difference it's because we can't speak them to mean the same they did over there.

8

Introduction

Nous voulions nous faire entendre,	We wanted to be heard,
nous voulions nous faire comprendre et . . .	we wanted to be understood and . . .
Ne croyez pas que nous en ayons du dépit,	Don't think we're angry with you,
nous savions que vous ne comprendriez pas,	we knew you wouldn't understand,
que vous ne croiriez pas,	you wouldn't believe,
car cela nous est devenu à nous-mêmes incroyable.	we hardly believe it ourselves.
Pourquoi iriez-vous croire	Why should you believe
à des histoires de revenants	in horror tales
de revenants qui reviennent	from ghosts who come back to haunt you
sans pouvoir expliquer comment?	and can't explain how?

9

1 Holocaust theatre and the problem of justice

ROBERT SKLOOT

The literature of trials is substantial. Playwrights throughout western history have acknowledged the usefulness of trials as a way of providing form, conflict and meaning to the stories they present. The only extant Greek trilogy, Aeschylus' *The Oresteia*, concludes with what may be the most famous trial scene in western dramatic literature, when the goddess Athena casts the deciding and pardoning vote on behalf of the matricide Orestes. Of course, the Greek plays have their rivals for our attention. Shylock's trial in Shakespeare's *The Merchant of Venice*, Volpone's trial at the end of Ben Jonson's play of that name, and Joan's trial in Shaw's theological tragicomedy *St Joan* compete for 'greatest trial scene', as might moments in Arthur Miller's *The Crucible*, Ibsen's *An Enemy of the People*, or *Inherit the Wind*, *The Caine Mutiny Court Martial*, *The Trial*, *Billy Budd*, and so on.

This chapter deals with plays that engage the Holocaust experience – of which there are a considerable number – plays that may vary in subject, style, language and intention, but which share the common feature of the search for a posthumous sense of justice following the terrors inflicted by the twelve-year Reich. In advancing these thoughts about the theatrical search for justice, I refer to plays that contain or allude to trials as a way of seeking after two complementary aspects of Holocaust dramaturgy: the rendering of the mind of the Nazi perpetrators, and the way in which this inquiry into the Nazi mind has, over the last decade or more, revealed deep and lasting changes in the way we think of the issue of justice when it is placed in the context of postmodern culture.[1] Later in this chapter, I will describe in greater detail how these two aspects are dealt with in several plays, but a brief, if general explanation is warranted here concerning contemporary critical practice.

The deeply problematic twist contained in the most recent criticism finds its origin in seeing everything as a text; additionally, in this view, the text is quite literally created by the reader/viewer. This is the postmodern idea. Thus, the process of representation sets aside (or even makes impossible) the assignment of ethical value to a work of art. Postmodernists claim that all writing becomes knowable only by approaching it through its linguistic activities. These have neither original source nor secure and agreed-upon meaning. Actions themselves, therefore, cannot be ascribed a value, i.e. judged as right or wrong, and the truth of an action must be indefinitely deferred. The focus of discussion shifts away from the event and its actors (in this instance, the Holocaust and its victims) toward commentary or explication of the linguistic confusions or paradoxes about the event. This postmodern approach to 'telling' the Holocaust story has elicited a strong response from critics whose condemnation of it is both vigorous and scornful.

> The inability of European postmodernist literary theorists and their followers in this country to face the implications of the recent cultural past of Nazism and of a genocide committed on, and in full view of, the European continent, has rendered contemporary criticism incapable of dealing with the human dimension in literature. In its concentration on the ontological

---

[1] Alice Kaplan was the first to apply the term *postmodern* to the trial of the Nazi Klaus Barbie, though her reasons for doing so are slightly different from mine. She wrote: 'The Barbie Trial was a postmodern trial because everything in it was at odds: the histories of the prosecuting groups, the motives of the defendant and the defenders, the huge gap of time itself between the event and the trial.' Alice Y. Kaplan, introduction to Alain Finkielkraut, *Remembering in Vain: The Klaus Barbie Trial and Crimes Against Humanity*, trans. Roxanne Lapidus and Sima Godfrey (New York: Columbia University Press, 1992; first published 1989), p. xxii.

status of fictions and on the epistemic status of literary criticism itself, contemporary literary theory manages to enact a perpetual deferral of human reality.[2]

The problem in 'explicating the Nazi mind' concerns the possibility of creating a situation of 'explaining away' the Nazis' crimes. There is a tendency to feel that in understanding the Nazi part in the Holocaust by delving into the psychology of the perpetrators, we make their crimes normative and in some way universal. This is the 'everybody can do what they did' phenomenon that becomes 'everybody did what they did' excuse, that is, all the 'actors' were governed in part by hatred, resentment, cowardice, ignorance or revenge. We recall that the traditional search for justice seeks after *motive*, and the divulging of motive, however hidden, is a time-honoured task of drama extending back to the theatre of ancient Greece.

In addition, contemporary literary and legal theory, as well as popular exposure to major attempts to 'find justice', has produced, and continues to produce, changes in the way evil is imagined. Of crucial interest has been the attempt by writers to restore earlier, more traditional images of evil and, concurrently, more traditional beliefs in systems of justice. As a result of investigating a selected number of Holocaust plays, I am suggesting that the ways justice could be defined and delivered, belief that was grounded in and validated by the Nuremberg trial, have been found inadequate. The multinational effort to bring Nazi war criminals to justice after the war became the touchstone, and provided the images, upon which later trials would be measured. I am suggesting that, in the 1990s, the fundamental assumptions of Holocaust writing and belief have been shaken because justice has been shaken, and one result has been the production of plays that, in their well-meaning way, are as 'revisionist' (although in no measure as

---

[2] David H. Hirsch, *The Deconstruction of Literature: Criticism After Auschwitz* (Hanover, NH: University of New England Press, 1991), pp. 115–16. See Hirsch's negative review of *Testimony: Crises of Witnessing in Literature, in Psychoanalysis and History in Holocaust and Genocide Studies,* 9.1 (Spring 1995), pp. 130–44 for the application of his critical objections to 'postmodern' writing.

heinous) as those pseudo-academic documents that seek to deny the Holocaust entirely.

I

In the spring of 1994, the cover story of one Sunday's *New York Times* magazine was called 'The Last War Criminal'. The article concerned the trial earlier that year of Paul Touvier, the Nazi police official in charge of intelligence and operations in the area in and around Lyon in 1944. Touvier was convicted and sentenced to life imprisonment, after fifty years in hiding, for crimes against humanity, specifically for the killing of seven Jews. The author of the article writes:

> The indelible moment at these trials was the recognition scene. The survivor, who had been marked for execution or deported to the death camps, appeared 40 or 50 years after the event on the witness stand to confront the man who had ordered his removal. The high level of emotion, the re-enactment of what transpired, the sense that justice was finally being done, taught a powerful lesson. In the end, it was as if history were being rewritten by a fairer and more benevolent hand, because some form of reparation had been made.[3]

Touvier's trial elicited a variety of responses in France: anger that justice had been so long delayed, indifference that so much effort should have been spent on old crimes committed by an even older man, relief or disgust that long-buried (and controversial) secrets had been publicly discussed, and vindication that those who commit heinous crimes can and should always be punished. Whether or not the punishment fits Touvier's crimes and evasions, what distinguishes the author of 'The Last War Criminal' from many other stories of trials of Nazis is the blatancy of his somewhat old-fashioned attempt to 'rewrite' the trial in his own 'fairer and more benevolent hand', as demanded by his traditional belief in the salutary nature of gestures of reparation.

---

[3] Ted Morgan, 'The Last War Criminal', *New York Times* magazine, 22 May 1994, pp. 31–2. See also Morgan's book on the Klaus Barbie trial of 1987, *An Uncertain Hour: The French, the Germans, the Jews, the Klaus Barbie Trial, and the City of Lyon, 1940–1945* (New York: Morrow, 1990). Morgan covered that trial for the *New York Times* also.

One method for measuring the history of the Holocaust in the popular consciousness is to trace the linkages and progression in the trials of the perpetrators of crimes against humanity. This trail of presumptive justice began with the Nuremberg trial immediately after the Allied victory, and extended chronologically through the Eichmann trial in Jerusalem in 1963, the Frankfurt trials of the mid-1960s, the Franz Stangl trial in Düsseldorf in 1970, the Barbie trial in France in 1987, the Demjanjuk (or 'Demjanjuk') trial in the early 1990s in Israel, and most recently in the spectacle of the unrepentant 79-year-old Paul Touvier in a French courtroom before three judges, nine jurors and, as the Chief Rabbi of France was reported to have said, 'in the presence of history itself'.[4]

Elsewhere, Hiam Goury assesses his memories of that trial: 'It was a trial, with all its dark implications, that unveiled the duality of our existence – the Jews as a murdered people and the story of Israel as a nation sitting in judgement.'[5]

After a half-century of trials, the idea of standing before history's judgement is a common one, even a cliché, though concluding that Touvier's trial would be the last of its kind is an extremely important, if

[4] Quoted in the *New York Times*, 20 April 1994. Trials, as a number of recent commentaries show, have distinctly national implications. Tom Segev's *The Seventh Million: The Israelis and the Holocaust*, trans. Hiam Watzmen (New York: Hill and Wang, 1993; first published 1991) describes in detail the importance of the Eichmann trial to the process of developing the Israeli character.

[5] Hiam Goury, 'Facing the Glass Booth', *Holocaust Remembrance: The Shapes of Memory*, ed. Geoffrey H. Hartman (Oxford: Blackwell, 1994), p. 155. In another notorious legal case, in early January 1997, the French Supreme Court ordered Maurice Papon to stand trial for the crime of ordering the deportation of 1,560 Jews, including many children, to Germany for extermination between 1942 and 1944. Papon, eighty-six years old in 1997, served in the Bordeaux office of the Vichy government during World War Two, and became a high-ranking minister in postwar France.

Papon, who attempted for years to keep his case out of the French courts, blames his current troubles on the Jews of France. It is certain that Touvier and Papon will be the only two Frenchmen to be tried for complicity with the Nazis' crimes against humanity.

accurate, cultural development.[6] The previous year, another fugitive Nazi in Argentina, 82-year-old SS-captain Erich Priebke, was arrested and in November 1995 was extradited to Italy to stand trial for his part in the massacre of 335 people in Rome's Ardeatine Caves in 1944. In August 1996, Priebke was found guilty by an Italian military court of 'complicity in violence with multiple homicide against Italian citizens', but unable to be punished because the statute of limitations on those charges had expired. Priebke was found not guilty of the charges of 'cruelty and premeditation' which could have put him in jail for the rest of his life.

The Italian government and citizens, and others in Europe, were outraged by the verdicts and the next day Priebke was rearrested. In July 1997 he was convicted and sentenced to five years in prison, a verdict against which he is appealing.

Clearly, a number of vital questions are raised by the playwrights who dramatize post-Holocaust consciousness through a series of formal or informal trials, because the very form, the *trope of the trial*, makes the inquiries inevitable: Who is guilty of Holocaust crimes? Who was complicitous in those crimes? What is the nature of good and evil? How does suffering affect memory/evidence and memory/evidence affect suffering? How does language/testimony affect belief and belief/ testimony language? And finally, what is justice and how can it be achieved? These are old questions of both law and history, all the more vexing because as the western world moves chronologically further from the Holocaust, it moves toward answers to these questions that offer neither acceptance nor certainty. Aeschylus' play, like all theatre, is more metaphor than legal precedent, though it may be all the more real and important for that. In the 'Age of the Last War Criminal', perhaps the struggle to establish justice by changing the Furies into Eumenides is effective *only as theatre*, and only as one kind of theatre with its origins in ancient Greece.

---

[6] Touvier died of cancer on 17 July 1996, in a prison hospital near Paris. He was eighty-one.

The trial of the unrepentant and arrogant Papon continues into 1998.

II

No matter how consistently the judges shunned the limelight, there they were, seated at the top of the raised platform, facing the audience as from the stage of a play. The audience was supposed to represent the whole world.

(Hannah Arendt, *Eichmann in Jerusalem*)

Hannah Arendt begins her book on the Eichmann trial with the words '"*Beth Hamishpath*" – the House of Justice'.[7] These words, shouted by the court usher at the start of every trial day, referred, as well, to the metaphorical place of the trial. (It was held in the *Beth HaAm*, literally the House of the People, Jerusalem's municipal auditorium. Klaus Barbie's trial took place at the Palais de Justice in Lyon.) Shortly thereafter, we find Arendt's evaluation of the legal events of the trial described as a theatrical experience, and one of a very traditional kind:

> It was precisely the play aspect of the trial that collapsed under the weight of the hair-raising atrocities. A trial resembles a play in that both begin and end with the doer, not with the victim . . . In the center of a trial can only be the one who did – in this respect, he is like the hero in the play – and if he suffers, he must suffer for what he has done, not for what he has caused others to suffer.[8]

The case Arendt puts forth in her study of 'the banality of evil', the sub-title of her book, is expressed within a theatrical concept of heroism and action derived from classical and neoclassical models. These models provided an aesthetic foundation for her political writing. To the extent that Adolf Eichmann, functionary and cipher, sought to evade respons-ibility and agency for the murder of millions, he brought specific jeopardy to the representation of evil seen as the protagonist in a tragic drama. The diminution of his character (a word from theatre and from life) was proportional to his own self-exculpation, and to his unpre-possessing appearance as well. The glass booth that encased him in the courtroom could be taken as a device to protect a creature more fragile

---

[7] Hannah Arendt, *Eichmann in Jerusalem: A Report on the Banality of Evil* (New York: Viking Press, 1964), p. 3.

[8] Ibid., p. 9.

than malignant. And because he was the sole representative of the terror and the slaughter at his trial, unlike the radically divergent personalities of the multiple defendants tried at Nuremberg, on his middle-aged shoulders alone fell the burden many hoped he would carry: the elevated image of heroic loathsomeness.

Eichmann's slight and solitary figure seemed to underscore his centrality to the drama, but, at the same time it attested to his inadequacy to perform well in it, and Arendt was brilliant in her detection of the tension that found immediate and intense expression as the trial took its course. Arendt was right in her traditional assessment of theatre, but, in the 1990s, it is not the only one that can be applied to Eichmann's trial. Central to *Eichmann in Jerusalem* is the remembrance of eternal battles of good against evil, as well as the awareness that the battle could not be joined in Jerusalem, and that some other conflict had to replace it. Seen as classical theatre, the play of justice had a shadow at its centre, although the articulation of the extent of the atrocity, the destruction of one-third of the world's Jews, insured that the wail of tragedy would be heard and wept over in the theatrical hall of justice.

With the world as the audience, the drama proceeded to a final curtain, but with the twist that provided Arendt's neoclassical text with its ironic sting: the trial presented not Aeschylus' Orestes defending his right and obligation to murder on behalf of the threatened *polis*, but Euripides' Orestes, weak and craven, simultaneously self-obsessed and distracted with a fate too big for him, like an oversized and shabby coat. In this view, Eichmann was the protagonist as anti-hero. Thus, because life usually refuses to provide the materials for high tragedy, and because life is lived often with diminished hope and sometimes with increased terror, the form of the Holocaust narrative rather than the characters who inhabit it is made to provide the shape for dispensing an elusive and long-delayed justice which is itself called into question by post-Auschwitz existence. (For good reason much of the attention at the Eichmann trial, and before it at the Nuremberg trial, and later at the Barbie trial, was given over to *legal* questions which were answered by recourse to historical incident if not precedent: for instance, could a country try someone whose crimes preceded the founding of the state, or whose presence was itself a statement of illegality

(Eichmann's kidnapping from Argentina)?) In deciding how to conduct the trial, the prosecution reaffirmed the form of justice that, in Arendt's estimation, could have provided both drama and catharsis had the protagonist only been better cast.[9]

The Eichmann trial defined, as did the Nazi trials that followed it and, I would argue, as was implied in the ones that preceded it, an image of both anti-hero and historical chaos that produced, according to the necessities if not the niceties of the legal structure, a momentary restoration of cultural equilibrium. As a result, it was possible to deliver the formal access to closure that the world left shattered by Nazi terror required, and that the Jews, decimated by the Nazi genocide, craved. But in the process a new category of character was liberated, a character familiar to literary and theatre critics, and belatedly to legal scholars: the Nazi as victim. This image, of course, is repugnant to traditionalists, which is to say to those who persist in the belief both in a fixed, knowable system of good and evil and a legislated, impartial system of justice. The character representing victimized evil is all the more startling because it comes to us contradicting historically validated positions of power and authority. These stage Nazis become yet more provocative and outrageous when, in the hands of postmodern playwrights or historical revisionists, the import of their heinous careers is detached from moral assessment and the meaning of their murderous actions is advanced as negotiable. The strategy becomes even more problematic when it appears as another character type, a variant and extension of the Nazi as Victim: the Nazi as Jew.[10]

(We should remember that in the grand eschatological structures which the Nazis established for themselves, the Jew is Satan and 'had to be extirpated completely, or else he would rise again'.[11] But, for the Allied victors, the mirror-image of the world rescued from destruction

---

[9] See also chapter 15 in this book, pp. 254–66.

[10] See ch. 4, 'Revisions and Reversals', in Robert Skloot, *The Darkness We Carry: The Drama of the Holocaust* (Madison: University of Wisconsin Press, 1988), pp. 68–93.

[11] Yehuda Bauer, 'The Place of the Holocaust in Contemporary History', *Holocaust: Religious and Philosophical Implications*, ed. John K. Roth and Michael Berenbaum (New York: Paragon House, 1989), p. 17.

prevailed: the Nazis were the negative force crushed by the power of good. Thus, it is common for writers on the Holocaust to refer to the Nazis as 'satanic' or 'demonic' in their evil. These are binary descriptions and affect keenly the creation of dramatic conflict and incident, and they are, in themselves, under heavy and negative scrutiny as retrograde holdovers from Aristotelian criticism. Terrence Des Pres, in his analysis of the Holocaust survivor, rejects imagining the concentration camps as 'a deliberate actualization of demonic tradition' because 'we end up seeing the SS as satanic monsters and the prisoners as condemned souls'.[12]

These developments correspond to a vision of life and art through the political and cultural lens of victimhood, a much-discussed feature of contemporary critical discourse. Thus, a quarter of a century after Eichmann's trial, Alain Finkielkraut reviews the conflict at Klaus Barbie's trial and the quality of Barbie's character. He refers to and further diminishes the images of forceful agency in the commission of genocidal slaughter, and he does so in terms that lament the condition of contemporary life and justice, while arguing for a pre-modern context to view them in. He writes,

> Was it necessary, in the interest of teaching a lesson or of
> delaying the fatal deadline of historicization, to pursue and
> judge forty years (two generations!) later the acts of this paltry
> underling, this monstrous subaltern, this poor man's
> Eichmann? What in fact is the chief of sections 4 and 6 of the
> Sipo-SD security police of Lyon in comparison to the great
> Nazi dignitaries who appeared at Nuremberg, at Frankfurt,
> or in Jerusalem?[13]

Finkielkraut answers with a particularly poignant reversal of expectation worthy of the English playwright Tom Stoppard, whose first great play appeared around the time of the Jerusalem trial of Adolf Eichmann: when Hamlet is absent, Rosencrantz or Guildenstern must be called to answer for the universe gone off its traditional, ethically normative

[12] Terrence Des Pres, *The Survivor: An Anatomy of Life in the Death Camps* (New York: Oxford University Press, 1976), p. 202.

[13] Finkielkraut, *Remembering in Vain*, p. 3.

track. What carries the endeavour forward is the memory of traditional literary narrative and conservative theatrical form.

> The argument of his insignificance, far from invalidating the trial, is its primary justification. . . The notion of crime against humanity is, precisely, to re-establish the link between the man and the crime . . . ; to recall, by treating the *cogs* in the Nazi apparatus as *persons*, that service to the state does not exonerate any civil servant . . . from his responsibility as an individual.[14]

In Finkielkraut's cosmology, the law is maintained as the traditional mechanism for retributive justice and humanistic example, a necessary corrective to ethical slippage in an age of mass murder and the collapse of aesthetic formalism. His is a project with more at its heart than denying sympathy for the devil.

III

In a number of Holocaust dramas, playwrights approach the subject of Nazi crimes with the intention of exploiting the popular understanding of courtroom or pre-courtroom dialectics, what lawyers and playwrights might agree to call 'discovery'. They use the trope of the trial (sometimes including a pre-trial) and the interrogation of the characters to propose some historical or psychological conclusions concerning the atrocities of the Holocaust and those who committed them. The form of the plays and their presentation are intended to comment on the issue of justice, its nature and its possibility. But the images they convey vary widely from one to another, and the conclusions they reach about the careers of the most powerful Nazis require profound reassessments of our understanding of history, law and the theatre.[15]

Among the best-known trial plays is Christopher Hampton's 1982 adaptation of George Steiner's *The Portage to San Cristobal of A. H.*[16] Its story concerns the hunt and capture of Adolf Hitler in a

---

[14] Ibid., p. 8.

[15] From a somewhat different perspective, I have analysed a number of these plays in 'Stage Nazis: The Politics and Aesthetics of Memory', *History and Memory*, 6.2 (Fall/Winter 1994).

[16] Christopher Hampton, *George Steiner's Portage to San Cristobal of A. H.* (London: Faber and Faber, 1983).

Brazilian jungle by a search party of Israelis. The captors are slowly defeated by disease, weather and doubt as they make their way back to 'civilization', and the play concludes with Hitler, whose strength has increased throughout, unleashing a furious tirade of invective against those whom he calls 'gentlemen of the tribunal' as he defends himself in the jungle space that has become a courtroom. Hitler's rhetorical onslaught is a mixture of confused history and self-promotion that is intended to confuse the documented facts of genocide and their commonly agreed-upon interpretation. His argument, based on three themes – that the Jews provided his ideology, that they deserved punishment, and that they benefited from the Holocaust through the founding of the State of Israel – defines a legal defence that is based less on fact than on cruel fantasy. And, as has been often discussed, by not providing Hitler's argument with *any* refutation, effective or otherwise, Steiner and Hampton have provoked both controversy and thought about their motives. Nonetheless, taken on its own terms, Hitler's presentation is entirely appropriate to the dynamics of courtroom procedure: the best case is being made to 'get the defendant off'. In notorious criminal trials of the 1990s (in America, the trials of Rodney King, O. J. Simpson, and the Menendez Brothers come immediately to mind), television audiences have been confronted with the ways legal structures are used to elide or obscure truth.

Clearly, there is a need to provide words of rebuttal and reproof for Hitler's self-defence, and in a conventionally structured and imagined play, it is likely some or many would have been provided. At the same time, we need to acknowledge that our common desire for artistic or ethical closure may be beside the point, and that Steiner's insistence upon the *audience* providing the response to Hitler may be appropriate in the light of more current and ambiguous theatrical and legal practices. In the courtroom, the system of law is used to structure the response to the problems of crime and punishment. Steiner's refusal to confront Hitler's arguments now seems to be the inevitable response to the failure of both law and history to the extent that he (and Hampton) are asking for another kind of ethical assessment of the Nazi genocide of the Jews. Older concerns with agency and responsibility which can be adjusted to ideologies of liberal humanism, neoclassicism, or traditional political conservatism are unavailing here. And Steiner's point, made to the press as well as in the theatre, insists that the tale be turned back to the jury/audience, as if to say 'Go find justice where you will, but you are least likely to find it in the systems of justice of any country.' Further, because the crime is without precedent, the language without conviction and the destruction without repair, remedies like 'simple justice' are as useless as the traditional theatre, though that may be the only place remaining to advance – with decreasing credibility or efficacy – images and explanations for events that leave only the irreparable and the opaque as their legacy.

It should not be surprising that when confronted with the 'playwright as lawyer', that its reverse has also appeared in the form of 'lawyer as playwright': Robert M. Krakow, a Washington attorney whose play *The False Witness* (originally called *The Trial of Adolf Hitler* and later subtitled *The Trial That Never Was*) appeared in 1995.[17] It would be easy to make light of this text for its lack of dramatic sophistication, and perhaps unwise to call attention to a play whose theatrical future is uncertain. Produced three times in Florida to 'commemorate the 50th anniversary of the concentration camps', the play's premise concerns the trial of Adolf Hitler before the 'Celestial Criminal Court of the High Tribunal' at 'the Gate of Purgatory'. 'If convicted', the author's note continues, Hitler 'will be sentenced to the final circle of Hell'.

The False Witness (it is not certain to whom this refers) is most interesting for its attempt to bring Hitler to justice with so flagrant a use of the trial trope in its most traditional way. To be fair to Krakow, we must acknowledge his sincerity and his determination to provide a context for the Nazis' destruction of the Jews. Thus, Hitler's actions are explained and defended by the witnesses who testify on his behalf: Martin Luther, Henry Ford, Richard Wagner, Franklin D. Roosevelt and Pope Pius XII. In excerpts from historical documents and through dramatized flashbacks, Hitler's genocidal crusade is shown to have extensive human precedent; in fact, his defence rests on the argument that 'he acted in accordance with the wishes of mankind . . . To condemn him is to condemn all mankind [for killing the Jews]'.

---

[17] The text of the play was sent to me by the author.

Krakow, who admits to spending five years researching and writing the play, lacks the theatrical gifts to make what is an extended legal argument in dialogue form into theatre that is emotionally captivating or intellectually satisfying. But for just these reasons *The False Witness* deserves attention in these speculations. It is exceedingly difficult to conceive of a more skilled or theatrically knowledgeable playwright engaging in this type of exercise. Of crucial interest is the playwright's use of the audience to serve as the jury in this imagined trial of Hitler, and secondarily the evidence he puts before them. The audience, in fact, is sworn in at the beginning of the play after they have *'been seated in such a way as to simulate a jury box'*, and likely serves its jury time with the commitment and attention of any committed actor. Virgil, the Latin poet who is the Prosecuting Attorney representing the 'Spirit of Man', concludes his summation to the jury thus:

> For these proceedings demonstrate beyond doubt that the
> death factories of the Nazi regime were conceived many centuries
> ago. That these assembly line murders were the ultimate
> embodiment of evil myths that were transformed through the
> millennia finding their perfection in the modern era of man.

This kind of argument is the exact provocation for Michael André Bernstein's recent study *Foregone Conclusions*, which argues for rejecting as in any way useful discussions of the Shoah that have 'so often been represented through a plot governed by a logic of historical inevitability. Such emplotment . . . provides the kind of totalizing master narrative against which the counter history proposed here can be heard most effectively.'[18]

Later, Bernstein's proposal to establish a revisionary historiography based on his theory of 'sideshadowing' delineates a number of contradictions contained within most discourse on the Shoah, one of which involves narrative: 'The contradiction is between insisting on the unprecedented and singular nature of the Shoah as an event and yet

[18] Michael André Bernstein, *Foregone Conclusions: Against Apocalyptic History* (Berkeley and Los Angeles: University of California Press, 1994), p. 14.

still using the most lurid and formal tropes and commonplace literary conventions to narrate it.'[19]

The False Witness may not be able to escape the criticism that so obviously limited a theatrical form can provoke; we can imagine the intense pressure on both performers and audience (who are also performers) to react with utmost seriousness to an enterprise that is in constant danger of losing its theatrical and historical balance. Still, Krakow is basing his play on the implicit understanding that many in the post-Holocaust world continue to seek simple theatrical *and* legal solutions to an overpowering and terrifying historical event.

It is surely one dimension of our postmodern condition that these attempts to deal with the Holocaust through legal judgement can only provoke disbelief or wonder that so much other history – of dramatic art, of human folly, of legal systems that are nothing better or worse than protection for vested or moneyed interests – can be set aside in favour of the articulation of images that hold closely to a belief in bringing the perpetrators of genocide to justice and new life to the humanizing power of theatrical endeavour.

Being on the jury where decisions and judgements will determine the future of humankind seems too heavy a burden to assume for the price of admission to a theatre performance. Even *acting* on behalf of the Spirit of Man cannot disguise the emptiness of the trope. Perhaps it is time to retire this seemingly resilient form from the service of the Shoah's explication, and accept solace or enjoyment in Aeschylus and Shakespeare 'played straight', as part of the 'good old days'. In the post-Shoah world, other means must be found to account for the loss of the victims and the triumph of their tormentors than the simple appeal to simple justice. Plays that turn the trope on its ear in order to show the folly of the form may be the way to do this.

[19] Ibid., p. 23. This 'weight of the whole modernist tradition – now dead', as Frederic Jameson wrote in his famous essay 'Postmodernism and Consumer Society' (1983), has produced in writers a reliance on the pastiche, 'the nostalgia mode' of 'seek[ing] the historical past, which itself remains forever out of reach'. In *Postmodernism and its Discontents*, ed. E. Ann Kaplan (London: Verso, 1988), p. 20.

IV

It is in the very nature of things human that every act that has once made its appearance and has been recorded in the history of mankind stays with mankind as a potentiality long after its actuality has become a thing of the past. No punishment has ever possessed enough power of deterrence to prevent the commission of crimes . . . The particular reasons that speak for the possibility of a repetition of the crimes committed by the Nazis are even more plausible.[20]

Arendt's assessment of the genocidal inheritance of Nazi crimes would seem to be validated in the appearance of atrocity all over the world, and it is an assessment that causes her classical preferences to sag badly under so crushing a historical weight.

Hampton's dramatization of Steiner's play reveals several of the features of postmodern theatre, in particular by resisting the temptation toward formal closure. The play puts on trial the man who was arguably the candidate for the most criminal man in history (though he does have competition), and provides him with a forum of self-defence that is released in a vituperative and perverse rhetoric with no apology. He appears as the exception to the rule of evil's banality, as a dominating, thrilling stage presence, and would seem to be an appropriate kind of character for Arendt's pre-modern vision. Most importantly, *Portage* allows Hitler to articulate theories of race, history and theology without effective refutation because the playwright's highly controversial strategy prefers to force us, as an audience, to provide the judgement of a jury in a situation that has raised issues that its author(s) want(s) us to see as both complex and resistant to justice. If atrocities flourish after the Holocaust, indeed if Nazism has in fact survived into our time, justice itself in the form of images and systems of retribution and compensation is what is found guilty. Under these conditions, finding Hitler guilty, as Krakow insists we do, is as irrelevant as it is meaningless.

In other plays, Eichmann, Goering, Mengele and other less powerful Nazis, are hauled into the court of theatrical opinion, where they can

---

[20] Arendt, *Eichmann in Jerusalem*, p. 273.

upset our ethical and aesthetic preferences. In some of them, the idea of history as fixed, of goodness as pure, of victims as worthy – or even victims at all – is deconstructed and revisioned. What remains constant in these plays is the venue of the courtroom where, a half-century after the Holocaust, the profession and trope of the law is employed either to reaffirm or reassess our common understanding of justice, history and the theatre as well. What is important to note is that it is cultural and political movements that provide the refutation of Finkielkraut's dire vision of our future, one so reminiscent of Aeschylus.

> Civilization established the Nuremberg Trial in order to *bring the law to justice*. We abandon this ambition if we allow entertainment to release humanity from continuity, from coherence, and from all forms of the law.[21]

[21] Finkielkraut, *Remembering in Vain*, p. 67.

2 The power and limits of the metaphor of survivors' testimony

HANK GREENSPAN

A few years ago, I gave a talk to a group of students at the University of Michigan Law School under the title, 'How to Listen to Holocaust Survivors Without Hearing Anything'. In fact (and this was, of course, my point), instruction is hardly needed. Over the past fifty years we have done very well not hearing what survivors have had to tell us – even without professional assistance.

As is now well known, during most of that time we neither heard *nor* listened to survivors. As different as were the contexts, survivors' experiences in Israel and the United States were strikingly similar in this regard.[1] Through the first quarter-century after liberation, survivors were admonished to put the past behind them and to move on. If they were noticed at all, they were noticed, in Wiesel's phrase, as 'sick and needy relatives' – 'misfits, kill-joys, carriers of disease'[2] – and that stigmatization further insured their silence. The recollection of Paula Marcus, a survivor of Auschwitz and Ravensbrück, is typical:

> People said, 'This is to forget! Life goes on. Hush up your bad dreams; it's not going to happen' . . . And also we were ashamed. We were made to feel ashamed. Because you were considered *crazy* if you talked about it. You were considered abnormal. So I had to really suppress it. I covered up. 'I'm fine, Joe! That's not

---

[1] See Tom Segev, *The Seventh Million: The Israelis and the Holocaust* (New York: Hill and Wang, 1991).

[2] Elie Wiesel, *A Jew Today* (New York: Random House, 1978), p. 196.

me! How are *you*!' . . . We tried to get along, you know, 'I'm an American too!'[3]

In the United States, survivors' isolation did not significantly begin to change until the late 1970s. Thanks largely to survivors' own efforts, but also in response to a new kind of popular interest, it was then that oral history projects, days of remembrance, and programmes of testimony suddenly began to develop. At the same time it was becoming apparent that it *was* possible to listen to survivors – even to listen again and again to survivors – and still not hear anything. Here is how Sally Grubman, like Paula a survivor of Auschwitz and Ravensbrück, described the transformation:

> There is a tremendous interest in the Holocaust that we didn't see when we came . . . but also some confusion about the reality. I get these frantic calls from twenty-five year old teachers [who] invite me into their classes to speak, but they do not want me to make the Holocaust a sad experience. They want to turn us into heroes and create a heroic experience for the survivors. There is this book they use, *The Holocaust: A History of Courage and Resistance*, but the Holocaust was never a history of courage and resistance. It was a destruction by fire of innocent people, and it's not right to make it something it never was.
>
> . . . And people have said, 'Sally, tell the children about the joy of survival.' And I see they don't understand it at all. If you're in a canoe and your life is in danger for a few moments and you survive, you can talk about the joy of survival. We went through fire and ashes and whole families were destroyed. And we are left. How can we talk about the joy of survival?[4]

---

[3] Paula Marcus's recollections of the first years after liberation are discussed in greater detail in Hank Greenspan, *On Listening to Holocaust Survivors: Recounting and Life History* (Westport, CT: Praeger Publishers, 1998), p. 89.

[4] Sylvia Rothchild, *Voices from the Holocaust* (New York: New American Library, 1981), pp. 381–2.

As Sally Grubman suggests, survivors are now invited – even frantic-ally invited – to speak. But they are expected – sometimes downright directed – to speak in certain ways. Affirmations of courage, resistance, and the joy of survival are all right. Helplessness and ashes are not.

Of course, as Sally's protest also expresses, survivors may *not* speak as they are directed. Indeed, to the extent they are able to convey it, and to the extent they themselves are able to bear it, they usually tell us the truth. So here, in order to listen to survivors but still not hear anything, I think we do something quite interesting: we ritualize the very act, even the very idea, of survivors' testimony. That is, we sur-round survivors' speech with so much hype, so much ceremonial and rhetorical fencing, that we are almost able to seal it off completely.

As a typical example, listen to this commentary from the American public television coverage of the first World Gathering of Holocaust Survivors that took place in Jerusalem in 1981. After the lead-in photographs of corpses and terrified victims with which every broadcast began, one of the commentators made these introductory remarks to the first broadcast of the series:

> Some five thousand men and women, just a remnant of the
> six million Jews who were tortured, gassed, and incinerated,
> are here today. In the opening sequence we showed you a
> glimpse – even a glimpse is enough – of the savagery of the
> Holocaust. We didn't do this to shock you, although it is
> shocking. We did it so that you can better understand the
> triumph of the human spirit . . .
>
> These heroic people who are gathered here today have
> not come to resurrect the nightmares of the past. They have
> not come to mourn. They have come to celebrate life. To
> bear witness. And to pass it on to their children and their
> children's children . . . This is their true legacy.[5]

From the start we must wonder, 'How is it possible to "bear witness" *without* mourning and *without* resurrecting "the nightmares of the past"?' In fact, the scenes from the Gathering that immediately fol-lowed – survivors grouped around computers and holding up signs in

[5] PBS, *Holocaust: The Survivors Gather*, 15–18 June 1981.

search of those they lost – seemed to have everything to do with mourning and resurrection. But even these remarks taken alone already convey the commentator's far greater involvement with the *idea* of survivors 'bearing witness' than with anything that witnessing is about. Of that – represented by the opening photographs – 'even a glimpse is enough'. In other words, *that* we know already. We do not need survivors' testimony for *that* at all. Thus severing the act of testimony from its content – disallowing terror but celebrating celebrating – we can indeed listen to survivors without risk of hearing anything.

In recent years, the rhetoric of inter-generational transmission – of 'true legacies' passed on 'to children and children's children' – has become particularly central in celebratory discourse about survivors and their recounting. Indeed, whether in speaking of a legacy of trauma, of testimony, of Hitler, of Schindler, of night, or of dawn, there is probably no single word used more often in connection with survivors than 'legacy'. Related references to survivors as 'storytellers', 'tellers of tales', or – more postmodernistically – 'weavers of narrative tapestries' are almost as ubiquitous.[6] As a single instance that could stand for many, listen to this foreword to a recent collection of survivors' testimonies. The person referred to as 'Howard' is the son of two of the survivors included:

> The stories of Howard's parents were important because
> they were becoming Howard's stories – and one day they
> would become the stories of Howard's children.
> And not unlike the Passover, when we are commanded
> to tell our children the story of the Exodus, perhaps we have a
> similar responsibility here: to tell the stories of the Holocaust.
> Maybe that was what was on Howard's face that day – the
> responsibility of the storyteller . . . that the story does not stop
> with those who valiantly died in or survived the Holocaust . . .
> that the story is now in the hands of those younger generations

---

[6] See Hank Greenspan, 'Making a Story From What is Not a Story: The Oral Narratives of Holocaust Survivors', in Joachim Knuf, ed., *Texts and Identities: Studies on Language and Narrative* (Lexington: University of Kentucky, College of Communications and Information Studies, 1995).

– to pass along to others . . . so that they will understand . . . and continue to tell.

And so for these stories – this book . . . It is our responsibility to be the storytellers.[7]

Now I am not a quantitative researcher, but ten evocations of stories or storytellers in just a handful of sentences cannot help but impress! Each is surrounded by the primal imagery of a people's narrative tradition and its transmission – a celebration of continuity, coherence, and cohesion on a biblical scale. In the grasp of such rhetoric – in the grasp of such theatre – we can almost forget that the coherence of stories and the continuity of legacies are precisely what remembering the Holocaust undoes.

Here, then, are some of the ways our very celebration of survivors' testimony works to deny and to disarm it. As a psychologist, my task has been to analyse such strategies. As a playwright – particularly of *Remnants*,[8] a play about survivors' recounting from which I will present a couple of excerpts – my task has been to exploit those strategies in order to reverse them.

Remnants attempts this reversal, first, through a kind of imitation. The work initially *appears* to be a presentation of survivors' oral testimony in a familiar format. There are six actors playing six survivors – three men and three women – each of whom performs a monologue. While the monologues are not verbatim transcription, all are based on actual reflections that survivors shared with me, which the audience knows from a programme note. The survivors approach the audience as public speakers, one at a time; and each talks only to the audience – there is no interaction between them. Six memorial candles are also typically part of the set, confirming that this is indeed a serious ritual of remembrance – as it absolutely *is*.

---

[7] Temple Emanu-El, *And So We Must Remember: Holocaust Remembrances* (Oak Park, MI: Temple Emanu-El, 1992).

[8] Hank Greenspan, *Remnants*, 1991. First produced in 1992 by the Michigan Radio Theatre, directed by Hank Greenspan and Ann Klautsch, WUOM-FM, Ann Arbor, Michigan.

What the survivors talk about, however, and the way they speak, are not traditional. For, along with remembering the Holocaust, a good part of their reflection explicitly concerns the problematics of this recounting situation itself. In different ways, each monologue raises the questions: 'How is it possible for me, for you, to speak at all about these things?' 'What are you expecting, even insisting, to hear from me as a survivor?' 'Could you bear it if I told you differently?'

Beyond simply raising these questions, part of the dramatic impact here comes, of course, from breaking the ritual mould. Simply establishing the metaphor of survivors' testimony is powerful enough, providing drama like *Remnants* with a kind of authenticity, not necessarily deserved, that is hard to attain in any other way. But the impact of violating that metaphor, the impact of survivors *not* staying within the usual confines and contents of testimony, may be more powerful still. Accurately or not, audiences experience these moments as more spontaneous and thus more emotionally 'real'. In a context as typically ritualized as survivor testimony, they have the sense that something else has somehow gotten through.

Of that, I should let you judge. But it is instructive to cite briefly two reviewers along these lines. One critic wrote about *Remnants*: 'I thought I had seen and heard everything about the Holocaust, but this play is fresh and original.' A second commented: 'In spite of the vast literature on the Holocaust, each of the segments of *Remnants* presents a new approach to this unspeakable crime.'

Now, how does one respond to comments like these? You celebrate, of course! But eventually reality sets in and you ask yourself: What does it mean for someone to think he had 'seen and heard everything' about the Holocaust? Could we imagine the same comment in any other context? For example: 'I thought I had seen and heard everything about the Russian Revolution', or 'I thought I had seen and heard everything about the battle of Leyte Gulf'? And then there is the man who credits me for going beyond 'the vast literature on the Holocaust'. How does he *know*? Has he read that vast literature?

It becomes clear, of course, that such comments express a *feeling* of substantive knowledge, not the reality. As the television commentator put it, up against the real terror of the Holocaust, it *feels like* 'even a glimpse is enough', it feels like this *must* be 'seeing and hearing everything'. And so it may follow that any work that causes us to look a little longer might seem, by contrast, 'fresh and original'.

Here, then, are two monologues from *Remnants* as they were performed in a 1992 radio production: 'Voice', with which the programme opens, and 'The Vanity' with which it closes – in other words, the 'book-ends' of the piece.

Opening monologue: VOICE, *spoken by the first female survivor.*

During the war I lost my voice. I literally lost my voice. I was a little kid at the time, a little *pisher* like we say in Yiddish. I was eight years old. And at that time, I lost my voice.

This was in 1943. In the ghetto. It was after one of those *Aktions* – you know, when the SS come in and they kill a lot of people. And they round up the others and they take them to the train. And the train takes them away.

After one of those *Aktions*, I lost my voice. I don't know why. But for two years, I did not speak a single word.

After the war, my voice came back. Not right away, but very slowly. This was in 1945, in a 'DP Camp', a camp for 'displaced persons', mostly for Jews who had survived the war. During the day in that camp I did not speak at all. But at night, when I was having a nightmare, I screamed. So that was how we knew I still had a voice. Because during the day I was completely mute. But during the night I screamed.

There was a doctor at that camp, a Jewish doctor, who said: 'If the girl can scream in the night, when she is asleep, so she can scream in the day, when she is awake. And if she can scream in the day, so she can also sing or cry. And if she can sing or cry, she can speak words as well. The voice can be salvaged. The screams can be refined into cries. And the cries can be refined into words.'

So the doctor tried to help me. He took me to run in the hills near that camp. And he had me run with my mouth open, so I could feel the air push up against my throat. And he told me to try to scream with the air in my throat, or to make any sound

1. **Hank Greenspan**, *Remnants*. Maria Orlowski (The Vanity) in a presentation from 1992.

at all. And soon I did start to scream when I was running. And then I was crying and making other different sounds. And eventually the sounds became a voice. I could speak words again, after two years of no words at all. [*pause*]

Today, we have *many* words about the Holocaust. We argue what does it mean? What should we do? What should we have done at the time? We argue for God and against Him. For Israel and against Israel. For reaching out to others and against reaching out to others. We argue and we reflect and we argue some more.

But to me, when I think about the Holocaust, I remember the doctor. And I remember myself, when I was a young girl, running in the hills. Because to me, *all* our words, *whatever* we say about the Holocaust, are just so many different refinements of a cry. And the cry is just barely salvaged from a scream. And the scream is just barely salvaged from the silence.

34

Closing monologue: THE VANITY, *spoken by the third female survivor.*

Whenever I am introduced as 'a survivor', I am a little bit uncomfortable. I mean, what do people want? What do they expect?

In the beginning, until just the last few years, nobody wanted to hear from us. Everybody said, 'This is to forget! Life goes on! Hush up your bad dreams!' Like – this may sound stupid – but we heard in this country, 'When you laugh, the whole world laughs with you. And when you cry, you cry alone.' So that's exactly what we did. We said: 'We're Americans too!' And we *are*. And we kept our memories to ourselves.

Now, today, everybody makes a big deal out of it. I mean, they don't just invite us to speak, but they turn us into some kind of heroes. They talk about the special wisdom we're supposed to have. And the precious legacy we're supposed to pass on. And all the tales and legends *(she becomes ironic)* we're supposed to be able to retell?

What is this, a *Bar Mitzvah*? A celebration of our Jewish roots? I mean, we, whose roots were totally destroyed, are supposed to have a precious legacy? And we, who can hardly speak at all, are supposed to tell you fabulous tales and legends?!

In the beginning people were silent. Today, they are stupid.

But I'll tell you, I'm stupid too. I don't have wisdom. I don't even know what I think. I mean, I lived through it. I remember it. But even *I* don't know what the Holocaust means or what we should believe about it.

One memory I will tell you because then maybe you will understand this stupidity of mine. You know, I was part of the time in Birkenau. Birkenau – that was the part of Auschwitz where they had the gas chambers in the shower rooms. And the crematoria. Birkenau was where they killed most of the people in Auschwitz. And I was in the group of prisoners who sorted the clothes of those who had already been gassed and burned. After they went into the shower room, the gas chamber, we came out and packed up the clothes they left behind.

And also in Birkenau there was the prisoners' latrine – you know, where we went to the toilet – which was really just a bench with a row of holes over a pit filled with quicklime. So this was where we went to the bathroom.

And, in the latrine of Birkenau, the SS took one lady, one of the prisoners, and they made her the *Scheisskapo*. This was a joke for the SS. It means, 'the shit commander'. That was her title. It was on a sign she wore around her neck. And her job was to watch the toilets and be like a kind of attendant. She had to keep it neat and clean.

And one day I noticed that this lady, the *Scheisskapo*, had managed to find a few boxes. Somehow, she got a couple of old crates made of wood. And she put them together with the little one in front, so she could sit on it. And she also had a little mirror that she probably found in the clothes – from one of the prisoners who had been killed.

So with the boxes and the mirror she made like a little bureau. She put the mirror over the big box and she sat on the little box and made like a little vanity in the corner of the latrine. A little vanity in the corner of the ladies' room. [*pause*]

Whenever people ask me, 'what does the Holocaust mean?' – or I ask myself, 'what does it mean?' – I think about this memory. It's not easy to do. Try to keep the picture – *all* the elements of the picture – together in your mind at one time: A vanity . . . In the latrine . . . In Auschwitz-Birkenau.

Now you tell me – you tell me because I don't know myself – does it inspire your hope, or your revulsion, that the attendant in the toilets of Hell made a place to put on her make-up?

Earlier I quoted from two reviewers of *Remnants*. Here is a third whose reflections raise another kind of question with which we should conclude. The reviewer wrote:

Some of the events described – the women's camp in Birkenau, for example – are well documented in other works on the Holocaust . . . [But] in general the reflections voiced in

> *Remnants* are not what survivors tend to share in public
> presentations . . . Rather, they are what survivors say only
> after trust and confidence have been established . . . They are
> personal stories, told between friends, at moments of special
> clarity and candour.

I should be candid – I like this reviewer's analysis! Certainly it expresses some of what I *wanted* to be true about the piece. And yet it also suggests a danger. Most moments between friends – survivors or otherwise – are *not* characterized by 'special clarity and candour'. Indeed, during most of the time I spend with my friends who happen to be survivors, we are not talking about the Holocaust at all – however much it may be implicit background. The monologues of *Remnants* are thus highly stylized, both in form and in content. Survivors are not 'survivors' in this way most of the time; and, of course, the 'candid survivor' or the 'reflective survivor' could become as limiting a metaphor as the storytelling, legacy bestowing survivor.

Let the final voice, therefore, be a survivor who tells us essentially this. It is Paula Marcus, whose memory happened also to be the primary model for The Vanity. Toward the end of one of our conversations, Paula reflected:

> But you know my wish is always – I don't know what I
> achieved in my own little circle, in my own family. Will they
> say, 'Well, my mother taught me this'?
> I don't know how they feel. Maybe – I'm sure they do
> – but I don't know it.
> What was I able to leave for them? What is that word I
> want to use? The word they always use? Legacy. I don't know.
> Do they look at me as a quote-unquote '*survivor*'?
> Do they have compassion because now they understand
> what happened? And they understand *me* instead of I
> understanding *them*? You know, it's a very, a very bothering thought within you.

Being a 'quote-unquote survivor' is here what contributes *least* to Paula's sense of 'legacy'. She then reflected further about what legacies, her own and others, actually entail.

But you know, on the other hand, every parent, every person who leaves a legacy in this life, it's a very little minor thing. I'm thinking of my own parents, especially my father, because unfortunately my mother I remember only vaguely . . .

When I go to the synagogue, which I don't do that often, but I always hear my father's voice. And I always recall, at certain prayers, how much joy he got out of singing that particular one. He wasn't extremely religious. He was just good-hearted, believing, so pure within his world . . . And he enjoyed singing *En K'elohenu*.[9] And he excelled! You know, his voice just – !! And every time I sing that, I feel that this is why I enjoy it – because my father enjoyed it . . .

So, actually, what is a legacy? It's a very, it's one little thing if you are going to make it a legacy. I can't. Whatever I work on, it's up to you what you take out of it. How you translate it for yourself. And for that you have to be fortunate. To be able to enjoy these little things that are given.[10]

For Paula, then, legacies *are* the 'little things that are given'. Far from emerging from the Holocaust, they are what can be salvaged and transmitted *in spite of* the Holocaust. They are made of the same biographic and cultural stuff, like father's voices and *En K'elohenu*, as our own. And, in fact, it is only through such remembered voices that legacies are *ever* made – once again, whether that be survivors' legacies or anyone else's.

Let me conclude, then, with what Jean Améry would have called an 'extravagant moral daydream':[11] a hope with no chance of realization, but still the right thing for which to hope. It would be that we, as listeners to survivors, are finally so full of their words, so shaken by them, so irrevocably transformed by them, that survivors and drama could part company forever. We would not have to dramatically represent them – which includes dramatically challenging the usual

---

[9] 'There is none like our God.'   [10] Greenspan, *On Listening*, p. 64.
[11] Jean Améry, *At the Mind's Limits* (Bloomington: Indiana University Press, 1980), p. 79.

dramatic representations – and, struggling within and against our rituals and rhetoric, survivors would not have to dramatically represent themselves. All of us would then be free to devote ourselves to our true legacies – the *real* remnants of whatever songs, and whatever voices, we find we have been able to salvage.

3 On the fantastic in Holocaust performances

FREDDIE ROKEM

It was very theatrical: in go people at one end and out comes
smoke at the other.　　　　　(Danny Horowitz, *Uncle Artur*)

Niemand
zeugt für den
Zeugen　　　　　(Paul Celan, 'Aschenglorie')

Israeli culture and its public discourses resonate powerfully with stories about the Holocaust. They have been central to the creation of a collective Israeli identity. The awesome dialectics between Destruction and Revival – *Shoah ve-T'kuma* – has been inscribed in the consciousness of every Israeli, including those not directly affected by the Holocaust, even the Palestinians who are Israeli citizens, as well as those living in the occupied and the autonomous areas, or in exile. Thus Sadam Hussein's threats during the Gulf War to bomb Israel with scud missiles equipped with poisonous gas naturally were interpreted cognitively and emotionally in the context of the Holocaust experience.

The Israeli theatre is no doubt one of the many seismographs measuring and confronting the extreme complexities of the Holocaust. The main issue I want to raise here is how the Israeli theatre, in performances about the Holocaust, has dealt with the incomprehensibility and the inherent difficulties of communicating what, in the words of KaTzetnik (Yehiel De-Nur) during the Eichmann trial, happened 'on the planet called Auschwitz'. Since the early 1980s the representation of the Holocaust on stage has manifested some new aspects not previously expressed in theatrical discourses.

40

It is possible to distinguish a mixture of at least three different genres or modes of representation in performances about the Holocaust appearing in the early eighties. The first-person testimony of the survivor is the rhetorical kernel on which these performances are based. Michael Bernstein rightly argues that 'One of the most pervasive myths of our era, a myth perhaps even partially arising out of our collective response to the horrors of the concentration camps, is the absolute authority given to the first-person testimony.'[1] But performances since the eighties have also been enhanced by two additional modes or genres of theatrical representation: first, by the documentary drama, either presenting a situation from the period of the Second World War, *in media res*, or showing the lot of the survivors in the present, with the more objective tools of theatrical realism; and, second, by dramatic and theatrical devices, which on the basis of the generic and structural distinctions made by Tzvetan Todorov could be termed 'fantastic'.

First I shall discuss two performances from 1981: *Uncle Artur*, a monodrama by Danny Horowitz, directed by the author and performed by Yossi Yadin at the Bet Lessin Theatre;[2] and *Adam's Purim Party*, a collective work, based on Yoram Kaniuk's novel, *Adam ben Kelev*, directed by Nola Chilton at the Neve Zedek Theatre Centre.[3] Both performances were based on testimonies presented from the point of view of the survivor. They also contained some form of direct address by a survivor/witness, who has 'too much' knowledge or experience, to a 'naive' listener inside the fictional world or on its borders, who has not experienced the Holocaust directly. This transmission of painful knowledge and experience to a listener, a strategy which through rhetorical means actively includes the spectators in the process of communication, is a very important feature to which I shall return later. The main aim of this device, however, is to make it possible for the 'naive' listener to understand, and at the same time to show that he or she probably never *really* will.

[1] Michael André Bernstein, *Foregone Conclusions: Against Apocalyptic History* (Berkeley: University of California Press, 1994), p. 47.

[2] Danny Horowitz, *Uncle Arthur* (n.d.) (manuscript of a play based on *The Reunion* by Gabriel Dagan).

[3] Yoram Kaniuk, *Adam ben Kelev* (*Adam Resurrected*, translated by Seymour Simckes, New York: Harper and Row, 1971).

In the Horowitz performance, *Uncle Artur*, Peter Stone, a survivor, not only wants to explain, but is intent to show his uncle, who fled Prague in the last train out, how it was possible for the Jews to react as 'cattle led to slaughter'. In the Neve Zedek production, *Adam's Purim Party*, the inmates of a mental hospital in contemporary Israel, all Holocaust survivors, have invited their 'relatives' (the spectators) to a Purim party, in which they perform the traditional story from the Book of Esther – a story of almost miraculous survival in ancient Persia – while reliving their own concentration camp ordeal and survival. Adam himself, a circus clown before the war, survived because he was willing to serve as the commandant's dog. He and all the inmates of the mental hospital paid a heavy price for their survival.

According to Mendel Kohansky, who reviewed this performance, its message is 'that the Holocaust, which ostensibly came to an end in 1945, still lives with us, not only as a nightmarish memory, but as a horrifying presence in those who had the misfortune to survive'.[4]

Ironically, Purim is the holiday celebrating the survival of the Jews facing extinction as it is told in the Book of Esther. The Purim party in the mental hospital offers an awesome balance between physical survival and spiritual disintegration. While the world goes on living normally, at least on the surface, it is in fact the mental patients in a madhouse, who have enabled their souls to integrate the pain, who are perhaps reacting to the Holocaust in the only 'normal' way possible.

In addition to establishing a direct communication inside the fictional frame between a survivor and a listener, both of these productions offered different kinds of documentary material which were dramatized in a realistic–objective mode, either presenting the experiences from the Holocaust itself, or the situation in which the testimony was given. In *Uncle Artur*, the playwright/hero Peter Stone, with the help of four puppets, performs a scene from a play he has written about the first selections of the Jews in Prague. The play-within-the-play is acted out to show the uncle, still unwilling or unable to understand, how the threats and the violence forced the Jews to comply with the Nazi commands.

---

[4] Mendel Kohansky, 'Perils of Realism', *Jerusalem Post*, 22 May 1981.

The re-enactment, through which uncle Artur is made to understand how such things really were possible, is both a 'rehearsal' of a play and a 'return' to the actual events themselves. The double meaning is implied by the Hebrew title of an earlier play by Gabriel Dagan, *Chazara*,[5] rejected by several Israeli theatres, and which served as a basis for Horowitz's version. The documentary aspect of *Adam's Purim Party* was achieved through the realistic presentation of the inmates' stories within the setting of the mental hospital. Through the Purim play 'performances' they were re-enacting and reliving their Holocaust traumas, in a way that some critics found too realistic and disturbing.

In these performances the humiliating and painful stories from the past are retold in a documentary, realistic style. But they also contain elements that could be termed 'fantastic' in the sense Todorov gives to this genre or mode of presentation. According to Todorov, 'the very heart of the fantastic' appears when 'in a world which is indeed our world, the one we know, a world without devils, sylphides, or vampires, there occurs an event which cannot be explained by the laws of this same familiar world'.[6]

Holocaust performances since the early 1980s have in several ways integrated the fantastic in an everyday world. These fantastic elements are probed as a means to address and confront the issues of the incomprehensibility and the incommunicability of the Holocaust. One of the aims of these performances is to show that what may seem too fantastic to be true has in fact taken place. This indirectly also shows that, paradoxically, some kind of aesthetization of the narrative is necessary in order to tell what has really happened.

The person who experiences an event which cannot be explained by the laws of our familiar world, Todorov argues,

> must opt for one of two possible solutions: either he is the
> victim of an illusion of the senses, of a product of the
> imagination – and the laws of the world then remain what

---

[5] See Ben-Ami Feingold, *The Theme of the Holocaust in Hebrew Drama* (Tel Aviv: Hakkibutz Hameuchad, 1989), pp. 116–18. In Hebrew.

[6] Tzvetan Todorov, *The Fantastic: A Structural Approach to a Literary Genre* (Ithaca, NY: Cornell University Press, 1975), p. 25.

they are; or else the event has indeed taken place, it is an integral part of reality – but then this reality is controlled by laws unknown to us.[7]

Testimonies of survival from the Holocaust, as they have been represented on stage and screen, communicate the sense that the victims in the ghettos and in the camps were living in a world controlled by laws unknown or incomprehensible to them. This in turn implies that their testimonies must also be viewed as expressions of the fantastic, a position which these performances in different ways also attempt to reproduce in their relationship to the spectator-participants.

Performances about the Holocaust insist on creating very direct and almost intimate relationships with spectators. This insistence is, according to Todorov, related to the notion of the fantastic. He argues that 'the fantastic also implies an integration of the reader into the world of the characters; [and] that world is defined by the reader's own ambiguous perception of the events narrated'.[8]

This ambiguity is one of the reasons why these Holocaust performances literally place a representative of the spectators inside the fictional framework of the performance, transforming him or her into an active participant. According to the scheme presented by Todorov, while the stories from the past are presented to the reader – or to the spectator in our case – he or she experiences a hesitation which is based on the incomprehensibility of these events. And to this Todorov adds the important remark that, 'the reader's role is so to speak entrusted to a character, and at the same time the hesitation is represented, it becomes one of the themes of the work'.[9]

According to Todorov's structuralist–functional formula, which I adopt here, the key to the fantastic lies in the representation of hesitation as one of the themes in the work itself. The articulations of such hesitations in Holocaust performances are manifold. One such recurrent articulation is the device of performance within the performance which, in these instances, serves as an epistemological experimentation and a measure of the dialectics between the real and the fantastic. In Horowitz's play, Peter Stone presents a *chazara*, i.e. a

[7] Ibid.   [8] Ibid., p. 31.   [9] Ibid., p. 33.

44

rehearsal of and a return to the past in order to change the uncle's preconceived ideas. Such an inherently ambiguous timescale also provides the basic concept of the Purim party, when Adam as impresario presents his performers in his Shoah show. It raises the question if what we are seeing on the stage/mental hospital is really a form of survival. In both performances the present moment is powerfully penetrated by the fantastic elements of the past embodied in the theatrical representation.

Joshua Sobol's *Ghetto* (1984) is also a mixture of the three genres or modes of representation I have distinguished above. Here too, the performance-within-the-performance holds a prominent position. By examining some of the different published and performed versions of the play it is possible to see how sensitive the balance between these genres is. *Ghetto* is the first part of a trilogy about the Vilna Ghetto, followed by *Adam* and *In the Underground*.[10] All three parts open with the testimony of a survivor and, through flashbacks, each play is transformed into a historical documentary drama. The dramatic action in all three plays is situated in the Vilna Ghetto. According to the stage directions of *Ghetto*, published after the première at the Haifa Municipal Theatre in 1984, the action starts in 'the living room of a middle-class apartment in Tel Aviv, 1984'.[11] However, the opening sequence of the play, together with several other details in the first printed version, were not included in the Haifa production directed by Gedalia Besser.

In all published versions of *Ghetto*, as well as in most productions, the action starts by allowing Srulik, the only survivor from

---

[10] Since I have already analysed the strategies of survival through different forms of theatrical disguise and deception in Sobol's *Ghetto* triptych ('Sobol's Ghetto Trilogy', in *Machanaim*, 9 (1995), pp. 304–11, in Hebrew; 'Jehoshua Sobol's Theatre of the Ghetto', in *Small is Beautiful*, eds. Claude Schumacher and Derek Fogg (Glasgow: Theatre Studies Publications, 1990), pp. 140–6; and 'Angels of History: Joshua Sobol's Theatrical Reconstruction of the Vilna Ghetto', in *Israeli Theatre* (Ann Arbor: Michigan University, Press)), I will not deal with these plays in detail here. See also Feingold, *Theme of the Holocaust*, pp. 93–113.

[11] Joshua Sobol, *Ghetto* (Tel Aviv: Or Am, 1984), p. 14. In English, see *Ghetto*, translated and adapted by Jack Viertel, in *Plays of the Holocaust*, ed. Elinor Fuchs (New York: Theatre Communications Group, 1987), and *Ghetto*, trans. David Lan (London: Nick Hern Books, 1989).

the Vilna Ghetto theatre company, to answer a question from an unidentified interviewer about the activities of the theatre:

> The last performance? No, I don't remember anymore . . . the last performance, you asked? It was on the evening before Kittel murdered Gens. (14)

After a brief account of that last performance, and some comments on the theatre in the ghetto, Srulik says that he will go and look in his library for one of the texts performed there. This rhetorical device clearly involves the spectators, who are in a way carrying out an interview with the survivor, like Sobol when doing his own research for the play, and the performance can be seen as the answer to the implied initial question.

According to the stage directions in the first published version, Srulik gets up with difficulty before suddenly rushing straight through one of the walls, which collapse. The whole stage is thus revealed with a heap of clothes and a library barely visible in the semi-darkness. On the back of the stage there is a piece of grey cloth hiding a shrine for the Torah scrolls. Sobol also mentions, in his stage directions, that this shrine, which can hold all the members of the theatre group, is situated at a height of three metres and has to be entered via a ladder. After the walls have crumbled, noises of locks and chains can be heard, a large gate is opened through which the shadow of a man in torn underwear appears. He approaches the heap of clothes, 'picks up the uniform of a German officer . . . gets dressed and is transformed, in front of the eyes of the audience, into the German officer Kittel' (16). After grabbing a machine-gun and a suitcase from the heap of clothes, he takes a torch from his pocket and shouts *'Tohu va-vohu!'* ('Chaos!'), an obvious reference to the biblical creation story: God also acts in the world through agents like Kittel, who create chaos and destruction, instead of introducing order into the chaos as God supposedly did through the creation. When another character enters Kittel immediately commands, *'Or!'* ('Light!')

I mention these details to point out how Sobol uses several modes of representation. As Srulik, the only survivor from the theatre, is addressing his first-person testimony to the audience, he starts to reminisce and through the act of memory he is brought back into the ghetto which is taking shape on the stage. This is an obvious

46

transformation from the first-person narrative to the multivocal, realistic dramatic situation. After the transition to the Vilna Ghetto, the play presents different highlights from the history of the theatre, how it was founded, which performances were presented during its brief existence, and how it was finally liquidated by Kittel, leaving a lone survivor, Srulik, sole witness to this short and desperate attempt at survival through theatre. The play ends with a return from the grim realities of the ghetto to the opening lines of the play – 'The last performance? The last performance you asked? Just a moment . . .' (115) – reinforcing the idea that we have been witnessing a testimony, which paradoxically ends where it began. This bracketing sentence frames Srulik's testimony, while his memory, which has been dramatized on the stage, constitutes the story of the ghetto theatre reconstructed as a documentary drama. The realistic document has been confined to the memory of the individual, and the work of art can thus liberate and communicate it.

But while the play moves from testimony to documentary drama there are also several details in the text which are quite enigmatic, giving rise to a situation where the fantastic can be perceived. A person running through the wall; a figure in underwear dressing up in Nazi uniform and using language from the biblical creation story, as if he were a divine figure, ordering people around on the stage; the presence of the Torah shrine in the ghetto: such disparate features make the spectators uncertain as to the kind of reality they are watching. The Torah shrine serves, according to the stage directions, as the refuge and hiding place for the actors in the last scene of their final performance, just before their execution. According to Sobol's initial conception of the play the shrine was supposed to remain on stage throughout the performance as a reminder of the kind of ambiguity from which the fantastic, as an otherworldly or even supernatural presence stems.

The Torah shrine is clearly a potential *deus ex machina*. It is also a direct reference to the visual language of the first act of the famous Vakhtangov production of *The Dybbuk*, where the Torah shrine signifies divine presence actively influencing the lives of humans.[12] In

---

[12] See Freddie Rokem, 'Das Deus ex Machina im Theater der historischen Avantgarde', in *Theater Avantgarde*, ed. Erika Fischer-Lichte (Tübingen and Basel: Francke Verlag, 1995), pp. 324–68.

Ghetto, however, this divine 'place' has been deserted and has become powerless: the power is now embodied in the figure of Kittel. But, as far as I know, the Torah shrine and the dressing of Kittel, taking the clothes from the heap, have never been realized on stage in any of the many productions of *Ghetto*.[13]

This change indicates how delicate and problematic the balance between the different modes of representation of the Holocaust can be in performance. By making Kittel put on his uniform in front of the spectators, they would perceive him as one of the actors in the theatre group rather than just a Nazi officer; but, at the same time, he also appears as a divine figure: this ambiguity (in the sense Todorov has given this notion), if it had been realized on the stage, would probably never have been solved by the spectator. Such a scenario would have made it impossible for the spectator to fix Kittel's identity unambiguously within the framework of the documentary sections describing the theatre in the ghetto, and according to Todorov's scheme it would have transformed the play into a narrative about the marvellous which no doubt would have been counterproductive. When he wrote his play, in 1984, however, Sobol probably wanted to show that anybody, including a Jew, can put on a uniform and become a Nazi. Kittel's use of biblical language, on the other hand, transforming the SS into the creator of the ghetto, is included in every *mise en scène*. It is a fantastic element which can easily be interpreted by the spectators.

In many Israeli Holocaust performances of the 1990s, the intricate balance between the three genres has radically changed and it is

---

[13] After working on the production at the National Theatre in London in 1989 and directing the play himself in Essen in 1992, Sobol published a revised version of the play (*Ghetto*, 2nd edn; Tel Aviv: Or Am, 1992). Now the opening location is 'the square of a city in a mist' through which Srulik appears on roller-skates (p. 15). The monologue begins as in the first version, but Srulik ends by saying that he remembers some of the songs and, as he skates to the back of the stage, he pulls on a rope and a heap of clothes and shoes fall down, waking up a group of some fifteen adults and ten children asleep on the stage. The noise of the gates can still be heard, but now 'the shadow of a Nazi officer: Kittel' (p. 16) is seen entering the stage accompanied by two German soldiers and a member of the Jewish police. As before, the dialogue begins with '*Tohu va-vohu!*'

possible to discern how the fantastic has been given a much more central position than before. Avishai Milstein's *Piwnica*, directed by the author at the Habima Theatre in 1994, was completely embedded in a metatheatrical context. The central narrative of this performance is the making of a Hollywood movie about a hiding place for Jews during the Holocaust. The father of the scriptwriter, a Holocaust survivor, appears on the set and only through his testimony is it possible to get the ending of the story right. In *Adam ben Kelev*, the Gesher Theatre 1993 version of Kaniuk's novel, which also served as the inspiration for the above mentioned Neve Zedek production of *Adam's Purim Party*, the whole performance takes place in a circus tent, so that the documentary aspects of the theatrical representation are completely bracketed by this metatheatrical context.[14]

Arbeit Macht Frei vom Toitland Europa, directed by Dudu Maayan at the Acco Theatre Centre in 1991, and still running in 1998, deserves much more attention than I can give it here. Its first major section is a guided tour, first by a Holocaust survivor called Selma and after that by Haled, a Palestinian, in the Holocaust museum of Kibbutz Lohamei Ha-Ghetaot. This situation also involves the spectators as 'naive' listeners. Selma, the main character of the performance, starts the tour by introducing the photographs and other exhibits document-ing the Holocaust as 'works' – *avodot* – the same word as 'Arbeit' in German, which can, in Hebrew, also be understood as works of art. The aim of the tour, Selma says, is to make the visitors to the museum understand how Europe was gradually transformed into 'a puddle of blood'; and the whole performance, as its full title indicates, is an attempt, through the work *of*, but also *in* the performance, to become liberated from 'Toitland Europa'.

---

[14] An analysis of Gesher's production can be found in my forthcoming book, *Performing History*. It is also worth noting that Motti Lerner's dramatization of the Kasztner trial (see Motti Lerner, *The Kasztner Trial* (Tel Aviv: Or va-Tsel, 1994), in Hebrew) is entirely set in the docu-mentary mode, but since this was a performance for television, it seems to follow a different genre mechanism than the mixture of genres or modes of representation in the theatre examined here. See also chapters 4 and 6 by Gad Kaynar and Dan Laor in this book.

The museum section creates a strong unification between the first-person testimony of the survivor and the objective documentation in the museum which gradually develops into what I understand to be the central theme of this very complex and multifaceted performance, a theme which is both metahistorical and metatheatrical – the idea that the writing and the performing of history is a form of theatrical inscription. As I have shown in an earlier article analysing this performance,[15] Selma, through different strategies of inscription, constantly places herself at the meeting point, or nexus, of testimony and documentation. This is realized by enabling the actress Smadar Yaaron-Maayan literally to transform herself into the character of Selma, which is her own 'work'. This not only makes large sections of the performance 'fantastic', but disturbing and deeply enigmatic, because it reaches far beyond the intensity and involvement that we are used to seeing on the Israeli stage.

In addition to introducing the museum as a place of objective documentation about the Holocaust, where Selma serves as a surviving witness, the performance also shows how the events as she describes them have become inscribed on her body. The performance literally re-enacts several of these inscriptions. One example is when a scene from the Polish postwar film *The Ambulance* is screened and Selma explains how the children were killed by diverting the fumes from the exhaust pipe into the closed car. While the film is shown Selma appears several times in front of the screen, pointing out the exact shape of the exhaust pipe and how the children were deceived. She is thus inserting herself in the film, as if she had been present at the scene itself as an omniscient observer and commentator. But the film is also projecting the past on her, inscribing the images of the past on her fragile body.

The past has been inscribed on Selma's body in more ways. We learn that she also has a number on her forearm. Returning from the museum to Acco on the bus (transport?) the spectators are ushered

[15] Freddie Rokem, 'Cultural Transformations of Evil and Pain: Some Recent Changes in the Israeli Perception of the Holocaust', in *German–Israeli Theatre Relations After the Second World War*, ed. Hans-Peter Bayerdörfer (Tübingen: Niemeyer Verlag, 1996).

into a dark room, where dim lights are focused on Selma, sitting in the centre. In this dreamlike sequence Selma slowly, and with a dumb pain, touches her arm with the inscription from the death camp. In the next section, where an exaggerated and parodic school ceremony of the Holocaust is taking place, we learn from one of the video screens that in creating her character Smadar Yaaron-Maayan tattooed her arm with a number, the date of the death of her father, who was able to escape from Europe. The inscription expresses the paradoxical dialectics between life and death – of her life-giver and his death, of the death camp and her father's survival.

Pointing at a wooden Muselman sculpture in the museum, in the first section of the performance, Selma says: 'I would give a fortune to know where this "Muselmanchick" hides the bread; millions to know where the scream comes out, the Bat-Kol.' Much later, in the wooden barrack structure which is Selma's 'home' in Israel, and after having eaten a full meal, the spectators get at least a partial answer to this crucial question of survival. The meal starts when the table filled with food descends in the midst of the spectators – another *deus ex machina* – and we are invited to share the food. After the meal the leftovers are lifted up, closing up the roof space. But almost immediately the table is lowered again with the thin, anorexic body of Selma lying naked on it. She is fondling her vulva and, screaming in a strange mixture of pain and ecstasy, she shows where the bread has been hidden inside her body. Her scream will continue to echo to the very end of the performance.

This remarkable performance shows how the Holocaust has become inscribed not only on the bodies of those who survived, but also on their children. Selma is the Muselmanchick – she has a number on her arm. Her body is neither, to use the term coined by the French historian Pierre Nora, a *lieu de mémoire*, like the museum, nor is she the source of a testimony. By inscribing the past *on* and *in* her body Selma is as fantastic and enigmatic as survival itself. And contradicting Celan's poem quoted above as my motto, she becomes a witness able to testify for the survivors, the real witnesses. In this sense her 'performance' is a response to the crisis which we are experiencing and which is soon going to become reality, when all the survivors will have died and it will be impossible to give a testimony.

When I told an old friend who spent two years just outside the gas chambers in Auschwitz sorting disinfected clothes from the victims, how difficult it is to write about theatre and survival, but in particular to understand, she immediately responded: 'You need a lot of fantasy to tell about that.'

4 The Holocaust experience through theatrical profanation

GAD KAYNAR

First example: the programme from the Israeli black mass and passion play *Arbeit Macht Frei vom Toitland Europa* (first prize at the 1991/2 annual Akko Festival of Alternative Israeli Theatre) depicts the image of the entire theatrical event. The overall framework consists of the most notorious entry gate of this century – the gate to Auschwitz. Under the inscription which pointedly subverts a naive ditty by Kadja Molodowska – 'We opened the gate we opened it wide it was hell and it was work' – we see a profane kitsch assemblage of the most trite iconography of Nazi evil, Zionist redemption and Jewish victimology: Hitler on top, with speech bubbles coming out of his mouth; below him, hands on barbed wire; Theodor Herzl's official portrait; the Israeli flag enmeshed in the railway leading to the gas chambers overprinted with 'Halt!'; Ben Gurion declaring the establishment of the State of Israel; and finally the headline '*Yiddische Meluche*' (literally 'Jewish Kingdom' and metaphorically 'Jewish Sovereignty'). All these symbols are thrown together, the unbridgeable contrast between their meanings and emotional imports questioned by being totally erased. They overshadow piles of corpses lying above lines of an unpunctuated, deconstructed text, self-contradictorily proclaiming among other clichés, 'I have no other country, I was born here in Israeli hell.' At the bottom of the page, in bold letters, is inscribed the impossible command, 'laugh', which is precisely what some of the spectators, including myself, did throughout the five-hour journey through the Dantesque hellish compartments in Akko, thereby arousing the indignation of others who still regard the memory of the Holocaust as holy, meaning something which demands that one go through the habitual, ceremonious motions of barren solemnity.

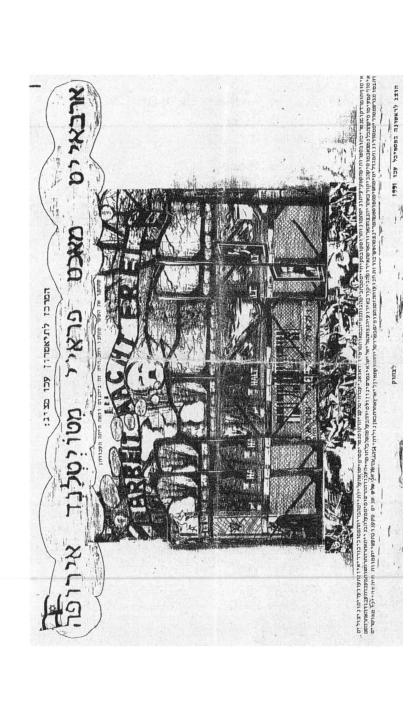

2. Programme for *Arbeit Macht Frei vom Toitland Europa* (Akko Festival of Alternative Israeli Theatre, 1991/2). The line under the title reads: 'We opened the door: we opened it wide. It was hell and it was work.' The single word at the bottom says 'Laugh!'

Second example: the 'Zionist terrorist' Arik, a Holocaust survivor, an all-Israeli paranoiac, an all-Jewish schizophrenic, destroys in
Shmuel Hasfari's *Hametz* the ur-symbol of Jewish survivability, the
Seder, the Passover meal, by negating collective memory through the
terrible act of extinguishing the most venerable symbol of Jewish resurrection – the eternal flame in the 'Yiskor' tent, the heart of Israel's holiest shrine, Yad Vashem. He leaves a blasphemous spiritual testament
before being driven to suicide by the black, Mephistophelean angel, the
inverted incarnation – in SS uniform – of Jacob's angel, who is supposed
to save the children from all evil. This angel, the avenging dead child,
a metaphoric–metaphysical victim of the Holocaust lunatic victims,
imposed the past on the present and murdered his innocence. Arik says:

> I'm destroying memory, I'm destroying history . . . And the
> children, if they are not dead, if they live and ask questions –
> let them watch a tree, a flower, a bird, and find answers . . .
> and forget. Do not 'remember what they did to your father',
> do not 'remember' anything . . . Kids, beware of museums for
> the History of the Jewish People . . . They'll take you to
> concentration camps, and you just fancy the bottom of the
> girl standing before you, and all the heroic acts will enter into
> your right ear and come out from the left.[1]

These examples of defiling the Holocaust's sanctity in and through theatre reify the nature and function of the metaphors which constitute
the most emphatic phenomenon in the rhetoric of recent Israeli Shoah
performances: the attempt to revive a genuine experiential, traumatic,
critical and actuality linked consciousness of the catastrophe, as well
as of its enraging present-day repercussions and manifestations, in the
minds of the second and third generations of Israeli spectators, who
are weary of the stock commemorative rites and their manipulative
aspects. This is achieved by a sophisticated strategy of sensory and
emotional manipulation, as well as the shock effects elicited through
the travesty of the most basic and vulnerable ingredients of Israel's

---

[1] Shmuel Hasfari, *Hametz*, rehearsal manuscript, Tel Aviv, Beth-Lessin
Theatre, 1995.

communal identity, which are rooted in the Holocaust. The paradoxical postulate that underlies these theatrical texts is that only arbitrary artistic invention, agnostically inspired by attraction to German culture and fascist aesthetics, can re-endow the Shoah with the truth it has lost within changing Israeli reality conventions. Joel, the young scriptwriter in Avishai Milstein's play *Piwnica*, says while vainly seeking a proper artistic ending to the real Holocaust ordeals of his father, aestheticized by him in a Spielberg-like documentary drama: 'I'm unable to use my imagination – to find an idea – to understand how it *really* was.'[2]

These new, blunt texts eliminate the traditional Holocaust consciousness from within by setting up new iconic codes to convey an updated Holocaust vision. Such codes are the result of an iconoclastic approach that breaches the holiest taboos to redeem them through the gutters, turning the sacred but outworn and ideologically abused sign language of the Shoah upside down.[3] The Shoah is decanonized and thus recanonized in the sense imparted by Herbert Lindenberger, albeit in a totally different context, to 'canon': 'a term we ignore when its referent remains in a stable condition, but that we invoke incessantly whenever it is threatened with change'.[4] I partially agree with Freddie Rokem that the Holocaust 'holds such a strong direct as well as symbolical presence in the collective Israeli consciousness that it is almost automatically triggered or activated at a time of crisis as a kind of coded

---

[2] Avishai Milstein, *Piwnica*, Tel Aviv, National Theatre Habima, 1994, p. 9, my emphasis.

[3] For a detailed discussion of the sociopoetic process that has led to this present stage in Israeli drama and theatre, see Gad Kaynar, ' "What's Wrong with the Usual Description of the Extermination?!" National Socialism and the Holocaust as a Self-Image Metaphor in Israeli Drama: The Aesthetic Conversion of a National Tragedy into Reality-Convention', in Hans-Peter Bayerdörfer, ed., *German–Israeli Theatre Relations After the Second World War* (Tübingen: Niemeyer Verlag, 1996), pp. 200–16. The Hebrew version of the article appeared in *Bama*, 138 (1994), pp. 73–92.

[4] Herbert Lindenberger, *The History in Literature: On Value, Genre, Institutions* (New York: Columbia University Press, 1990), p. xiii.

and well-prepared defence mechanism'.[5] Yet it is precisely this 'well-preparedness', over-codification and automated 'humpty-dumptiness' of the Holocaust sign repertory that conduces to its experiential erosion. The gas chamber, the tattooed number, the death-skull insignia and the transports deteriorate to the level of ready-made and mechanically applicable semiotic vehicles projected on transitory circumstances, losing with each manipulation a little more of the authentic horror originally imbued in them. The shockingly unorthodox idioms of recent theatrical texts such as *Arbeit Macht Frei*, *The Child Dreams*, *Piwnica*, *Chametz* and *Adam Son of a Dog* revitalize the Holocaust experience through the tensions engendered by deliberately misusing the eroded Shoah sign repertory within intertexts in which the past experience is – in a Gadamerian vein – dehistoricized, merged with the contemporary horizon, and its inner truth sought after *via negativa*, that is, through utterly irreverent and incongruent metaphorical prisms with an underlying, eerie expressionist syntax. When Smadar Yaaron-Maayan proudly boasts in *Balagan*, the German documentary on *Arbeit Macht Frei* – 'For me this work is sacrilege: to take something and turn it into "Balagan" ' – she refers to a repertory of symbols profaned simply by transcontextualization and the invasion of their purist immunity as exclusive Shoah signs, such as the immense erotic pleasure that she, in the character of the perverted survivor Selma, derives from the images, screened on her body, of an SS officer's experimentation with the effect of exhaust pipe fumes on some Jewish children in the Polish semi-documentary *The Ambulance*; the presentation of the Treblinka model by a Palestinian guide 'in love' with the Holocaust theme; the blasphemous and sadistic 'selection game' that Selma imposes on her son; the associations Yaaron-Maayan draws between the Horst Wessel Lied and Israeli independence war songs; and her pulling out a piece of bread from her vagina or spitefully tattooing her arm and then trying to erase the number. She refers, in one word, to the venture of once again turning the Holocaust consciousness of the

---

[5] Freddie Rokem, 'Cultural Transformations of Evil and Pain: Some Recent Changes in the Israeli Perception of the Holocaust', in Bayerdörfer, ed., *German–Israeli Theatre Relations*, pp. 217–38 (see n. 3).

spectators into a 'Balagan', namely, into something that evokes the chaotic experience which it had originally exerted, yet is still entirely up to date. This sacred act is all the more profane, paradoxical and dialectic since in order to expose an Israeli audience to such mental cruelty you have to admit and let loose the 'little Nazi' in you, as George Tabori says in *Jubiläum*.[6] Little wonder, then, that Tabori is not exactly the favourite dramatist of Israeli artistic directors.

The most prominent among these 'profane' and decorum-breaching strategies is the use of the self-referential and self-reflective theatrical performative idiom. This subject has been intensively and extensively researched by Feingold,[7] Urian and Yaari,[8] and many others. These lucid explications appear to undermine the most fundamental aspect of resorting to theatricality when dealing with the Holocaust, namely, *theatricality itself*. Shoah in its traditional phenomenological position (in Israel) as a religion, on the one hand, and theatricality, on the other, constitutes a contradiction in terms. I do not refer, as in *Ghetto*, to the theme of a theatre operating within the historical, or pseudohistorical, context of the Holocaust, nor to theatrical patterns exploited as analogous filters to convey the horrors. What I do refer to is the presentation of the *Shoah-as-performance*, to the Holocaust constructed in terms of self-conscious theatricality. Theatricality, first and foremost, imbues the catastrophe with connotations of a pretence, or a myth. This is offensive, because such performances are designed to give Israeli society, in the 'legitimate' and 'appropriate' context of the theatre, that necrophilic thrill on which it thrives – or, more precisely, they unravel this thrill to condemn it – and to expose the truly theatrical, mannerist, routine and empty character of our ritualistic attitude to the Holocaust. The profane foregrounded theatricality of recent Shoah performances incorporates the option of *repeating the performance*, thus institutionalizing and denouncing the stock and well-rehearsed

---

[6] George Tabori, *Jubiläum*, *Theater Heute*, 2 (1983), p. 39. See also chapter 16 by Anat Feinberg in this book.

[7] Ben-Ami Feingold, *The Theme of the Holocaust in Hebrew Drama* (Tel Aviv: Hakkibutz Hameuchad, 1989).

[8] Dan Urian and Nurit Yaari, 'Ghetto – From Play to Performance', in *Bama*, 98 (1989), pp. 116–36.

identification with the dead as it is practised by us in reality (demonstrated, for instance, by the parody of a school commemoration ceremony in *Arbeit Macht Frei*). Precisely by committing the sacrilege of stressing theatricality, these performances make it clear, in Eli Rozik's terminology, that 'the single and ultimate referent of theatrical sense is the spectator alone'.[9] Moreover, only by forcing the Israeli spectators to adopt the perspective of the hangman's death through kitsch aesthetics, and to be carried away by it (as in Hanoch Levin's *The Child Dreams*[10]), only by engendering the sensory conviction that brutality is far more 'artistic' than the presentation of impotent victims, can the spectators experience the horror which lies in the theatrical temptation of evil and mass murder, and, hence, grasp its relevance to the present. It may, of course, be rightfully maintained that the contiguity between Nazi demonism and performative decadence has, since Visconti's *The Damned* (1969)[11] and Saul Friedländer's *Essay on Kitsch and Death*,[12] become a cliché and, consequently, an ineffective artistic device. This, however, does not apply to the new approach in the Israeli theatre of amalgamating the 'sub-standard' popular show with the specific theme of the persecution and murder of the Jews.

The harshest defamiliarization of the habitual artistic and cognitive patterns for dealing with the Holocaust and reactivating its memory by defaming it is achieved by resorting to grotesque, irreverent, infamous and 'oversimplified' performative genres, such as the operatic spectacle, the multimedia show, the lewd, infantile vaudeville, the below-the-waist cabaret skit, the mock-happening or the drag show. Some of these stylistic features typify the cabaret 'numbers', which expressly debase the Holocaust's spiritual heritage in my main example,

---

[9] Eli Rozik, *The Language of the Theatre* (Glasgow: Theatre Studies Publications), p. 152.

[10] Hanoch Levin, 'The Child Dreams', in *Plays (4)* (Tel Aviv; Siman Kriah-Hakkibutz Hameuchad, 1991), pp. 261–331. Performed at the National Theatre Habima and Haifa Municipal Theatre, May 1993.

[11] See Ilan Avisar, *Screening the Holocaust: Cinema's Images of the Unimaginable* (Bloomington and Indianapolis: Indiana University Press, 1988), pp. 152–7.

[12] Saul Friedländer, *Reflections of Nazism: An Essay on Kitsch and Death*, translated by Thomas Weyr (New York: Avon Discus Books, 1986).

Adam Resurrected (or in a literal translation of its Hebrew title, *Adam Son of a Dog*), premièred in September 1993 by the renowned Russian immigrants' theatre, Gesher, under the direction of Ivgenye Arieh. I shall not attempt an exhaustive analysis of this highly complex performance, but will focus instead on a few aspects of its profane theatrical language. The following notes are based on a strict differentiation between, on the one hand, the intentions of the Russian–American adapter and the director, who was a novice on the Israeli stage, and, on the other, the intentionality imbued in the performance itself as designed to be perceived by its Israeli-implied spectator, whose features likewise emerge from the show (a persona distinct both from actual Israeli spectators, as well as from foreign audiences such as those who viewed the performance on its tour to Germany, Austria and Switzerland).

Adam Resurrected is a stage adaptation by Alexander Chervinsky of the Israeli writer Yoram Kaniuk's novel, which was published in 1968. It is the expressionistically visualized inner tragedy of Adam Stein, a mentally sick patient hospitalized in an Israeli bedlam – or, as both the novel and the play present it, in 'bedlam Israel'. Stein, a genial clown and former circus owner, suffers from the symptomatic syndrome of guilt for the death of his wife and daughter while he had managed to survive by becoming the performing dog of the 'benign' Klein, the commander of a circus-like concentration camp. Adam eases the way of the victims, his own family included, to perdition in the gas chambers through his pranks and violin playing. Chervinsky and Arieh transcribe Adam's surreal reminiscences and hallucinations, in contrast to the madhouse setting of the novel, into circus and cabaret metaphorics. These inform the identity, the performative and body language, the kinetics, the proxemic relations, the costumes, the props and the entire contexts of the personae, places, periods and elements which intermingle in Adam's perfectly normal sick mind in a synchronous interpolation: past and present; Nazi Germany and Israel; the state of mad Jews, who are identical with the camp and asylum inmates seeking their Messiah in the archetypal Holocaust survivor and their God in the Nazi commander, who is saved by Adam after the war and transformed into Dr Gross, the chief psychiatrist of the mental clinic.

The sacrilege, intended to estrange, criticize and revitalize the spectator's numb Shoah experience, ensues not merely from the tense

3. **Alexander Chervinsky** and **Yoram Kaniuk**, *Adam Resurrected* (Gesher Theatre, Tel Aviv, 1993). Commander Klein (Israel Demidov) and his mistress (Natalya Voitulevich-Manor) breathe in some fresh air away from the stench of the crematoria.

imposition of the semiotic co-ordinates of such a cheap, infantile and sheer entertainment-oriented variety genre as the circus on the *sanctum sanctorum* of the Holocaust, but also from the recognition that both history and performance are, in fact, demetaphorized through their inscription within pure theatre. The director insisted on performing *Adam* in a circus tent, emphasizing that he did not want 'a stage set but a real circus'.[13] Arieh, in other words, was not seeking an artistic metaphor which would furnish the spectator with the convenience of an uninvolved onlooker who would be able to tell the dancer from the dance; namely, to detach – in Brechtian manner, as Sobol in *Ghetto* – the present signifying parable – the circus – from the absent signifieds – the historical atrocities and his or her own reality. Quite the contrary. If, according to Friedländer, 'Nazi death is a show, a production, a performance. For the viewer, everything signifies fascination, terror, and ecstasy,'[14] then this is precisely the aim: to put the spectator, against his or her will, in the position of the arch-spectator, the camp commander Klein, and force him to enjoy this theatre of cruelty – the extermination circus – staged on his behalf. At the same time, the spectator should retain the awareness that he or she is watching a funny, delightful and horrendous show together with the victim characters – the Stein and Fein families. The actors playing these characters are seated among the spectators, who are thereby also stamped as potential victims. On top of everything, the spectator has to acknowledge that his or her crazy, perplexed, stereotyped and ahistorical Holocaust consciousness is in fact just a histrionic make-believe, like this Adam circus horror show in which everything is lethal and nothing is real or serious: the actors play performers who cause or suffer a paradoxically terminal and pretended death (unlike *Ghetto*, in which show is show, and death is death), as demonstrated by the hallucinatory scene of the birth of Ruth, Adam's daughter, directed and acted as an exaggerated clownish act. This act leads – in the fashion of a condensed circus number inspired by silent-movie rhetoric – from a sugar-coated cabaret song by the Nazi trio, through the disclosure of the pregnancy of Adam's wife to the

---

[13] In Lihi Hanoch's semi-documentary television feature *Adam Circus*, Israeli Television, Channel 1, 1994.

[14] Friedländer, *Reflections of Nazism*, p. 16.

performing circus artist. This is followed by Adam's accidental fall and leg breaking, leading to the arrival of the slapstick Mack Sennet ambulance, which takes the husband instead of the wife, and to Ruth's birth behind the circus arena screens, which simultaneously indicate the gas chambers. The festive adoration of the baby, a grotesque doll, is followed by its destruction by the medical staff, i.e. the SS murderers, and the chaining of the maddened Adam to the hospital bed. The perfect blending and overlapping of the juxtaposed contexts has the curious effect of converting alienating burlesque stimuli into an embarrassed pondering over the real intentionality of this unusual theatrical syntax, namely, over the true, chaotic, unexpected and currently relevant meanings of the Holocaust.

The architecture and proxemic substructure of the circus sustain the multivalent functions of the blended performance-past-present-future horizons within a 'real circus', a 'round arena, without beginning or end'.[15] This structure accords with the circular, non-chronological pattern of the show, which embodies the dehistoricized postmodern conception of the Shoah. This should not be regarded as a failure to present the horrible ontology of 'the thing itself' according to some critics,[16] but as constituting the thing itself from our present, over-loaded and impure vantage point: as a timeless, placeless and infinitely veiled phenomenon in which 'past-present-and-future are mutually contained circles'.[17] The circus arena is, furthermore, 'egalitarian' and democratic in shape, and thus permits the striking alternation of roles between perpetrators and victims. In accordance with circus aesthetics, each 'number' or episode is autonomous, circumscribed only by the clear demarcation lines of entrance and exit, which in contrast to the conventional apron stage enables a reorganization of the characters' hierarchical relations with each new 'act'. These relentlessly changing proxemic relations manifest the more flexible views, within the Israeli reality convention and theatre, on the relative and changeable positions of perpetrator and victim roles (which, of course, do not reverse

---

[15] *Adam Circus* (see n. 13).

[16] See Shimon Levy's review in *Yediot Achronot*, 3 December 1993.

[17] Miriam Yachil-Wachs, 'Circus as a Madhouse', *Yediot Achronot*, 22 October 1993.

the fixed underlying structure of the Nazi as the persecutor and the Jew as the persecuted).

The most evident architectonic feature of the intertextualized Holocaust circus is the curtained entrance gate: that 'usually soft gate of circuses through which tigers, elephants and acrobats enter, becomes here a hard "transit" gate, a hell emitting dense smoke and reddish light, in which the Holocaust victims often disappear'.[18] True, but not entirely: the 'hard' entrance into the gas chambers does not lose its function as a 'soft' circus gate, and inasmuch as the smoke and the red glow are signs of those infamous ovens, they are also enchanting performative effects, and our childish fascination – as with all kitsch ingredients of the circus – makes us oblivious to what is happening in the outer-stage area, on the other side of this beautified entrance to the death chamber. Thus *Adam*'s theatrical idiolect subtly points an accusing finger at our waning Shoah consciousness, and turns our circus bench into the dock of the accused.

The gist of the homeopathic approach of redeeming this regressing consciousness is embodied in the figure of the protagonist, Adam, the Jewish Everyman converted into a performing dog. The presentation of a human being as an animal belongs to the 'common' fare of attractive and amusing deformations provided by the circus, like the Biggest/Smallest Man in the World, the Rubber Maiden, the Man With Two Heads, and so on. There is a sudden acknowledgement that this Jew-dog, this personification of a trite anti-Semitic metaphor, is nothing more than another exemplar of those dehumanized 'Freaks of Nature' which arouse our laughter. This shows how easy it is to slip into the position of the victimizer or the silent majority, even if we are aware of the exceptionality of this circus. All the more so, in view of the fact that almost every circus feat is a gladiator's act of survival, and the greater the risk taken, the greater our amusement; not to mention our secret longing to be those spectators rewarded by seeing the acrobat fall from the tightrope and crash on to the ground. This mixture of identification by spectators who are – in a double sense – on the victim's side, of brutal as well of fun-and-games expectations, makes the

---

[18] Shimon Levy, in *Yediot Achronot*, 3 December 1993.

4. *Adam Resurrected*. Adam (Igor Mirkurbanov) is transformed from a smart circus manager into Commander Klein's dog by the drag-show trio (*l–r*) Ruth Heilovsky, Roland Heilovsky and Michael Assinovsky.

strategy employed in *Adam Resurrected* to demythicize our superficial Holocaust perception much more effective, complex and realistic than the merely flattering recognition, fostered by plays like *Ghetto*, 'that the theatre had been a source for physical and spiritual survival'.[19]

The bankruptcy, the abuse and the distortion of Shoah as a living and fertile consciousness are at their worst when it comes to the usual reduction of the experience to the level of signs. These have been emasculated by the collective memory and perverted from particular icons, anchored in a specific reality, into becoming trite incantation symbols and fetishes: the soap, the nakedness of the victims, the heaps of clothes, of spectacles and other personal belongings, the striped inmates' uniform, the SS helmets and riding breeches, the railway, the smoke, and so on. These are the implied referents of Primo Levi's contention: 'Memory can be replayed so often that it becomes fixed in a

[19] Rokem, 'Cultural Transformations', p. 10.

stereotype.'[20] The provocative and cruel misreading of this sign reservoir in blasphemous, catharsis-denying entertainment terms in *Adam* demystifies this theological vocabulary by lending it semiotic density. Terror lurks in daily objects, in the most innocent pleasure and in the dirtiest jokes, gestures and fantasies. This becomes manifest in one of the most shattering and, at the same time, most fascinating scenes in the performance, which shows Mrs Fein lured into entering the gas chamber with a smile on her face. A close observation of this scene from the viewpoint of its estranged Shoah semiotics yields some interesting and surprising insights.

The ominous black uniform of the Nazi commander, the arch-murderer Klein, is in fact the tail coat of a master of ceremonies, which also determines his behaviour, just like Mr Fein's Beckettian bowler hat and Adam's clownish inmate's garment. Klein offers the potential victims an immaculate, pink slice of ordinary soap – the unbearable connotation of soap made out of human fat is thus emphasized – as one would offer a prize in an amusing children's contest. Mr Fein is a gentleman: he graciously allows his wife to go to perdition before him. Shoah experience is thus rescued from the alienating clutches of bleak metaphysics. It is presented as having its fine dramatic ironies, which only the immune Israeli spectator and the Nazis can relish. The officer throughout tries to make Mrs Fein's death as pleasing to her, and as fascinating to the audience, as possible. He leads her in a round, as if presenting the star number or the prize horse in a circus performance. The cabaret trio strips her of her clothes and belongings, one by one, in a fashion which is both discreet and public. They shelter her from the audience's view, simultaneously shielding her modesty and raping her, and at the same time presenting Mrs Fein's items to the viewers as if they were performing some magic trick, thus satirizing the absurdity in the customary depersonification of the dead and apotheosis of their material, lifeless property. As the hermaphroditic drag-show trio leave the perplexed victim, she is seen standing alone on a small pedestal, trying to hide her nakedness. The taboo sign of the female victim's bare flesh in the familiar Holocaust documentation is here marked

---

[20] Primo Levi, *The Drowned and the Saved*, trans. Raymond Rosenthal, (New York: Summit Books, 1988), p. 24.

and pushed to the foreground by the pornographic context, sustained by Klein's erotic game with the victim turned into a sexual object – especially since she has to bare her breasts in order to get the soap – as well as by the attractiveness of the non-Jewish looking actress which negates the documented historical images. Our filthiest and most profane associations are triggered and legitimized, transforming the Shoah into a private, sensual and intimate experience indelibly – and therefore much more painfully – connected with an entire field of pleasurable, vivid sensations from which it had been excluded with the result of becoming aloof, demonic, ceremonious and bereft of true experiential meaning.

These recognitions engendered through incongruous contexts bring us to the last argument. In her semi-documentary television feature on the show – *Adam Circus* – the director Lihi Hanoch asks each of the actors whether he is Jewish. This curious interrogation is neither tasteless nor pointless, since several of Gesher's artists are not Jewish and, therefore, perhaps not 'entitled' to deal with the subject considering the mute monopolistic attitude to the Holocaust in Israel, not to mention the ingrained dogmatic code of relating to it. This is especially so since apparently there is hardly any theme to which Marvin Carlson's contention that 'the interpretation of signs is of course culturally generated, but so is the recognition of signs as signs'[21] more appropriately applies. It is precisely Gesher's outsider's perspective, the theatre's unorthodox, insensitive, almost obtuse meddling with canonical sign systems and its 'ungodly' practice of matching totally inconsistent contexts, that renders the reception of *Adam Resurrected* a genuinely existential experience.

Yet Gesher's (subliminal) 'impertinence' goes even further, for neither Natalya Voitulevich-Manor, who plays Mrs Fein, nor Igor Mirkurbanov, who plays Adam, nor the other actors, look Jewish, speak like Jews or Israelis, or have the 'appropriate' body language. They look like pretty 'Goyim', and their physiognomy is more Aryan than Aryan. Moreover, their heavy Russian accent – when they utter German words or sing the greasy nationalistic folk-songs and the schmaltz-dripping

---

[21] Marvin Carlson, in *Theatre Semiotics: Signs of Life* (Bloomington and Indianapolis: Indiana University Press, 1990).

5. *Adam Resurrected*. Mrs Fein (Natalya Voitulevich-Manor) is lured into the gas chamber.

cabaret refrains from the Third Reich – totally deforms the pure German dialect of 'our' (i.e. the non-German speaking Israeli spectator) standard Nazis. In a word, they are outrageously ethnically and politically incorrect. How dare they touch 'our' Shoah? What entitles them to 'colonialize' our catastrophe? In view of these questions, it seems that the casting is the most ingenious thematic and rhetorical accomplishment of the show, even if it was unintended in this sense by the director. It subtly, obliquely, yet very shrewdly brings out the latent racists in us, and turns *Adam Resurrected* into a performance about ourselves.

Freddie Rokem refers to a strange and theatrical act executed by Smadar Yaaron as Selma in *Arbeit Macht Frei*, and asks, 'What does it mean to tattoo a number on the arm in order to perform a Holocaust survivor?'[22] I have tried to propose an answer: to profane a symbol by staging a theatrical – namely, public – act of estranging it, recontextualizing it, misusing and abusing it and thereby crassly demartyrologizing or undemonizing the typology of character – structures connected with it, means to regenerate the real experience for which this trite and overprotective symbol pretends to stand by renouncing, or rejuvenating, the hollow sign. It is, thereby, not only an aesthetic but also an ideological and political act that erases the mythical and mystical uniqueness of the Shoah in order to revive it as a recharged and meaningful paradigm which bears on our present existence.

[22] Rokem, 'Cultural Transformations', p. 17. See also chapter 3 by Freddie Rokem in this book.

5 Ben Hecht's pageant-drama: *A Flag Is Born*

ATAY CITRON

A Flag Is Born was staged in New York in 1946, just one year after the end of the War. This probably makes it the first postwar Holocaust drama to be staged anywhere. The term 'Holocaust drama', however, is not entirely appropriate for *A Flag Is Born*, for although the background of its plot was the Treblinka death camp, the play itself focused on the survivors' right to an independent state of their own. *A Flag Is Born* differs from other Holocaust dramas in yet another respect: it was conceived not as a reflection on the experiences of the victims or the victimizers, but rather, for three immediate political purposes:

1 To draw the attention of the American public to the fate of the 100,000 Holocaust survivors, who had been labelled 'Displaced Persons' or 'DPs', living in DP camps in Germany and Austria. The living conditions of these Jewish DPs were described by Earl G. Harrison, President Truman's representative to the Inter-Governmental Committee on Refugees, as 'horrible'. In his report, Harrison stated that 'those who have suffered most and longest [namely, the Jews] should be given first and not last attention'. In another paragraph he said, 'We appear to be treating the Jews as the Nazis treated them, except we do not exterminate them.'[1] *A Flag Is Born* dramatized that chilling analogy most effectively.

[1] Reprinted by United Jewish Appeal for Refugees, Overseas Needs and Palestine, pp. 6–9, Palestine Statehood Commission Papers, Sterling Library, Yale University (hereafter, PSC-Yale).

2 To agitate the American public against the British White Paper policy of 1939, which prevented the DPs from entering legally into Palestine.

3 To gain moral and financial support for a large illegal repatriation effort, as well as for an armed struggle for Jewish independence in Palestine.

A Flag Is Born was a propaganda pageant-drama. It was militantly anti-British and, at the same time, it was a bold attack on the Jews of the free world for having failed to come to the rescue of their brethren who had been slaughtered in Europe.

It took guts and conviction to lash at the British liberators right after the end of the war. Even more so, perhaps, to point an accusing finger at the mourning Jewish community, which, with wounds still open, was hardly ready to cope with its feeling of guilt. This combination of guts and conviction, seasoned with plenty of talent, hot temper and a giant ego, characterized Ben Hecht, the creator of *A Flag Is Born*. Since 1941, Hecht had been writing belligerent propaganda pieces for a small, radical Jewish organization known as the Bergson Group. At the peak of his career – he was the most highly paid screenwriter in Hollywood, the winner of three Academy Awards, the author of many novels, newspaper columns and Broadway plays – Hecht became the leading campaign writer for the Bergson Group. His full-page advertisements, appearing in America's largest newspapers, were a continuous outcry against the abandonment of the Jews by the leaders of the free world.[2] His writing style, fusing bitter sarcasm and poetic pathos, was highly effective with non-Jewish Americans. The Jewish establishment perceived Hecht's collaboration with the Bergson Group as a dangerous act of dissidence, and later, even as treason. In the early 1940s, the leaders of American Jewry tried to silence him by using their influence on Federal officials, politicians and media personalities. Toward the end of the war and immediately following it, they realized that their efforts had largely failed and declared an open war on the Bergson Group. For

---

[2] I borrow the term from the title of David Wyman's book, *The Abandonment of the Jews* (New York: Pantheon Books, 1984).

6. **Ben Hecht**, *A Flag Is Born* (Alvin Theater, New York, 1946). Cover of the souvenir programme.

the duration of its run, *A Flag Is Born* stood at the centre of that bitter inter-Jewish feud.

The origins of the anti-Nazi Jewish pageant in America

Hecht did not invent the Jewish propaganda pageant. *A Flag Is Born* was the last in a series of four gigantic anti-Nazi pageants staged by

American Jews. First in this series was *The Romance of a People*, which was produced by the Jews of Chicago for the World's Fair of 1933. This spectacular, Cecil B. DeMille-like pageant was most probably the largest show ever produced in America. Staged in Soldier Field Stadium with a cast of 5,000, it presented highlights of 4,000 years of Jewish history, from the creation of the world to the rebuilding of modern-day Zion. Emphasizing the Jewish contribution to civilization, it was designed to counter the Nazis' anti-Semitic propaganda. It was seen by close to 1,000,000 spectators in Chicago, New York, Philadelphia, Cleveland and Detroit, and of its net profit of $200,000, half went to the Central Refugee Fund, to pay the ransom required by the German government to allow the repatriation of German Jews to Palestine.

Following the success of *The Romance of a People*, its producer, a Zionist activist named Meyer Weisgal, commissioned a similar (yet more professional and artistically refined) pageant from Max Reinhardt – the prince of the German-speaking theatre at the time. Reinhardt, himself a victim of Hitler, asked Franz Werfel and Kurt Weill to collaborate with him on the new pageant.

Werfel's play, *The Eternal Road*, is the story of a persecuted Jewish community in Europe, which finds refuge in a synagogue and spends the night before going into exile, reading the great biblical narratives which come alive on the desert hills, designed by Norman Bel Geddes on the vast stage of the Manhattan Opera House. After three years of preparation and ten postponements, the show finally premièred on 7 January 1937 to raving reviews. The cost of mounting this lavish spectacle could not be covered, however, by ticket sales, and after 153 performances it had to close. In terms of Jewish or Zionist propaganda, its achievements were meagre (especially in view of Weisgal's high expectations), although the spectacle itself and the extensive media coverage aroused considerable sympathy for the plight of the Jews of Germany (and one must remember that in 1937 many Americans were responding favourably to isolationist, racist and Nazi groups).

In 1941 Ben Hecht stepped in. In this limited space, we can only trace the most significant stations in his personal transformation from a fanatic individualist and a totally assimilated Jew into a leader of an anti-Nazi crusade; from a writer of gangster movies and situation comedies into a zealous Jewish propagandist.[3]

Hecht and the Bergson Group

In the late 1930s Hecht began publishing anti-Nazi articles in his personal column in the New York daily, *P.M.* What characterized these articles was Hecht's preoccupation, not only with the brutalities in Europe, but with the rage, helplessness and shame (not to mention simple fear) felt by American Jews while reading or listening to the disturbing news. This preoccupation was forcefully expressed in Hecht's *The Book of Miracles* (1939). In October 1941 it took a different form, when Hecht and his regular collaborator, Charles MacArthur, joined forces with the producer Billy Rose and the composer Kurt Weill to create the Fight for Freedom pageant, *It's Fun to be Free.* The pageant was the central feature of a large anti-fascist rally in New York's Madison Square Garden. Its main point – that freedom was a traditional American ideal worth fighting for – led to the conclusion that the United States should participate in the war.[4]

Hecht was still thinking at that time more as an American than as a Jew. This changed as a result of his meeting with a small group of young Jewish men who had arrived in the US from Palestine and Europe. The Group had links with the Irgun T'zva'i Le'umi (National Military Organization) – a small, militant anti-British militia in Palestine, which was ideologically associated with Ze'ev Jabotinsky's Revisionist Zionism. The leader of the group, Hillel Kook, was operating in America under the alias Peter Bergson, hence the group's name. The Bergson Group's first goal was to recruit American support for the idea of establishing an army of stateless and Palestinian Jews that would fight the Nazis with the Allies. The British strongly objected to this for fear of escalating the Arab–Jewish conflict in postwar Palestine. But the

---

[3] For a fuller description of this process, see Ben Hecht, *A Child of the Century* (New York: Simon and Schuster, 1954), pp. 515–23, and William MacAdams, *Ben Hecht: The Man Behind the Legend* (New York: Charles Scribner's Sons, 1990), pp. 211–27.

[4] *It's Fun to be Free*, souvenir programme with the full script, at New York Public Library's Billy Rose Theatre Collection.

Bergson Group's imaginative campaign of full-page advertisements in the leading newspapers was very effective. Soon, the idea of a Jewish army won the support of high-ranking officials, politicians and other public figures. Hecht became co-chairman of the new Committee for a Jewish Army.

The surprising success of the Bergson Group's campaign was met with strong antagonism from within the Jewish establishment, headed by the president of the American Jewish Congress, Rabbi Stephen Wise. Wise supported the Haganah, the armed resistance forces of the Jewish Agency in Palestine, and adopted its hostile attitude to the Irgun dissidents. Besides, the Bergson Group's propaganda presented Wise and his fellow Jewish leaders as passive, if not incompetent.

In November 1942, Wise confirmed to the press the long-suppressed reports of the systematic extermination of 2,000,000 Jews. His announcement, which appeared on page 10 of the *New York Times*, goaded Hecht and the Bergson Group into action. They felt that unless public opinion exerted pressure on the Roosevelt Administration, it would not take steps to stop the genocide. Such pressure, they believed, could be generated only by bold, unusual and extravagant acts. *We Will Never Die*, the pageant they created, was exactly that.

It was devised as a memorial to the first 2,000,000 Jewish victims of the Nazis, as a solemn religious ritual, played in front of two giant Tablets of the Law with Hebrew inscriptions. Its tone was bitter and angry, its images bold and simple. It opened with 'The Roll Call', in which the narrators, Paul Muni and Edward G. Robinson, recited the names of the great Jews who had made a major contribution to humanity – from Abraham to Albert Einstein. With each name that was called out, a group of performers in black garb entered the stage, bearing burning white candles. At the end of the roll call, the stage was vibrantly illuminated by candles symbolizing the Jewish gift to civilization.

Another moving scene was the Kaddish prayer, chanted by a group of frail, old rabbis, refugees from the ghettos of Europe. The second episode, 'Jews in the War', showed the heroic fighting of Jews under the flags of eighteen Allied countries. But it was the closing episode, 'Remember Us', which was the most effective. It depicted the peace table at the end of the war, with representatives of the Allied Nations seated across from the Germans, Italians and Japanese, who were ready to sign their surrender. Only the Jews were missing, because, as the narrator explained,

> There will be no Jews left in Europe when the peace comes.
> They will have been reduced from a minority to a phantom.
> Nothing and no one would represent the Jews at the peace table,
> but the sad, faint phrase Remember Us, which would drift in,
> uncalled for through the open windows of the hall of
> judgement.[5]

A small group of grey-faced Jewish ghosts entered through the gap between the Tablets of the Law and stood at the Peace Table. One of them stepped forward and gave a brief yet detailed testimony on the circumstances of their slaughter by the Germans. The first group was followed by a second, then a third, a fourth – seven groups altogether, – each recounting the story of its own massacre, opening and closing with the plea, or the decree, 'Remember Us!'

Forty-thousand people saw *We Will Never Die* in two performances at New York's Madison Square Garden. Thousands who could not get in listened to the pageant through loudspeakers. The day of the performance, 9 March 1943, was proclaimed by Governor Dewey as a Day of Mourning and Prayer in the State of New York, despite Rabbi Wise's attempts to have the governor cancel his proclamation.

The impact of the pageant was tremendous. For the first time, the American public was exposed to the gory descriptions of the slaughter. Its response was that of horror and rage. The *New York Post* editorial of the following day concluded with the emotional appeal, 'What are we waiting for? . . . Each day that passes means death to hundreds who wait!'[6]

We Will Never Die was performed again in Washington, DC, with many dignitaries, politicians and state officials in the audience. Eleanor Roosevelt, who also attended, commented in her personal column, 'No one who heard each group come forward and give the story of

---

[5] Ben Hecht, *We Will Never Die* (New York: Committee for a Jewish Army of Stateless and Palestinian Jews, 1943), p. 32, the Billy Rose Theatre Collection, New York Public Library at Lincoln Center.

[6] *New York Post*, 10 March 1943.

what had happened to it in the hand of the ruthless German military, will ever forget those haunting words: Remember Us!'[7] Yet even the first lady's impression did not prompt the president into action.

Audiences in Philadelphia, Boston, Chicago and Los Angeles were also stirred by *We Will Never Die*. Hecht and his Bergson Group associates received thousands of letters of support, in which contributions were enclosed. Still, the Roosevelt administration avoided the Jewish problem. Only in January 1944 did the president set up the War Refugee Board, which eventually rescued some 200,000 Jews. According to its own director, John Pehle, the board did too little and much too late. Pehle also admitted that the formation of the board was, to a large extent, the result of the continuous pressure and propaganda activities of the Bergson Group.[8]

A Flag Is Born: the circumstances of the production

Encouraged by the impact of *We Will Never Die*, the Bergson Group continued to initiate anti-Nazi rallies and smaller stage presentations, some of which were sharply anti-British.[9] The feud between the group and organized American Zionists intensified in 1944, after the group had announced the formation of the Hebrew Commission of National Liberation (HCNL) and the American League for a Free Palestine (ALFP) – two organizations with the avowed goal of achieving independence for the Jews in Palestine. The hostile reaction of the World Jewish Congress was released to the press by Dr Nahum Goldman. It included such terms as 'fraud', 'traitors' and a call to exclude the Bergsonites from the Jewish community. In a confidential meeting at the State Department, Dr Goldman was even more belligerent. He suggested either to deport Bergson or to draft him immediately, explaining that Rabbi Wise 'regarded Bergson as equally as great an enemy of the Jews

---

[7] The Miami *Herald*, 17 April 1944.

[8] Wyman, *Abandonment of the Jews*, p. 287. Also Pehle to Bergson, 30 November 1944 (PSC-Yale, box 3, folder 65).

[9] Most notable among those performances was *A Jewish Fairy Tale*, which was presented at a mass meeting in Carnegie Hall on 4 December 1944, following the British reaction to the assassination of Lord Moyne by two Irgun members.

as Hitler, for the reason that his activities could only lead to increased anti-Semitism'.[10]

When the war ended, the Bergson Group focused its propaganda and fundraising campaign on the repatriation effort. The goal was to compete with the large-scale illegal immigration operation run by the Haganah. In that operation, DPs were loaded on small boats in European ports and smuggled into Palestine. Although many of the boats were seized by Royal Navy destroyers and their human cargo placed in detention camps, the operation seemed successful enough, both from a practical and a political point of view. The Irgun was therefore determined to start a similar operation of its own, but its agents lacked the experience and resources of the larger organization. The difficulties in obtaining the necessary boats in Europe were enormous, and while Hecht and his colleagues at the ALFP were launching their repatriation campaign with much fanfare, no real progress was made.

The failure to take part in the most important postwar Zionist activity caused frustration within the Bergson Group. The feeling of crisis was deepened by the escalating attacks of the Zionist leadership, which were clearly having an impact: popular support of the ALFP significantly decreased and branches of the administration, particularly the State Department, treated the Bergson Group with suspicion and hostility. Once again, there was an urgent need for an extraordinary deed, and once again it was Hecht who was asked to create it – in the theatre!

A Flag Is Born was written swiftly. It was conceived as a pageant-drama – a hybrid of a Broadway spectacle, Yiddish melodrama and agitprop theatre. It was designed to stir public opinion and to raise funds for the repatriation operation. Its theatrical success was supposed to open the gates of Palestine.

The hero of Hecht's new, ambitious pageant-drama was Tevya, modelled after Sholem Aleichem's Tevya the Milkman.[11] The original

---

[10] Confidential memorandum of the meeting with Dr Goldman, the representative of the Jewish Agency for Palestine and the World Zionist Organization in Washington, 17 May 1944 (PSC-Yale).

[11] Hecht had previously used the character of Tevya in *A Jewish Fairy Tale*, in 1944. It was then played by Luther Adler.

7. *A Flag Is Born.* Three survivors of the death camps meet in a Jewish cemetery on their way to Palestine: Tevya (Paul Muni), Zelda (Celia Adler) and David (Marlon Brando).

character was left intact, with all the qualities that had made him so popular: incurable optimism, a down-to-earth common sense and a self-mocking sense of humour. Hecht, who admired Sholem Aleichem, also preserved Tevya's humane and tolerant traditionalism, as well as his colloquial language, studded with equivocal proverbs and wittily distorted quotations from the Scriptures. He perceived Tevya as the ultimate representative of the old Jewish world, which had been annihilated by the Nazis.[12]

In Hecht's play, Tevya and his wife Zelda are survivors of the Treblinka death camp. They have lost all their children in the gas

[12] Years later, a very similar Tevya became the emblem of Jewishness all over the world, as the hero of the American musical hit *Fiddler on the Roof.*

8. *A Flag Is Born*. Tevya (Paul Muni) appeals to the Mighty of the World.

chambers, and they are roaming through war-beaten Europe, wishing to reach Palestine. When the play begins, they stop to rest in a Jewish cemetery. There they meet eighteen-year-old David – another survivor on his way to Palestine. David has lost faith in God and in his fellow humans. He believes in nothing except the clear vision of a bridge that must be crossed on the way to Palestine. Tevya fails to see that bridge, but he has his own visions, which fill him with nostalgia and hope. He sees the synagogue of his shtetl and he encounters the biblical kings Saul, David and Solomon. He draws strength from his ability to communicate with them and is almost euphoric when granted permission to address the Council of the Mighty – a parody of the League of Nations. His speech to the world's leaders is one of the highlights of the play – an emotional argument for the survivors' right of a state of their own. The Mighty, however, are indifferent to Tevya's plight, and both he and Zelda die of despair and exhaustion.

Left alone, David is about to stab himself, when he is stopped by the fighters of the Hebrew resistance in Palestine, who encourage him to cross the bridge and to join them in the fight for independence. David takes the prayer shawl that covers Tevya's body and turns it into a flag by placing a blue Star of David at its centre. Carrying the newborn flag on a branch, he crosses the brightly illuminated bridge and joins the armed fighters in their singing of Hatikvah, the Zionist anthem.

Preparations and casting

For maximum effect and highest possible profit, Hecht decided to stage his play on Broadway and to cast it with stars: Paul Muni and Celia Adler were Tevya and Zelda. Muni, at the peak of his Hollywood career, could fill the house for the entire four-week run. With Celia Adler – the reigning queen of the Yiddish theatre – playing opposite him, the play was a sure hit, at least with the Jews of New York. Celia Adler's half-brother, Luther Adler, was chosen to direct the play, but according to all sources, it was Hecht himself who did most of the staging. It was Luther Adler, however, who found the actor for the part of David. The unknown young actor had studied with Luther and his other sister, Stella, at the Dramatic Workshop of the New School. His name was Marlon Brando, and although he was not Jewish, he sympathized with the Bergson Group and had previously volunteered for a few of its fundraising projects.

Another non-Jew in the cast was Quentin Reynolds – one of America's most famous author-journalists, a war correspondent and a radio commentator who had enjoyed tremendous popularity in Great

9. *A Flag Is Born*. David (Marlon Brando) holds the Zionist flag as he joins the Hebrew resistance fighters in Palestine.

Britain during the war. Reynolds, who was to appear as the Narrator in the play, volunteered to do the part without pay.

Muni, Celia Adler and Luther Adler were also donating their services, while the rest of the cast – seventy actors, dancers and extras – consented to take the minimum wages allowed by their unions. Kurt Weill, who composed the musical score, joined Hecht in giving up his royalties. The commitment to the cause seemed to unify the cast and the production team. It inspired manufacturers and suppliers of costumes, lighting equipment and scenery to provide their merchandise gratis or at cost. The same spirit attracted celebrities and public figures to join the production sponsors' list, which included the Mayor of New York, William O'Dwyer, Eleanor Roosevelt, Maxwell Anderson, Leonard Bernstein, Lion Feuchtwanger, Harpo Marx and many others.

Propaganda tactics

'It is 1776 in Palestine!' was the promotion slogan for *A Flag Is Born*. That slogan was obviously intended for the American democracy-and-justice-lover, for whom the mention of 1776 would evoke a strong sympathy for a people fighting to gain its independence from Britain. The analogy between American and Jewish freedom fighters was illustrated on the production poster and programme cover. The main image was that of three muscular young men: the first carried a gun, the second, the Zionist flag, and the third, a hammer and shovel on his shoulder. Floating at the centre of that 'social-realist' drawing was an image of another group of three – the two drummers and the piper that became the icon of the American Revolution (see p. 72).

The basic argument of the play is that a free Palestine is the only solution to the Jewish problem after the Holocaust. The only way to gain independence, in view of the failure of prayers, pleas and diplomatic efforts, is through an armed struggle that will force the British out of the Jewish homeland. The Jews will rise from the ashes and, turning from victims into freedom fighters, use their despair as fuel for their fighting spirit. The old Jewish world, Hecht suggests, has been totally annihilated. Those who survived the gas chambers but preserve their old, naive values and their endearing Sholem Aleichemesque sense of humour, are also doomed. Their corpses are added to those piled in the mass grave called Europe. Only the youths, who have lost faith in humanity and who are ready to fight with fury, stand a chance of surviving and of changing the course of Jewish history.

While the argument was immersed in the plot, fragments of it were inserted in 'ideological capsules' – speeches and dialogue, which had no purpose other than articulating Hecht's convictions. The 'ideological capsules' were spread in measured intervals throughout the play. Some theatre critics, who were judging the production according to dramatic norms, found those 'ideological capsules' redundant and arbitrary. In retrospect, however, it seems useful to examine *A Flag Is Born* not as a regular drama, but as a piece of propaganda theatre, with its specific conventions and mechanisms. Hecht's goal was to manipulate the spectators to accept his argument in its entirety, without reflection or evaluation. All artistic means were to serve that end.

The part of the Narrator may serve as a good example. From a dramatic point of view, it seems superfluous. The Narrator's comments add little to the information received from the stage action. As Tevya and Zelda were walking into the graveyard, for instance, the

Speaker commented, 'Beyond this shambles of a graveyard two figures are moving down a dark road.' By stating the obvious – that which can be immediately verified – the Speaker establishes an irrefutable credibility for himself. All he has to do in order to extend this credibility beyond the realm of visible facts is to interject his (or, rather, the playwright's) opinions and arguments and have them appear as facts. Generalizations, subjective analogies and interpretations thus passed, hardly noticeable, and penetrated the subconsciousness of the audience. The casting of Quentin Reynolds as the Narrator certainly helped establish the authority of the 'objective' commentator.

Agitprop, melodrama and pageantry

In the principal conflict, the world-view of the old couple was juxtaposed with that of the youth. Tevya and Zelda, the archetypal old-world Jews, were characterized as sick and frail, soft-spoken and ironic. Their bitter-sweet dialogue was studded with Yiddishisms ('Choochem', 'Ballabatim', Malachamuves'), witticisms ('In a graveyard, a good Jew is among friends'), and was altogether devoid of self-pity. The old couple behaved as if the Holocaust had not changed their basic belief in human decency. David, on the other hand, neither looked nor spoke like a Jew. Wearing dungarees and a black turtle-necked sweater, he was 'gaunt and grim looking', with 'the cold look of a lord high executioner'. In a flat, cold voice Brando delivered his first speech, which appeared as if directed at Tevya, but was delivered directly to the audience.

> Jewish prayers can't get to God, Tevya, without an English visa.
> This is the new law. Yesterday our prayers needed a German
> visa. And the day before yesterday, they required a Spanish visa.
> You see, our trouble is, Tevya, we have been praying in the
> wrong countries.

The long speech was accompanied by a marching theme, hinting at David's destiny as a potential soldier. At the end of the speech, the music changed into a Jewish folk tune, introducing the first flashback.

It was the Sabbath eve and Zelda lighted two candles on a tombstone. As Tevya started praying, a small synagogue appeared in the back, as if floating in the sky (in fact, on an elevated platform backstage, behind a gauze scrim). While the Torah scroll was being held aloft, the cantor and the small choir were singing the prayers and the dream slowly faded out. That brief, nostalgic tableau marked the beginning of Tevya's trip to his past – the past of the Jewish people, and that of many of the spectators in the auditorium. Theatrically, the scene served as a transition from the sombre cemetery drama into realms of lavish pageantry and propaganda of agitation.

The second vision depicted King Saul with his armed captains, receiving a delegation of the people of the besieged town of Jabesh Gilead. Each of the three delegates represented a different generation: the Old One, dressed in tattered robes, was scared and beaten, but his hope and courage were easily rekindled by King Saul's brave words; the Young One, a warrior in armour, would not surrender to the Ammonites: speaking bitterly about the cowards who were ready to yield all of Israel to the enemy, his words were directed against the Middle-Aged One – the richly dressed, well-mannered man, whose voice was 'unctuous and appeasing'. In the face of catastrophe, he wanted to present a balanced picture to Saul. Suggesting to deal 'sensibly' with the enemy, he said, 'Who knows? Perhaps we can make friends with the Ammonite . . . do nothing to anger him . . . show him how learned and law abiding we are . . . woo him by turning a kindly face to him.'

Those words were written, no doubt, to strike the audience with the worst possible memories. They were not the words of the Bible, but those of many Jewish leaders in Europe and in America who had refused to take Hitler's intentions seriously. According to Hecht, they were also the words of the Zionist leaders who were willing to give up their country to the British invaders, as long as they could keep their wealth and power. History keeps repeating itself, Hecht suggested, but those who have much to lose are blind to its patterns and bring disaster on the rest of the people. Analogies were thus drawn not only between the Middle-Aged One and the Zionists, but also between Tevya and the Old One, between David and the Young One, and naturally, between the Ammonites and the British. As in previous Jewish–American pageants (and in nationalist pageantry in general), a direct line was drawn from the past to the future. The old ones were presented as closest to the ancient, glorious past. Though weak and beaten, they were hopeful and strong in spirit. The young ones were closest to the bright future. Their determination would eventually restore the glory of the past. In this scheme, the present, represented by the Middle-Aged One, was an obstacle that must be removed. Self-centred and petty, the Middle-Aged One was lacking any sense of destiny and history.

Resolved to defend his kingdom, King Saul delivered a national-ist manifesto. As he was about to leave, surrounded by his army of farmers and shepherds, he identified Tevya and addressed him. Startled by the possibility of a dialogue between the present and the ancient past, Tevya asked the King to point out to him the direction to Eretz Yisrael. The King mentioned a bridge that had to be crossed, and disappeared.

After a brief interlude, presenting David, the boy-king, singing and playing the lyre, it was time for Zelda's flashback of a Friday night meal at home with the children around the festive table. Staring into a spotlight in front of her, Zelda began talking to her children, as if they were sitting around the Sabbath table:

> How nice everybody looks! What are you doing, Rochella?
> Enough, Lukshen! Leave some room for the fish! Yusella –
> Yusella – use a napkin! Don't wipe your hands on the table
> cloth! Estherel – you are not eating. Stop sitting in a dream –
> and eat.

By the time Miss Adler reached the end of her speech, there were many quiet sobs and wet eyes in the auditorium. This was exactly the effect Hecht was after. Being familiar with Yiddish melodrama, he undoubt-edly knew that Jewish spectators were conditioned to cry at that type of scene, when, from the depth of her misery, the heroine reminisced about her lost happiness. Such scenes were standard in Yiddish melo-drama, and were always received with the same cathartic response. Knowing that Zelda's children had perished in the gas chambers, like so many of their own relatives, the spectators were even more likely to react intensely.

Still following the Yiddish melodrama routine, Hecht led the scene to a climax with a lullaby. In the Yiddish theatre, the melancholy recollections would normally lead to a well-known sad song, which (as a pretext) the hero or heroine remembered from childhood. There has never been a safer way to crush a Yiddish theatre audience than by doing the flashback lullaby routine, and there has never been a more perfect lullaby for that routine than the one Hecht chose for Miss Adler – 'Rozinkes mit Mandeln' ('Almonds with Raisins') by the founding father of the Yiddish theatre, Avrum Goldfaden.[13]

Hecht was not merely paying homage to the theatre of his child-hood. The purpose of Zelda's vision became clear only during David's speech in the following scene. David, who had been standing with his back to the audience, suddenly rose and looked wildly over the audi-ence. Standing in front of two strong shafts of light, he delivered his 'J'accuse!' in a voice full of pain. The shift from the sentimental, melan-choly flashback to the direct, angry accusation was abrupt and violent. It cannot and should not be explained in dramatic terms, since no dra-matic development led from Zelda's scene to David's. It was important, however, that the spectators who had wept during Zelda's vision were softened, disarmed and absolutely vulnerable. David's furious speech, coming out of nowhere, exploited that vulnerability.

> Where were you – Jews? Where were you when the killing was going on? When the six million were burned and buried alive in the lime pits, where were you? Where was your voice crying out against the slaughter? We didn't hear any voice. You Jews of America! You Jews of England! Strong Jews, rich Jews, high-up Jews; Jews of power and genius! Where was your cry of rage that could have filled the world and stopped the fires? Nowhere! Because you were ashamed to cry as Jews! A curse on your silence! That frightened silence of Jews that made the Germans laugh as they slaughtered. You with your Jewish hearts hidden under American boots. You with your Jewish hearts hidden behind English accents – you let the six million die – rather than make the faux-pas of seeming a Jew. We heard – your silence – in the gas chambers. And now, now you speak a little. Your hearts squeak – and you have a dollar for the Jews. Thank you. Thank you.

Exhausted and broken, Zelda lay down. As she expressed her last wish – that Tevya would pray for her in a synagogue – a procession of garlanded

---

[13] The song is probably the most popular Yiddish theatre song, and it was originally performed in the operetta *Shulamis* as part of a similar routine.

girls paraded in the sky – on the upper level of the stage, behind the scrim. The light brightened, the music swelled, and Solomon's Temple was seen in all its glory. Incense smoke curled out of the Temple, the King on his throne, flanked by robed priests and armoured warriors, read a long portion of the Song of Songs, as a group of female dancers circled the dais to the sound of strings, pipes and cymbals. The pageantry reached a climax in a still tableau, after which the King called out Tevya's name. In his wisdom he detected bitterness and tears in Tevya's voice, and after some persuasion, Tevya agreed to spell out the name of his enemy. 'The name of my enemy is the WORLD', he said. Encouraged by the King to speak and express his complaint, Tevya was ready to address the Council of the Mighty.

The satirical scene ridiculed the hypocrisy and cynicism of the world leaders. Here a different Tevya appeared: not a soft-spoken, good-natured Jew, but a stubborn representative of his people, showing no sign of exhaustion, and using his wit to embarrass the statesmen. Particularly sardonic was his exchange with the English statesman, whom he ostensibly mistook for a German. The verbal battle between the lonely Jew behind the tombstone and the formally dressed statesmen continued until faint, distant voices were heard, speaking to Tevya in Yiddish. They asked him to speak for them – for all the dead and the living. They sounded like an echo of the dead Jews in *We Will Never Die*.

Tevya's long speech, created as the climax of the play, cannot be properly analysed here, for lack of space. Its main point should be quoted, however.

> How nice it would have been if you had . . . not hired German Hessians to fight the young Americans as you are hiring Arabs to go fight the Jews now . . . You have never won a war against a people that wanted to be free.

Tevya's speech was received by the statesmen with excited exclamations and applause. A unanimous resolution to open the gates of Palestine to the Jews was received, but the English statesman slyly demanded the appointment of an investigative commission to deal with the ways and means of opening the doors to Palestine. Consequently, the matter of the Jews was put on the following day's agenda. The statesmen repeated the word 'agenda' several times and began to chuckle. Their laughter rose as Tevya, with arms stretched out, was pleading not to be left alone with 'a promise that dies'.

It was Zelda's death, followed closely by Tevya's, that brought David back to centre stage. Having covered Tevya's body with his talis (prayer shawl), David pulled out a pocket knife and was ready to plunge it into his heart. The sound of Hatikvah, sung by three uniformed soldiers who were standing on the illuminated bridge, stopped him. They told him to cross the bridge and to join them in the fighting, in which 'Jews die singing and chanting tomorrow's victory'. As the music grew louder, more soldiers, carrying submachine-guns, crowded the stage, and called David to help them 'give birth to a flag'. Removing the talis from Tevya's body, David took a blue Star of David out of his pocket and put it on the centre of the talis. The sound of guns was heard through the singing of Hatikvah, as David tacked the talis-flag to a branch and crossed the brightly lit bridge.

The impact of the pageant

A Flag Is Born opened on 5 September 1946 at the Alvin Theatre and was a huge success. Although the professional critics were divided in their opinions of Hecht's script, they all sensed the tremendous effect it had on the audience. Commenting on the play's final scene, one critic wrote: 'It was an oversimplification of the Jewish resistance in Palestine, but what is important is that the audience, constituting the jury, indicated by its applause its vindication of all and any means Jews may use to obtain their ends – freedom in Palestine, freedom from DP camps.'[14] Spectators also translated their emotions into action. Many of the pledge cards (looking exactly like blank cheques), which were inserted in the programmes, were filled out with large sums. As the *Hollywood Reporter* critic wrote: 'Ben Hecht has written so moving a pageant, that we have been moved to pen not only a congratulatory critique – but to write a check to aid the American League for a Free Palestine in its repatriation program.'[15]

---

[14] Bernard Lerner, the Atlantic City *Jewish Record*, 25 September 1946.

[15] Irving Hoffman, the *Hollywood Reporter*, quoted in 'Critics Acclaim A Flag Is Born', a two-page handout filed in the Palestine Statehood Committee Papers, Sterling Library, Yale University.

The success surpassed even the most optimistic expectations. The original four-week run was extended, with the show moving from the Alvin to the Adelphi Theatre, then to the Music Box Theatre, then again to the Broadway Theatre. During those extensions, Muni returned to Hollywood and was replaced first by Luther Adler, and later by Jacob Ben-Ami. Brando, too, was on his way to Hollywood, and he was replaced by Sidney Lumet.

Apart from the excellent box-office receipts, the success of *A Flag Is Born* was in the controversy it provoked. The play and the issues it raised were discussed in personal columns, letters to editors and radio programmes. The Zionist leadership protested vociferously, but Hecht also received letters of support, often expressing the will of their authors to volunteer for the ALFP, or even for fighting in Palestine.[16]

The success of the pageant boosted the activities of the ALFP. In addition to the box-office receipts and contributions received by mail, new ALFP branches opened all over the US and in Mexico. Bergson believed that the events were leading to the eventual establishment of a provisional Jewish government in Palestine. 'I know now and I will know then', he wrote to Hecht, 'that it was *A Flag* which provided the Archimedes point which gave us the lever with which to lift this heavy ballast.'[17]

The British press reacted very strongly. The New York correspondent of the *Evening Standard* described the show as 'the most virulently anti-British play ever staged in the United States'.[18] Both Hecht and Quentin Reynolds wrote long letters to the editor, refuting that description, and announcing plans to stage the show in London. The British press did its utmost, however, to prevent a London staging of the play. In exaggerated reports of the production's success in New York, the press presented it as a serious threat to British foreign policy. Some newspapers went as far as arguing that *A Flag Is Born* would have an influence on the results of the presidential elections in the US.

---

[16] The letters are filed with the Ben Hecht papers at the Newberry Library in Chicago.

[17] Bergson to Hecht. Undated, second page of letter, at the Newberry Library, Chicago.

[18] Quoted in the *Answer*, the ALFP weekly newspaper, 8 November 1946.

Whereas the plans for a British version of *A Flag* were quickly abandoned, a US-wide tour began in December, with performances in Chicago, Detroit, Baltimore and Philadelphia, where Stella Adler joined the cast in the role of the Narrator. The two weeks of performances in Philadelphia were the most controversial in the entire run of the show. Local branches of Zionist organizations and youth movements staged large street rallies against the show. Pickets were arranged in front of the Erlanger Theatre, with placards calling, 'Do no attend this play!', 'Watch your pockets!', and 'Do not contribute as the money is being wasted!' Flyers were distributed, exclaiming in bold-type letters:

WORDS ON THE STAGE ARE NOT ENOUGH!
Disciplined constructive work will build Palestine.

The flyers urged the public to support only the legitimate Zionist organizations, which 'bring Jews to Palestine; buy land in Palestine; build in Palestine; support Palestinian defence'. The League, the flyers said, 'creates chaos within the Palestinian Jewish community (Yishuv)', and stated that supporting it was actually harming Eretz Yisrael.[19]

The massive opposition to the play in Philadelphia may be explained by the fact that the show's opening night, 27 January, was also the date of a Zionist meeting at the Benjamin Franklin Hotel. Dr Bernard Kahn, a physician present at that meeting, said he was approached at the hotel by at least a dozen people who pleaded with him not to attend the play. In a letter to a local Zionist leader, Dr Kahn wrote that despite the pleas he did go to see the play and was appalled to discover the Zionist pickets in front of the theatre. 'Do you realize that many non-Jewish people attend the play also?', he protested. 'What an impression on them to watch the disgraceful display of disunion among the Jews!', he continued, 'I can hardly express myself adequately the bad taste and disgust I felt . . . and still do, of this nasty affair perpetuated in the name of the Zionist Organization of America.' As for the play itself, Dr Kahn was unequivocal in his praise: 'I have benefited more spiritually by this play than all the Zionist meetings I ever attended. It is a shame that a great number of timid souls heeded your idle gossip and innuendoes and stayed away from this masterful play,

[19] PSC-Yale, box 9, folder 71.

thus depriving Jewish leaders and artists of a well deserved income . . . This play portrays vividly the life and death and the spirit of the present Jewish existence. There is no better piece of propaganda than this play.'[20] Hardly surprising was Dr Kahn's conclusion to transfer his regular $100 contribution from the Zionist Organization of America to the American League for a Free Palestine.

A Flag Is Born closed six months, instead of four weeks, after its opening. A South American tour of the play, starring Jacob Ben-Ami, began in the summer of 1947, and reaped similar acclaim. According to the Answer, the League's weekly newspaper, the play was also staged in a British internment camp in Cyprus in Hebrew, by Jewish refugees.[21]

Two months after its Broadway opening, A Flag Is Born produced an income of $275,000. The money was transferred to the repatriation commissioner of the Hebrew Committee in Basel, Switzerland, who began to organize a group of DPs for illegal immigration. In the meantime, the Bergson Group purchased a small boat, the SS Abril, in an auction of surplus ships belonging to the American government. Following extensive renovations, the ship and its American crew sailed for France in December. The departure was the strongest evidence of the success of A Flag Is Born and of the idea behind it. As Congressman Will Rogers, Jr put it in his letter to ALFP supporters: 'The first of a fleet of A Flag Is Born ships sailed from an American port.'[22] As soon as the boat left the French territorial water, loaded with some 600 DPs, it was renamed SS Ben Hecht, thus publicly expressing the DPs' gratitude to the playwright.

The public learned about the SS Ben Hecht soon enough. Postcard-size photographs of it, with its new name written on its bow, were mailed to sponsors together with 'a call to action'. At last, there was hard evidence that the League could be trusted; that it fulfilled its promises, and that A Flag Is Born was more than just a theatrical success.

On 8 March 1948 the Ben Hecht was captured by two British destroyers off the Palestine coast, near Jaffa. The passengers were transported to a

[20] Bernard Kahn to Michael Engal, 6 February 1947 (PSC-Yale).
[21] Answer, 4 April 1947.
[22] A draft of a letter by Will Rogers to the League's supporters, PSC-Yale.

detention camp in Cyprus, and the American crew was arrested on charges of aiding and abetting illegal immigration. The diplomatic incident between the US and Britain had been planned by the Bergson Group, and was very effectively exploited by them. The American press and the American Congress were both outraged by the arrest of American seamen. Public opinion united against the arrest, forced the British to release the seamen, who received a heroes' welcome organized by the American League for a Free Palestine in New York.

The drama of *A Flag Is Born* extended far beyond the boundaries of the stage. Stimulating a vivid debate, the production made Americans aware of the fate of the Jewish DPs. Opposite the victims, the play succeeded in portraying the British as the villains in the Palestine arena (significantly, it avoided an elaborate reference to the Arab inhabitants of that country). It also exploited the guilt feelings of Jewish and non-Jewish Americans, thus causing increased moral and financial support in the American League for a Free Palestine. With its predecessor, Meyer Weisgal's *The Romance of a People, A Flag Is Born* is among the few productions in theatre history which had a real and immediate impact on the fate of people who had not even seen them.

I wish to thank the British Council in Tel Aviv for the travel grant which made it possible for me to attend the 'Shoah and Performance' conference at Glasgow University in 1995, where an earlier version of this chapter was read.

6 Theatrical interpretation of the Shoah: image and counter-image

DAN LAOR

The general context of this chapter is the change in attitude toward the Holocaust which has taken place in Israeli society in recent decades, as reflected in public discourse as well as performance. Our test case will be the treatment on stage and screen of two historical figures – Hannah (Anna) Szenes and Israel (Rezso) Kasztner. Both Szenes and Kasztner are Hungarian Jews, each of them related in his own particular way to the tragic events which took place in Hungary during the last phase of World War Two, following the unexpected occupation of that country by the Nazis in March 1944.[1]

Hannah Szenes, born in Budapest in 1921, was a highly talented writer and poet. Daughter of the famous Jewish Hungarian writer Bella Szenes, she came from a well-assimilated family, immigrated to Palestine in 1939, and two years later became a member of Kibbutz Sedot Yam, near Ceasarea. Together with other youngsters from Palestine – thirty-seven in all – she volunteered to parachute into Nazi-occupied Europe in order to aid her Jewish brethren. In March 1944 she was dropped with her fellow parachutists in Yugoslavia, where she spent three months with Tito's partisans. Early in June she entered Hungary, hoping to take part in saving Jews in the country in which she was born. But soon after crossing the border she was caught by the Hungarian authorities, put in prison, tortured, tried for treason and finally shot

---

[1] The spelling of the names of both Hannah Szenes and Israel Kasztner follows *The Encyclopaedia of the Holocaust*, ed. Israel Gutman (New York and London: Macmillan, 1990), except for titles or quotations in which these names are spelled in a different way.

by a firing squad. In 1950 her remains were brought to Israel, where she was buried in the national military cemetery on Mount Herzl.[2]

Since her execution in November 1944 at the age of twenty-three, Hannah Szenes, as Abba Eban put it, 'has become a consecrated image in her people's memory'.[3] The book of her diaries and poems has reached its fifteenth edition; a ship, a forest and two farming settlements have been named after her; thirty-two streets in Israel bear her name. Since the late forties, many plays have been written about her, and the story of her life and sacrifice was put on stage several times. Some of these plays were widely circulated in amateur theatres, schools and youth movements. In the late fifties the emerging Israeli film industry considered producing a film about her life, and in 1964 Menachem Golan, the producer of the American movie *Hannah's War* (1987), was commissioned to write a script on Hannah Szenes. A traditional ceremony in memory of Hannah Szenes takes place every year in Kibbutz Sedot Yam, as part of the Holocaust Remembrance Day's ritual, where readings of her diaries and poems and singing of her songs are intermingled with a military parade of Israel Defense Forces (IDF) paratroopers. Kibbutz Sedot Yam is also the location of *Beit Hannnah* ('Hannah's House'), a memorial site where visitors can watch a seventeen-minute audiovisual presentation dedicated to her life.[4]

Interestingly enough, the first treatment of this theme in Israeli drama was in a play written by Yitzhak Sadeh, the first commander of the Palmah, the permanently mobilized strike force of the Haganah (Israel's pre-state army). As early as 1947, Sadeh had published the third act of a 'memorial play' entitled *Darkah shel Hannah* (*Hannah's Road*), later to be included in *Lohamim* (*Warriors*), a posthumous volume of dramatic works which deal with modern Jewish heroism. In this context, Sadeh fosters the heroic image of the Holocaust, presenting

---

[2] See A. Masters, *The Summer that Bled: The Biography of Hanna Senesh* (London: Mitchell and Valentine, 1972).

[3] Hannah Senesh: *Her Life and Diary*, introduced by Abba Eban (New York: Schocken Books, 1972), p. vii.

[4] See Judith Tydor Baumel, 'The Heroism of Hannah Senesz: An Exercise in Creating Collective National Memory in the State of Israel', in *Journal of Contemporary History*, 31.3 (1966), pp. 521–46.

the Jews not 'like sheep going to slaughter', but rather as courageous warriors who rebelled against the Nazis. The theme of Hannah Szenes – whom Sadeh happened to meet in person before her departure to Yugoslavia – was more than appropriate for this purpose: 'Watching the way in which she faced the firing squad raised respect in the heart of every soldier', says the investigator to Hannah's mother following the execution. 'Shit, it cannot raise but respect. If she were not Jewish, I would be proud that someone like her was a native of Hungary.'[5] Sadeh was not a professional playwright, yet his long-forgotten play, staged only once by an amateur group,[6] was a significant expression of the need to locate Hannah Szenes, the symbol of Jewish and Zionist struggle against the Nazis, at the foreground of Israeli consciousness.

For this same reason, the idea of using Hannah Szenes as a dramatic figure became extremely attractive to many writers and playwrights throughout the 1950s. Sadeh was followed by Aharon Megged, a writer and playwright of fame and an ex-member of Kibbutz Sedot Yam, who produced his own 'memorial play' based on his personal acquaintance with Hannah Szenes, as well as on written and oral evidence. *Ha-Sneh ha-Bo'er* (*The Burning Bush*), a small sketch on Hannah Szenes' last days, was published in the spring of 1955 in a literary periodical, and was later issued as a booklet for amateur groups, particularly in schools.[7] In January 1957 Eliezer Barot, also a member of Sedot Yam, published in a Kibbutz periodical the first act of a play dedicated to Hannah Szenes' Hungarian mission.[8] Later that year, the National Theatre Habima announced a competition for a play on Hannah Szenes, to be performed in 1958 as part of the celebration of the tenth anniversary of the State of Israel. Behind this contest was the idea that the proper way to treat the Holocaust in the context of celebrating

---

[5] Yitzhak Sadeh, in *Lohamim* (Tel Aviv: Hakibbutz Hameuchad, 1953), p. 58. First published in *Leahdut ha'Avodah*, 165, 13 November 1947.

[6] This information was provided to me by Zevi Dror, the biographer of Yitzhak Sadeh (*Mazbi-le-Lo Serara* (Tel Aviv: Hakibbutz Hameuhad, 1966)).

[7] *Orot*, 4.23 (1955), pp. 31–43. The mimeographed booklet was issued by the Department of Culture and Education of the *Histadrut* (General Union of Workers).

[8] Eliezer Barot, 'Hannah', *Mibifnim*, 19.2–3 (January 1957), pp. 258–9.

Israel's statehood was through the character of Hannah Szenes, who represented the heroic image of the Holocaust, and was directly associated with the limited involvement of the Yishuv (the Jewish community in Palestine) in the military struggle against the Nazis. Six plays were submitted, and as none of them was found worthy of theatrical production, all sank into oblivion, except for one written by the Hungarian-born writer Avigdor Hameiri, an old friend of the Szenes family, who produced a long epic play in which he intermingled the realistic presentation of Hannah's biography with references to Jewish legends and myth associated with martyrology. Hameiri called his play *Ashrei ha-Gafrur* (*Blessed Be the Match*), following Szenes' highly popular poem, with the match turning into a mystical emblem identified with the light of the Messiah, the long-expected redeemer of the Jewish people.[9]

The work finally staged was a two-act play commissioned by the National Theatre from Aharon Megged, who was known not only as an experienced writer and playwright but also as a man deeply committed to Hannah Szenes' memory. The new play was an extension of Megged's earlier piece, *Ha-Sneh ha-Bo'er* – with both plays cultivating the widely accepted image of Hannah Szenes as a national heroine: 'The generation of catastrophe, the generation which lost millions of our people', wrote Megged in an essay which he contributed to a Hannah Szenes volume in 1946, 'this generation has chosen as its hero the emissary and the pioneer, who had sacrificed her life by leaving her country and by going to a foreign land to save her brethren from the trap of death.'[10] Megged located his play in the Budapest jail in the summer of 1944, with episodes from Szenes' previous life both in Hungary and Palestine introduced through flashbacks. The artistic intention was to describe the mission of Hannah Szenes as a saintly mission. Shaw's *Saint Joan*, first performed in Israel in 1952, inspired Megged's writing, as this defiant speech testifies:

> I have been accused here of a number of crimes which I do not
> deny. I did cross the border from the partisans in Yugoslavia

[9] Avigdor Hemeiri, *Ashrei ha-Gafrur* (Tel Aviv, 1958).
[10] Aharon Megged, *Hannah* (Sedot Yam, 1946), p. 71.

– I admit it. I was sent here by the Allies. I admit it . . . I came
to save Jews from death – I'm proud of it. But the charge that
I betrayed the country of my birth, and planned its destruction,
I categorically deny.[11]

Megged also explicitly compares Hannah to other martyrs from the European Christian tradition, such as John Huss, John Wyclif and Galileo, as
well as with Jewish martyrs like Hannah and her seven sons.[12]

The 1958 performance of Megged's *Hannah Szenes* was one of
the most prestigious and successful productions of the Habima. A careful examination of this particular production is extremely enlightening
as to the centrality of Szenes in the Israeli imagination at that time. The
cast was the best Habima could assemble: the role of Hannah Szenes
was played by Miriam Zohar, a Holocaust survivor herself, and the
most promising talent among the young generation of the national
theatre. Next to Zohar were Hannah Rovina, Aharon Meskin and
Yehoshu'a Bertonov, who were among the founding fathers of the
Habima in Moscow, and definitely three of the most celebrated actors
on the Israeli stage. Long previews were written about the production,
which included a detailed report about the sentimental journey taken
by the actors to Kibbutz Sedot Yam, as well as their meeting with the
'real' people behind the play – one of them was Katherina Szenes,
Hannah's mother. An exhibition on the life of Hannah Szenes and her
mission was prepared specially for the occasion and shown in the theatre's lobby. The opening night, which was attended by state dignitaries as well as by Hannah's fellow paratroopers, turned to be a highly
emotional event which received full press coverage. Daily newspapers,
weeklies and children's magazines were full of cover stories and
articles related to the production, and of extensive writing about the
so-called 'legend' of Hannah Szenes. Shortly after the première the
play was published, and the first edition was soon sold out.

---

[11] Aharon Megged, 'Hannah Szenes', translated by Michael Taub, in
Modern International Drama, 27.1 (1993), p. 129.

[12] Ilan Avisar, 'The Evolution of the Israeli Attitude Toward the Holocaust
as Reflected in Modern Hebrew Drama', in *Hebrew Annual Review*,
9 (1985), p. 35.

10.   **Aharon Megged,** *Hannah Szenes* (Habima Theatre, 1958). Hannah Szenes
(Miriam Zohar) with her mother Katherina Szenes (Hannah Rovina).

Megged's *Hannah Szenes* became a major success at the Habima. Though most reviewers were rather critical of the text itself, all of them thought that the performance of the play was of great significance: 'In a show like this one', wrote the critic Leah Porat, 'how unpleasant is the role of the critic, who is obliged to mention all the possible flaws. Indeed, for quite a long time we haven't seen a theatrical show which is so important to be seen, which is so good to identify with, which enables you to say: go and see it in droves, because it is part of yourself, a flesh of your flesh, a pure golden ring in the chain of your own history.'[13] During the 1958/9 season it was performed 116 times, while productions of other plays never went beyond 50 performances. It was revived in 1964, with only minor changes, which is an unusual phenomenon in Israeli theatrical life. Matinées were offered for young audiences, and special performances were organized for IDF paratroopers. On the eve of Holocaust Remembrance Day, when all theatres in Israel are closed by law, Habima remained open for a special performance of *Hannah Szenes*. No less than five different adaptations of the play were written for the young; these were largely circulated among dramatic troupes in schools and youth movements. All this could happen because Megged's *Hannah Szenes* was the right play at the right time, interpreting the Holocaust in a way which would perfectly fit into the Israeli ethos. As such, it was also considered worthy of cultural export: an English version of the play was staged in 1964 at the Princess Theatre in Los Angeles (under the title *The Legend of Hannah Senesh*) and, in 1969, Habima performed it at the Burgtheater in Vienna.[14]

In subsequent years the theme of Hannah Szenes was still on the agenda of the Israeli theatre, yet it was treated in a totally different way. In 1973 a group of young actors and singers under the direction of Shimon Levi and Nissim Givati produced a theatrical pot-pourri based on the diaries, poems and songs of Hannah Szenes, as well as on selected parts of Megged's play. This production, which had more than 300 performances (mainly in schools, small towns and agricultural

---

[13] *Lamerhav*, 6 June 1958.

[14] For the American production, see Margaret Harford's review, '*Hannah Senesh* – Drama of Wartime Hero', in the *Los Angeles Times*, 8 May 1964.

settlements), was defined by its producers as an attempt 'to take the figure of the Israeli paratrooper down from the national pedestal and to represent her as a sensitive, cautious woman'.[15] It was followed in 1979 by the short-lived Haifa Municipal Theatre performance of *Kenafayim* (*Doves*), a theatre–dance evening produced by the American choreographer Anna Sokolow in co-operation with the Israeli poet and playwright Israel Eliraz, who made it clear that he and Sokolow were not interested in treating 'a national symbol, charged with pathos, who lacks a face of her own', but rather a girl who had a lust for life, who searched for love, who had experienced solitude, and who was ready to make a personal commitment and pay the full price for it.[16] Another production, though marginal, was offered at the Israel Festival for 'Alternative Theatre' in Acco in 1987, where the playwright Dudu Palme's intention was to analyse the formation of the myth of Hannah Szenes rather than reproduce that myth once again. The glorious days in which Hannah Szenes was staged at the national theatre as a local version of Joan of Arc, with the performance of the play turning into a major cultural event as well as a commercial success, were over.[17]

Ironically, the man who was taking Hannah Szenes' place on the Israeli stage as a symbol of the Holocaust was none other than Israel Kasztner, the Hungarian Jewish leader who was accused of collaboration with the Nazis, and whose victimization took place just as Hannah Szenes had her heyday on the Israeli stage and in public discourse at large. The emergence of Kasztner as a significant presence in the Israeli theatre and media has definitely been a by-product of a new interpretation of the Shoah. 'This particularly glaring ideological representation started crumbling with the Eichmann trial, and subsequently faded out

[15] *Yeditot Aharonot*, 26 February 1973. The play is titled after a poem by Hannah Szenes – 'Kol Kara, Ve-Halakhty' ('I Heard a Voice. I Went').

[16] Quoted from Israel Eliraz's presentation in the programme of the Haifa Municipal Theatre production (1979). Anna Sokolow's production was later performed with a local company at the Harold Clurman Theater in New York in 1953. See Elenore Lester's review, 'The Story of a Wartime Heroine Comes to the Stage', *New York Times*, 23 January 1983.

[17] Dudu Palme, *Rak ha-Kokhavin Hayu Kerovim Kol Kakh* (*Only the Stars Were So Close*), unpublished play, Hannah Szenes Archive, Sedot Yam.

of the main public discourse', says the historian Saul Friedlander.[18] Beside the trial itself, Friedlander points to a number of social and political factors which have lead to a new and more complex attitude of Israelis toward this national trauma, reflected in historiography, public discourse, novels, plays, museology, ceremonies, and so on. In this new phase, Israelis became less interested in heroes and martyrs, trying instead to get to know more about the victims themselves. This led, among other things, to a new understanding of the dilemmas of those individual Jews who were in a position of leadership in Nazi-occupied Europe, mainly the *Judenrat* (the Jewish councils who operated under the Nazis), traditionally regarded as reflecting the moral failure of Jews during the war, and as a symptom of the rather despised *galut* (Diaspora) mentality. The publication by Yad Vashem (The Holocaust Authority) of a Hebrew version of Isaiah Trunk's seminal book *Judenrat* (1979), followed by Ruth Bondy's biography of Jacob Edelstein, the head of the Jewish council in Theresienstadt (1981), are early expressions of this new understanding.[19] It was in these circumstances that the shift from Szenes to Kasztner was made possible, even necessary.

Israel Kasztner, who was born in Cluz (Transylvania) in 1914, was a lawyer, a journalist and a Zionist leader, who served as the vice-chairman of the Jewish Relief and Rescue Committee in Hungary during the war. After the German conquest of Hungary in March 1944, Kasztner negotiated with the Nazis, particularly with Eichmann, on the possibility of exchanging 'merchandise for blood' (*'ware für blud'*). Kasztner finally managed to rescue 1,684 Jews, who left Budapest by a special train in June 1944. The historian Yehuda Bauer credits Kasztner for being involved in saving the life of several thousands of Jews in Hungary and elsewhere. In 1954, already in Israel, Kasztner brought a lawsuit against Malkiel Grünwald, who blamed him for collaborating with the Nazis. The Grünwald trial was soon turned by attorney

---

[18] See Saul Friedlander, 'The Shoah Between Memory and History', *Jerusalem Quarterly*, 53 (Winter 1990), p. 118.

[19] Isaiah Trunk, *Judenrat: the Jewish Councils in Eastern Europe Under Nazi Occupation* (New York and London: Collier–Macmillan, 1972); see also Ruth Bondy, *Elder of the Jews: Jacob Edelstein of Theresienstadt*, translated by Evelyn Adel (New York: Macmillan, 1989).

Shmuel Tamir into a Kasztner trial, which ended by a verdict in which Justice Benjamin Halevi, the president of the Jerusalem district court, went as far as to describe the vice-chairman of the Jewish Relief and Rescue Committee in Budapest as someone 'who sold his soul to the devil'. Kasztner was found guilty of collaboration with the Nazis, and following a highly emotional testimony by Katherina Szenes, he was also blamed for the desertion of her daughter Hannah while she was imprisoned in Budapest. About a year after the verdict was handed down, Kasztner was murdered by national extremists, who took Justice Halevi's words literally; only after his death did the supreme court exonerate him from all accusations (except the charge that he helped Nazis escape justice).

A dramatic shift in the public attitude towards Kasztner took place in 1982, when a two-part documentary by Yehuda Kaveh, commissioned by Israeli television, adopted an extremely favourable position toward him and his role during the Holocaust, and, therefore, criticized the judicial procedures which led to his indictment by the Jerusalem district court. Kaveh's treatment of this controversial material was warmly welcomed by most columnists and reviewers.[20] Two years later, in 1984, David Levine, then Habima's director, wrote (in collaboration with Miri Shomron) a trial drama named *Reszo* which challenged the previously accepted notion about Kasztner and called for his rehabilitation. This line of thought was followed in 1985 by a highly successful production by the Tel Aviv Chamber Theatre of Motti Lerner's *Kasztner*, as well as by this playwright's three-part television drama, *Mishpat Kasztner* (*The Kasztner Trial*), produced by Israeli television in 1994.[21] That same year the Israeli composer Arie Shapira presented a new opera with the same title (*Mishpat Kasztner*), whose libretto was based on selected quotations drawn from the transcripts of the trial of 1954. Originally Shapira planned to write an opera for the stage, but as he turned to electronic music, his piece was

---

[20] Yehuda Kaveh (producer), *Kofer Nefesh* (*Ransom*), and *Pesak Din* (*Verdict*), Israeli Television Archive, Jerusalem.

[21] Motti Lerner, *The Kasztner Trial* (Tel Aviv, Or-Am, 1994). An English translation by Emre Goldstein's is included in the same issue of *Modern International Drama* (27.1 (1993)) which provides the translation of Megged's play, pp. 33–94.

broadcast only on Israeli radio, and later recorded on CD by the Israeli Association of Composers. In 1994, Shapira won the prestigious Israel Prize for composition.[22] Kasztner's role during the war also received much credit in a book written by Dov Dinur in 1987, and most recently in a new, most favourable biography written by the historian Yehiam Weitz.[23] Both Dinur and Weitz were involved in the various Kasztner productions: the manuscript of Dinur's book was used by Lerner for the writing of his 1985 play, whereas Weitz operated as a historical advisor to Lerner and Barabash in their work on the 1994 television drama. No wonder, then, that the cover of Dinur's *Kasztner* included a picture showing Oded Teomi and Ilan Dar, the two actors who played the roles of Kasztner and Eichmann in the Chamber Theatre production which took place prior to the publication of his book.

The production of *Kasztner* by the Chamber Theatre in 1985 can be seen as the antithesis to Aharon Megged's *Hannah Szenes* performed by Habima almost thirty years earlier. Whereas Megged and Habima had chosen to celebrate Hannah Szenes, the anti-Nazi woman fighter, Lerner wrote a play about the Holocaust by focusing on someone who had been perceived for years – particularly as a result of the 1954 trial – as being diametrically opposed to the mythical Szenes. And it was this kind of 'anti-hero', also associated with the Hungarian chapter of the Holocaust, which Lerner was committed to put on stage: 'There is great heroism in one's ability to stand in front of Eichmann, to negotiate with him', he declared. 'We are not used [to appreciate] this thing. We think still of heroism in terms of using a pistol and a hand-grenade. This was heroism of a different kind.'[24] Like Megged before him, Lerner had also produced a semi-documentary drama, in which he reconstructed the

<hr />

[22] Arie Shapira, *The Kasztner Trial: Electronic Opera in 13 Scenes* (1991–4). Compact disc published by the Society of Authors, Composers and Music Publishers in Israel (ACUM), cat. no. AS-001. The libretto is rendered in English translation.

[23] Dov Dinur, *Kasztner: Giluyim Hadashim al ha-Ish u-Fo'olo* (*Kasztner: New Revelations on the Man and his Deeds*) (Haifa: Gestlit, 1987); Yehiam Weitz, *Ha-Ish She-Nirzah Pa'amayim* (*The Man Who Was Murdered Twice*) (Jerusalem: Keter, 1995).

[24] Quoted from a television debate (1 October 1985). Israeli TV Archive, Jerusalem.

11. **Motti Lerner**, Kasztner (Tel Aviv Chamber Theatre, 1985). Kasztner (Oded Teomi) meets Eichmann (Ilan Dar).

devastating situation in Budapest after the Nazi occupation in March 1944, exposing with great empathy the dilemmas, the motives, the code of behaviour of the man who stood at the centre of his play: Kasztner facing Adolf Eichmann, Kasztner facing the Jewish community, Kasztner facing his own self. The chain of events is broken only in the final episode, which dramatizes the assassination of Kasztner in Tel Aviv in March 1957; by doing so, Lerner, just as Megged before him, is using the moment of execution as a vehicle through which he manages to present his innocent hero as a victim of evil forces, thus reaching for his ultimate sanctification.

Lerner's *Kasztner* was one of the best, most successful and highly debated productions of the Israeli theatre. It had a tremendous press coverage, including a special television feature produced by Yehuda Kaveh, who had been in charge of the television documentary of 1982 which marked the turning point in the treatment of the Hungarian Jewish leader by the Israeli media. Naturally, this production became the focus of renewed public debate on Kasztner, and though the old accusations were reiterated – mostly by attorney Shmuel Tamir, who had been instrumental in leading Halevi to his verdict in 1954 – new voices, absolutely pro-Kasztner, were heard in the Israeli arena. An eminent spokesman who expressed a pro-Kasztner position following the theatrical production was Yehudah Bauer, who presented Kasztner once again as a person who 'struggled with the devil' for the purpose of saving Jews, finally managing to save at least some of them; the critical reference to the district court verdict of 1954 was more than obvious.[25] The polemics of the 1980s over the idea of associating *shoah* ('Holocaust') with *gevurah* ('Heroism'), cemented in the 1950s, was getting here its full expression. This was also the reason why most reviewers, who may have been sceptical as to Lerner's dramatic genius, responded favourably to what he had done.[26] As *Hannah Szenesz* in 1958, this was also the right play at the right time. In the daily *Ma'ariv* – a rather right-wing paper – Gabriel Strasmann wrote

---

[25] Yehuda Bauer, 'Yoter Mal'akh mi-Shed' ('More of an Angel than a Devil'), *Davar*, 1 August 1985.

[26] Boaz Evron, 'Mi la-Hayim, Mi la-Mavet' ('Who is for Life, Who is for Death'), *Yediot Aharonot*, 31 July 1985.

that *Kasztner* by Lerner should be performed everywhere, particularly in schools; it should even become part of the curriculum, because this play raises some of the major issues embedded in the Holocaust. Public interest was so great that long before its publication in book form, the full text of the play was printed in a weekend magazine of the daily *Davar*.[27] In 1987 *Kasztner* was performed by the Chamber Theatre in Wiesbaden, Germany, as it was considered by its producers to be an appropriate product for foreign consumption. Finally, the play won the 'Aharon Meskin Prize' of the Israel Centre of the International Theatre Institute (ITI) in 1986. The award was presented to Lerner by the Minister of Education and Culture, Yitzhak Navon, in a ceremony which took place at Habima, in the same hall where Megged's *Hannah Szenes* was performed three decades earlier.[28]

The success of the Chamber Theatre production and the change of the public climate towards Kasztner paved the way for the television production of *The Kasztner Trial* in 1994, written by Motti Lerner and directed by Uri Barabash. This time Lerner followed David Levine's model, composing a trial drama based on the transcripts of the trial but definitely not identical with them. In his script, Lerner cultivated the line presented in his theatrical production of 1985 by characterizing Kasztner as a genuine and courageous Jewish leader, the true 'hero' of the Holocaust period. Yet this production was still located in Hungary, with Israeli society and its judicial system being criticized only indirectly, whereas the television drama – located in Israel of the 1950s – was a direct and most aggressive attack against the victimization of Kasztner by the Israelis. This attack was carried with the full aid of the Israeli cultural establishment: *The Kasztner Trial* was the most ambitious television drama ever produced in Israel, it was in three parts, it had the best possible cast, it was transmitted on national television during prime time on three consecutive nights, it was highly promoted before and after, a special film was even produced by Israeli television describing the very process of production. All this effort was put into a performance which treated favourably a man who three decades earlier

---

[27] *Davar ha-Shavu'a*, 27 December 1985.
[28] For the jury decision, see *Modern International Drama*, 27.1 (1993), pp. 37–8.

was considered a war criminal. With the presentation of the three-part television drama on the Kasztner trial, the Israelis found themselves paying tribute not to the 'hero', the war fighter, but rather to the negotiator, the manipulator, the politician, maybe even to a villain, to a man who 'co-operated' (though not 'collaborated') with the Nazis in order to rescue as many Jews as he could, not through useless revolts, but through acts of diplomacy; this kind of human breed, incarnated by Kasztner, turned out to be the legitimate representative of the Holocaust in the texture of Israeli memory. 'Since the trial and death of Israel Kasztner', writes Yehiam Weitz in his introduction to the booklet of *Mishpat Kasztner* published by the Israel Broadcasting Authority, 'a radical change in the image of this man and in the evaluation of his activities has taken place. This change is meaningful, because Kasztner is in many ways a mirror which reflects the change which Israeli society has gone through since the days in which it had passed judgement.'[29]

The tremendous public attention directed to the television drama was very much enhanced by an off-stage drama which took place a few days before the screening of the Lerner–Barabash production. A sensational preview made it known that the original script of *The Kasztner Trial* included a scene in which Kasztner suggested that Hannah Szenes, while imprisoned in Budapest, betrayed her friends. This, one should note, was never said by Kasztner, not during the trial, nor anywhere else. This was never said by anybody, was contrary to all available historical evidence, and even the producers were ready to admit that it was just 'poetic licence'. So, while paving the road for Kasztner to become the legitimate representative of the Shoah, the producers of the television drama made an attempt to go one step further by desecrating Hannah Szenes' memory, the previously highly cherished heroine of the darkest period in the history of the Jewish people. The long-time rivalry between Kasztner and Szenes over the Israeli memory of the Shoah was finally taken into the open.

This move was unanimously rejected by public opinion: the Szenes family took the case to the supreme court, which decided on a majority rule that the omission of the controversial scene would not interfere with the continuity of the programme, but left it to the Israel

---

[29] *Mishpat Kasztner* (Jerusalem: Israel Broadcasting Authority, 1994), p. 10.

Broadcasting Authority to take the final decision. The suggestion of the court was respected by the Broadcasting Authority, and Kasztner's statement as to the betrayal of Hannah Szenes was removed. The issue was also put on the agenda of the Knesset, the Israeli parliament, and, in a debate which took place on 9 November 1994, Hannah Szenes received the absolute backing by members of all parties. Eli Goldschmidt (Labour) declared: 'Hannah Szenes, as far as I am concerned, and I believe that every Jew and Israeli feels the same, is the ultimate expression of the very essence of Jewish and Israeli existence, which is both heroic and tragic . . . A nation which negates its symbols is negating its own self.' Newspapers were full of articles, interviews and letters to the editor in favour of Hannah Szenes; one of these articles, by Aharon Megged, vehemently condemned the scriptwriter for trying to be 'politically correct' by desecrating 'the myth of Hannah Szenes', whose heroism – to the best of his knowledge – was no myth, but an absolute reality.[30] The general attitude taken by the various agents of public opinion was that Kasztner had got his share, his 'rehabilitation' being by and large accepted, but that it was absolutely unnecessary to grant him a pardon through the unjust desecration of Hannah Szenes.

Yet in spite of the tremendous backing which Hannah Szenes received from the court, the parliament and the press, the public focus still remained on Kasztner, not on her. Incidentally, the television drama on Kasztner came out on the night of 9 November 1994, just two days after the fiftieth anniversary of Hannah Szenes' execution (Budapest, 7 November 1944). While Israeli television produced this prestigious, high-cost production about Kasztner, Hannah Szenes got a small share in the framework of a marginal programme called *Ha-Hodesh* (*This Month*, 22 October 1994) which included interviews, some biographical sketches, and of course excerpts from Aharon Megged's drama, this time performed by second-rate actors.[31] Another place where this event was commemorated is Kibbutz Sedot Yam, where a memorial symposium was specially organized. A large audience,

[30] Aharon Megged, 'Al Rezah Giborim' ('On the Murder of Heroes'), in *Shishi*, 24 February 1995. See also David Pedhazur, 'Mishpat Szenes' ('The Szenes Trial'), *Davar*, 11 November 1994.
[31] Israeli Television Archive.

including more than 100 women soldiers, gathered in the Kibbutz dining hall, early in January 1995, to attend a round-table discussion on 'The Personality of Hannah Szenes and her Mission'; among the participants were Aharon Megged himself, the arch-builder of the Szenes myth, the veteran Labour leader Yitzhak Ben-Aharon, the general secretary of the United Kibbutz Movement, Muki Tsur, and, last but not least, Gyora Szenes, Hannah's younger brother. Yet this symposium, impressive as it was, was no more than a local event; the national rostrum, at least for the time being, was taken by Kasztner.

7 Inadequate memories: the survivor in plays by Mann, Kesselman, Lebow and Baitz

ALVIN GOLDFARB

Elie Wiesel, in his essay 'The Heirs', concludes that his best students are children of the survivors. They ask the most perceptive questions:

> Some are intrigued by the killers, others by the victims. How does one become one or the other. And how is one to understand the onlookers? Nor do the children of survivors understand the survivors. Why did they close the book after their ordeal ended? Why did they not choose vengeance? Why did they re-enter a society that had repudiated them? Why did they marry? And why did they have children? What right did they have to bring us into the world?[1]

In the past two decades, there has been increased interest in the survivors and increased debate over and re-evaluation of their postwar existence, especially with the realization that fewer and fewer now survive the passage of time. The oral history projects of Yale University and Steven Spielberg, of course, generate immense media interest.[2]

---

[1] Elie Wiesel, *A Jew Today*, translated by Marion Wiesel (New York: Random House, 1978), p. 41. While I would not be presumptuous enough to compare myself with Wiesel's students, I, too, struggle with the very same questions: my mother and father were both survivors.

[2] As an example of the kind of attention oral history projects are generating, a press release of March 1995 announced that Steven Spielberg's Survivors of the Shoah Visual History Foundation received a $1.3 million donation of computer technology and engineering support from Silicon Graphics, a leading manufacturer of 3-D graphics work stations and digital media servers.

Like Wiesel's students, psychologists, psychiatrists, historians, critics and literary artists pose similar questions. Scholarly works proliferate, with marked differences over how the post-liberation lives of survivors are characterized.

For example, the psychoanalyst Aaron Hass, in *The Aftermath*, citing his interviews of fifty-eight Jewish survivors, points out the fallacies he perceives in generalizing about their experiences; he optimistically concludes: 'This is a book about the incredible resilience of human beings. This is a book about those who survived the Holocaust and reassembled lives which had been completely and violently shattered.'[3] While, on the other hand, Lawrence Langer, in *Holocaust Testimonies: The Ruins of Memory* (1991), analyses the oral histories of survivors – or former victims, as he refers to them – housed at Yale, coming to the darker conclusion that 'Available vocabulary educes a unified view of the self, which invites us to adapt the Holocaust experience to ideas of heroism *during* the event and process of *recovery* afterward that are inconsistent with the realities of the disaster' (p. 171).[4]

The plight of the survivor has, in a similar fashion, intrigued many postwar playwrights, also leading to many disparate points of view regarding the survivors' Holocaust pasts and their present lives, as well as marked differences in dramatic strategies used for representation. In my selected bibliography for Elinor Fuchs' *Plays of the Holocaust*, almost half of the works I cite deal with the survivor.[5]

Of particular interest to me, however, has been the increasing number of traditionally structured plays by contemporary American dramatists in which a survivor is a leading character and which have been produced by institutionalized regional theatres in the United States; among these are: Emily Mann's *Annulla: An Autobiography*;

---

[3] Aaron Hass, *The Aftermath: Living with the Holocaust* (Cambridge: Cambridge University Press, 1995), p. xi.

[4] Both of these very recent works provide intriguing insights into the lives of survivors and will be cited frequently in relationship to my discussions of dramatic representations.

[5] Elinor Fuchs, ed., *Plays of the Holocaust: An International Anthology* (New York: Theater Communications Group, 1987), pp. 303–10.

Wendy Kesselman's *I Love You, I Love You Not*; Barbara Lebow's *A Shayna Maidel*; and Jon Robin Baitz's *The Substance of Fire*.[6]

For the most part, there has been little scholarly analysis of the dramatic strategies employed in representing the survivor in these recent works. For example, Mann's and Lebow's works are thoughtfully discussed by E. R. Isser, who writes: 'In the 1980s Emily Mann and Barbara Lebow transcended the limitations of these earlier [stereotypical and sexist] representations [of Holocaust characters] by creating female protagonists who are fully developed characters.'[7] However, Isser overlooks Kesselman's *I Love You, I Love You Not*, as another possible American feminist representation of the Holocaust written in the same decade, and does not examine the issue of Holocaust survivor representation in these plays.

What I hope to do then, after providing a brief production history and synopsis for each play, is draw some conclusions about the shared dramaturgical techniques employed by these playwrights, in their attempts to stage lives of survivors and point out what are the shared shortcomings of the texts in representing the former victims.

Annulla: An Autobiography is based on an interview with the Holocaust survivor Annulla Allen, a relative of Emily Mann's college room-mate, which the playwright recorded in England in 1974. The play, originally entitled *Annulla: Autobiography of a Survivor*,

---

[6] Jon Robin Baitz, *The Substance of Fire* and *The Film Society* (Garden City, NY: Fireside Theater, 1991), Wendy Kesselman, *I Love You, I Love You Not* (New York: Samuel French, 1983), Barbara Lebow, *A Shayna Maidel* (New York: Dramatists Play Service, 1988), Emily Mann, *Annulla: An Autobiography* (New York: Theater Communications Group, 1985). Among the other plays dealing with survivors which have recently premièred at regional theatres or off-Broadway are: Donald Margulies' *The Model Apartment* (Los Angeles Theater Center, 1988), Sybille Pearson's *Unfinished Stories* (Mark Taper Forum, 1992), Diane Samuels' *Kindertransport* (a British play produced in the United States at the Manhattan Theater Club in 1993) and Cynthia Ozick's *Blue Light* (Sag Harbor, New York's Bay Street Theatre, 1994). References to these works are hereafter cited parenthetically in the main text.

[7] E. R. Isser, 'Toward a Feminist Perspective in American Holocaust Drama', in *Studies in the Humanities*, 17 (December 1990), pp. 139–48.

premièred as a one-woman show at the Guthrie Theater Minneapolis in 1977, directed by Mann and starring Barbara Bryne, and later revived at the Goodman Theater in Chicago in 1978. In 1984/5, for a production at the Repertory Theater of St Louis, Mann revised the work, adding a 'narrator's voice'. Staged at a number of other regional theatres, *Annulla* was presented in 1988 at the New Theater of Brooklyn, with Linda Hunt starring.

The revised play, which is the published text, presents Annulla's recollections of pre-war Europe, the early years of the Nazi rule, her escape, and her current political points of view, interspersed with commentary by a narrator who is looking back on her meeting with the survivor. Annulla survived the early years of the Nazi era by masquerading as an Aryan, obtained her husband's release from Dachau, and fled first to Italy and then to England.

A Shayna Maidel was produced at the Academy Theatre in Atlanta in 1985 and 1986, then at the Hartford Stage Company, and off-Broadway in New York in 1987. In 1992, *Hallmark Hall of Fame* produced a television adaptation, *Miss Rose White*. Lebow's play is a more traditional family drama, dealing with the reunion of a survivor, Lusia Weiss, with her Americanized sister Rose White – not Weiss – and her father Mordechai, both of whom had come to New York prior to the Holocaust. The excessively proud Mordechai, who refused to borrow money, was unable to save the rest of his family from the Holocaust. Lusia's mother and her infant daughter Sprinze were gassed; her pre-war and concentration camp compatriot Hanna died of typhus immediately after liberation. Lusia spends the dramatic action of the play searching for her husband, with whom she is eventually reunited. In addition, the play uses a number of 'fantasy scenes', in which Lusia interacts with her mother, Hanna, and her husband Duvid.

The Actors Theater of Louisville presented *I Love You, I Love You Not* during its 1982/3 season as part of the 'shorts festival' of one-act plays and then by New York's Ensemble Theater Studio in June 1983. It was restaged by New York's American Jewish Theater in 1987. The play will probably gather more public recognition after the release of its film version, starring the American television teenage star Claire Danes, and the renowned French performer Jeanne Moreau. Kesselman's work is also a family drama, in which Daisy, a troubled teenager, struggling with her adolescence, personal insecurity, and Jewish identity, visits her survivor grandmother.

Jon Robin Baitz's *The Substance of Fire* premièred at the Long Wharf Theater in 1990 and was subsequently produced by New York's Playwrights Horizons in 1991. The play's first act presents Isaac Geldhart battling with his children in his attempt to hold onto his business and to keep publishing what he considers quality works. The second act takes place three and a half years later. Geldhart is interviewed by the social worker Marge Hackett, who has come to evaluate his ability to care for himself, on the instigation of his eldest son. Geldhart is a survivor of the Second World War, who remained in hiding while the rest of his family was annihilated.

As can be seen from these brief summaries, on the surface the four plays and their survivor characters all seem quite distinct and individual because their Holocaust experiences are so disparate. Annulla masqueraded as an Aryan and fled Austria prior to the Final Solution. Isaac Geldhart was in hiding in a basement. While Lusia Weiss and Nana were both interned in camps, they were at different moments in their lives: Lusia, whose camp is unnamed, was a parent who lost her child and her mother; Nana, an older sister, lost her siblings and parents in Auschwitz.

Furthermore, while Kesselman and Lebow present positive nurturing images of the Holocaust survivors, Mann and Baitz present survivors with apparent human flaws. Kesselman's Nana begs Daisy to eat and supports her voracious reading; she is constantly making pancakes and purchasing books. Lebow's Lusia struggles to find her husband Duvid, never believing that he could have perished in the Holocaust. Mann's Annulla, on the other hand, is not as positively represented. She, as one critic notes, 'verbally abuses her invalid sister, even as she makes chicken soup for her, nonchalantly chopping and dismembering the bird'.[8] Isaac, in *The Substance of Fire*, has a troubled relationship with his children, due to his own headstrong arrogance. Frank Rich, in his review of Baitz's play, suggests that, 'All of Isaac's struggles, of course, date back to a war in which his parents and grandparents

---

[8] Richard Kramer, 'Annulla', in *Studies in American Drama, 1945–Present*, 4 (1989), p. 288.

died in the camps while he escaped incarceration. If Isaac has his share of survivor's guilt, he also has a survivor's arrogant omnipotence' (267).

The playwrights' portrayals exemplify Aaron Hass's analysis that 'Survivors of the Holocaust, particularly Jewish survivors, are often seen as a unitary phenomenon by both mental health professionals and lay persons. And yet the experiences of individual Jews during Word War II varied markedly'[9] since there is 'significant diversity in survivors' post-Holocaust adjustment' (The Aftermath, p. 7).

Yet, while creating such disparate characters, all four authors employ many similar structural techniques to represent the plight of the survivor. Some of these techniques are directly related to the structural qualities of the oral histories on which three of the four – Annulla, I Love You, I Love You Not, and A Shayna Maidel – are based. (While, as noted earlier, Annulla is a transcription of Emily Mann's meeting with a survivor, the other two authors also indicate indebtedness to specific survivors for being the models for their protagonists.)

In his study of oral testimonies, Langer notes, 'A complex kind of "reversible continuity" seems to establish itself in many of these testimonies, one foreign to straight chronology that governs most written memoirs.'[10] Or, in a less scholarly and more personal discussion, one survivor's child remarks, 'no matter how often we heard her [their mother's] war stories, we could never quite figure out how they fit together'.[11] In all four of these plays, the chronological representation of the survivors' experiences does not follow a traditional linear pattern but instead is given to the audience in a fragmentary fashion.

---

[9] Hass, The Aftermath, p. 1. Let me again insert a personal note. In my family, the experiences were quite diverse. My father spent the war as a slave labourer at the Flossenburg labour camp. My mother spent her teenage years hiding in the Ukrainian forest with her aunt and the man she would marry after the war. My parents' closest friend was an Auschwitz survivor. Some of my most unsettling childhood recollections are debates over dinner regarding who had it worst.

[10] Lawrence L. Langer, Holocaust Testimonies: The Ruins of Memory (New Haven: Yale University Press, 1991), p. 20.

[11] Aron Hirt-Manheimer, 'The Long Road to Liberation', in Reform Judaism, 24.1, (Fall 1995), pp. 10–19, p. 11.

In *Annulla*, the protagonist immediately warns us that 'my life is in terrible disorder' (p. 1), referring to her present life and the messy state of her apartment but, in reality, commenting on her narrative of the past. Annulla moves back and forth between her pre-war, Holocaust, and postwar lives, forcing the audiences to help construct the narrative. In *A Shayna Maidel*, the fantasy scenes do not follow chronological order either; liberation, for example, precedes Lusia attempting to convince her mother to flee the ghetto with a Gentile employer. In both *I Love You, I Love You Not* and *The Substance of Fire*, the revelations of the past are fragmented and must be pieced together by the audience and the on-stage listeners. In Kesselman's play, we are given part of the story of a Gentile girl who turned away from her Jewish friend just prior to the deportation, then the story of the capture of the children by the Angel of Death, and then an explanation for the chronologically earlier event.

According to many commentators, oral testimonies often reflect the 'partitioned self' of the survivor: the fact that they see the world both through the eyes of their contemporary 'normality' and the eyes of their incomprehensible experiences. In addition, 'researchers report that the vast majority of survivors have vivid and intrusive memories of Holo-caust experiences almost daily' and that 'references to the Holocaust become almost reflexive'.[12]

In all four plays, there are moments when the split persona and the reflexive intrusion of the Holocaust are powerful dramaturgical techniques. When Nana reviews Daisy's German with her granddaughter, the older woman whispers to herself, 'Links, rechts, links, rechts' (p. 35), the command for selection at the arrival platform in Auschwitz, and then orders Daisy to make the bed in German, as if reverting to her past life. Nana further reflects her partitioned personality when talking about her and her sisters' capture and selection. The survivor always refers to herself by what is probably her given name, as if that name belonged to the fictional character, Annushka. In addition, Nana accidentally begins to describe her deportation in the third person, as if she had been a divided person both observing the horror and taking part in it: 'Midnight that night – at midnight, they, we – we were –' (p. 14).

---

[12] Hass, *The Aftermath*, p. 108.

Lusia's fantasies in *A Shayna Maidel* reflect a partitioned persona, blurring her present post-liberation world with her past. The fantasy scenes develop out of and merge into her present, thereby forcing the audience to see the world in this double fashion. When Rose gives Lusia too much to eat, the survivor thinks of those times when there was nothing to eat. The most striking example occurs when Mordechai brings the last letter his wife has written for her American daughter Rose, and Lusia relives her impotent attempt to convince her mother to flee the ghetto. The Holocaust past intrudes on and reflects each present moment, and frequently Lusia exists in moments of duality, literally moving from her fantasy into the 'real' world and back again.

In *Annulla*, the present is also continuously compared to the past and the references to the Holocaust are 'reflexive', invading the protagonist's interaction with the narrator/interviewer. For example, when the unseen voice says the word *Nazis*, 'Annulla is stopped by the word' (p. 15). At the close, the 74-year-old survivor says, 'it went by so fast. Do you know everything has gone by so fast' (p. 18), while having great difficulty in saying 'good-bye'. Again, it is apparent that she is talking not only about the present interview but also her past life.

In *The Substance of Fire*, Isaac specifically describes himself as partitioned, as someone who has lived in two worlds but for whom the dual existences merge and become reflexive:

> And then I got out of the basement and into the wrecked world. I came to this country. You reinvent yourself. Make it as a *bon vivant* in Manhattan. Meet this woman – this extraordinary woman. Marry. Have these kids. Go to so many cocktail parties, host so many more . . . and they . . . haunt. (*Beat.*) I have kept my eyes closed to the world outside of the basement for so long. The wrecked world all around us. But I can no longer close my eyes. (p. 32)

As has been noted frequently, many survivors – though not all – have great difficulty in speaking about the Holocaust.[13] Langer suggests that

---

[13] My own personal observation is that some survivors are compelled to speak, to bear witness, while others find it too painful. My mother, who was a teenager during her years of hiding in the forest, spoke constantly

'The seeds of anguished memory are sown in the barren belief that the very story that you try to tell drives off the audience you seek to capture. Those seeds often shrivel in the further suspicion that the story you tell *cannot* be precisely the story as it happened. Reluctance to speak has little to do with *preference* for silence.'[14] Hass, in his analysis of survivors, also notes that 'some survivors have not spoken because they have felt it was useless. Words could not articulate the full measure of their ordeal. They are also convinced the unmarked can never imagine or understand.'[15]

In all four American plays, the dramatists use the reluctance to speak about the Holocaust and its absence to underscore the horrors: the playwrights are quite careful to make certain that the absence forces the audience to feel more palpably the omnipresence of the Holocaust in the postwar world. The former victims' silence, then, is both the dilemma of the survivor characters dramatized in these plays and an underlying dramatic strategy. Each of the characters is impotent to describe the actuality of the Holocaust.

In terms of the horrors, Annulla only says, 'So my mother went to Poland with my older sister where they were killed; they were shot by the Nazis, my mother and Czecha, before they got to the concentration camps' (p. 10). Lusia never specifically talks of her past, her place of internment remains unnamed; instead, she recites to her father a list of where – not how – people in the family died. Nana can only talk of being captured after fleeing the ghetto with her younger sisters and their separation, as if it were a third-person children's tale; Daisy even begins the story like a fairytale: 'Once there were . . . three little girls. Annushka. Maruchka. And Varuchka' (p. 36). In *The Substance of Fire*, Isaac screams to the social worker, 'You can't even imagine. You have no idea' (p. 66).

The dramatists also use the inability to speak concretely about the Holocaust to force the audience to confront more fully its absent horrors. By making its absence a constant presence in the plays, the

---

of her experiences. My father, who was ten years older, could never bring himself to tell us of his life in the concentration camp; his nightmares died with him.

[14] Langer, *Holocaust Testimonies*, p. 61.   [15] Ibid., p. 118.

audience is forced to realize that there is no escape from the horrors of the Shoah for these survivors in the postwar world and, at the same time, the impotence of the characters and, by implication, the playwrights to present the Holocaust dramatically.

Barbara Lebow, in her notes, specifically requires that 'There should be no visual or auditory images suggesting a concentration camp' (p. 5). And in none of these plays are there any visual or auditory images suggesting the ghettos, concentration camps, or any of the other horrific circumstances of the Shoah. Instead, in all of these dramas, the palpability of the Holocaust is recreated through metaphorical elements in the *mise en scène* or through stage action.

In *A Shayna Maidel*, Rose, the American sister, marks herself with a pen; she tattoos herself in an impotent gesture to understand her sister's history. In *I Love You, I Love You Not*, Daisy screams selection commands in German – using words from her vocabulary lesson – and then throws open the stove and shouts, 'You wouldn't want me to go in there, would you?' (p. 49). In *The Substance of Fire*, the obsessive desire to publish books detailing the Nazi era and Isaac's postcard painted by Hitler reflect the reverberations of the past on Isaac's present. Annulla's manuscript, in which she tries unsuccessfully to make sense of the horrors of the twentieth century, sometimes using broad generalizations which the audience realizes make no sense, reflect her entrapment in the past.[16]

Yet, despite these dramaturgical strategies, ultimately the authors are not totally successful in their representation of the Holocaust survivor.[17] All of these recent plays oversimplify the representation

[16] Annulla's historical generalizations, particularly those in which she blames the victors of World War One for inflicting economic chaos on Germany and thereby for being responsible for the Second World War, are shockingly like the Nazi's propagandistic attacks. Annulla illustrates Hass's conclusion that 'Most survivors know little of the general history of the Third Reich and its programme for the Jews' (*The Aftermath*, p. 112).

[17] I should point out that I am uncomfortable about being too critical of the dramas' weaknesses. As Vicki Patraka has argued, when the film *Schindler's List* was being discussed at the 'Shoah and Performance' conference, University of Glasgow, September 1995, these plays, like

of the survivor and of their Holocaust pasts, draw analogies which diminish the magnitude of the Shoah, as well as strive to provide emotional reassurance to their audiences through simplistic plot resolutions.

While the plays do present characters whose Holocaust experiences and postwar lives are highly individual, three of them provide too simplistic an analysis of the Holocaust survivors' psyche. Except for *Annulla*, all represent characters as burdened by melodramatic guilt for having either lost loved ones or having been spared. Guilt is too simplistic a dramatic reduction and, unfortunately, moves the focus away from the victimizer to the victim. As Hass suggests in describing those survivors he has interviewed: 'I did not find this phenomenon [survivor guilt] so widespread as we have been led to believe . . . Approximately one half of those I interviewed articulated an uneasiness [note the choice of word, by Hass, it is not *guilt*] about their reprieve' (*The Aftermath*, p. 25). In these plays, repressed and suddenly expressed guilt, not complex memories, dominate the moments of dramatic revelation.

Furthermore, the real focus of all of these dramas is not on the survivor but on the 'other' who struggles to understand. *I Love You, I Love You Not* is Daisy's coming-of-age play. Nana is a device to help her through adolescence. Nana's experiences are meant to help Daisy grow up, not help her – or the audience – grapple with the experiences of the Holocaust survivor. Mel Gussow, in his review of the Ensemble Theater Studio production of 1983, described the play as 'about the growing pains of a girl named Daisy', never once mentioning that Nana is a former victim of the Holocaust.[18]

In the revision of *Annulla*, the intrusion of the commenting voice shifts the focus to the narrator's quest to understand her own

that film, are popular pieces of dramatic literature which are being produced throughout the United States in regional and university theatres, often in uninformed communities with small and sometimes marginalized Jewish communities. Because of their accessibility, they have moved the Holocaust into the consciousness of their audiences. For example, *A Shayna Maidel* and *I Love You, I Love You Not* have been produced at Illinois State University and each production generated much greater interest than the few lectures that have been given on campus by survivors or by myself.

[18] Mel Gussow, 'The Short Form', *New York Times*, 1 June 1984, p. 4.

past: 'I wanted to know – I wanted to know everything' (p. 5). *The Substance of Fire* splits its focus between Isaac's children, who suffer because of their survivor father's intolerance of their lifestyles, and the social worker of act 2, who suffered personal losses in her life, and becomes Isaac's tool of redemption.

The *shayna maidel* of Lebow's play is Rose, not the survivor Lusia. The Americanized sister is the upstanding woman who accepts her sister with open arms, struggles to understand her circumstances, and helps rebuild a family.

While none of these playwrights suggests that their audiences can comprehend the Holocaust experiences of the survivors, by focusing on the 'other', they reassure spectators that there is an inherent willingness to listen. Of course, their reassurance flies in the face of a more common, harsh reality; as has been pointed out, 'In America, the survivors were met by Jews who soon made it apparent that they did not want to hear about what happened in the concentration camps . . . Their ignorance of the unprecedented savagery experienced by their cousins did not inhibit the offers of demoralizing analogies.'[19]

These playwrights – like the welcoming American Jews – also draw analogies, suggesting similarities between the Holocaust and other personal, social, and/or political circumstances. Baitz draws parallels between the suffering of Isaac and that of the social worker whose husband committed suicide due to political scandal. At one point, the world of New York City is compared to the world of the Holocaust:

> I came from the worst place. People turning one another in for
> a hustle, for a piece of ass, for a piece of black bread, whatever.
> You get it, sweetie? I mean, if they thought you were a Jew or

---

[19] Hass, *The Aftermath*, p. 17. Again, a personal recollection: my mother's aunt had an American brother who sponsored my mother's and the aunt's immigration to the United States. They were his only surviving relatives. He, like Mordechai in *Shayna Maidel*, had come to the United States prior to the war's outbreak. While he helped bring them here, he spent little time with these survivors, was not central to their lives, and, furthermore, was often described by his sister and his niece as a 'stranger', not simply because he had left the Ukraine before they were born, but because they believed he shut his ears to their experiences.

not. Or *not*. If they were just pissed off at you 'cause you slighted them. But this city wins on points. You got me? This city wins on points. (*The Substance of Fire*, p. 62)

Daisy's adolescent pain is given comparable weight to that of Nana's loss, and Rose's separation from her mother and control by her domineering father is paralleled to Lusia's horrors.

Only Emily Mann seems uncomfortable in diminishing the Shoah by drawing parallels. She has Annulla attack Brecht's allegorical representation of Hitler in *The Resistible Rise of Arturo Ui*: 'This moronic man, this Brecht, makes Hitler *funny*! Did he think no one in the audience had gone through this? You know, Brecht had not. He was in America. To make Hitler into a gangster, this shows ignorance' (p. 16). Even so, Mann's text suggests analogies between the Third Reich and Stalinist oppression, a comparison which has been cogently negated by Jean Améry, himself a survivor, in *At the Mind's Limits*. When Mann's protagonist compares Stalinists to Nazis, she twice uses the generic term 'men's barbarism', which echoes Améry's fear that the Holocaust will be submerged and diminished because it will be historified 'as regrettable, but in no way unique. Everything will be submerged in a general "Century of Barbarism".'[20]

But possibly the greatest weakness of these playwrights is that they fall into the trap of what Langer calls 'moral oversimplification'.[21] All of these plays romanticize the wartime and postwar existences of the former victims. Furthermore, the four dramas all epitomize the type of Holocaust play that, according to Elinor Fuchs, 'always took on the conventions of melodrama or family drama, dramatic patterns that in their very familiarity, including the familiar focus on the individual, seemed to offer a subtle reassurance to the spectator' (*Plays of the Holocaust*, p. xii). And all four suggest a universe in which there is always familial redemption following the Holocaust.

---

[20] Jean Améry, *At the Mind's Limits: Contemplations by a Survivor on Auschwitz and its Realities*, translated by Sydney Rosenfeld and Stella P. Rosenfeld (Bloomington: Indiana University Press, 1980), p. 80.

[21] Lawrence L. Langer, *Admitting the Holocaust: Collected Essays* (New York: Oxford University Press, 1995), p. 166.

Lebow's play most clearly exemplifies the problem. She presents the audience with a romanticized, Americanized liberation, which stands in strong contrast to the following description found in Yad Vashem's internet presentation, 'The Anguish of Liberation': 'The story of the liberation is not the good ending to the bad story, it is a harsh story in its own right. It is the successful conclusion of the struggle for physical survival, but the start of the longer mental struggle.'[22] Using the well-made play formula, Lebow allows for a reconciliation between Rose and her mother by having a letter – à la Ibsen – delivered following the war. Duvid survives and the family is resurrected; there is 'a small echo of the old days' (p. 66). In the last fantasy scene, there is a well-made resolution which transcends the death camps; even those who perished in the Holocaust are reunited with those who did not. The final stage direction has all of the surviving members of the family, including the oppressive Mordechai, embrace. Even Lusia's husband's name – Duvid or David – implies a rebirth, since the Messianic hopes of the Jewish people are traditionally tied to King David's descendant.

In *A Shayna Maidel*, the family is always a moral, redemptive tool: staying with one's child and parent is an easy choice during and after the Shoah, even in the face of much survivor testimony that reflects the opposite. Consider, for example, how much the Holocaust dehumanized the mother described by Emmanuel Ringelblum in his Warsaw Ghetto journal, and whether Lebow's play allows the audience to consider the obscene extent of dehumanization by the Nazis:

> Terrible case of three-year-old refugee child. En route, the guard threw the child into the snow. Its mother jumped off the wagon and tried to save the child. The guard threatened her with a revolver. The mother insisted her life was worthless for her without her child. Then the guard threatened to shoot all the

---

[22] The URL for Yad Vashem's discussion of liberation is http://www.yad-vashem.org.il/LIBINDEX.HTM. Langer provides a similar description of postwar life: 'Liberation is displaced, in meaning and fact, by the ordeals preceding that experience, ordeals from whose thrall he cannot be released' (*Holocaust Testimonies*, p. 119).

Jews in the wagon. The mother arrived in Warsaw, and here went out of her mind.[23]

Yet, as mentioned earlier, most of these plays have similar redemptive dramatic resolutions. At the close of *The Substance of Fire*, the social worker is so moved by Isaac's revelation of his survival that she promises he will not be placed under his children's control. In addition, there is a hint of a relationship between the survivor and the suffering social worker and a reconciliation between Isaac and his younger son, Martin. To suggest his letting go of his obsession with the past, Isaac burns the postcard painted by Hitler.

In *I Love You, I Love You Not*, Nana tries to arrive at a rational reason for her Gentile friend refusing to recognize her just before deportation:

> Maybe they told her things, and maybe, maybe she believed
> them. Maybe she had to, maybe they forced her to. Maybe she
> was afraid. Maybe that day she saw them stringing up the lights
> and she came all the way to the ghetto to see me, only to turn
> and walk away from me. Maybe Daisy, maybe, who knows?
> Maybe that was the day she found out, six hours before we did,
> where they were taking us, where we were going. Don't be
> afraid, Daisy. Don't ever be afraid.   (p. 56)

Compare this with the Israeli novelist Aharon Appelfeld's unromanticized representation of Austrians' reactions to a deportation, as remembered by his survivor protagonist in *For Every Sin*:

> They left the police building . . . At the windows women and
> children stood and watched their progress in silence. No one
> called out, no one opened his mouth . . . At the end of the street
> a paint contractor called out, 'Death to the Jews, death to the
> merchants . . .' The synagogue, without worshippers for years,
> was gripped by flames at that moment . . .

---

[23] Emmanuel Ringelblum, *Notes for the Warsaw Ghetto*, trans. and ed. Jacob Sloan (New York: Schocken Books, 1974), p. 131.

>On Schimmer Street a few women stood on a balcony,
>and a kind of malicious glee dripped from their eyes.[24]

Kesselman's play closes with Nana promising Daisy, 'I'll be here.' While an understandable sentiment for the neat resolution of well-made family drama about adolescent *angst*, the horrors of the Shoah ask audience members to consider less reassuring possibilities. Think of the testimonies of those who returned from a ghetto errand to find 'no one there'. The Holocaust undermines the facile familial reassurance, 'I'll be here.'[25]

Even Emily Mann, who attempts to undercut the romanticized notion of the Holocaust, chooses to recount a story of family reconciliation. Her protagonist tells of being reunited with a son who had been sent to Sweden, and with her husband, who survived internment in Dachau.

However, Mann does not provide simple reassurance to audiences; her drama does not have a neat denouement. Mann warns us through her narrator that 'there's no time', making us painfully aware that the repositories of the horrors of the Shoah, the survivors, are disappearing. Yet, the narrator's quest to understand also fails; she cannot gain a true access to or understanding of the Holocaust. As she tells us,

>I went to Ostrolenka [in Poland, where her family had come
>from and her great-grandfather was murdered by the Nazis].
>I saw where my grandmother's family had lived; I tried to get

---

[24] Aharon Appelfeld, *For Every Sin*, trans. Jeffrey M. Green (New York: Weidenfeld and Nicolson, 1989), p. 165.

[25] Avraham Tory, in his Kovno Ghetto diary (*Surviving the Holocaust: The Kovno Ghetto Diary*, translated by Jerzy Michalowicz (Cambridge, MA: Harvard University Press, 1990)), gives a horrific example of parents who discovered their children weren't there: 'I could not explain to Miller [the Nazi overseer of the ghetto] that before the war our women had never performed such strenuous labour in the capacity of hired hands . . . Nor could I tell him that we are not very eager to set up a kindergarten in the Ghetto. We do not want to deliver our children to destruction. In October 1941, more than 160 children and babies then in the hospital were executed' (p. 258).

into Bucovina where my father's family had lived but it was in
Russia and they wouldn't let us in. There is a wonderful fairy
tale about a young girl who loans her relatives to another young
girl who doesn't have any. You see? It's been eleven years since
I visited Annulla.   (18)[26]

There is no romanticized, well-made solution to the problem of lost
family, lost memories, or lost lives. In the St Louis Repertory production, 'the sound of a clock ticking was a background for the young
woman's voice', underscoring how much more the passage of time will
obliterate the possibilities for comprehending.

Ironically, however, Mann the director cannot escape a desire for
a consoling representation. When discussing the underlying message of
the production she staged in Brooklyn, she claims: 'The play is about
how one generation teaches another, and how systems of values and
morals are passed down.'[27] As many commentators argue, the Holocaust flies in the face of this rational notion. What clear-cut morals
and values survive in the face of Auschwitz, Majdanek, Treblinka,
Belzec, Sobibor and all the other places of horror? Mann's play more
clearly represents this moral quagmire than her directorial statement
about it.

What do we then conclude about these American dramatists'
attempts to represent survivors? Simply stated, while all are well
meaning, their focus on the non-survivor and their use of traditional,
well-made dramatic techniques and formulae diminish the complexity
of the subject matter and let the audience members off the hook too
easily.

Since all of these plays present successful familial reconciliations, they avoid the harsher moral and human implications of the
Holocaust. By providing neat, well-made play resolutions to the family circumstances, the authors reassure their audiences but avoid the

---

[26] Just to note a coincidence: Aharon Appelfeld, the Israeli novelist cited
earlier, was born in and emigrated from Bocovina, the area where the
family of Emily Mann's father had lived.

[27] Amy Hersh, 'A Survivor's Voice', in *American Theater*, 5.8 (November
1988), pp. 8–9.

incomprehensibility and the lack of logic inherent in the Holocaust universe. The structural and plot resolutions of these plays ultimately diminish the enormity of the dehumanization and depersonalization that took place during the Shoah.[28]

Since Lebow's Rose, Kesselman's Daisy, Baitz's social worker, and Mann's narrator all valiantly struggle for insight into the Holocaust survivor, the implication is that there is a universal, reassuring willingness to listen and to try to know. None of the four playwrights, however, chooses to stage the nightmare of concentration camp internees that Primo Levi so painfully describes and which stands in stark contrast to the Americans' reassurances:

> They had returned home and with passion and relief were describing their past sufferings, addressing themselves to a loved one, and were not believed, indeed were not even listened to. In the most typical and cruellest form, the interlocutor turned and left in silence.[29]

---

[28] Even if these are based on documented accounts of actual lives, one wonders why it is only positive resolutions that attract the playwrights? Langer's criticism of the conclusion of Spielberg's *Schindler's List* (1993), a film he greatly admires, seems applicable to these plays:

> To no one's surprise, some relics of Hollywood infiltrate *Schindler's List*, reminding us of how powerful a hold the culture of consolation still exerts over the culture of dread . . . deplorable is his warning to the SS guarding his factory at the war's end that they could return home as murderers, or as decent men. That was no longer a choice for such troops in 1945, and even though there is some evidence that the real Schindler uttered those very words, Spielberg was free to reject them for the sake of the artistic logic of his film. His lapse suggests that even he was reluctant to leave his audience on the brink of the moral chaos to which Nazi Germany had led the Western world . . . [E]ven a blunt film like *Schindler's List* decides to leave us with memories of a healing wound rather than a throbbing scar.
>
> (*Admitting the Holocaust*, p. 11)

[29] Primo Levi, *The Drowned and the Saved*, translated by Raymond Rosenthal (New York: Summit Books, 1986), p. 12.

None gives the audience an uncompromising representation of the life of the survivor.[30] And none is able to shed greater light on the questions posed by Elie Wiesel's best students.

[30] For a more successful dramatization of the enigmatic existence of the survivor, see Yehuda Amichai's radio play *Bells and Trains*. The Israeli poet uses an old people's home, that a relative of one of its female residents visits, as a way both of depicting the dehumanizing camps and their omnipresence in former victims' lives. The visitor left Germany with his immediate family prior to the war; the woman in the home, while referred to as Aunt Henrietta, is his mother's cousin. Existence in the old people's home, which is populated almost exclusively by survivors, parallels existence in the concentration camps. The trains, dogs and bells remind the audience of the sounds of the camps. Routines in the home parallel those in the camp: men and women communicate through intermediaries; the food is described as nothing more than bread and water. What Amichai does is illustrate the omnipresence of the camps in the survivors' contemporary lives through this symbolic home. In addition, there are no well-made revelations or sentimental familial reconciliations in the universe Amichai creates. Few visitors come to visit; there is no false reassurance of universal interest in the Shoah. The survivors remain in this institution – in their impenetrable world – the nephew returns to Israel. His aunt warns him in the last lines of the play: 'Hans, Hans! At 3.30 there is an express from Singburg . . . Don't come back . . . At 3.30 . . . Hans . . . Hans' ('Bells and Trains', in *Midstream*, 2 (October 1966), p. 66).

8 Performing a Holocaust play in Warsaw in 1963

SETH WOLITZ

Man brennt etwas ein, damit es im Gedächtnis bleibt:
nur was nicht aufhört, *wehzutun*, bleibt im Gedächtnis.

(Friedrich Nietzsche)[1]

The hurt of the Shoah has not ceased to haunt the existence of the Jews. Theatre, treating the theme of the Shoah, not only pricks the hurt but can hypostatize the painful memory into a commemorative monument and art: 'consciousness released into structure'.[2] As Robert Skloot notes, 'five objectives of serious playwrights who are drawn to the forbidding part of our history [should be] honouring the victims, teaching history to audiences, evoking emotional responses, discussing ethical issues, and suggesting solutions to universal, contemporary problems'.[3] The theatre can perform all these functions and can reward didactically and with responsibility. However, the Holocaust play I saw in Warsaw 1963 failed on most of these objectives; yet it was highly applauded.

The context, meanings and performance of that play are the parameters of this chapter. I shall show how a Polish–Jewish Communist

---

[1] Friedrich Nietzsche 'Zur Genealogie der Moral', in *Werke*, 3 vols. (Munich: Hanser Verlag, 1966), vol. II, p. 802. 'One brands something so that it can remain in memory, only that which does not cease to cause pain remains in memory.' (Translation Wolitz.)

[2] Herbert Blau, *Take up the Bodies: Theater at the Vanishing Point* (Urbana: University of Illinois Press, 1982), p. 163.

[3] Robert Skloot, *The Darkness We Carry: The Drama of the Holocaust* (Madison: University of Wisconsin Press, 1988), p. 10.

dramatist wilfully manipulated the historical events of the Shoah to create a play which served the ideological and political interests in 1963 of the Polish People's Republic in which he believed. The drama distorts events and creates clichéd scenes and dialogues. The playwright weaves together many political elements: he consciously exaggerates Polish–Jewish co-operation and friendship; oversimplifies the exploitation of the Jewish workers by the Jewish bourgeois *Judenrat*; insists on the Communist role in organizing the Warsaw Ghetto Uprising; and casts aspersions on the Zionists and national parties. This play provides an exemplum of early Holocaust revisionism and underscores the extent to which a Jewish Communist and dramatist was prepared to express his loyalty to the regime. The work, furthermore, displays the limits of mimesis in treating the Shoah, particularly within the confines of socialist realistic dramaturgy.

There are few plays in Yiddish about the Holocaust, and for good reason.[4] Yiddish speakers were its major victims and the survivors hardly needed aesthetic mimesis to jog their memories. What Yiddish theatre there was after the Shoah sought to preserve a lost world and to entertain with a strong ethnic tonality. Allusions, direct and oblique, to the Shoah traversed the stage, but very few performances were given of the few Yiddish plays directly inscribing the Holocaustal experience.

---

[4] The Jewish State Theatre of Poland performed the majority of the Yiddish plays treating the Shoah and therefore its repertoire provides a useful panorama of the plays and their dates of production (1945–74). Anna Shvirtshinski, *Shosn oyf der Dluga-gas* (*Gunfire in Dluga Street*; 1948); Khayim Sloves, *Haman's Mapole* (*Haman's Defeat*; 1950); Bine Heler, *A hoyz in geto* (*A House in the Ghetto*; 1953); Mikhl Mirsky, *Der Kheshbn* (*The Bill*; 1963); Khayim Sloves, *Tsen Brider zenen mir geven* (*Once we were Ten Brothers*; 1968). Out of the 104 plays in the repertoire produced between 1945 and 1974, only 5 plays treated the Holocaust directly. See Shloyme Kleyt, 'Der Repertuar fun yidishn melukhe-teater', *25 yor yidisher melukhe-teater in folks-poyln* (Warsaw: Arkady, 1975), pp. 48–51 (Solomon Kleyt, 'The Repertoire of the E.[sther] R.[okhl] Kaminska Jewish State Theater', *25 Years of the Jewish State Theater in the Polish People's Republic* (Warsaw: Arkady, 1975), pp. 41–4). The distinguished Soviet Yiddish poet, Perets Markish, composed a Holocaust play, *Der Oyfshtand fun geto* (*The Ghetto Uprising*; 1946–8), which was produced in the Soviet Union.

The yearly ceremonies have served as the normal frame for commemorating the events.

The Polish Communist government under Wladyslaw Gomulka prepared carefully for the twentieth anniversary of the Warsaw Ghetto Uprising; full press coverage was given, and government officials attended the various events throughout the week leading to 19 April, the actual date of the uprising.[5] The Jewish Cultural Organization, an official part of the government, had worked with the various Jewish cultural institutions to prepare for the welcome of international guests.[6] At the Jewish State Theatre founded in 1950, the crown jewel of the Polish–Jewish cultural institutions, a brand new play directed by Ida Kaminska, *Der Kheshbn*, by Mikhl Mirsky (in English, *The Final Bill, Account* or *Reckoning*, and in Polish, *Rachunek*) was in final rehearsal.[7] The dramatist served as a long-time party member and played an important role in the Jewish Cultural Organization.[8] It was the première of this play that I witnessed along with many other 'guests' at the Teatr Polski on 15 April 1963.[9]

In April 1963 the Polish–Jewish condition of Warsaw, in historical perspective, was quasi-stable. The Polish regime provided the approximately 30,000 Jews left in Poland with their own schools, a publishing house, cultural centres, and underwrote the Yiddish State Theatre. The Polish–Jewish Communists had seen, of course, the obliteration of Yiddish culture in the USSR in 1952, but that was Stalin's time, and the 1956 instabilities in Poland were now eased. As Jaff Schatz states: 'all retained their basic belief in the purity of the

---

[5] 'Rirende stsenes in Varshe bay ehren di geto-kedushim', *Forverts* (*Forward*), New York, 21 April 1963, pp. 1 and 9.

[6] A. Kvaterko, 'Lekoved undzer teater', *Folksshtime*, Warsaw, 2 April 1963. Reprinted in *Morgen Freiheit* (*Morning Freiheit*), New York, 23 April 1963, p. 5; in *Folksshtime*, 13 April 1963, p. 1.

[7] Ida Kaminska, *My Life, My Theater*, edited and translated by Curt Leviant (New York: Macmillan, 1973), pp. 221–30; Nahma Sandrow, *Vagabond Stars: A World History of Yiddish Theater* (New York: Harper and Row, 1977), pp. 359–62.

[8] Mikhl Mirsky, *Lexicon fun der nayer yidisher literatur* (New York: fun altveltlikhn yidishn kultur-kongres and Tsiko, 1963), vol. v, p. 671.

[9] *Folksshtime*, 17 April 1963, p. 1.

Communist vision'.[10] Mikhl Mirsky belonged to this cadre and was a committed Communist. He believed in a secular Yiddish progressivist culture and, with others of his generation, paid a heavy price to secure it temporarily. His play was intended to commemorate the Shoah and to place his ideological perspective in an honourable light. The typescript of the play was officially submitted on 26 March 1963, and was used as the working script for the production.[11] Certain pages reveal considerable rewriting in pen (of an unknown hand), toning down some of the more ideological passages and intensifying the dramatic dialogue. The play has never been published.

Ida Kaminska, the heir to one of the most famous Yiddish acting families in Warsaw, going back to pre-World War One days, not only directed the Jewish State Theatre but personally directed the new drama. This theatre, the only subsidized Yiddish theatre in the world with the exception of the 'provincial' Rumanian Jewish State Theatre, brought pride to the Polish–Jewish Communists, for it symbolized to them living Yiddish culture and served as their ideological rebuttal to the Habima, the Hebrew-speaking National Theatre of Israel, as well as symbolizing for them their victory over Hitler! The Polish government supported it for ideological and propaganda purposes, and the company stayed well inside the boundaries of folkloric and socialist realism. (No Polish Laboratory Theatre experiments here!) In retrospect, it is clear that the Kaminska Theatre was part of a Potemkin Village. The younger actors in the troupe were Polish actors who learned their Yiddish lines by rote.[12] In the small theatre in which they performed,

---

[10] Jaff Schatz, *The Generation: The Rise and Fall of the Jewish Communists of Poland* (Berkeley: University of California Press, 1991), p. 281. Other texts consulted on the Gomulka period of Communist Poland are: Norman Davies, *Heart of Europe: A Short History of Poland* (Oxford: Clarendon Press, 1984); R. F. Leslie, *The History of Poland Since 1863* (Cambridge: Cambridge University Press, 1984).

[11] The manuscript is listed as originally number 130A, but changed to 138 in the archive of the Panstwowy Teatr Zydowski Im. E. R. Kaminskiej (Jewish State Theatre): Mikhl Mirski, *Der Kheshbn*, drame in 2 tayln/7 bilder.

[12] The Jewish State Theatre normally performed in a little theatre on Krulevske 13 in Warsaw. Because of the large number of participants at the Twentieth Commemoration, the performance of Mirsky's play took place at the Teatr Polski, the most elegant theatre in Warsaw at the time.

most of the patrons, Jewish and Polish, sat with earphones on listening to a Polish translation!

Ida Kaminska was a *kluge Yidene* who maintained lines to the ruling élite. She served up to 1964 as a member of the Jewish Cultural Organization. Travelling with her troupe around the world, she scored propaganda points for the regime and brought it legitimacy: the new Poland is not anti-Semitic and supports its minority cultures! For a Yiddish actress, where else in the postwar period could one find economic security, a subsidized theatre and official honours?

A true professional, Kaminska took Mirsky's script and blocked it for production, adding tableau scenes not listed in the script, but which I remember and are confirmed by another 'foreign guest' and by a Polish critic who commented on one of them in his review.[13] Ironically, she never mentions Mirsky, the play, or her directing of it in her memoirs, *My Life, My Theatre*, written for an American 'capitalist' audience after her flight from Poland in 1968!

Der Kheshbn was written especially for the twentieth anniversary celebrations of the Warsaw Ghetto Uprising and as such seems conceived as a *Festspiel*.[14] More narrative than dramatic, *Der Kheshbn* is an epic retelling of the liquidation of a large ghetto – any ghetto,

[13] The Polish critic Roman Szydlowski, 'Epica opowiesc o tragedii getta', *Trybuna Ludu*, 25 April 1963, p. 6. A Jewish foreign guest, Charles Baron (Paris), in a telephone conversation and in private correspondence, confirmed the tableau scenes.

[14] Synopsis of *Der Kheshbn*

> *I. Exposition*
> *Scene 1*. In the foyer of a ballroom. Summer. Pre-war Poland. Students. Daniel Marshak arrives to inaugurate the new Jewish housing. Bronke, his daughter, talks to the Polish student Silvester Dobroczynski who is in love with Esther, a close friend of Bronke and a Jewish student activist. He brings bad news that Hitler is deporting Jews. Selek, a cousin of Bronke, is in love with Bronke and dislikes Silvester having dances with her. She will distribute handouts at a student protest. The love plots, the political and ethnic lines, the Marshak family are established.
>
> *The Judenrat*
> *Scene 2*. During the Hitlerian Occupation at Marshak's apartment. Marshak named head of the *Judenrat*. Simon, his father, warns him to reject the position. Bronke tells of transports and mass murders.

Warsaw, Lodz, Vilna – in occupied Poland, interpreted through a Communist optic. The play brings together a large cast – showcasing the entire troupe – representing all the social classes and various political perspectives. At its heart is the divided family as microcosm of the larger Jewish community. Mirsky dubs the work 'A Drama in two parts with seven scenes.' Part 1 illustrates the collaboration and the resistance. Part 2, one long suspension, depicts moments of survival until the massive deportation. The *fabula* establishes the generation gap

Violent debate between father and daughter over his role. Esther comes and begs for decent food for the orphanage. Father hears of more transports. He defends himself. Bronke flees house. A survivor from transport arrives and reveals mass murder.

Tableau: the cattle car and hands imploring from barbed wire window.

Decision for Uprising

Scene 3. At Bronke and Esther's place. Selek is a ghetto policeman. He warns Bronke not to flee the ghetto. He loves her but is rejected. Student youth leaders enter representing various political factions under pseudonyms for Communist, Bundist/left socialist, and Zionist organizations. Silvester and Kaplan, Communists, argue for Uprising. Left socialists agree. Zionists join in willy-nilly. Jewish police enter. Confrontation and stalemate.

II. Zionists collaborate with Judenrat

Scene 4. Marshak's apartment. Yankev, a Zionist leader, needs money for a deal with Red Cross and the Gestapo to ship halutsim to safety. Marshak will find the cash if Yankev hands over old men for deportation. Simon warns Marshak not to enter into deals with the Gestapo.

Pity the innocent

Scene 5. Orphanage. Esther discovers children are aware of death lurking.

Love theme: Polish/Jewish ties

Scene 6. At Esther's and Bronke's place. Silvester enters. Esther wants to save the children. They declare their love. She invites him to spend the night with her.

Betrayal and repentance

Scene 7. Marshak's apartment. Mass deportation order. Marshak shocked. Everyone on *Judenrat* prepared to sign deportation lists. Selek explains that he signed list to transport orphanage in Marshak's name. If Marshak refuses to sign the new list, he will. Simon wants his name placed first on the list. Daniel Marshak will sign his own name too!

Final tableau: The students move forward to front of stage with arms and saluting. A red light illuminates the background.

(scene 1) between the father, Daniel Marshak, who becomes the acquies-
cent member of the *Judenrat* (scene 2), and the activist student generation
of his daughter, Bronke and her politicized friends, Mikhl, Esther and
her Polish boyfriend, Silvester Dobroczynski, and so on, who plan an
uprising (scene 3). Scene 4 reveals how the Zionist youth, Yankev, plots
with Marshak, head of the *Judenrat*, to save young *halutsim* (young
pioneers) in deals with the Gestapo. Scene 5, in the Orphanage, reveals
an orphan's awareness of ultimate deportation. Scene 6 brings the Polish
Communist Silvester and Esther together in a night of full Polish–
Jewish fraternization. The denouement (scene 7) reveals the iniquity
of the *Judenrat* who, to save themselves, are prepared to deport everyone in compliance with Gestapo orders. Marshak (an avatar for Adam
Czerniakow, head of the Warsaw *Judenrat* who committed suicide)
now fully realizing his collaboration, accepts his religious father's
request to be placed on the list and signs his own name, thus repent-
ing before death! Each scene is a quasi-independent act with minimal
linkage.

The work elicits the image of a tragic pageant in which each
character and setting represents metonymies of a greater whole. The
diffusiveness of dramatic interest undercuts any concentration on a
character or the building of sustained plot tension. There is, in fact, no
real dramatic action created or sustained among the protagonists. The
obstacles which exist are either rapidly resolved or left unsolvable. Each
scene is a fragment, a theatrical postcard from a tragic era. Scenes 4, 5
and 6 are totally interchangeable. The ordering or external structure
of the script follows a seemingly more chronological ordering than any
dramatic one. We are in the spirit of socialist realism in which a broad
picture is painted of typical people in 'typical' settings who, opposed to
passive and solipsistic positions, choose positive collective action.[15]

---

[15] Herman Ermolaev, 'Socialist Realism', in *Handbook of Russian
Literature*, edited by Victor Terras (New Haven: Yale University Press,
1985), pp. 429–30; Katerina Clark, *The Soviet Novel: History as Ritual*
(Chicago and London: University of Chicago Press, 1985), pp. 98–9;
Spenser Golub, 'Charlie Chaplin, Soviet Icon', *The Performance of
Power: Theatrical Discourse and Politics* (Iowa City: University of
Iowa Press, 1991), p. 202.

By refusing to particularize a specific ghetto, or use the actual names of heroes and traitors, by using pseudonyms for the political organizations and even creating a pseudonym for Auschwitz called here Trishevitz, Mirsky creates a generalized condition which is both dramatically weak and factually inadequate. Mirsky must have considered this broad generalizing a means of being inclusive, as well as a clever way of eschewing the historical fine points which might impinge upon his ideological perspective.

Central to the dramatic intention of the script is the celebration of the student activists who vote for the Uprising and an appreciation of the role of the Communists among them as an inspiring force to action. The final scene, a tableau, reveals students with arms in hand going off to battle, illuminated from behind by a red light. If the students are collectively the heroes of the play, the role of women is underscored, particularly Bronke, who breaks off from her father and boyfriend, Selek, her cousin and ghetto cop, and her friend Esther! Dialectically the playwright represents and reprimands the passive or collaborative forces in the ghetto. To effectuate these intentions in dramatic terms, Mirsky constructed the play with two loci of dramatic interest: (a) the family of Marshak, and (b) the love duets.

The family provides a locus of dramatic interest and economy by reflecting the communal distress, dislocation and discontinuity. By having Marshak's father, Simon, represent the tradition, with his old-fashioned religious values intact, he sets off his son, Daniel, head of the *Judenrat*, who has lost his moral compass as a participant in the selection process. The bourgeois wife, Etl, is also guilty by her sin of omission. She seeks to avoid any knowledge or engagement and retreats into total passivity. The activist daughter, Bronke, in her confrontation with her father, discovers her sense of self and communal honour by abandoning the household. By contrast, Daniel's sister's son, Selek, represents extreme selfishness in order to survive. The collapsing family serves as the microcosm of the ghetto's psychological condition and desperate options. Mirsky, however, condemns the family on class grounds. By serving as a member of the *Judenrat*, Daniel Marshak ships off the workers and protects his own class under the guise of rescuing those who can be saved. By making Simon the ultimate *raisonneur* in the drama (he condemns his son) the ideological purity of the play seems compromised or at least problematized, for surely Simon's sacred Talmudic vision is in contradiction to the secular ethics of Marx, Engels and Lenin, the guiding ideology of the play. Or is this a unique Talmudic–Marxist moral *rapprochement* against 'bourgeois morality'? The Marshak family, a microcosm of desperate ghetto options, is held to an absolute moral standard in an impossible condition while the German oppressor is placed beyond good or evil! The drama concludes in a moral myopia! Mirsky indulges in ideological coercion.[16]

The love duets create 'dramatic interest' and make use of the cardboard figures as sounding boards for either positive or negative ideological persuasions. The Silvester Dobroczynski (*dobro* meaning *good* in Polish) and Esther relationship is placed in a positive light and the Bronke–Selek relationship in a negative one. The latter reveals a selfish, jealous Jewish bourgeois male who seeks to subjugate Bronke, his first cousin, and who looks upon Silvester as a possible rival and an ethnic enemy. Obviously such a relationship is doomed by scene 3. The Silvester–Esther relationship, however, is of crucial interest to us, for it goes to the heart of Mirsky's Communist ideological intentions, which are translated into dramatic representation.

A central policy during the sixties in countries of socialist persuasion was the propagation of *Völkerfreundschaft* (international brotherhood), particularly among socialist lands haunted by long-standing rivalries and hatreds. Not only was it a pragmatic policy, it was a bedrock position of the Communist Party, with its universalist ideals of humankind. In Poland, the Party paid it much lip service and the Jewish Communists truly believed in it and pushed for it, if only for practical reasons of combating anti-Semitism. By constructing a love duet of ideal types whose authentic love goes beyond ethnic boundaries and yet appreciates the partner's original culture, Mirsky gives Communist universality a kind of 'transubstantiation'. The name of Esther here is no less significant than Dobroczynski for, in the Bible, Esther married Ahasuerus, a Gentile, and saved her people, and one Estherke was the legendary mistress of King Casimir the Great, another

---

[16] Anthony Kubiak, *Stages of Terror: Terrorism, Ideology, and Coercion as Theater History* (Bloomington: Indiana University Press, 1991), p. 5.

rapprochement which spawned many lively stories among Poles and Jews. True *Völkerfreundschaft*! Ethnicity must not stand in the way of true passion! As in the neo-Platonic ideal, their love fulfilled their intellectual *noblesse* and expresses the Communist position of universality.

Mirsky's cartography of society is phallocentric and implies either ideological disjuncture or an essentialist distortion. Masculinity defines not only a positive body type, but political and social activity. In this ideologically charged setting, Silvester the Pole emerges as the ideal type. Passivity denotes femininity and solipsism. Opposite Silvester is Selek, the negative image: the co-opted Jewish ghetto cop. The Jewish students, male and female, appear on the spectrum of masculinity and femininity according to how close they approach the ideal of Silvester. The Communists and leftist socialists are closest. The Zionist Yankev, with his deviousness, abuts Marshak and Selek. The women, Esther, Bronke and Shifra approach the moral masculine ideal by their social consciousness and their political commitment. They define emancipated women from bourgeois conformity and yet are supportive, nurturing and not passive. Silvester may represent the new man of socialism but the woman is still cooking the potatoes (scene 3) and serving men. This contradiction reveals an incongruity in the play's normative ideological commitment to gender equality. It also raises concerns of Mirsky's depiction of Jewish society as regressive.

By making a Pole the masculine and ideological ideal of the Holocaust drama, Mirsky serves the Communist ideological position that the Uprising (read: Warsaw Ghetto Uprising) was led by Communists for non-nationalist universal principles of socialist justice. The Pole acts as a purer and nobler Communist than the 'interested' Jews, for Silvester comes to share their plight out of principle! The model for Silvester is the party leader in Soviet social-realist literature. The Jews consequently appear inferior. This raises serious questions of authorial subservience. The roots of the Uprising are distorted from that of Jewish victims *qua* Jews seeking a last honourable but doomed defence to a proletarian Uprising led by Communists in the person of a virile Polish Party member. The dramatist appears to use ideological loyalty to occlude his Jewish self-contempt or Jewish self-interest. Mirsky displays the colonialized mind hiding in universalist ideology: what Sartre would call acting in 'bad faith'! By using a Pole as the heroic ideal in a Holocaust play, Mirsky denies a national basis to the Uprising and curries favour with the Polish Communists.

More serious is the moral discrepancy into which the play falls, by functioning unconsciously inside the dramatic world-view inherited and derived from the classical tragedy and the well-made play. By eschewing any confrontation of victor and victim, German and Jew, and insisting only upon the depiction of the ghetto inhabitants, Mirsky has placed the Germans in the role of fate: they are provided a divine role. They are used as a plague in some Artaudian dramaturgy. No judgement can be made upon them for they are placed above and outside the human realm of the drama. In this play structure and world-view, German brutality escapes any real condemnation! By equating Nazis as evil gods of fate, the playwright unconsciously cedes to the real human enemy a role he craved: superman!

This drama places upon the Jews the burden of impossible moral responsibility and moral conduct in a world of fate which is abnormal, unnatural, debased and evil, for it is the construct of another human posing as a god through imposed terror. Fate, here, is reduced to the fact that Jews will be murdered sooner rather than later. What type of free will is there in this condition? The Jews are placed in an impossible situation and are judged by an implacable playwright through the prisms of his own ideological bias, which does not even recognize fate, normal (divine) or abnormal (Nazis), but only recognizes a socio-political historical condition. Yet Mirsky constructs a traditional fate play that allows no real free will and still insists that free will must exist! Thus, for Mirsky, he who cedes to Nazi fate is a moral coward and he who resists is morally correct. The *Judenrat* is evil for succumbing to Nazi fate and the students are good by their doomed resistance.

The play's theatrical moral presuppositions are as if it were the world of Sophocles' *Antigone*, where Creon is the *Judenrat* and Antigone is a student revolting against the *Judenrat*. But in *Antigone* service to the divine order is placed over service to the human one. Creon fails to recognize this fact and becomes a victim of divine judgement. Had he recognized the divine law of honouring the dead, his family would have remained alive. The gods in *Antigone* are just. In Mirsky's play the 'divine' is evil and the *Judenrat* is forced to be its earthly representative in the ghetto. The student revolt is against both:

the Undivine and the *Judenrat*! But the *Judenrat* members' hubris is to serve the Undivine order as an accommodative strategy for personal and communal survival. Privately they are as opposed to the Undivine as much as the students. Their sin is to arrogate to themselves power that the Nazi fate has demonically proffered by their use of selection. Their desperation was human: to survive. Creon's hubris was to oppose divine will which gave honour to man in death! The *Judenrat* yielded to the Undivine will to stave off its only free-will choice: how to die. The students in the play, who are more realistic, recognize that every Jew's fate is death and so it is how to choose one's death which is the only act of free will! All Jews in the ghetto are in an untenable condition, but Mirsky uses this impossible situation to render moral judgements unfairly.

The play ends with the Germans morally scot-free and alive. The *Judenrat* is condemned and in need of repentance, of which death in Trishevitz with all the other Jews is the moral good! Is this *der Kheshbn*? Is this the final bill? The final accounting, the Reckoning? Is this all the title and the play are about? Making the bourgeois *Judenrat* pay? What we have is a serious disjuncture between the operating world-view in the generic presuppositions of the drama clashing with the playwright's ideological vision. The play ends in moral confusion if not squalor.

Mirsky has also served the Communist Party by playing fast with history, for he places not only a Communist as a prime instigator for the Uprising, but a Pole ready to wear the yellow badge of Jewish shame! This is shameless historical fabrication. That Mirsky gives the Communists a leading instigating role is not surprising given this period of harsh ideological conflict between east and west, in which the Jews of that surviving generation had serious ideological stakes. In the west, the Bundists and the Zionists both took negative positions toward the Jewish Communists. The feelings were mutual. (And the conflict is not dead, even today.) The historical record was at stake: who initiated the idea of a joint uprising in the Warsaw Ghetto? Yitzhak Zuckerman declares: 'Ber Mark (head of the Jewish Historical Society in Warsaw) published his book (on the Warsaw Ghetto Uprising) in Warsaw during the worst years of Stalinist Poland; he distorted many facts to show that the Communists initiated and organized the Uprising, thus "legitimizing" the Uprising and cleansing it of the stigma of a Jewish national effort.'[17] Mirsky, therefore, uses Silvester, the Polish Communist, in a conscious manner to make the Uprising more than a Jewish act of self-defence. When in the discussions of what to do in scene 3, Khayim, the representative of Hatsofa, a pseudonym for the Jewish socialist youth organizations, declares his distrust of the Poles who 'give over our people to the Gestapo', Silvester retorts, 'Khayim, you throw into one pot the Polish Revolutionary Proletariat with a bunch of blackmailers and extortionists. Each folk has its flowers and its dungheap!' Mirsky gives Silvester some of the most idealist lines. The playwright serves the Communist Party line by rewriting history and inscribing '1963 *Völkerfreundschaft*' into this historical play for the twentieth anniversary of the Uprising. Long live Polish–Jewish friendship!

The playwright also clearly intended to denounce the Zionist role in the Uprising as recalcitrant, narrow-minded and devious, as opposed to the Communists and socialists. In *Der Kheshbn*, Yankev, the representative of the L'aretz (Zionists), is less than convinced that the Uprising is for the best, for it will hasten the total destruction of the ghetto. He joins reluctantly. But in the following scene (scene 4) he negotiates with the enemy *Judenrat* to save Zionist *halutsim* at the cost of delivering up for transport three old Jews! In scene 7 we learn that the manoeuvre failed and that the *halutsim* were sent to Trishevitz: so the episode is presented as one more piece of Nazi deception into which fell both the *Judenrat* and its accomplices. Instead of horror, the play implies such are the just deserts for Zionist collaboration. Mirsky is a Communist ideologue and the play reveals his bias.

---

[17] Yitzhak Zuckerman, *A Surplus of Memory: Chronicles of the Warsaw Ghetto Uprising* (Berkeley: University of California Press, 1993), p. 184, n. 28. The book was published in Hebrew in 1990, as *Those Seven Years*. Ber Mark was a Jewish–Communist writer and historian who published many studies on the Warsaw Ghetto and on Polish–Jewish history. The first edition of *Der Oyfshtand in Varshever geto* (*The Uprising in the Warsaw Ghetto*) was published in Moscow in 1947. In 1953 he published *Dokumentn un materialn vegn oyfshtand in varshever geto* (Warsaw). In Polish he published *Powstanie w Getcie Warszawskim na Tle Ruchu Operu w Polsce* (1953), and *Walka i Zaglada Warszawskiego Getta* (1959).

The play in manuscript does not conclude on the uplifting act of tragic resistance by the students, but applauds the self-destruction of the Marshak family. The evil of the Nazis and the impossible conditions imposed on the Jews is of no concern here. The only justice is the self-condemnation of the bourgeois *Judenrat* leader for his malignant performance of selection at the expense of the weak, the proletariat. The play serves only as a vehicle for making propaganda points by exploiting the Holocaustal condition. The drama distorts history and also fails both on dramatic and aesthetic levels.

The difference between the manuscript text and the production underscores ideological and aesthetic tensions. Having witnessed the première at the Teatr Polski, I noted that the scene which made the strongest impression on the audience and on a Polish critic was a tableau interpolated in the first part, just after scene 2. This was a creation of the director, Ida Kaminska, and her assistants. The curtain opened to a stage prop of a railway freight car, the typical European one which transports cattle and, in the Shoah, Jews. From out of a small rectangular window high up toward the side that was criss-crossed with barbed-wire, hands, many human hands were flailing, desperate, appealing, silent . . . The applause was thunderous. Why was this mimetic silent scene the most appreciated? Perhaps because it was the most truthful. It confirmed hypostatically the message: the Holocaust wiped out the Jews whose desperation was not heard and all that is left is the silence of memory.

A final, animated but silent, tableau concludes the play. It was created to bring a positive note of closure. After the condemnation of the *Judenrat* and the Marshak family, the curtain rose on the students led by Silvester Dobroczynski, arms-in-hand, bathed in the red light of the Uprising. The applause was intense. In the youthful resolve, the play could grasp at hope against despair. Irony was not intended. This was calculated Yiddish melodramatic manipulation and a traditional Yiddish *shund teatr* (popular theatre) device: a rapid reversal of the emotional engines. Let the audience leave content. The production inverts drama into pure nineteenth-century melodrama. The director understood her audience better than the dramatist. The theatre sought success on the level of performance; the dramatist was determined to push his ideological intentions. The last page of the manuscript reveals

a hotchpotch of scratchings and deletions, rewritings and more eras-
ures without any final resolution. Ida Kaminska used the last tableau as
an astute theatrical – if old-fashioned – technique to play on traditional
Jewish theatrical expectations which garnered what she, as a thespian,
wanted most: wild applause, success and appreciation.

The audience, mostly Yiddish speakers, survivors, and I suspect
mainly leftists and pro-Communists, came from all over the world. I
remember large delegations from France, Israel, Belgium and Great
Britain. This audience came to the theatre to celebrate life, to hear their
mother tongue in an aesthetic setting, to hear it honoured and to commemorate the martyred dead, and perhaps to exorcise any guilt of having survived. The play even offered the audience a chance, a malicious
one, I believe, to vent their spleen against – not the German – but the
Jewish bourgeois collaborators. However, I do not recall the audience
expressing any negative feelings. Did they really buy this ideological
drama of cardboard characters and clichéd set-pieces? I frankly believe
they were oblivious to it on a cognitive level. They bought it on an emo-
tive level, in whole cloth. They wanted it to be a wonderful play and as
Pirandello has taught us, 'It is so, if you want it to be!' The fact that the
play was panned later probably reflects the attitude of the audience
after the intoxications of that memorable evening, when Yiddish was
alive again![18]

The play soon disappeared from the repertory of the Jewish State
Theatre. It is noted only in passing in a celebratory publication of the
Polish government, *25 Years of the Jewish State Theatre in the Polish
People's Republic in 1975*. By that time Ida Kaminska had left Poland as

---

[18] Andrzej Wroblewski, 'Smiech Na Pogozelisku' ('Laughter on a Heap of
Ashes') *Teatr*, 20 (October 1963), p. 16. 'Mirsky's attempt to show the
tragedy of the ghetto was a failure. The play was artificial and written
according to some schemes and clichés (schematycznie prawidlowa
– 'politically correct'). This tragedy cannot be captured in the framework of a simple realistic play.' Szydlowski, 'Epica o powies c o Eragedii
getta': 'Mirsky's play cannot be discussed in purely artistic categories.
Emotional and political elements play an important role in its reception.
I think this tragic topic is waiting for a great playwright.' (Translations
by Professor Garbowska of the Marie-Curie State University, Lublin.)

had Mikhl Mirsky. The victory of the Zionists in the Six-Day War of 1967 had caused a shift in foreign and domestic Polish Communist policy. Gomulka denounced Israel as an aggressor and a Party purge of Jews began. The Jews were seen as a 'fifth column' and anti-Semitism filled the streets and threatened the Jews. Devoted Polish–Jewish Communists were denounced. Half of Poland's last Jews left the country, psychologically defeated. Ida Kaminska came to America in 1968, hoping to produce a 'high-class' Yiddish theatre like that in Poland. It was not to be. Mikhl Mirsky settled in Copenhagen in 1968, and as one leftist Yiddish writer informed me, 'sat there waiting to be called back'.[19] He died in 1993, embroiled in vituperative polemics. None of the people associated with the play and production of *Der Kheshbn* ever seemed to have mentioned it again, at least not in print. And yet this play in 1963 was, seemingly, at the high point of Polish–Jewish Communist hopes at the twentieth anniversary of the Warsaw Ghetto Uprising. Or was this hope of renewal just part of the ceremonies in a Potemkin Village?

The play stands out as a striking example of ideological manipulation and a conscious distortion of Jewish history regarding the Holocaust. It provides a negative example of how art and theatre can be exploited by a regime and an artist to reconfigure the past in service to the present. The collaboration of Mirsky with the Communist regime in 1963, to consciously produce a drama with such malevolence and national self-hate, for propaganda purposes in order to promote Communism, marks a painful example of Jewish subalternity in twentieth-century Jewish history. In terms of theatre, *Der Kheshbn* underscores the limits of social-realism or any mimesis based on realistic aesthetics. It concludes a unique strain in postwar Jewish theatre history, the plays of the Jewish leftist and Communist tradition whether produced in the Soviet Union, the People's Republics of Poland or Rumania, the Artef productions of New York City or the postwar Yiddish Communist productions in Paris. This Jewish–Communist contribution to Yiddish theatre must not be erased from Jewish memory. It is part

---

[19] A telephone communication from the editor of *Yidisher Kultur*, Itche Goldberg, New York City.

of Jewish theatre history and reflects a portion of Jewish history of the twentieth century. Its absence would lessen the whole of Jewish theatrical creativity in this century of the Shoah.

This chapter is dedicated to Professor Monika Garbowska of the Marie-Curie University of Lublin, and to Mrs Krystyna Szmeruk who provided unstinting collegial help in obtaining the manuscript of the play and other archival materials in Poland. Their generosity is unforgettable.

9 Reality and illusion in the Theresienstadt cabaret

ROY KIFT

There are many records of the abundant activities in the world of theatre, opera and classical music by the Jewish prisoners in the garrison camp at Theresienstadt.[1] But, to my knowledge, there is little or no material in English on Kurt Gerron's cabaret known as the Karussell, which, in 1944, played to packed and enthusiastic houses in the confines of a room in the Hamburg barracks. If at first sight the juxtaposition of comedy and concentration camps seems to be not only impossible but also morally indefensible, how much more grotesque must it seem that comedy, songs and laughter in the form of cabaret were almost a daily experience in the Theresienstadt camp.[2] But since

---

[1] The two standard works on Theresienstadt are by H. G. Adler, *Die verheimlichte Wahrheit, Theresienstädter Dokumente* (Tübingen: Mohr, 1958), and *Theresienstadt, 1941–1945. Das Antlitz einer Zwangsgemeinschaft, Geschichte, Soziologie, Psychologie* (Tübingen: Mohr, 1960). The most important publications in English are Gerald Green, *The Artists of Terezin* (New York: Hawthorne Books, 1959), Joseph Karas, *Music in Terezin, 1941–1945* (New York: Leo Baeck Institute, 1985), Zdenek Lederer, *Ghetto Theresienstadt* (London: Goldston, 1953; New York: Fertig, 1983), and Ruth Schwertfeger, *Women of Theresienstadt* (Oxford: Berg, 1989). This last includes many documents previously only available in German, has a good short history of the camp and an excellent bibliography. Abundant material on Theresienstadt can be found in the Theresienstadt Archive and Museum, Givat Chaim Ichud, Israel 38935. See also Helen Lewis's autobiographical account, *A Time to Speak* (Belfast: Blackstaff Press, 1992).

[2] Gerron's cabaret was neither the first nor the only cabaret in the camp. Others were run by Karel Svenk, Felix Porges (both Czech), Egon Thorn, Hans Hofer, Bobby John, Ernst Morgan, Walter Steiner and Walter Lindenbaum.

12. Bedrich Fritta, *For Kurt Gerron!* Theresienstadt, 1944.

the inmates themselves considered laughter to be a perfectly accept-
able response to their predicament, there may be valuable lessons here
to be learnt for modern writers trying to find an appropriate formal
approach to tackling the Holocaust in performance.[3] In this chapter I
will examine the programme of the cabaret and try to distinguish some
recurring themes in the songs and sketches, in the light of how they
confronted the audience with the harsh realities of camp existence – or
attempted to avoid them by promoting illusions.

The essence of good cabaret is an incisive and up-to-date satirical
view of current events in the world at large. In Theresienstadt, the
inmates had no contact with the outside world: or, to put it another
way, their world *was* the camp. This meant that the only material the
artists could deal with was their own and their audience's immediate
situation and problems. Consequently, the shared bond of interest
between performer and audience here was of necessity much more
intense than in any normal cabaret. If the illusion the Nazis wished to
present to the outside world was of Theresienstadt as a modern spa
town and old people's holiday camp, with leisure opportunities for all
to enjoy – a lie which has been left to us in Kurt Gerron's so-called documentary film, *The Führer Gives the Jews a Town* – the reality was much
more brutal and out of joint.[4] Many inmates, especially the elderly, had
been tricked by the Nazis into handing over their homes and wealth in

---

[3] The most prominent contemporary dramatists to have tackled the
Holocaust through comedy are Peter Barnes (*Laughter!* (London:
Heinemann Educational, 1978)), and George Tabori. See chapter 16 of
this volume, 'George Tabori's Mourning Work in *Jubiläum*'.

[4] Only a twenty-minute fragment of the film is known. It was shot
between 16 August and 11 September 1944. See Käthe Starke, *Der
Führer schenkt den Juden eine Stadt. Bilder – Impressionen – Reportagen
– Dokumente* (Berlin: Haude und Spenersche Verlagsbuchhandlung,
1975); Adler, *Theresienstadt, 1941–1945*; B. Felsmann and K. Prümm,
Kurt Gerron – Gefeiert und Gejagt (Berlin: Hendrichs Verlag, 1992);
G. Harms and M. Schmidt, 'Kurt Gerron und das schwärzeste Kapitel
der deutschen Filmgeschichte', in *Film*, 7 (Frankfurt-on-Main, 1996);
K. Margery, 'Theresienstadt (1944–45): The Nazi Propaganda Film
Depicting the Concentration Camp as Paradise', in *Historical Journal
of Film, Radio and Television*, 12.2 (1992). Margery has written an
academic thesis on the film.

exchange for promises of rest and comfort in the up-to-date health resort of 'Theresienbad' (note the allusions to other spas like Carlsbad, Marienbad), and the shock on arrival must have been traumatic.

To give some idea of the illusions of new arrivals, what was high-lighted and how it was debunked, I shall first examine a musical sketch by Leo Strauss, one of the two main writers for the cabaret.[5] The sketch is called *Theresienstadt Questions*, and is a conversation between a finely dressed lady in plaid carrying a birdcage, who has just arrived in the camp, and another woman in overalls, who is part of a brigade responsible for keeping the streets clean.[6]

FIRST LADY: I've just got in from the country
And here I've no friend or relation
Would you be so kind as to tell me
Where I can get hold of some information?
CLEANER: At your service, dear lady, in short
Every wish is for me a command
I came here on the Vienna transport
And know this place like the back of my hand.
BOTH: Theresienstadt, Theresienstadt, hooray!
Is the most up-to-date ghetto in the world today.

We are presented with the tensions between expectations and reality, ignorance and knowingness.[7] For many members of the audience the shock of recognition must have given their laughter a bitter edge. The

---

[5] Leo Strauss also ran his own cabaret before joining Gerron's Karussel. He was the son of the operetta composer, Oscar Strauss.

[6] The original text of the song can be found in Ulrike Migdal, *Und die Musik spielt dazu* (Munich: Piper, 1986), which contains an intro-ductory essay, many German texts and a wealth of reports and reviews written in Theresienstadt itself. The texts can be found in the archives in Yad Vashem. All the translations in the chapter are mine. For the original text of *Theresienstadt Questions*, see Migdal, *Und die Musik*, pp. 71–4.

[7] For a stimulating approach to 'knowingness' and internal codes of communication in variety theatre, see Peter Bailey, 'Conspiracies of Meaning: Music-hall and the Knowingness of Popular Culture', *Past and Present*, 144 (August 1994), pp. 139–70.

13. *Lit. Kabarett*, Theresienstadt, 1941.

sketch goes on to deal with everyday problems such as health, food and lodging. But the very first theme which Leo Strauss chooses to tackle comes as something of a surprise.

FIRST LADY: It strikes me as very bizarre
        That I should be ordered to wear a star
        Not to speak of the shock when I heard the news
        I'd be thrown in the middle of Polish Jews
CLEANER: There's many a person rubbing their nose
        Putting on airs, adopting a pose
        But most of these poor braggadoccio hacks
        (are themselves) . . .
        Nothing but tinkers and Tarnopolacks.

Tarnopol was a region and a town in Poland where roughly half the inhabitants were Jews. Here we are confronted with the first of a series of references, vocabulary and slang which were common knowledge to the inmates of the camp and which, as we shall see, consistently crop up in the cabaret material.

BOTH: Theresienstadt, Theresienstadt, hooray
Is the most anti-Semitic ghetto in the world today.

The tensions and antipathies between the various national and social groups in the camp – all of them Jews – is a theme which is taken up again in a far harsher manner by another writer, Manfred Greiffenhagen, in a song called *The Oxen*, where he makes a direct appeal for this nonsense to stop. For, as he says, 'Here in this very special case there's no difference between a person and a cow. For we are all Jews – and only Jews – just as oxen are only oxen.'[8] The specific tensions in Theresienstadt, which reflected general attitudes in Europe at the time, were between middle-class German-speaking Jews, many of whom considered themselves more Austrian and German than Jewish, and the Yiddish-speaking, poorer peddlers and street hawkers from the east, with whom they had very little in common. That said, the reference to Tarnopol is very strange since there were, to my knowledge, few or no Jews from Eastern Europe in the camp, which was populated overwhelmingly with Germans, Austrians, Czechs and Danes.

To return to the sketch: the refined, middle-class lady is gradually robbed of her illusions but also receives a few tips on survival and an introduction to camp jargon. For example, she learns that the best way to stay healthy is always to have a sick note, because sick people qualify for double rations. 'Hunger' is a word no one uses: it is called 'vitamin deficiency'. As for 'a place to live / Simple but not primitive': the street cleaner tells her that 'with a little fantasy / A house will be your just reward / All your dreams' reality / When sleeping on your wooden board.' For 'Theresienstadt, Theresienstadt, hooray, is the dreamiest ghetto in the world today.' The newcomer then wants to know 'What's the code for evening dress?', because she'd really 'hate to look a mess'. She receives the following reply:

> There's one or two as put on airs
> But most folks opt for casual wear
> To be quite honest, what the heck!
> My husband dresses like a wreck.

---

[8] The original is rhymed. See Migdal, *Und die Musik*, pp. 105–6.

... in ... 'the most mundane ghetto in the world today'. The new arrival learns that she will have to wait months before she can get a bath in ... 'the most hygienic ghetto in the world today'; that she can forget about her belongings, which have been confiscated on her arrival, because there is no room for them anyway. The song reaches its climax with the most absurd problem of all: the newcomer asks not only how she can get food for her pet bird, but she insists on the very best quality. When we consider that people were in a permanent state of semi-starvation in Theresienstadt, this is an absolutely lunatic question. And, sure enough, it is treated as such in an untranslatable answer. There is a German phrase for someone who is a bit crazy: *er hat einen Vogel* (literally, 'he has a bird'). Accordingly, the street cleaner tells the newcomer to give the bird away immediately, for anybody who has a bird is a candidate for the *cvokarna* or camp madhouse.[9] *Verzwockt*, which might be translated as 'zwokky', was camp slang for 'crazy' and, consequently, 'Theresienstadt, hooray is the zwokkiest ghetto in the world today'. But after this eruption of humour the sketch ends on a note of bitter irony which brings the audience down to the level of the victim they have been laughing at and reminds them of their own common fate.

> LADY: One last question, please don't groan
> I'd like to write a letter home
> And put my family in the clear ...
> How long will we be staying here?
> CLEANER: Now that request I can't refuse
> Ain't you 'eard the latest news?
> According to reliable rumours –

At this point the stage directions say that her words are drowned out by a cacophony of noise from the musicians in the band, leaving everyone in a shared state of ignorance and uncertainty. I can well imagine that, as the band stopped, the whole room was left hanging in a state of silence for a few moments before the tension was resolved by the final

---

[9] Czech slang was rife amongst the inmates. Amongst the most common terms were *balicek* (packet), *cetnik* (camp police), *buchten* (cakes), *turin* (turnips) and *dvakrat* (twice, or double portion).

choral duet, probably accompanied by the audience in a way very similar to the participation in the Victorian music hall.

> Theresienstadt, Theresienstadt, hooray!
> Is the most up-to-date ghetto in the world today.

The audience participation strengthened the bond of solidarity between performers and listeners and attempted to cauterize the pain of their predicament through song and laughter. But this was more than simply a culture of solidarity. It was also a form of inner, spiritual resistance in the face of their powerlessness to combat the threat of physical destruction.

If many people had travelled to Theresienstadt under the illusion of being able to find some peace in a rural spa town, the brutal reality of the camp stripped away such deceptions. But, paradoxically, the camp was at one and the same time reality and illusion. This was the Potemkin Village *par excellence* and an illusion presented as reality when it was 'embellished' by the Nazi authorities in order to deceive the International Red Cross delegation and to allay the fears of the world at large as to the fate of the Jews.[10] In this respect, Kurt Gerron's film was crucial to the Nazis' intentions, especially since it was to be directed by a Jew himself. One of Theresienstadt's most recent chroniclers has described the camp as being both 'the best of all camps', and also 'the worst of all camps'.[11] Unlike at other camps, the inmates at Theresienstadt were able to take advantage of an immense range of cultural and educational activities. But, nonetheless, like all other camps, Theresienstadt was catastrophically filthy, hopelessly overcrowded, ridden with lice, bugs and disease, and the prisoners were tortured by ever-present hunger. Not the sort of hunger which we today call hunger, when we have gone from breakfast to teatime without a bite to eat. But

---

[10] In order to prepare for the embellishment, 7,500 inmates were sent to Auschwitz in May 1944. The Red Cross visit took place on 23 June 1944 and the delegation was completely taken in. See their reports in Adler, *Die verheimlichte Wahrheit*, p. 312.

[11] Ruth Kluger, *weiter leben* (Gottingen: Wallstein, 1992). Kluger gives an excellent account of the camp as she experienced it in her childhood.

a continual gnawing, obsessive, unsatisfied pain in the belly, simultaneously soothed and aggravated by insufficient amounts of thin, watery soup made up from potato peelings and the rotting remains of turnips, which was the staple diet of the inmates. Over and above this, everywhere there was the constant threat of death – from disease in the camp and the fearful uncertainty of transport into the unknown. In this so-called transit camp no less than 33,000 inmates, over a quarter of all internees, died as the result of hunger, sickness or the sadistic treatment meted out by their captors. This is the reality of the environment into which the inmates were thrown, and many of the new arrivals fell into states of hopeless depression and lethargy, if not madness. It was to counter such damage to morale that Rabbi Weiner, who was the first official responsible for leisure activities in the camp, suggested the introduction of a broad range of cultural activities with an emphasis on the maintenance of a specifically Jewish culture.[12] At first the activities were clandestine, but after they were discovered by the camp authorities they were tolerated and finally officially promoted. Such activities fitted in perfectly with the Nazis' cynical plans to present the world with a show camp of happy Jewish inmates in an oasis of peaceful work and carefree leisure.

If camp life was intolerable, one way of making it more bearable was to try to relativize it by comparison with something even worse. In a song entitled *Invitation*, Leo Strauss uses a typical comedy technique of reversal when he claims that the problems of Jews living under restrictions outside the ghetto are in fact far more considerable than those inside Theresienstadt – an absurd assertion, but, when you listen to the text, you are almost fooled into the illusion of agreeing with him.

INVITATION
Friends and loved ones, do you suffer
From a life of want and fear
Are things at home becoming tougher?
Pack your bags and join me here.

---

[12] See Weiner's reports on leisure activities in Migdal, *Und die Musik*, pp. 131–60.

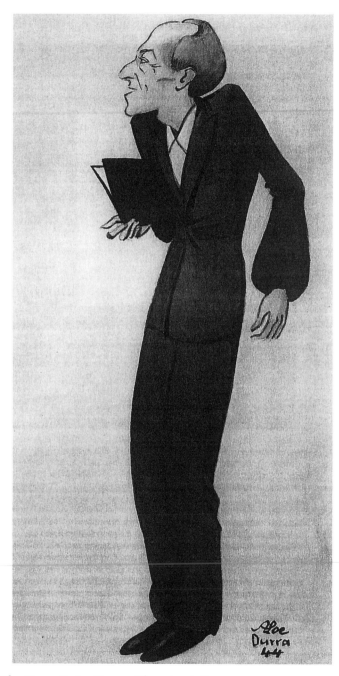

14.   Aloe Durra, *Dr Leo Strauss*, Theresienstadt, 1944.

Reality and illusion in the Theresienstadt Cabaret

Do you live in trepidation?
Is your life a vale of tears?
I'm offering you some consolation.
Pack your bags and join me here.

Are you owing lots of money?
Sunk in debt from ear to ear?
Such a state is far from funny
Pack your bags and join me here.

Is it hard to find some work, sir,
In the current atmosphere?
Enough to make you go berserk, sir?
Pack your bags and join me here.

Had enough of constant moving?
Different houses every year?
Need a home that's calm and soothing?
Pack your bags and join me here.

Are your vases all in pieces?
Got a broken chandelier?
Stains on cloths and mantelpieces?
Pack your bags and join me here.

Got a woeful constitution?
Too much nicotine and beer?
There's clearly only one solution
Pack your bags and join me here.

When neighbours see the star you're wearing,
Do they start to scowl and jeer?
Had enough of hostile staring?
Pack your bags and join me here.

Are your stock and shares still sinking?
Servants' wages in arrears?
Nurse has gone and nappy's stinking?
Pack your bags and join me here.

Are you sick of penny-pinching?
Shops and markets far too dear?
Tormented by eternal scrimping?
Pack your bags and join me here.

Do you dream of ease and pleasure,
Tea and coffee, wine and beer,
Concerts, theatre, endless leisure?
Pack your bags and join me here.

Here's a wacky world of show biz,
So stunning that I can't explain.
The only thing we'd like to know is
How we all get out again.[13]

Here the performer is adopting and embodying the rhetoric which the Nazis used to lure many of their victims into the camp. By so vehemently exaggerating the propaganda he or she is not only exposing it for the lie it is, but using illusion to make reality bearable. Once again, we note the repetition of the catch line and its invitation to the audience to share in and laugh at the sheer absurdity of the comparison. And as in *Theresienstadt Questions*, the situation is reversed at the end. After having continually asserted that life inside the camp is better than outside, the performer returns to what we all know to be the truth – that conditions outside, no matter how harsh, are infinitely preferable to the hell inside, which has just been presented as paradise.

For those who specialize in theatre practice, there is a well-known Stanislavskian exercise, known to English-speaking practitioners as *endowment*, where the actor is asked to trick his or her imagination and trigger his or her belief in the illusion he or she is being asked to present as reality by the words *as if*. The idea behind this is that the imagination cannot be forced but has to be coaxed into believing an illusion.[14] By coincidence another of Leo Strauss's songs is called *As if*. It goes like this:

---

[13] For the original, see ibid., pp. 61–3.
[14] For the best summary of endowment, see Uta Hagen, *Respect For Acting* (New York: Macmillan, 1973), pp. 112–19.

I know a lovely little town
This town is really spiff
The name I can't quite place for now
I'll call the town 'as if'

This town is not for everyone
This town's a special place
You've got to be a member
Of a special 'as if' race

The townsfolk are quite normal there
As if in life, forsooth!
They greet all rumours from outside
As if they were the truth

The people in the crowded streets
They rush about their biz
And even if there's nought to do
They act as if there is

They've even got a Kaffeehaus!
With customers so toff-ee
Who sit and swap the latest tosh
By cups of 'as if' coffee

You come across some shameless folk
Back home, nonentities
But here they strut about the streets
As if they're VIPs

At meal times what a queue for soup
They scramble round the pot
As if the water had some meat
As if the soup was hot

At night they lie upon the ground
As if it was a bed
They dream of kisses, love-bites – ow!
They've bugs and fleas instead.

They bear their burden with a smile
As if they knew no sorrow
And talk of future happiness
As if it were . . . tomorrow[15]

Here the whole camp is presented as an illusion and the inmates as
fools who are living out their illusions as reality. Whether the end of the
song was performed in a melancholy fashion – following the text – or
against it, is something I have not been able to discover. It would indeed
be a profitable area of research for scholars to interview survivors of
Theresienstadt to try and establish performance styles and attitudes.
All we can note here are the tensions between the community, people
elbowing for survival in the pecking order, the appalling discomfort of
the beds with their never-ending plague of lice and above all hunger,
hunger, hunger.

One author (who has not been identified) tried to deal with this
issue by persuading his audience that life was really quite tolerable
Ohne Butter, Ohne Eier, Ohne Fett (without butter, eggs or lard). 'Even
if we've got no meat or fish and are suffering in other ways', he says,
'we're all looking a picture of health. And, whatever happens, we can
put up with it "ohne Butter, ohne Eier, ohne Fett".' After assuring his
audience that everything is fine and peaceful 'ohne Butter, ohne Eier,
ohne Fett', he ends with some words of reassurance and an attempt
to bind his spectators into a sense, not only of community, but a
specifically Jewish community.[16]

In this world there'll always be stars
Without butter, eggs, or lard
We're proud of the star on our chest
And know it cannot be suppressed
Without butter, eggs, or lard
And even if we're short of *achile*

---

[15] The original has one verse more. Because this is almost untranslatable
I have incorporated its salient points into the 'Kaffeehaus' verse. For
the original, see Migdal, *Und die Musik*, p. 106.

[16] Might this be also another indication of internal tensions in the Jewish
community in the camp? For the original, see ibid., pp. 95–6.

In the end it'll all come to *nile*
Without butter, eggs, or lard
We're free of guilt, no sins to bewail
Long live *Schma Yisrael*
Even without butter, eggs, or lard.

Achile is Yiddish for food and *nile* is a word derived from the Hebrew *Neilah*, which is the final prayer at Yom Kippur. In Theresienstadt this word had particular force, for the expression *Es geht auf Nile* ('It's coming up to Nile') or *Einmal geht es doch zu Nile* ('Nile's got to come sometime') came to be expressions of the longed-for day of liberation. *Schma Yisrael* are the first two words of the prayer *Hear Me Israel*. To some this might seem an extremely audacious, even outrageous, combination of satire and religion. But on closer consideration the pairing of the two is not only justifiable but necessary, for the author is transcending the needs of the flesh and appealing to and confirming the immortality of the spirit. Given the brutal reality in the camps, it would be easy to dismiss such a viewpoint as being hopelessly idealistic and romantic. Nonetheless, it has some validity. The artists in Theresienstadt might have been murdered in the most appalling circumstances, but they have one thing which gives them final victory over their torturers. They survive and will continue to live on through the works they left behind. And this is what makes these texts so important. They are not only of artistic and historic value, but also bear witness to human resilience and resistance.

There are many other songs about food, and how to get it, by chicanery, by sick notes, or contacts with the right people. There are songs about bureaucracy, money and dealing in goods. There is one in praise of the cabaret (probably written as a tribute by a member of the audience), for the moments of pleasure it brought, for its ability to take the audience back to the carefree life in Vienna or Prague and to wipe out, albeit temporarily, the pain and homesickness. Not only the cabaret, but all aspects of cultural life were immensely popular: academic lectures, reading, theatre, opera and classical music. One song called *The Theatre Ticket*, by Hans Hofer, deals in a Kafka-like (or Karl Valentin) manner with the problems of how to get hold of the eponymous ticket. The poor would-be theatregoer is sent from block to block, from room

15. Bedrich Fritta, *Synagogue and Theatre*, Theresienstadt.

to room and from person to person, he is continually being told he will get one tomorrow, next week, next month, for this show if not for that, providing it has not been postponed from this day to that. Finally he decides that the only place he will get into is the *Zwockhaus*.[17] Few aspects of life in the camp were omitted. There is even a song in praise of a former chemist, a Mr Pick, who repaired all the musical instruments.[18] The one area which was taboo was satire of the Nazis – for obvious reasons.[19] The fact that authors and performers (and the audience) were unable to hit out at their captors might partly explain why they turned a lot of bitterness and anger on themselves, albeit mostly in a mild and ironic form.

What I have not been able to establish is how much and in what way the texts and performances were mediated by the music to which they were set. Sometimes music was specially composed for the texts.

[17] Ibid., pp. 90–3. [18] Ibid., pp. 100–1.
[19] The few radical attempts to criticize the Germans seem to have been censored by the camp *Judenrat*. See Felsmann and Prümm, *Kurt Gerron*, p. 96.

But on many occasions the texts were written to fit in with well-known melodies from Strauss waltzes (one of the songs is called *From the Family Strauss*), choruses from popular operettas or songs of the day such as *Und die Musik spielt dazu* (literally, 'And the music plays along'). In this parody of a hit song by Rosita Serrano, Walter Lindenbaum tackles one of the central points of pain in the camps and a feature which has been censured very strongly by critics, both from within and without: while people were starving to death, being tortured, murdered or loaded like cattle on to transports, there was always a band nearby playing jolly music. *Und die Musik spielt dazu* is full of bitter sarcasm for those who could think of 'brightening' this man-made hell to the accompaniment of light-hearted melodies. The words 'infernal', 'hell' and 'evil dwarf' turn up in the first five lines alone. And another section of the song goes as follows:

Oh yes it's only good manners to keep to the beat
And at the last hole we'll still be whistling strong
And no one gives us a second of peace
Because the music never stops playing along.

Whether Meyerbeer or Mozart
It all sounds like genteel art
For here a *forte* would be seen as naughty
Although the music here is chronic
And the way we live here disharmonic
So many still play haughty-taughty
And we all want to stand in the middle
Leading the rest on first fiddle
And every man wants to wave the baton
Or at least call the tune with top hat on.[20]

We should not forget that the Jewish officials who were forced by the Nazis into taking responsibility for the transport lists were in an impossible dilemma. Most of them were only too aware of the transports' destination, and they were powerless to stop them. Critics must ask

[20] For the original, Migdal, *Und die Musik*, pp. 108–9.

themselves: would it have been any less reprehensible had the victims been accompanied by solemn funereal marches, thus destroying any last remaining hope? At least a medley of favourite light-hearted melodies might have given them some courage to accompany them on their way – even if it were only maintaining an illusion. For sometimes illusions, like painkillers, are indispensable. Nor should we forget that when the music stopped, life stopped. The musicians were literally playing for their lives. Or so they believed. For as long as they were needed to play, they would be spared the fate of the transports: yet another illusion. As the war neared its end, in the autumn of 1944, with the advance of the Soviets, the transports grew more and more frequent, as the Nazis hastily loaded more and more artists on to the trains to be murdered in Auschwitz – amongst them the leader of the cabaret, Kurt Gerron, whose last act had been one of forced collaboration in filming the lie of the gentle life at Theresienstadt.[21]

Even the transports were the subject of a song by Manfred Greiffenhagen. He starts by ironically congratulating the survivors for their achievement; then, in apocalyptic terms, he evokes the world aflame, the total destruction in the midst of which millions of people are being moved forwards and backwards, from coast to coast, setting new organizational records in transportation. The third verse deals with the gap between the Jews' prior knowledge of the transports and the inconceivable horror of the direct, personal experience when they are finally driven out of their homes, rounded up like cattle and taken away on the trains. But unlike most other songs that start with illusion and end with reality, Greiffenhagen takes the opposite course. Having treated his listeners to a ruthlessly hard description of realities, he ends on a note of hope and illusion.

> For one thing remains, will remain ours till death
> The belief that our victory is just round the bend
> That this will all be an episode, short as a breath
> And sometime, sometime the war must end

[21] Gerron was in fact transported to Auschwitz before he had time to complete the film. The direction was taken over by a Czech called Peceny. See the interview with the cameraman, Ivan Fric, in Felsmann and Prümm, *Kurt Gerron*, pp. 140–4.

Then we won't ask of victory or speak of defeat
We'll only ask, when are you coming back to us?
Peace in our time is all we Jews entreat
And somewhere our fair share of happiness.

Transport, transport
Blasts out the report!
We'll see them again
Our women and men
Laughing and crying
United undying
At the final chord
Transport.[22]

An illusion maybe. But in a way there was no alternative but to cling on to this illusion, to hope against hope. This, I would suggest, was the great achievement of the Theresienstadt cabaret: its ability to bolster up the will of its audiences to cling on to hope and refuse to capitulate even in the midst of the most appalling circumstances. Songs not only dealt with the hope of a common future back home in a world of peace and contentment. The cabaret also traded in the consolation of memories. Since I have mainly dealt with comic reversals, it is appropriate to close with *Karussell*, written by Manfred Greiffenhagen and performed by Kurt Gerron in person,[23] probably the opening song at all *Karussell* performances. It starts by recalling the carefree times of childhood and uses the image of the whirling carousel as a symbol of innocent joy. But as the song progresses, 'going round in circles without a destination', 'having lives full of sensations', and 'being carried along in a dizzy whirl', the lyrics gradually take on other, darker implications.

---

[22] Original in Migdal, *Und die Musik*, pp. 109–11.

[23] Migdal gives the author as Strauss but Felsmann and Prümm (*Kurt Gerron*, p. 99) claim the song might in fact have been written by Manfred Greiffenhagen. This is confirmed by the composer Martin Roman, who was a member of the cabaret and of the Ghetto Swingers, and who later enjoyed a successful musical career in the USA. Roman's music to this song is the only original score I have been able to track down. It can be heard on a CD of 'Chansons und Satiren aus Theresienstadt' released in 1993 by BMG Ariola Musik, number 43211 74532.

I

In time out of mind, so long long ago
When we were just kids beginning to grow
There was one thing we longed for like hell.
If our folks wished us out from under their feet
Or simply wanted to give us a treat
Why! All us kids would begin to yell
Carousel, oh please, carousel, carousel.

We're riding on old wooden horses
Round and round in a clippety-clop
Longing to get fizzy and whizzy and dizzy
Before the roundabout grinds to a stop

O ain't this a funny old journey,
A journey with no destination –
Going round in circles, it really is weird
Our lives are so full of sensation

And the hurdy-gurdy music
We'll never ever forget
When the images fade before our eyes
This melody lingers yet

We're riding on old wooden horses
Round and round in a clippety-clop
Where we land at the end of our journey
We'll only find out when we stop.

II

For most of the time our life is so hollow
But what makes it worth living is passion not sorrow
That's what gives it some sense
Careers, the markets, blondes, brunettes
Movies, football, cigarettes
We've all got our favourite bents
Don't rob us of thrills and amusements
Illusions, oh please, please illusions.

We're riding on old wooden horses
Round and round in a clippety-clop
Longing to get fizzy and whizzy and dizzy
Before the roundabout grinds to a stop

O ain't this a funny old journey,
A journey with no destination –
Going round in circles, it really is weird
Our lives are so full of sensation

And the hurdy-gurdy music
We'll never ever forget
When the images fade before our eyes
This melody lingers yet

We're riding on old wooden horses
Round and round in a clippety-clop
Where we land at the end of our journey
We'll only find out when we stop.

III
Even when sunk in attrition a man's still got his ambition
And here there should be no objection.
How we relish to shout
With the down and out
And those in utter abjection
Hear the song of the ghosts, their pleas so intense
For difference, oh please, difference!

We're riding on old wooden horses
Round and round in a clippety-clop
Longing to get fizzy and whizzy and dizzy
Before the roundabout grinds to a stop

O ain't this is a funny old journey,
A journey with no destination –
Going round in circles, it really is weird
Our lives are so full of sensation.

And the hurdy-gurdy music
We'll never ever forget
When the images fade before our eyes
This melody lingers yet

We're riding on old wooden horses
Round and round in a clippety-clop
Where we land at the end of our journey
We'll only find out when we stop.

Is there a more appropriate motto for this chapter than the last two lines?

This chapter is dedicated to my friend Edit Weisz, in Budapest, who was rescued from Belsen-Bergen in 1945 and who was the first survivor of the camps I ever met.

10 Liliane Atlan's *Un opéra pour Terezin*

YEHUDA MORALY

They say of Auschwitz, if you didn't enter it, you can never
enter it, and once you have entered, you can never leave. But
you, Liliane Atlan, you were never there, yet you are always
there.

> (A camp survivor to Liliane Atlan, during the reading
> of *Un opéra pour Terezin* in Jerusalem.)

In her autobiographical novel, *Les Passants* (*The Passers-by*),[1] Liliane
Atlan writes about how, at the age of fifteen, she starved herself after
hearing stories of concentration camps. She was born in 1932 in
Montpellier to a Jewish family from Saloniki. After the war, her father
adopted a camp survivor. It was the stories of her adopted brother that
determined the direction of her literary career. In all her plays, she
speaks of the camps where she never was, but which, in her mind, she
can never leave.

Her first play, *Monsieur Fugue, ou le mal de terre* (*Mr Fugue, or
The Earth Sickness*; 1967), tells of a trip in a truck by four children
sentenced to death by the Nazis. In the truck the children act out the
life they only know about through their parents' conversations. Over
several decades, Liliane Atlan's creative energies were almost solely
dedicated to the Shoah, and to the problem of being Jewish in the
world.[2] But it is *Un opéra pour Terezin* (1986) which seems to me to be

---

[1] Liliane Atlan, *The Passers-by*, translated by Rochelle Owens (New York:
Henry Holt and Company, 1993).

[2] In *Les Messies ou le mal de terre* (Paris: Le Seuil, 1969), there is an old
rabbi tortured by the Nazis and the description of a pogrom. This was

169

the high point of her career. This theatrical epic has not yet been produced, but it was twice broadcast on French radio (France-Culture) in an eight-hour presentation, in 1989 and in 1992.

The Terezin camp

Before the war, Theresienstadt (*Terezin* in *Czech*) was a little town sixty kilometres from Prague. It was to become a transit camp where many intellectuals, artists, painters and musicians were imprisoned. Faced with the horror of their existence, there was only one thing for them to turn to: artistic creation. They played and composed music, they performed cabaret, and created an opera, *Brundibar*. They also sang Verdi's *Requiem*. When the Red Cross obtained permission to visit the camps, the Nazis took them to Terezin, but only after killing all the sick and emaciated prisoners. A film, *The Führer Gives the Jews a Town*, was made with the inmates in order to show how contented they all were in their new existence.[3] Three weeks after completing the film, the Jewish director, actors and musicians were sent to the death camps. Atlan tells us how she decided to write a play about Terezin, the gateway to hell:

> Je suis retournée à Terezin, au début de l'automne, vers le nouvel an juif. Au cimetière, le gardien m'a montré une petite boîte en carton où reposent les cendres d'un détenu anonyme, la seule qui n'ait pas été jetée dans l'Ohre. C'était l'heure où dans les synagogues on sonne du shoffar, j'ai juré de raconter l'histoire – irracontable – de ces personnes disparues en fumée, de faire en sorte que chaque année on les entende.[4]

followed by *La petite voiture de flammes et de voix* (Paris: Le Seuil, 1971) and *Les Musiciens, les émigrants* (Paris: Oswald, 1976), where in a Jerusalem asylum, inmates tell stories about their pasts in the camps, about the orchestras which performed in front of the gas chambers.

A special issue of the *Nouveaux Cahiers* has been dedicated to the playwright (Summer 1996) with texts by Myriam Anissimov, Pierre Vialle, Andrée Chedid, Leonard Rosmarin, Bettina Knapp, Roland Monod, Irène Oore, Danielle Dumas, and extracts from *Un opéra pour Terezin*.

[3] On Kurt Gerron's film, see note 4, p. 149.

[4] I went back to Terezin at the beginning of autumn, round about the time of the Jewish New Year. At the cemetery, the watchman showed me a little cardboard box in which rested the ashes of an unknown

Four overtures or the four cups

Such an intense subject could not be treated within the limits of traditional theatre. Atlan chose the framework of the Pesach Seder. This ritual meal recalls the failure of the first Holocaust attempted by Pharaoh. The story is told through elementary symbols: an egg, unleavened bread, bitter herbs. Atlan links the remembrance of the Shoah victims with the Exodus, not in a sense of a ritual meal of salvation and hope, but as a commemoration of despair.[5]

In Atlan's *Opéra*, the ceremony is to be conducted all night long in several places around the world and in different languages. All the different groups taking part in the ceremonies scattered across the world are to commune through audiovisual, high technology links. Like the Seder, the ceremony consists of a meal preceded and followed by rituals. The four children (the wise one, the simple one, the wicked one and the one who does not know how to ask) ask questions and get answers. There are four overtures, each corresponding to one of the Seder's four cups of wine. Each one uses a different type of dramaturgy.

The first part is closest to the traditional Seder. In each of the places where the ceremony is conducted, a table is laid out. Around each table sit the four children, the narrator and the participants. In *Un opéra pour Terezin*, the participants are not passive spectators, for they are there to tell the story of this new Seder, and even play the parts of the musicians of Terezin. On each table, as in the Seder, there is a three-tiered Seder plate with yellow wheels, needles, scissors, black thread, potatoes, canned foods and chalk. Near the Seder plate stand children's

---

prisoner, the only ones that had not been thrown into the river Ohre. It was the hour when they were blowing the Shofar in the synagogues, I swore that I would tell the story – impossible to tell – of these people who went up in smoke. And I swore I would make sure that every year their story is heard.

(Liliane Atlan, *Un opéra pour Terezin*, Paris: L'Avant-Scène, 1007–8 (1–15 April 1997), p. 108.)

5 The idea of linking the Seder with the Shoah appears in several Haggadot that were published in the years after the war. A Haggada, published in Algeria, was called *La Haggada nouvelle*, because it linked the remembrance of the Shoah victims with the Exodus.

little toy suitcases. As in the original Seder, the ceremony begins with an announcement of the different parts of the ritual:

> Cette nuit, nous et nos enfants, nous serons ces musiciens qui composèrent, à Terezin même, un opéra pour Terezin, dont le livret a disparu. Nous serons, nous et nos enfants, ces musiciens qui allèrent à la mort en chantant pour eux-mêmes le *Requiem*. *On boit le premier verre . . .*[6] (p. 18)

The second cup is closer to conventional theatre. The table becomes the house that the participants are forced to leave when they receive their transport orders to the camp. The area around the table represents Terezin and its different parts. Almost forty scenes show us the fate of these fictional inmates (whose characters are based on authentic documents), the life and the death of the musicians who rehearsed Verdi's *Requiem* and who played in the film *The Führer Gives the Jews a Town*. All the participants in the ritual are asked to sew a little yellow wheel on their clothing before introducing themselves as the characters of the play. The Germans never appear. The inmates bow in front of them, mime the blows they receive, but the German torturers are invisible. There are no long scenes in this part of the opera. Everything is like the brief shots of an imaginary film, like speaking slides from hell.

Four couples rise above all the various characters. The first couple consists of Vaclav Taussig, a well-known architect, and his wife Erika Taussigova, who gives up the opportunity to escape to America in order to join him in Terezin. In some very short scenes, we witness the death process of this elegant woman, accustomed to luxury, who plunges into hell. At first she is happy because she finds her husband alive, she adapts to the concentration camp life, works hard without complaining, but, when the Nazis kill her newborn baby, she sinks into despair. She prostitutes herself, for food and for fun. 'Enjoy yourself' is her motto. However, when told about the suffering orphans from Bialystok, she sacrifices herself:

[6] Tonight, we and our children, we will become those musicians who composed, in Terezin itself, an Opera for Terezin whose libretto has disappeared. We and our children will become those musicians who went to their death singing the *Requiem* for themselves.
(*The first glass is drunk . . .* (p. 18))

EMIL, *allant et venant*: On demande des médecins et des infirmières volontaires pour s'occuper des enfants de Bialystok.

ERIKA: Moi.

EMIL, *à voix basse*: Tu n'en reviendras pas.

ERIKA, *emballant ses affaires dans un petit drap jaune*: Je n'ai pas pu m'occuper de mon enfant, je m'occuperai d'eux. *Elle embrasse Ludmilla et dit*: Tu es vraiment l'Etoile de Terezin, Ludmilla.

LUDMILLA: Tu es une grande dame, Erika.

ERIKA: Si faible.

STELLA, *à Erika*: Si grande. *Elles s'embrassent.*

ERIKA, *s'en allant*: Bonne chance.[7] (p. 63)

Ludmilla Hanselova and Reiner Lederer are united in their love for music: Ludmilla was a famous opera singer and Reiner a would-be orchestra conductor. They meet again in the camp and they decide to direct an opera, Smetana's *The Bartered Bride*. Ludmilla organizes the women, Reiner the men. The secret performance of the opera brings back confidence to the inmates, but Ludmilla falls in love with Vaclav, thus creating a second couple. Their romance lasts only one night (it is Vaclav's last night in the camp), but in these few hours they act out the whole life of a couple, from engagement to golden wedding. Later Vaclav escapes from the Oswiecin concentration camp to tell of the horrors that he witnessed there, but his appearance has changed so much that no one, not even Ludmilla, recognizes him, and no one believes him.

---

[7]   EMIL, *toing and froing*: They're asking for volunteer doctors and nurses to look after the Bialystok children.

ERIKA: I'll go.

EMIL, *in a low voice*: You'll never come back.

ERIKA, *bundling up her things in a little yellow sheet*: I wasn't able to take care of my own child. So I'll take care of them. *She embraces Ludmilla and says*: You are the real star of Terezin, Ludmilla.

LUDMILLA: Erika, you are a great lady.

ERIKA: So weak.

STELLA, *to Erika*: So great. *They embrace.*

ERIKA, *as she goes*: Good luck.

Emil tirelessly writes plays and operas (*The Slave Market*, a play for a finger and some matches, *The Non-Beloved*, and so on). When he is sent east, towards almost certain death, he gives Stella his last manuscript:

> EMIL: Stella, je te confie mon opéra. Fais-le jouer. Rendez-vous
> à la fin de la guerre, tous les soirs vers six heures, sur le Pont
> Charles jusqu'au jour où nous nous retrouverons et je
> t'épouserai . . . Ils ne m'ont pas laissé le temps de devenir un
> écrivain.[8] (p. 67)

The fourth couple is perhaps the most pathetic. In her youth Lilka had been the star of the Prague opera. Here, in the camp, this elderly woman is put in the insane asylum. But the performance of *The Bartered Bride* restores some of her courage and it is defiantly that she walks to her death:

> LILKA: Je veux chanter la Reine de la Nuit comme on doit la
> chanter. Donner, dans un son-limite, et le cri et la sérénité,
> puisée à je ne sais quelle source intérieure cachée, résistant
> à l'horreur absolue, je m'exprime très mal . . . *On la frappe.*
> Je dois vous quitter.[9] (p. 54)

The end of her male counterpart, Felix Kahn, is less dignified. This famous old writer, who was given a private room (a fantastic privilege) in order to write the story of Terezin, cannot write any more. Half-crazed, he begs some food from the children and, seated on a pile of little suitcases (which, in the ceremony, symbolize coffins), he awaits death, glancing wildly around him.

---

[8]   EMIL: Stella, I entrust my opera to you. Make sure it's performed.
When the war ends, let's wait for each other. We'll wait every night,
at about six, on Charles Bridge, until the day we find each other again.
Then we'll get married . . . They never did give me time to become a
writer.

[9]   LILKA: I want to sing the Queen of the Night as she should be sung.
To reach the very limit of sound. Find the place where the purest note
meets the loudest shriek and find a way to express both. To draw on
I don't know what hidden inner source. To resist absolute horror . . .
I . . . can't put this into words . . . *They beat her.* I must leave you.

16. Bedrich Fritta, *In the Attic*, Theresienstadt.

After *The Bartered Bride*'s performance, the whole camp is burning with a desperate desire for culture: they publish their own newspapers, perform poetry recitals, and puppet shows. But the second part
ends with the execution of all the musicians and actors of the film:

> *Chacun retourne à son ancienne table, on sent le vide laissé*
> *par les absents.*
>   *Ludmilla prend l'un des verres de vin, le boit, chacun boit,*
> *comme elle, debout et en silence.*
>   LUDMILLA *dit*: La plupart des verres resteront pleins, comme
> on laisse une flamme allumée pour signaler les disparus.[10]
>
> (p. 80)

In the ritual of the third cup no more characters appear. The participants read real documents from Terezin: letters and poems by prisoners.

---

[10]   *Everyone goes back to their old table. We feel the void left by all those*
   who are absent.
     Ludmilla picks up a wine glass and drinks. Everyone drinks, like
   her. Standing, in silence.
     LUDMILLA *says*: Most of the glasses will remain full. Just as one
   leave a candle burning to stand for the disappeared.

17 and 18. *Brundibar*. Children perform an opera in Theresienstadt, 1944.

They show photos, films shot by Shoah survivors. Atlan prefers to leave this part of the service open. Ideally children should search for new documents every year, and the different groups would exchange by fax, by radio, by any means whatsoever, the new documents they have discovered.

The children act out the ritual of the fourth cup. The ceremony (the last of the night) is based on drawings, projected on screens, drawn by artists in Terezin. All the children in the various groups performing the ritual simultaneously throughout the world watch images projected on screens or walls. They are images realized by painters of the camps, amateurs or professionals: *The Seder* by Eva Meitner, *In the Attic, The Transport has Arrived*, or *The Only Means of Transport* by Bedrich Fritta, *Mass Burial, Camp Commander, Execution*, or *Theatrical Performance* by Leo Haas, and so on. Each picture is linked to one of the ten plagues of Terezin: sand, lice, typhus, flies, killers, hunger, theft, people, fear, mass murder. Sometimes scenes are acted out that express the themes within the pictures. The author suggests a dialogue between the groups in her written text, but Atlan's dream is that the dialogue should emerge freely between the different groups celebrating the rite in the four corners of the world, and should continue until dawn. On a computer screen, a picture by Fritta would appear: Anna, from Kiev, would respond to it and key in her reaction; Deborah, from Acco, answers; Jim, from Chicago, adds something of his own, and so on.

Atlan calls this new form of dramaturgy the *'rencontre en étoile'* (the star-shaped meeting):

> Un événement majeur de l'Histoire récente de l'Europe . . . sera revécu, par la force d'un rituel, pendant toute une nuit, comme au présent, dans notre chair.
>
> La cérémonie commence au coucher du soleil. Elle se célèbre en famille, dans des maisons. On sait que d'autres familles célèbrent, dans d'autres lieux, dans d'autres langues, en même temps, le même rite – comme si l'espace ne nous séparait pas.[11]
> (p. 148)

---

[11] A major event of Europe's recent History will be relived by the power of a ritual, for a whole night, as if actually happening, in our own flesh.

This approach may seem very innovative, but it has its roots in ancient Jewish tradition. Purim is a Jewish festival commemorating another would-be Holocaust. Haman, King Achashverosh's chief minister, planned to wipe out the entire Jewish population dispersed throughout the Persian Empire. To commemorate the failure of his plan, Jews celebrate a festive meal similar to the Pesach Seder. On Purim, there is a special *mitzvah* (commandment) for each person to send at least two presents of food to a friend. Symbolically, all Jews eat together at Purim, despite their dispersion throughout the Diaspora. The aunt who sends a cake from New York drinks wine received from Tel Aviv, and eats chocolate from Geneva. In Atlan's rite, instead of food, Jews across the globe exchange messages and images through their fax machines and their computers. The goal is identical. The Jews remaining after the Shoah must feel united.

A work of science fiction
The opera's text is surrounded by dialogues in the way the Talmud is surrounded by commentaries. The dialogues involve four characters living in the year 2182 (i.e. 3,000,000 years after the catastrophe). Bernard Bouquet lives in Aix-en-Provence. He is the last editor of his galaxy and his printing press is protected by the cultural affairs minister like some prehistoric site. This man from the past, who is the last to feel suffering, the last to be preoccupied by books, has discovered the text of an opera, and he invites children to rehearse and perform the work with him.

Amandine is a sex maniac who lives for physical pleasure. But she is very astute and it is she who succeeds in deciphering the prehistoric notes of the *Requiem*. Socratine is the intellectual. Working from sketches designed by the artists of the camp, she builds the musical instruments of the past that will make the opera possible. Romarin is the cynic. He is Amandine's favourite lover and, for her sake, he has taken on the terrible responsibility of organizing the choir, but he never

The ceremony begins at sunset. It is celebrated in families, at home. We know that other families are celebrating the same ceremony, in other places and in other languages – but at the same time . . . as if distance did not separate us.

misses a chance of making fun of the ceremony. We recognize the four sons of the Seder, the wise (Socratine), the simple (Amandine), the wicked (Romarin) and the one who does not know how to ask (Bernard Bouquet), whose trouble, suffering and perplexity look so much like those of Atlan herself.[12] With this romantic quartet[13] (Amandine flirts with Bernard Bouquet and Socratine and Romarin are jealous), Atlan incorporates both poles of her work. The frenzy of the Shoah and that of Eros (the theme of most of her poems). Seen from the vantage point of the end of the twenty-second century, the Shoah is the only myth remaining from our own generation.

The *Scrolls of Testimony* and the *Opéra*

Like the Seder, the *Opéra* has its structure, its rhythm, its questions. Two Israeli experiments also use the rhythm, structure and questions of the Pesach Seder: the Theatre-Seder organized by Michal Govrin in the Jerusalem Bama Theatre and Aba Kovner's *Scrolls of Testimony (Megilot Ha-Edout)*.

In the Jerusalem Bama Theatre, Michal Govrin organized an event which, like Atlan's *Opéra*, lasted all night. There was no stage, but in the middle of the room, a table and, on it, thousands of heads of lettuce, an hallucinating sculpture by Frida Klopkotz, an artist who assists Govrin in all of her experiments. Sitting around the table were various representatives of Israeli society, kibbutznikim, businessmen, soldiers, students, artists, and so on. Each one was supposed to prepare a short performance, speech, play or ballet. The event attempted to create an image of the entire Israeli society, unified around the theatre table, like at a family Seder.

In the *Scrolls of Testimony (Megilot Ha-Edout)*, Aba Kovner writes a new Pesach Haggada whose purpose is to commemorate the Shoah.

---

[12] Bouquet lives in Aix-en-Provence; Liliane Atlan was born nearby, in Montpellier.

[13] Like Fellini with the number seven or Genet with the number five, Atlan is obsessed with the number four and all her works have a four-part structure. Why? Maybe because there are four stages in the Jewish prayer and Atlan writes hidden prayers?

Before it is too late, we must make it clear that the Shoah is not just the obsession of a few survivors, and the union with six million victims is not the only preoccupation of those who saw the horror in their flesh, but is a part of the collective memory of the Jewish people.[14]

Scrolls of Testimony is modelled after the Talmud as are some Pesach Haggadot. The central section is autobiographical and tells the story of the Shoah from 31 January 1933 until Kovner's departure for Israel on 14 February 1947. The text itself is surrounded by various commentaries, biographies, footnotes, the questions of a child to his father, snatches of dialogue (for example, the dialogue between a priest begging for the lives of 10,000 Jewish children and Pierre Laval, prime minister of the Vichy regime, who wants their death), documents, like the tracts distributed in the Vilna Ghetto in 1942. Like Atlan, Kovner wants his text to be the basis for an annual commemoration of the Shoah. And, like Atlan, he found his inspiration in the Pesach Seder, another commemoration of an attempt to destroy the Jewish people.

But Atlan's Seder, like Govrin's and Kovner's, is a human Seder. Atlan negates the miracle. Artistic creation and human relationships replace faith. For Atlan, Terezin is a metaphor. Inside or outside Terezin, faced with death and suffering, the only solution is artistic creation pursued hopelessly and with rage. Never mind if the world is absurd and revolting! Let us sing the *Requiem.* Let us run all over the world to realize the *Opera for Terezin:* let us sing together, each holding his and her friends' hands through their fax machines. But Liliane Atlan does not really believe in this glorification of the artistic enterprise. All the opera's musicians are like her; obsessed with the realization of their works, yet conscious that what they are doing is absurd. Like Atlan, they mock themselves in the most tragic moments. The opera is a cry of revolt and, simultaneously, something comic.

The musical structure forms a model for the structure of the play. The text has been conceived from a musical perspective and it contains solos and arias. The dialogues seem to have been written very simply, but each detail performs a particular musical function. Atlan is

---

[14] Aba Kovner, *Megilot Ha-Edout* (Jerusalem: Mossad Bialik, 1985), p. 7.

19.   Leo Hass, *A Theatre Performance*, Theresienstadt.

a poet, a great one. The translators will need to translate both the intent and the music, which will make their job a difficult one.

A new form of theatre

In *Un opéra pour Terezin*, Atlan has invented a new form of theatre – a specifically Jewish one, something all those involved in producing Jewish theatre have been dreaming about, as Jewish themes require to be expressed in a unique form. Michal Govrin (*Morning Prayer, The Yearly Cycle, Gog and Magog*), Serge Ouaknine (*1492, Sara*), Aliza

Elion-Israeli and Gabi Lev (*Bruria's Story*), all tried to invent a new theatrical form based on the Talmud and the Midrach. Liliane Atlan has
found with *Un opéra pour Terezin* a fascinating form that combines
ritual and theatre.

Had I only read the text of *Un opéra pour Terezin*, I would have
remained sceptical, but I have witnessed how powerfully effective this
form is. A few years ago, Atlan gathered a group of fifty people in
Jerusalem to try out her ritual. At the start the participants were waiting somewhat nervously, seated in front of their wine and their text.
Yet without a narrator, without a master of ceremony and without
actors, we began to read the text out loud, one by one, and, periodically,
together. It was an unforgettable experience. Just reading the text powerfully connected us to the victims of Terezin. Our emotions might have
been linked to the absence of theatrical elements. It is impossible to
'act out' the Shoah, but there, in that hall in Jerusalem, there were no
actors, no costumes, and the members of the audience were themselves
the participants. We were thrown off balance because the theatrical
conventions were circumvented and thrown into confusion, and the
text spoke directly to the participants/spectators.[15]

On that night, a musician, a survivor from Auschwitz, said to
Atlan:

> They say of Auschwitz, if you didn't enter it, you can never
> enter it, and once you have entered, you can never leave. But
> you, Liliane Atlan, you were never there, yet you are always
> there.

Prison is often linked with theatre. In several plays, inmates of a prison
rehearse a play within a play: *On répète Tête d'Or* (Claudel, 1949),
Haute surveillance (*Deathwatch*; Genet, 1949), *Marat-Sade* (Weiss,
1964), *Les Hommes* (Charlotte Delbo, 1978),[16] *Ghetto* (Sobol, 1983), and
so on. For people without hope, acting is all that is left. Atlan's ex-
perimental work is not simply another play that puts theatre into

---

[15] In a different register, one is reminded of *Six Characters in Search of an
Author*: the suicide of the boy is deeply moving because of the confusion
between theatre levels.

[16] See chapter 13, 'Theatre as a means of survival'.

prison. Atlan does not want to write another play about the Holocaust. She wants to continue a tradition that commemorates attempts at destruction of the Jewish People by a living memory experience. While Passover has its Seder, Hanukah its candle light, Purim its carnival with exchange of gifts, the Temple's destruction the fast of Tish B'Av, the Holocaust has no commemoration ceremony. When Atlan's work is published and translated in many languages, the Holocaust will have found its rite.[17]

---

[17] An English translation by John Clifford, a German translation by Rüdiger Fischer and a Hebrew translation by Emmanuel Pinto are now available through the editor of this book.

In March and April 1998 the University of Glasgow, the Freie Universität Berlin and the Université de Paris III (Sorbonne-Nouvelle) gave workshop performances of *An Opera for Terezin*.

Translation into Italian and Arabic are also being prepared and further performances are planned for 1999.

11 History, utopia and the concentration camp in Gatti's early plays

JOHN IRELAND

'Je porte en quelque sorte les stigmates de mes débuts. Je ne viens pas du théâtre. Ce n'était pas mon monde. Le théâtre pour moi est né dans le camp de concentration . . . Si on ne comprend pas ça, on ne comprend rien à ce que je fais.'[1] This statement, given to Michel Séonnet in an interview in 1991 is important in two ways: on the one hand it under-lines Gatti's experience of the camps as both the origin and the sub-ject of a series of innovative dramatic experiments; it also stresses an intense, sustained and parallel reflection on theatre as an institution. I shall explore these two facets of Gatti's involvement with theatre, focusing primarily on his first plays written in the late fifties and early sixties, with some reference to the very different projects of the last ten years.

It was as a Resistance fighter and not as a Jew that, in the winter of 1943, the eighteen-year-old Gatti was deported from France to the Neuengamme camp (and thence to the Lindermann Kommando on the Baltic coast, where inmates built submarine pens and mined salt). In Gatti's world, then and ever since, the concentration camp and its place in the twentieth century cannot be dissociated from his experience as a 'maquisard'. This association helps us understand Gatti's intense

---

[1] 'Gatti – le théâtre des exclus', in *Magazine littéraire*, 290 (July–August 1991), p. 100. 'In my theatrical work, I often feel that I carry the stigma of my beginnings. I don't come from the theatre. It was never my world. Theatre for me was born in the concentration camp in which I was interned . . . If you don't realize that, you cannot understand anything of what I do.' All translations from cited French editions and journals are my own.

involvement in other periods of social conflict and oppression: the Spanish Civil War and subsequent diaspora, Guatemalan genocide, the anarchist tradition, Hiroshima and Nagasaki, Vietnam, to identify only some of the issues his huge dramatic corpus has confronted. Even the plays that focus specifically on the camps remind us of the non-Jewish populations that suffered there – the Spanish Republicans, the gypsies, the Communists, and Gatti takes particular care never to forget members of the German Resistance to Hitler as well. In other words, Gatti's involvement with what the French call *l'univers concentrationnaire* has, at least initially, very different resonances than the Hebrew word *Shoah*. And yet, Gatti is truly fascinated by Judaism, by its philosophical and hermeneutic traditions. And, above all, by its alphabet. But even more importantly, when Gatti maintains that all his theatre stems from the concentration camp in which he was interned, he is also referring to a uniquely Jewish spectacle he witnessed there that changed his life. He explains:

> C'était un groupe de Juifs lituaniens. Ils avaient décidé de monter une pièce de théâtre. Dans le camp! Avec tous les risques de délation. Et la pièce tenait en trois mots: 'Ich war, ich bin, ich werde sein' ('J'étais, je suis, je serai.'). Une psalmodie.[2]

In a setting that denied their existence at every level, they showed Gatti for the first time what theatrical space could achieve – the assumption of language as a fundamental act of resistance. 'Les gens risquaient leur peau. C'était quelque chose qui combattait avec l'homme. Qui permettait à l'homme d'échapper à l'état végétal auquel il était réduit et de redevenir vraiment un homme.'[3] For the few moments during which the inmates forgot their desperate situation and reclaimed their identity as human subjects, theatre proved stronger than the camp. But that

---

[2] Ibid. 'There was a group of Lithuanian Jews. They had decided to put on a play. In the camp. With all the risks of being informed on. And the play was made up of three words: "Ich war, ich bin, ich werde sein" ("I was, I am, I shall be"). A psalmody.'

[3] Ibid. 'These people were risking their lives. In a struggle for human identity and dignity. Which made it possible for them to escape the vegetable condition they had been reduced to and become men again.'

play stayed with Gatti for another reason: this was a theatre whose primary motivation was, as he understood the term, anti-theatrical: 'Dans le camp, ce qui motivait le choix du lieu, c'était quoi? Passer inaperçu. Un théâtre qui faisait tout pour qu'on ne sache pas qu'il avait lieu.'[4] How could such an act become a model for theatre outside of that life-and-death context? How, after the Liberation, in 'normal' life could one reconcile, let alone reproduce, an experience like that with those comfortable cultural institutions we call theatres, whose essential preoccupations are critical reviews and, even more importantly, box-office receipts? Ultimately, Gatti's evolving response to these questions addresses an even larger question: what does it mean to affirm one's existence theatrically? Or, alternatively: in what kind of space can performed language become an act of those proportions?

It took Gatti more than ten years to formulate his initial response: his first plays (among which are three devoted to the camps) were not written until the late fifties and not staged until the early sixties. In the immediate postwar period, while working as a journalist, Gatti spent eight years trying to dispel his terrible memories of the camps in an interminable narrative, provisionally entitled *Bas-relief pour un décapité* (*Frieze for a Beheaded Man*) that ran through more than forty versions before it was finally abandoned. Instead of freeing him from the camp, confessed Gatti later, it was as if the words he selected and rejected, aligned and effaced on sheet after sheet of white paper became yet another convoy in deportation taking him back every night to a place he could not escape. But Gatti was also discovering concurrently with other survivors of the camps the fundamental aporia of writing about the concentration camp experience, well summarized by Colin Davis as the absolute moral imperative of bearing witness, accompanied by a terrible awareness of its impossibility.[5]

---

[4] Ibid. 'In the camp, what was the reason for the space that was finally chosen? Passing unnoticed. A play that did everything to ensure that nobody would know that it was taking place.'

[5] For an interesting account of the diverse strategies employed simultaneously to confront and circumvent this paradox, see Colin Davis, *Elie Wiesel's Secretive Texts* (Gainsville: University of Florida Press, 1994).

Gatti himself describes the impasse in graphic terms: 'Apocalypse en grec veut dire "révélation". Paradoxalement le camp fut pour moi une révélation. Et plus paradoxalement encore, elle fut d'ordre grammatical.'[6] For Gatti as for other writers, the first victim of the camp was language: How could one not be dazzled, he asks provocatively, by the two letters *K* and *Z*, capable of putting all the others to flight? 'Dès l'entrée de la grande porte, la grosse Tor franchie, des pans entiers de langage et ses significations s'effondrent.'[7] This image of a language in ruins is a commonplace of Shoah survivors. One thinks of the passage in Elie Wiesel's *Night* when he evokes the only household term that remained real to him in the camp – the chimney – or the paragraph in Primo Levi's *If This Is A Man* when he despairs of communicating, to an audience that had never known the camps, what the coming of winter meant to an Auschwitz inmate: 'We say "hunger", we say "tiredness", "fear", "pain", we say "winter" and they are different things. They are free words, created and used by free men . . . If the Lagers had lasted longer a new, harsh language would have been born.'[8] Gatti, too, speaks of the inexorable hollowing-out of language in the camp, the sudden paralysis of certain adjectives, the insipid vanity of words he had previously thought 'poetic'. There are echoes of Primo Levi's despair of language in some of Gatti's writing, for example, when he tries to describe the effect of the Baltic wind scouring the *Appellplatz* before daybreak in January, just one element of an experience of desolation and deprivation that became, as Gatti puts it, 'un vêtement et j'ai parfois l'impression – le vent de la Baltique n'ayant jamais cessé de souffler – de ne jamais l'avoir quitté. Parfois ce vêtement part tout seul. Il fait le tour du monde en une seule nuit. Et c'est

---

6 In Marc Kravetz, *L'Aventure de la parole errante. Multilogues avec Armand Gatti* (Toulouse: L'Ether vague, 1987), p. 79. 'Apocalypse in Greek means "revelation". Paradoxically the concentration camp was a revelation for me and, even more paradoxically, that revelation was primarily grammatical.'

7 Ibid., p. 79. 'As soon as one entered through the great door, *das grosse Tor*, whole strata of language and meaning collapsed.'

8 Primo Levi, *If This Is A Man*, translated by Stuart Woolf (London: Bodley Head, 1960), p. 144.

une nuit de camp.'[9] For Gatti, as for Wiesel, Kafka is a constant reference. Indeed, Gatti's first film, *L'Enclos* (*The Compound*), set in a concentration camp (filmed among the ruins of Mauthausen in 1960), was
made with money originally intended for an adaptation of *The Castle*
which he was to direct. For Gatti, the transposition from one project to
another was not hard. In each case, he concludes, 'c'était ouvrir la pa-
renthèse d'un monde condamné par des lois obscures mais implacables
à l'irréalité'.[10] But where does one find the elements of a language that
will convey the reality of an unreality whose aim was genocide?

The short answer is China. Having become a prominent journalist, Gatti was one of the first French visitors to travel extensively in
China and, in the heady days of the 1950s and the 'great leap forward',
he encountered a language and a culture that provided a fascinating counterpoint to western conventions. Above all, he discovered in
Chinese opera a new model of creation and communication:

> Les tréteaux ne sont que l'indication d'un espace imaginaire
> illimité. L'espace, les lieux, l'endroit où se déroulent une pièce,
> ce sont les acteurs qui le créent à chaque instant. Le jeu de
> mimes et de significations d'accessoires donnent à la scène une
> infinité d'existences différentes dans le temps et dans l'espace.
> De ce fait, le public devient co-producteur ou co-créateur d'un
> spectacle.[11]

In Chinese theatre, Gatti found the techniques of abstraction he felt
he needed to confront the unreal reality of the concentration camps.

---

[9] Kravetz, *L'Aventure de la parole errante*, p. 75. 'A kind of garment which
– since the Baltic wind has never stopped blowing – has never left me.
From time to time, it suddenly takes flight and circles the earth in a
single night, the space of a night in the camp.'

[10] Ibid., p. 72. 'One opened up the parentheses of a world condemned by
strange but implacable laws to unreality'.

[11] Armand Gatti, *Chine* (Paris: Le Seuil, 1956), pp. 162–3. 'The physical
stage delineates a limitless imaginary space. The locations, the different
spaces in which a play unfolds are created from moment to moment by
the actors. Together with a few accessories, their gestures give the stage
an infinite number of different existences in space and time. And these
techniques make the spectator a co-producer or co-creator of the play.'

20.   **Armand Gatti**, *L'Enfant-rat* (Théâtre International de Langue Française, Paris, 1996; director Hélène Châtelain).

Adapting them to his purpose, he turned conventional western realism on its head. Conceding the impossibility of any set 'reproducing' the ambience of a concentration camp, Gatti turns to abstract representations of subjective experience as the only purveyor of truth. Constantly moving back and forth in time, *L'Enfant-rat* (*The Child Rat*; first staged in Vienna in 1961) evokes the trauma and obsessions of six survivors of a concentration camp who were once members of the same work detail and who continue to live out the rest of their lives in relation to one another, despite the fact that one is a police inspector in Monte Carlo, while another is a circus proprietor in Germany and a third an unemployed machinist in France. Each gospel, representing the point of view of a central character, becomes a particular lens through which fragmented details of the salt-mine in which their shared past was forged are gradually revealed. Surrounding the central character of each gospel, the other subordinate characters will intervene in roles analogous to their situation in the mine. One of *The Child Rat*'s most striking innovations is that it identifies characters only by numbers, reflecting the practice of the camps themselves. Thus Number 9, who starts out as a kapo in the mine, will become an informant in the first gospel, a bear in the circus gospel, a policeman in the next, and so on. Constantly moving back and forth between moments in the mine and each character's present situation, the question of identity is both determined and undermined by the actantial sequences that lock these characters into the patterns of compulsive repetition that define them. Rarely has obsession found a more perfect theatrical form. There is no setting as such; the stage remains essentially bare. Events in the mine are evoked using minimal props conjured up in the deliberately distorted prism of each character's traumatized memories and fantasies. Indeed, Gatti's attack on conventional realism is even carried into the dramatic action itself. In one sequence he terms a 'sub-gospel', he specifically sets out to confound the spectator with preconceived ideas about the appearance of a concentration camp: barbed wire everywhere, search lights sweeping the compound, sinister SS guards snapping riding crops against gleaming black boots, and so on. The problem with commonplaces, Gatti reminds us, is that as conventions, they cannot communicate individual experience. From the outset, Gatti is committed to destroying an essentially *melodramatic* perspective of concentration camp history.

Of all the plays dealing with the camps, *The Child Rat* is the one that comes the closest to Gatti's own experience of deportation. But it is also unique among the concentration camp plays in that it tries, notably in the gospel of the machinist Joseph Claravel, to relate the oppression and degradation of the camp to the failure of the political revolution that the working-class Resistance fighters had hoped would 'liberate' France after their own liberation from the camps. Hence Claravel's lament:

> Autrefois (chiffre, matricule!) j'appartenais à une communauté de poumons mordus par le sel, de pupilles perpétuellement dilatées: je me reconnaissais à travers elle, et les autres se reconnaissaient en moi.
>
> Il y avait ceux qui pliaient le genou, ceux qui s'abattaient la face contre terre.

Mais nous étions aussi impérissables que les montagnes et
nous le savions.
L'épreuve finie, nous avons tous cru que les montagnes
allaient se mettre en marche.
Elles n'ont pas bougé.
Chacun s'est retrouvé seul.[12]

The grim and pessimistic progression mapped out by the gospels
acquires a more urgent political resonance as they proceed through
books of the Old Testament to the birth announced by the New Testament, the birth that gives the play its title, not of a Messiah but of a
child-rat, fathered by the century, already adapted to circumstances. 'Un
rat est capable de vivre n'importe où. Qu'un enfant né en déportation
lui ressemble, c'est à n'en point douter un trait de génie. L'homme de
l'avenir, le voilà!' (p. 128).[13]

The notion that the concentration camp experience forced
survivors into terrible modes of isolation is also very present in Gatti's
second venture into *l'univers concentrationnaire*, but *La Deuxième
Existence du camp de Tatenberg (The Second Existence of the
Tatenberg Camp*; 1962) constitutes a very different kind of theatrical
experiment. Tatenberg, as such, has no place in historical fact, but
its description and imaginary location in a granite quarry cut from the
hills above the Danube suggest that Mauthausen was Gatti's principal
model, although features of other camps come into play. In any case,
the whole question of historical past and present in relation to the

---

[12] Armand Gatti, *Œuvres théâtrales* (Paris: Verdier, 1991), vol. I, p. 108.
Page numbers in parentheses following citations refer to this edition.

Before (a numeral, a number) I belonged to a community of lungs
ravaged by salt, of perpetually dilated pupils. I recognized myself in
the others and they recognized themselves in me. There were those
who gave in, those who crawled, their faces pressed to the earth.
But we were as indestructible as mountains and we knew it. When
we were freed, we all thought the mountains would start walking.
They never moved.
Each one found himself alone.

[13] 'A rat can live anywhere. That a child born in deportation can resemble
one is a stroke of genius. Here is the man of the future.'

21. **Armand Gatti**, *La Deuxième Existence du camp de Tatenberg* (Théâtre des Célestins, Lyon, 1962).

camps' reality is precisely *Tatenberg*'s focus. Significantly, its two principal characters are attached to a travelling fair. Ilya Moïssevitch, a Jew from the Baltic states, miraculous survivor of the Tatenberg camp, is the owner of a musical robot with which he makes his living. His traumatic past is set against that of Hildegarde Frölick, a German war widow, also attached to the fair, whose husband was a German soldier shot for desertion on the Eastern Front. She is the owner of a puppet theatre with which she obsessively enacts imagined versions of her husband's death. As the play opens, the Danube, witness to so much twentieth-century suffering, has overflowed its banks, the memories it contains have resurfaced and Moïssevitch is once again plunged completely into a past that now blurs with his present. But what is the truth of that past, what really did happen? Moïssevitch is no longer sure and, in tortured dialogue with other figures who emerge from the gloom of Tatenberg, he desperately confronts his own guilt as a survivor. In particular, Moïssevitch is tormented by the memory of a kapo he helped kill when the camp was liberated:

> MOÏSSEVITCH: A la libération, Baltes et Polonais se sont
> battus à son sujet . . . (Vous connaissez l'histoire?) *Nous*: C'est
> un traître! *Eux*: C'est un héros! *Nous*: Il frappa avec la dernière
> des brutalités. *Eux*: Il a sauvé quinze vies au péril de la sienne.
> Finalement, Antokokoletz fut enlevé par les Baltes et lapidé.
> (J'ai lancé ma pierre; aujourd'hui encore je sens son poids
> dans mes mains.) Et le voilà revenu. (Est-ce lui? . . . N'est-ce
> pas lui? . . .)   (p. 583)[14]

And later, he confronts the kapo himself, or is their encounter merely imagined?

> MOÏSSEVITCH: C'était toi, le kapo du Goldpilz, Abel? C'était
> toi, n'est-ce pas?
> ANTOKOKOLETZ: . . . Pouvons-nous revenir sur les lieux où le
> feu brûle?
> MOÏSSEVITCH: Ce n'était donc pas toi.
> ANTOKOKOLETZ: Je le deviendrai, Ilya – Je le deviendrai pour
> pouvoir t'ouvrir les yeux.
> MOÏSSEVITCH: Est-ce un aveu?
> ANTOKOKOLETZ: Voilà que tu veux être juge, maintenant – Tu
> l'as déjà été pour le kapo que tu as liquidé. Si tu tiens tellement
> à recommencer son procès à travers moi, c'est qu'au fond tu te
> sens coupable.
> MOÏSSEVITCH: On est toujours coupable de quelque chose.
> Est-ce pour cela que tu es revenu?   (pp. 588–9)[15]

---

14   MOÏSSEVITCH: When we were liberated, Balts and Poles came to
     blows about him. (Do you know the story?) – *Us*: He's a traitor! *Them*:
     He's a hero! *Us*: He used to beat us like a brute. *Them*: He saved fifteen
     lives at the expense of his own. In the end, Antokokoletz was
     kidnapped by the Balts and stoned to death (I threw my stone too – I
     can still feel it now, feel the weight of it in my hand). And here he is,
     back again. (Is it him? . . . Isn't it him . . .)

15   MOÏSSEVITCH: You were the kapo of Goldpilz camp, weren't you,
     Abel? It was you, wasn't it?

The haze created by the tawdry lights of the fairground is reflected in the unreality of the false Tatenberg station where Moïssevitch holds these anguished exchanges and arguments with ghostly figures from the camp – victims or survivors, we can never be sure. As they argue, in the shadow of the painted clock on the fake station wall (these hastily built sets to reassure deportees arriving at the camps), as they enter into the same insoluble polemics undercut by their uncertain memories, the camp rises up again to assume its second existence. In the midst of Moïssevitch's confused and guilt-laden conjectures over the death of the kapo, he is joined by another figure from the past, Manuel Rodriguez, a Spanish Republican and a fellow camp inmate:

RODRIGUEZ: Pourquoi revenir là-dessus? C'est peut-être pour cela que chacun d'entre vous ne trouvait d'issue au fatal engrenage que dans la résignation ou la haine désespérée de son frère de souffrance.
MOÏSSEVITCH: En effet c'est toujours pénible, surtout lorsque nous nous souvenons du cordon (appelons-le sanitaire) que les détenus chrétiens mettaient entre les Juifs et eux. (Et c'était dans le meilleur des cas!)
RODRIGUEZ: Chrétien? Moi?
MOÏSSEVITCH: Tu me comprends fort bien. N'est-ce pas vous (les Espagnols) qui avez refusé la participation des Juifs lorsque le camp s'est soulevé?
RODRIGUEZ: Les décisions étaient prises par le Comité international. Si vous n'avez pu être contactés, c'est que vous étiez les derniers arrivés et sans aucune organisation.

ANTOKOKOLETZ: Can we ever return to places where fires still burn?
MOÏSSEVITCH: Then it wasn't you.
ANTOKOKOLETZ: I'll become him, Ilya. I'll become him so that I can open your eyes.
MOÏSSEVITCH: Is that a confession?
ANTOKOKOLETZ: Ah, you want to be a judge now? Just as you were when you killed the kapo. If you insist on using me to put him on trial again, it's because, deep down, you feel guilty.
MOÏSSEVITCH: We're always guilty of something. Is that why you came back?

MOïSSEVITCH: Et après. C'est quand même nous qui avions le plus souffert.

RODRIGUEZ: Peut-on mesurer ces choses-là?

MOïSSEVITCH: Au nombre – oui!

RODRIGUEZ: Le nombre n'a fait que rendre plus cruelle la réalité. Les intellectuels rivalisaient en platitude, les commerçants en bassesse – Un seul point vous liait: l'acharnement que vous mettiez à vous dénoncer et à vous traiter de sale Juif!

MOïSSEVITCH: Tous n'étaient pas ainsi.

RODRIGUEZ: Ils étaient bien cachés.

MOïSSEVITCH: Quant à l'écroulement des autres – les nazis ne l'auraient peut-être pas obtenu sans votre participation (et pour tout dire votre complicité).

RODRIGUEZ: Attention! Mes frères espagnols sont enterrés à cent mètres d'ici.

MOïSSEVITCH: Pourquoi passes-tu en jugement des millions d'innocents?

Les deux dernières répliques ont été prononcées presque en même temps . . . Les deux hommes se regardent avec consternation presque.

RODRIGUEZ: Moïssevitch! Le camp continue d'exister.

MOïSSEVITCH: C'est vrai – Quel que soit l'endroit où nous sommes – il est autour de nous.   (pp. 583–4)[16]

16   RODRIGUEZ: Why go over that ground again? That's why none of you escape the treadmill of your minds other than through resignation or hatred of those who suffered with you.
MOïSSEVITCH: Yes, it's always painful, particularly when you remember the cordon (let's call it sanitary) that the Christian inmates put between the Jews and them. (And that was in the best of cases!)
RODRIGUEZ: A Christian, me?
MOïSSEVITCH: You know what I mean. Wasn't it you, the Spaniards, who refused to let Jews participate when the camp rose in revolt?
RODRIGUEZ: The decisions were made by the International Committee. If no one could contact you, it's because you were the last to arrive with no organization.
MOïSSEVITCH: Even so. We were the ones who suffered the most.
RODRIGUEZ: Can one measure those things?

Once again, the dominant theme of the play – the uncertainty of the past, coupled with its hegemonic power – is well served by the abstract *mise en scène* on both sides of the ribbon of blue silk that dissects the stage, marking the line of the Danube. When Hildegarde Frölick's puppets emerge to enact the events leading to their execution, a white ribbon is superimposed on the blue, evoking the snow storm on the Russian steppes that separated the three German soldiers from the main body of their army. Otherwise, the stage is dominated by the gaudy booth of the puppet theatre – a microcosm of the carnival and of Vienna itself (the city of illusion) which unravels little by little the etymology of the camp (Tatenberg – literally mount of deeds or of facts) and any objective communicable past.

Chroniques d'une planète provisoire (*Chronicles of a Provisional Planet*), first written in 1963 and then rewritten in 1967, is the last play that Gatti would write about the camps for more than twenty years. Its approach is very different again from its two predecessors. In what is probably a brief nod to Bradbury's *Martian Chronicles*, a small group of astronauts leaves on an expedition to explore a planet that has always defied human understanding. Ultimately, what the astronauts encounter is another earth ravaged by war and suffering.

MOÏSSEVITCH: In terms of numbers, yes.

RODRIGUEZ: The numbers only make the reality worse. Your intellectuals outdid each other in platitudes, your merchants in ignominy. You only had one thing in common: the enthusiasm with which you denounced each other and called each other Dirty Jews!

MOÏSSEVITCH: That wasn't true of every Jew.

RODRIGUEZ: The exceptions were well hidden.

MOÏSSEVITCH: As for the capitulation of the others – the Nazis might not have managed it without your complicity and, to put it bluntly, your help.

RODRIGUEZ: Watch it! My Spanish comrades are buried a hundred metres from here.

MOÏSSEVITCH: Why are you passing judgement on millions of innocent people?

The last two lines are spoken almost in unison . . . The two men look at each other in consternation.

RODRIGUEZ: Moïssevitch! The camp still exists.

MOÏSSEVITCH: It's true. Wherever we find ourselves, we find it around us.

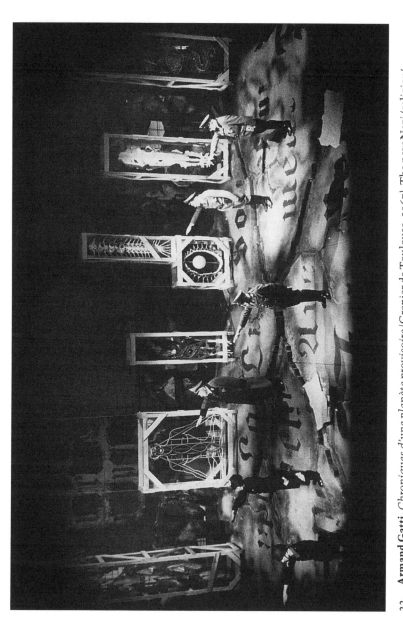

22. **Armand Gatti**, *Chroniques d'une planète provisoire* (Grenier de Toulouse, 1967). The new Nazi 'religion'.

However, the space voyage allows for an ingenious framing device: the stage perceived by the audience becomes the space ship's monitor in which the astronauts capture a succession of moments from around the provisional planet. In many ways, this staging device creates, I think, the most distanced perspective of all Gatti's Holocaust plays, an impression reinforced by a very strong burlesque element that is also comparatively rare in his work. As the space ship arrives, a warmongering Barberoussia is invading a large country called Tolstoievski. Other countries include the Rousseauist Republic, the Starry States, and last but not least, Picadilicircus. Among the Barberoussians, First Big Chief is a largely absent Hitler, Little Rat and the Apprentice Angel are grotesque characterizations of Himmler and Eichmann respectively. Along with the war on its eastern front (which is going badly), Barberoussia is also exterminating Jews. In *Chronicles of a Provisional Planet*, the hyperbolic Guignol-like presentation of Nazi figures and Nazi ideology contrasts sharply with some of the most moving and searing accounts of documented episodes from the camps. In one of the chronicles, for example, Gatti abruptly changes the metre and in spare blank verse, pays homage to the memory of Janusz Korczak, a teacher and director of an orphanage who, when 400 very small Jewish children were deported and finally killed, refused to leave them and even led them into the gas chamber himself, telling them stories so that they would not be frightened. And not once but twice, Gatti mentions the little boy Abracha in his father's arms, wrestling with a perplexing question as they wait in line to be gassed: '– Papa, est-ce que tu connais des chats qui parlent?' '– Des chats comment?' '– Des chats noirs.' '– Il faut beaucoup voyager, Abracha, pour en connaître' (p. 655).[17] In a sense, one can consider all of Gatti's theatre as an extended meditation on that brief exchange, at that moment.

The central theme of the *Chronicles* is provided by an extraordinary story that seems to have been unjustly relegated to the footnotes of history: In 1944 Eichmann was authorized to set up a deal with the

---

[17] 'Daddy, do you know any cats that can talk?' 'What kind of cats?' 'Black cats.' 'You know, Abracha, you have to travel very far to meet cats like that.'

23. *Chroniques d'une planète provisoire.*

Allies using as an intermediary a certain Joël Brand, the representative of a clandestine Jewish organization, whereby 1,000,000 Hungarian Jews would be exchanged for 10,000 British and American army trucks to be used on the Russian front. The deal was never concluded since nobody on the Allied side was prepared to assume responsibility for resettling this displaced community or contributing to the German war machine. In an effort to pressure the Allies to speed up the stalled negotiations, Eichmann reminded them dryly that the 1,000,000 men, women and children are 'perishable goods'. Seven hundred thousand of them will indeed perish in Auschwitz.[18] At the end of the play, the Apprentice Angel, Eichmann, condemned by the astronauts, not to death, but to live with the responsibility for genocide as his only

[18] See Raul Hilberg, *The Destruction of the European Jews* (New York and London: Holmes and Meier, 1985), vol. III, pp. 1132–40; and chapter 6, 'Theatrical Interpretation of the Shoah: Image and Counter-Image' in this book.

companion, retorts: 'Qui de votre bonne conscience ou de nos cré-
matoires a tué davantage?' (p. 715)[19]

On this provocative and disturbing note of shared guilt, the play
comes to a close; Gatti will not write another play about the camps for
more than twenty years. And when he does return to the camps, it will
be with a very different conception of theatre and of language, in which
a new sense of the Holocaust experience plays an essential part.[20] What
is remarkable about Gatti's work, long viewed as 'political', is that
its aesthetic development as a whole is determined from beginning to
end by his endless ruminations on the camps. The challenge posed by
the concentration camp to theatrical language never stops resonating
throughout all of Gatti's theatre. During the period of these first concentration camp plays, a radical example of this influence is found in
*Chant public devant deux chaises électriques (Public Lament in Front
of Two Electric Chairs)*, Gatti's treatment of the Sacco–Vanzetti affair.
Instead of staging an account of the famous trial, he elects to stage five
different audiences in five different countries reacting to a play about
Sacco and Vanzetti that the real audience never sees. From the various
and often conflicting reactions of these different spectators, the real
audience must infer what is happening in the invisible play, all the
while realizing that the different reactions of the spectators on stage are
conditioned by their particular situation, by their race, their social class
and their current preoccupations. The innovation is considerable and
quite ingenious since ultimately Gatti inserts the real spectator into
the very process he has staged. In order for the play to become coherent,
the spectator is forced to create, as Gatti puts it, 'in parallel' and thus
become an active participant in a process of continuous invention. For
Richard Coe, this association of subjectivity and identification has
even more far-reaching consequences. It is by a process of identification
with a particular depiction of or reaction to a character, that the spectator becomes active in the historical problem created by the play. But,
notes Coe, 'since he cannot actually become that character or wholly

---

[19] 'Who is responsible for more deaths, our crematoria or our clear
consciences?'

[20] See the following chapter, Dorothy Knowles, 'Armand Gatti and the
Silence of the 1059 days of Auschwitz'.

abandon his own identity, what he is doing is to create, through the fusion of his present-Self with his subjective interpretation of the past-Other, a third, *parallel* identity'.[21] It is in the space forged by this particular creative activity that Gatti locates the utopian dimension of his theatre. In all simplicity, Gatti concludes, the theatrical act is a meeting at the summit of all life experience.

It goes without saying that Gatti's aesthetic research entails an implicit parallel reflection on history, language and epistemology. Denying any objective sense to history, Gatti sees historical truth only in terms of subjective refraction; for him, history, when it suffers the deliberate distortion of individual passions and obsessions, is simultaneously and by that very act made real. The realism of his theatre – and for Gatti, the paradox is only apparent – lies in the continuous operation of subjective imagination. This tendency is reinforced by Gatti's frequent recourse to forms of mythology and open-ended symbolism that function as catalysts to extend the process of identification and interpretation still further. Is it too much to claim that in his dialogue with what Elie Wiesel has termed the Age of Testimony, Gatti's theatrical aesthetic is a compelling and coherent epistemological response to what Shoshana Felman has referred to as our 'radical historical crisis in witnessing'?[22] By denying any possibility of representing history, Gatti cuts the Gordian knot, insisting that our only meaningful access to history is creative endeavour. From this perspective, the concept of parallel creation, the basis of Gatti's aesthetic credo, is not an attempt to solve the question of the subject's relationship to truth or language but an effort to show by means of illustration the variety of creative responses to history theatre can both stage and provoke.

What I have presented of Gatti's theatre is valid until about 1970. But I want to suggest, as my final point, that the radical transformations that characterize Gatti's theatrical projects of the seventies and eighties are precipitated by the driving ambition to push this

---

[21] Richard Coe, 'The Theatre of the Last Chance: Catastrophe-Theory in the Plays of Armand Gatti', in *Australian Journal of French Studies*, 20.1 (1983), p. 84.

[22] See Shoshana Felman and Dori Laub, *Testimony: Crises of Witnessing in Literature, Psychoanalysis and History* (New York: Routledge, 1992).

process ever further. With one enormous difference. The Lithuanian Jews, largely absent as a reference throughout the many plays and interviews of the sixties (although they are briefly mentioned in the *Chronicles*), become an omnipresent icon in the increasingly metatheatrical research of the eighties and nineties, an ideal of the theatrical act itself for which Gatti must constantly construct a new forum. Having stretched institutional theatre to its limits throughout the sixties, Gatti abandoned it completely in the early seventies, a move that reflected his now unshakable conviction that theatre in all its vital urgency could not be realized as the product of a purely professional collaboration. In his search for a fundamentally different kind of motivation to fuel his theatrical work, Gatti returned again and again to the exemplary spectacle he had witnessed in the camps. The focus of his endeavours over the last ten years in particular has been to found a 'secular' context in which his work with groups of dispossessed and damaged young people can acquire its greatest autonomous performative value. Disputing the finality of historical chronology – the fixed syllables of recorded time – Gatti's work strives to realize the most important legacy of the camps enacted by the Lithuanian Jews: the creation of a significant theatrical space in which other suppressed voices from largely unrecorded history will have another chance to say: 'Ich war, ich bin, ich werde sein.'

12 Armand Gatti and the silence of the 1059 days of Auschwitz

DOROTHY KNOWLES

'Je ne suis jamais sorti du camp de concentration.'

This confession is still repeated by Armand Gatti[1] in interviews, public debates, even at rehearsals of his own plays. Captured by the Vichy police in a Resistance *maquis* in 1943, Gatti ended up in the Nazi concentration camp of Neuengamme. He was moved from there to Hamburg to work in appalling conditions 200 metres down on the sea-bed in a cement diving bell, 'an unwilling pioneer' of Himmler's crazed belief in a *concave* world in which rockets could be fired in a straight line from Hamburg to London!

In 1955, as the year's prize-winning investigative journalist, he toured, at his special request, Displaced Persons' camps in Germany and Austria, including the camp at Mauthausen where he spent several nights in the company of former prisoners, 'déportés à vie', like himself, who returned to the camps to sit and talk by the fires they lit in the huts which were the only homes they then knew. There, when the gates

---

[1] Armand Gatti, playwright and, since 1986, artistic director of 'La Parole errante', Centre International de Création, 3 rue François-Debergue, 93100 Montreuil-sous-Bois (Seine-Saint-Denis). Files and other documents can be consulted at the centre, also at the 'Fonds Gatti', at the University of Paris VIII.

Adam quoi? has not yet been published. Quotations have been made from various typed acting copies (much changed, cut, and so on, during rehearsals) of the various 'chapters', some bearing titles, some identified by a capital letter. Other quotations are from documents issued by La Parole errante, referred to here as File.

24. **Armand Gatti**, *Adam quoi* (Marseille, 1993). The opening scene: the disused marshalling yard of the Seita tobacco company with rail-track and dilapidated wood freight trains recalling the transportation of prisoners to the camps. Alphabet/actors performing on the painted Star of David using kung fu *gestuelle*.

were shut, so Gatti confided to Marc Kravetz, he felt as shut in as when he himself was imprisoned in a camp.[2]

These combined experiences led, in his early literary works, to the creation of an imaginary camp on the Danube which he called *Tatenberg*. Over time the imaginary camp came to be replaced by a real camp, Auschwitz, even though Auschwitz was no part of his personal experience, and personal experience is at the root of all his creative work. This difference of inspiration explains the complete change which came over his work with his two plays on Auschwitz.

The years of continuous controversy over the 'myth' of the existence of extermination camps, even of the gas chambers – in France one could cite the so-called historian, Paul Rassinier, writing in *Rivarol* in 1964 under the name of Jean-Paul Bermont and accusing the judges at

---

[2] Marc Kravetz, *L'Aventure de la parole errante, Multilogues avec Armand Gatti* (Toulouse: L'Ether vague, 1987), pp. 52, 73.

the Nuremberg trial of convicting on 'documentary evidence later re-cognized as false' – moved Gatti to want at all costs to 'entrer dans le silence des 1059 jours d'Auschwitz' (his actual words) no longer with an imaginary Tatenberg, but using the hard evidence of authors/survivors like Primo Levi, Elie Wiesel, Charlotte Delbo, and others. There was also unpublished testimony written by prisoners *in* the camp at the risk of immediate execution. Some of this had been collected and stored in tin or cement containers by Sonderkommandos working at the camp crematorium, then hidden under the mounting piles of human ashes or under bodies stacked up in blood-drenched trenches or pits waiting to be covered with a thin layer of soil.

The end result of the work done by Gatti on such documentary evidence was his play (if that is the right name for it) *Le Chant d'amour des alphabets d'Auschwitz*, written in 1989. At the request of the director of the Théâtre et des Spectacles, Robert Abirached, Gatti gave a reading at the Maison de la Culture at Bobigny, in a working-class suburb of Saint-Denis, near Paris. The house was packed – I was there – and the reading took six hours. The production of *Le Chant* scheduled at the Deutsches Theater in Berlin in 1991 was, on the contrary, effect-ively silenced by the authority's refusal to grant a subsidy. The ban, for that is what is was, was a challenge that Richard Martin, director of the Tousky Theatre in Marseille, decided to take up with Gatti. He pro-posed to Gatti that they should put on in Marseille a production of *Le Chant* that would be 'à la mesure de toute la ville', that is to say a production that would involve everyone and everything, townsfolk, dockers, institutions of all kinds, even the municipal buildings, and make Gatti and Auschwitz the talk of the town. It was not, however, with *Le Chant* that Gatti undertook this task but with a complete rewriting of the play under the new title of *Adam quoi*, with as its starting point the tragic events of 1943 in the docklands of Marseille. From that moment, for this play, Marseille became for Gatti his *lieu-écriture*.

Five months before Gatti put on his rewritten *Adam quoi* (July 1993), his son Stéphane with Michel Séonnet gave a 'Présentation' of *Le Chant* in Seine-Saint-Denis in February 1993, which I attended. The Présentation was Stéphane's answer to the request of the Conseil Municipal de Montreuil to devise, in his father's absence in Marseille, something 'unofficial' to counter the general public's obvious dis-interest in the recent history of its own town of Paris, which it demon-strated by failing to turn up at the Vélodrome d'Hiver for the official commemoration of the round-up, fifty years before, by the Vichy police of 13,000 Paris Jews, and their dispatch to German extermination camps.

Though the subject matter of Le Chant is taken by Gatti from books by authors/survivors of Auschwitz and other camps, the 'play' must not be seen as a patchwork of excerpts lifted from their writings. Gatti is here, as always, a creative artist. Furthermore his reactions to the happenings in the camps did not match theirs. Whereas they had all been deported to extermination camps, he had been sent to a concentra-tion camp – to be *worked* to death. What is more, he had managed to escape: he had not known the deliberate slow disintegration of the human being as planned by the Nazis. For him, the camp 'avait été une découverte aussi importante que celle de l'Amérique pour Colomb. J'ai découvert le judaïsme, un univers, un continent, une intelligence du monde',[3] and both the content and the dramatic technique of Le Chant testify to this discovery. With Le Chant, Gatti offers a Talmudic read-ing of existing texts on Auschwitz, and when his resulting 'textual commentary' of the books consulted was given a theatrical 'Présenta-tion' by his son and Michel Séonnet, a whole line of very differing commentaries was opened up through the work of the three directors, their 'actors', the composer, his musicians, and so on, down to the spec-tator as he or she watched Le Chant take on physical shape before his or her eyes. The two producers were very conscious of this development and noted in their commentary: 'Notre travail ne sera jamais rien d'autre que l'écriture dans l'Espace et dans le Temps de ce processus d'appropriations successives.'[4]

---

[3] 'had been a discovery as important as that of America for Columbus. I discovered Judaism, a universe, a continent, an intelligence of the world'. (File: *Le Chant d'amour*, Seine-Saint-Denis, 'L'Heure lettriste', no. 5 (January 1993))

[4] 'Our work will never be anything other than the writing in Space and Time of the process of successive appropriations.' *(Le Monde juif* (September–October 1993), 'Un travail de mémoire par S. Gatti et M. Séonnet')

With the Talmudic 'appropriation' and 'interpretation' of the textual evidence of people who had been through the purgatory of Auschwitz, any attempt at an imaginative creation of a dramatic plot, as in 'Tatenberg', would have been as out of place as it would have been ineffectual. Nor could the 'characters' of such a 'play' be SS men and their victims. They had to be abstractions, 'porteurs de paroles' – to use Gatti's terminology – having as their dramatic role the 'interrogation' of existing texts on the 'innommable', the 'unspeakable' – Auschwitz. They became Alphabets. Alphabets who for fifty years had been involved by authors/survivors in various attempts to 'dire' Auschwitz, to couch it in words.

For *Le Chant* Gatti created ten Alphabets; behind each one can be heard the voice of an author/survivor; that of Primo Levi, mainly from *Si c'est un homme*,[5] is distinctly audible behind the 'Alphabet de la Question', while the 'Alphabet du Principe Espérance' speaks for Ernest Bloch, who had managed to escape the Nazi dragnet for the camps. For *Adam quoi* Gatti created sixteen Alphabets and, he roguishly added, 'some more'. Amongst the 'some more' was the Alphabet d'Auschwitz or Inca Alphabet used by the Brigadists to pass on information during the Spanish Civil War, then by the Brigadists in Nazi concentration camps. This Alphabet consists of lengths of string knotted singly or doubly, according to some sort of Morse code, and was sent to Gatti by a Brigadist who had seen *Le Chant* in Seine-Saint-Denis. Although he had finished rewriting his script, Gatti incorporated it in *Adam quoi* and it made its first appearance in Marseille on the stage of the Greek-style open-air theatre, La Sucrière. There, alongside the camp gibbet with its dangling noose reserved for ceremonial hangings, mainly of attempted escapees, and always to music by the camp orchestra, it stood for the spirit of RESISTANCE.

When planning the 'Présentation' of *Le Chant,* the two producers decided not to expect spectators to attend at a given site in the *département,* but to take their product instead to the very doorstep of the inhabitants of Seine-Saint-Denis and to group the fifteen 'chapters' on seven sites in the area. This was possible because, there being no plot to develop, *Le Chant* is not written in acts and scenes but

---

[5] See chapter 14, 'Primo Levi's Stage Version of *Se questo è un uomo*'.

in 'chapters' which are more suited to the Alphabets whose role is purely discursive. The sites were a school, a museum, a psychiatric hospital, two libraries and the University of Paris VIII. The 'Présentation' at each site lasted about an hour, and together with the transport of the spectators from site to site and a short break for refreshment it took ten hours in all.

> Nous voyons chaque jour un peu plus ce que nous aurions perdu à enfermer cette pièce dans un théâtre. D'autant que pour nous, le but n'est pas le spectaculaire, c'est cette appropriation. Les vagues successives d'appropriation.[6]

Le Chant was Gatti's first theatre marathon. With its performance space restricted to a *département*, and the duration to ten hours, it could however offer only a meek apology for the Auschwitz-Birkenau camp which covered 2,500 square kilometres and lasted 1059 days.

With their choice of a school at Drancy for the opening 'chapter', the producers intended to bring the spectators up sharply against REALITY: the reality of a concentration camp on their own doorstep in France. The camp at Drancy had been opened in 1941 for French political prisoners, but by 1944 it had taken in prisoners of every category, finally becoming 'l'anti-chambre d'Auschwitz' and of Sobibor. By presenting the text in institutions as different as a school and a psychiatric hospital, the producers sought to enlighten spectators and 'actors' alike – the 'actors' were for the most part local volunteers – on the full significance of what was being performed and said. The matter of debasement of language in the camps was also broached. To take as an example the word *alphabétisation*, the official term used by the infamous Dr Mengele and his fellow-doctors for children being 'selected' for 'treatment' in the camp hospital. Its real meaning was 'le meurtre

---

6   'Each day we see more clearly what we would have lost by confining this play within a theatre's walls, especially as, for us, the aim is not in the theatrical element but in the "appropriations", in the successive waves of appropriations.'

(File: *Le Chant d'amour*, 'Parler d'Auschwitz' by S. Gatti and M. Séonnet, 12 January 1993)

sur la table de dissection . . . Les Alphabétiseurs ont découpé, charcuté, trituré, pour trouver de quoi écrire sur l'Homme Nouveau. Aux pieds de la table de dissection, le foie, les entrailles, les poumons dans les baquets.'[7]

What went on *in* the camps is covered up by this 'altération' of the language – this linguistic 'silence'. Silence of another kind hung over the tragic events of 1943 at the Gare d'Arenc, in the Marseille dockland, when 804 Jews living in the Panier district were rounded up during the night of 23–24 July and dispatched from that station to the extermination camp of Sobibor. At the Gare d'Arenc, Gatti noted the existence of a plaque commemorating the death of Railway Resistance fighters and the absence of any plaque commemorating the fate of 804 Jews. These had neither name nor camp registration number as they did not go through the 'Selection' parade but were marched from the station straight into the gas chamber. They were 'merchandise' – in camp parlance, *viande gazée*. Gatti was not prepared, even fifty years on, to let these 804 Jews be just 'smoke emitted from the chimney of a camp crematorium'. They had been human beings with names and addresses. Serge Klarsfeld's timely discovery in the Marseille police archives of their names and addresses provided Gatti with the opportunity to give them some sort of physical presence by setting eighty of his *stagiaires* (his 'actors') the task of hunting down the date and place of birth of each of the 804, and any other relevant detail. This meant visits to the Panier district, destroyed on Hitler's orders to 'nettoyer ce cloaque de l'Europe'[8] but since rebuilt. It meant also the writing of 804 letters to the newly found addresses (of these 405 were returned by the postal service marked 'unknown at this address', 'no street of this name'). One reply only was received. It was from a relative born three months before the police raid. It said 'Il y a quelques années tout le monde se souvenait. C'était la mémoire du vécu. Il aurait fallu la remplacer par la mémoire de l'appris. Ton travail est important. Il fait de toi un messager

---

[7] 'murder on the dissecting table . . . The Alphabetizers cut up, butchered, ground to powder, to discover what was needed to create (écrire) the New Man. At the foot of the dissecting table, buckets containing the liver, entrails, lungs.' (File: *Adam quoi?*, 'chapter' *L'Oiseau*)

[8] 'clean up this European sewer' (*L'Humanité*, 31 July 1993).

pour les autres.'[9] The letters were all put on view in the EXPOSITION set up by Stéphane to parallel his father's text, in the huge premises long since abandoned of the Seita tobacco company in the Friche Belle de Mai behind the Gare Saint-Charles. His aim, Stéphane said, was that 'la ville [de Marseille] certifie la disparition de ces personnes. Qu'elle contresigne le constat.'[10]

For *Adam quoi* the Panier district was the home port of the dramatist Gatti, his *lieu-écriture*. Everything in this second play on Auschwitz, even to the poster advertising the performance, is tied to what happened there. In the centre of the poster was an owl designed by Stéphane: the owl of Pallas-Athena, who gave the gift of writing to man, was the emblem of Gatti's initiative. The owl also announced the final destination of the 804 Jews, Sobibor – Sobibor, set as it was, in the 'Forest of the Owls'; and it was the owls of the forest which, as Gatti remarked, were the sole witnesses of the fate of the 804 Jews, all of whose names were printed on the poster round the owl emblem.

The style of presentation of *Adam quoi* (26–31 July 1993), Gatti's second theatre marathon, followed the pattern set by *Le Chant* but was more extensive and more elaborate. Each performance extended over two days – I was there too – from 1.30 p.m. to 1 a.m. on the first day and from 5 p.m. to 1 a.m. on the second day. Three performances in all were given. Of the fourteen self-contained 'chapters' eight were presented in sites in the city, each indicated by a plaster-cast owl made for the event by the civic workshop, Lieux Publics, where also one 'chapter' was presented. The rest were put on in the Friche in areas marked off by curtaining. Tickets cost 150 francs for the two days and included a substantial meal, served between the presentation of two 'chapters' on trestle tables set up in a large unused space under the roofing of one of the buildings of the Friche. A camp stool issued with each ticket was for use on sites where there was no seating. At other times it was stored in the bus which ferried the spectators from site to

---

[9] 'A few years ago everyone remembered. It was a living memory. It should have been replaced by a learned memory. Your work is important. It makes of you a messenger for the others.'

[10] 'the town should certify the disappearance of these persons and should countersign the affidavit' (*L'Humanité*, 22 July 1993).

site. During the transit a video was shown of a *stagiaire* hunting down at the Gare d'Arenc or elsewhere the information requested by Gatti on the 804 Jews.

For the opening scene of *Adam quoi?* the spectators were seated on their stools in the vast high-walled enclosure of the Friche under the blazing sun. In the background, rusty railway lines and dilapidated wood freight wagons inevitably conjured up a picture of the deportation of the 804 Jews from the Gare d'Arenc fifty years before. In the foreground a huge star of David painted in white on the concrete-covered ground was the 'stage' on which the Alphabets sang a full-throated tribute to a companion of Gatti's, captured in the *maquis* like him then deported without trace. Their song was accompanied by the expressive *gestuelle*, or gesture, of the kung fu, and was the only scenic language used by Gatti in the Auschwitz play. When his *'porteurs de paroles'*, the Alphabets, had something to say he required them to say it with their bodies as well as with their words, hence his recourse to the rigid discipline of kung fu. An explanatory stop-off was arranged by him at the Alhambra cinema to show a short film of the *stagiaires* at their daily two-hour training in kung fu.

I have space to comment only on the first and last of the 'chapters' of *Adam quoi?*. Taken together, they ask and answer what must be the main question raised by the Holocaust for a creative artist.

The first port of call on the theatrical circuit was the Ecole Yavné, which is linked with another school, la Rose, not in the Panier district. The extended title of the stop mentioning 'les enfants de la Rose qui ne sont pas revenus d'Auschwitz' explains the link: they were among the million-and-a-half Jewish children who had 'gone up in smoke' during the Holocaust and whom, even today, Gatti cannot dismiss from his mind. The chapter is centred on a doll separated from its loving owner, despite the yellow star she had sewn on its chest to be sure of having it with her for ever: 'on asphyxie aussi les poupées', wrote Gatti quoting Charlotte Delbo. Gatti was passionate in his demands for such a doll to be set up somewhere in Marseille for all to see, so the doll became the centrepiece of the setting he devised for this 'chapter': it proved to be the most telling, the most moving of all.

The spectators seated on their stools, this time in a garden under the shade of the trees, were confronted by the school's façade, of which

25. *Adam quoi?* The Ecole Yavne, first stop on the theatrical circuit, the 'crucified' rag-doll amid banners bearing the names of some million-and-a-half Jewish children sent to the gas chambers, with Alphabet/actors in the foreground.

the central windows were obscured by a monumental circle bearing cabalistic signs. At its centre was an equally monumental Star of David, on which was crucified a stuffed rag-doll six metres tall, with a big yellow star on its chest, and its arms and legs spread out as in Leonardo da Vinci's drawing *Human Proportions*. The windows on each side of the doll were covered with banners bearing letters of the alphabet, later to become names – Tordjman René, nine months old; Blumfeld Mireille, four years old. On the raised terrace where the action took place, the windows and doors were sealed with large sheets of white paper with black lettering in Hebrew, through which the Alphabets had to burst to enter the stage and engage in their dramatic discussions, described as 'ressemblant à un commentaire infini, tissé par des talmudistes qui auraient vingt ans et parleraient avec l'accent des cités de Marseille'.[11] One of the themes discussed was the

---

[11] 'resembling an unending commentary woven by Talmudists who would be twenty years of age and would be speaking with Marseille accents' (*Libération*, 30 July 1993).

possibility or not of music in the camps, given the unspeakable horrors witnessed there. This provides the link with the final 'chapter' of the itinerant spectacle *Adam quoi?* entitled 'Lorsque les livres brûlés répondent à Adorno', in which Gatti replies to the German philosopher Theodor Adorno's contention that 'after Auschwitz all culture is filth', quoted already in the Ecole Yavné sequence by a Lecteur d'Alphabet with his added comment, 'Et nous, sous les ordures, nous vomissons.'[12]

Not only does Gatti give his answer to Adorno's specific contention that after Auschwitz music no longer had the right to exist, he also joins in the contentious and long-continued argument about the role played by music in the camps and, in the Tousky Theatre, he does so with music and in a staging that was extraordinary. An orchestra, complete with fourteen music stands, arrived very ostentatiously and installed itself between the stage and auditorium which they faced just as ostentatiously. Soloists who performed under the conductor's baton were scattered in the auditorium, three or four speakers on one side, three or four professional singers on the other. In the balcony on both sides of the auditorium stood the Alphabets, ready to take part in the discussions. The spectators were seated *on* the stage with three Lecteurs d'Alphabets, also called Scribes and so, by definition, spectators like the rest. Behind them loomed six large disjointed panels of a cabalistic version by Stéphane of Leonardo da Vinci's *Man*, as it was featured on the programme of *Adam quoi?* with the 'chapter' titles and the sites of its performance signalled round the body. The fourteen music stands, the pride of the orchestra, had been inherited by Auschwitz-Birkenau from the show camp at Theresienstadt after the disappearance of the orchestra itself, unexplained but understood, just like that of the uncomfortably notable figures, deported to the 'luxury' camp to be 'allowed to die in comfort', no questions asked. The conductor of the Marseille orchestra, Jean-Paul Olive, who also composed the oratorio they were about to play, took up his baton with a significant gesture and, facing the spectators on stage declared: 'The *Orchestra* is the reply to Adorno' – and for Gatti also the reply to the 'unspeakable' – *l'Innommable* – AUSCHWITZ.

---

[12] 'And we, under the filth, we vomit.'

26. *Adam quoi?* The final scene, at the Tousky Theatre. Photo taken from backstage, showing the auditorium reserved for the Alphabets and Soloists; in front the orchestra, with its conductor facing the audience on stage, give to music Gatti's answer to Adorno on the *need* for culture after Auschwitz.

Many were the texts Gatti had read on Auschwitz. Of them he had said:

> Si une écriture ne peut répondre au camp, cette écriture n'a pas
> de sens – elle n'est pas écriture . . . Si des mots ne peuvent
> répondre au silence d'Auschwitz, ils perdent leur statut de
> mots . . . (et les lettres du mot Auschwitz signalent la mort
> du langage car son silence arrête le jeu des correspondances
> possibles – et de ce qui en fonde et le sens et la responsabilité).[13]

Several texts had, however, told of deportees who, knowing they were on their way to the gas chamber, had burst into song. Gatti's 'commentary' on one of these occasions ended with the words

> Et ils chantent. Auschwitz devient chant . . . Pendant plusieurs
> secondes (peut-être une minute) Auschwitz a cessé d'exister.[14]

---

[13] If writing cannot recall the reality of the camp, it is meaningless – it is not writing at all . . . If words can give no answer to the silence of Auschwitz, they lose their standing as words . . . (and the letters of the word Auschwitz sign the death of language because its silence puts a stop to the interplay of possible correspondences – the root of both meaning and responsibility).

      (File: *Kepler, Le Langage nécessaire,* at La Laiterie, Strasbourg, 1995, article by H. Châtelain, p. 6)

[14] And they sing. Auschwitz becomes song. For a few seconds (a minute perhaps) Auschwitz ceased to exist.

      (*Le Chant d'amour des alphabets d'Auschwitz,* in Armand Gatti, *Œuvres théâtrales* (Paris: Verdier, 1991), vol. III, p. 1036)

13 Charlotte Delbo: theatre as a means of survival

CLAUDE SCHUMACHER

I first met Charlotte Delbo in August 1974.[1] A French theatre publisher, Pierre-Jean Oswald (who was in dire financial straits) was selling his stock at knock-down prices. Among the thirty titles I ordered was *Qui rapportera ces paroles?* This *tragédie en trois actes*, set in a nameless extermination camp, is the most powerful theatrical text that I have ever read. And, on a very trivial level, it was a godsend for a theatre director working in a university drama department: it has a cast of twenty-three women! But the aesthetic, moral and linguistic problems raised by the play needed time to be properly addressed, and it was not possible to rush into production. Fortunately, another of Delbo's exceptional plays, *La Sentence*, just as dramatically powerful, but in a less daunting way, allowed me to stage my first Delbo play. *La Sentence* presents the plight of Basque militants under the Franco dictatorship (Burgos trial, 1970) from the point of view of the prisoners' womenfolk – girlfriends, wives, mothers, sisters. The production was shown at the Edinburgh Fringe Festival in 1974. Madame Delbo kindly joined us for the last rehearsals and the run of the play – it marked the beginning of

[1] Charlotte Delbo was born 10 August 1913 at Vigneux-sur-Seine, Seine-et-Oise – she died 1 March 1985 in Paris. She joined the Young Communists in 1932, where she met her future husband, Georges Dudach. They married in 1934. During the thirties, Charlotte Delbo worked with Louis Jouvet as literary assistant and administrator. She left France to tour South America with Jouvet's company in May 1941; returned from Rio de Janeiro on 15 November 1941, and became active in the Resistance. She was arrested, with Georges Dudach, on 2 March 1942 in the rue Molière, close to the Comédie-Française, and both were incarcerated in La Santé prison, in Paris. See following main text for the rest of the chronology.

an exceptional friendship and artistic collaboration, which lasted until Charlotte Delbo's death in 1985. After *La Sentence*, I staged *Qui rapportera ces paroles?* (*Who Will Carry the Word?*; 1978), *Une scène jouée dans la mémoire* (1980; unpublished) and *Kalavrita des mille Antigone* (1982).

Charlotte Delbo and her husband Georges Dudach were arrested for acts of Resistance on 2 March 1942. Dudach was shot as a hostage on 23 May at the Mont-Valérien. Charlotte Delbo was transferred to Romainville (a transit camp) on 24 August and deported to the Auschwitz-Birkenau extermination camp from Compiègne on 24 January 1943, in a transport of 230 women. She was liberated on 23 April 1945 by the Swedish Red Cross and returned to France in June 1945.[2]

What makes Madame Charlotte Delbo's destiny particularly remarkable is that as soon as she reached the camp, she declared her will to survive and to come back among us in order to bear witness to the horror and the atrocity she endured and saw at Auschwitz-Birkenau. To a journalist, she declared, 'Quand je suis rentrée du camp, j'ai voulu témoigner. Il fallait que quelqu'un rapporte les paroles, les gestes, les agonies d'Auschwitz.'[3] She always knew that her testimony would use the language of poetry and, more precisely, that of the purest tragedy: 'Chacun témoigne avec ses armes . . . Je considère le langage de la poésie comme le plus efficace – car il remue le lecteur au plus secret de lui-même – et le plus dangereux pour les ennemis qu'il combat.'[4] She concludes: 'Je me sers de la littérature comme d'une arme, car la menace m'apparaît trop grande.'[5]

[2] On her return from Auschwitz, Charlotte Delbo resumed her work with Jouvet, at the Théâtre de l'Athénée, from September 1945 to 7 April 1947, when she accepted an appointment to work for UNESCO in Geneva.

[3] François Bott, 'Entretien avec Charlotte Delbo: "Je me sers de la littérature comme d'une arme" ', *Le Monde*, 20 June 1975. 'When I came back from the concentration camp, I felt the urge to testify. The words, the gestures, the agonies of Auschwitz needed to be told.'

[4] Ibid. 'We all testify with our own weapons . . . I consider the language of poetry as the most effective – because it stirs the reader [and, or course, the spectator] deep down in their soul – and as such, it is the most dangerous weapon against the enemies it fights.'

[5] Ibid. 'I use literature like a weapon, because the danger is so great.'

27.   **Charlotte Delbo**, *Qui rapportera ces paroles?* Dumfries, 1978. Director
Claude Schumacher.

Charlotte Delbo has written five plays inspired by Auschwitz.
These are, in the chronological order of history: *Une scène jouée dans
la mémoire*; *Les Hommes*; *Qui rapportera ces paroles?*; *Et toi, comment as-tu fait?*, *Ceux qui avaient choisi*; *Kalavrita des mille Antigone*. Only two texts are published: *Qui rapportera ces paroles?* ('scenes
of Auschwitz') and *Kalavrita* (a dramatic poem which describes an
atrocity carried out on 13 December 1943 in the Peloponnese by the
retreating Nazi armies).

Les Hommes

The text that presently interests us is *Les Hommes (The Men)*. Written
during the summer of 1978, the play, which bears witness to Charlotte
Delbo's fierce determination to survive both intellectually and spiritually, a determination that took hold of her from the first moment of
her captivity, recounts an episode of Delbo's life as a prisoner *before*
deportation. It is always dangerous to confuse author and creation when
analysing a work of fiction, in this instance author and character, or –
more precisely – Charlotte Delbo and her principal character, Françoise.
But here we can safely assert that Françoise, present in all the 'Auschwitz

plays', is clearly the writer's double and speaks on Charlotte Delbo's behalf. The plays are essentially autobiographical while retaining some degree of 'objective reality' (in the tradition of *The Persians*, whose author, Aeschylus, Charlotte Delbo particularly admired).

In the 1930s Madame Delbo worked closely with Louis Jouvet, and the theatre was her *raison d'être*. In an interview with Madeleine Chapsal in 1966 – from which I shall quote freely – she said: 'J'avais été la secrétaire de Jouvet. Je connaissais des pièces par cœur, les jeux de scène, les éclairages. Je pouvais les réciter en racontant le jeu des acteurs. Je le faisais pour celles qui étaient groupées tout près de moi [i.e., at Romainville and during deportation].'[6] In *Qui rapportera ces paroles?* one of the deportees, Renée tells a fellow-prisoner who is faltering: 'Redresse-toi, Marie. Si nous trouvons un petit coin sec pour nous asseoir pendant la soupe, nous demanderons à Françoise de nous emmener au théâtre. Quel programme lui demanderons-nous? Elle raconte bien et elle fait les voix. On croirait entendre les acteurs.'[7]

But before arriving at Auschwitz, Françoise does more than tell stories: she puts on a show. At the Romainville fortress, between August 1942 and January 1943, where men and women await deportation (but where they are, of course, kept apart), the anxiety of the women is made worse by the fact that – without any warning – their companion might be shot as a hostage. To take their minds off this danger, Françoise, whose husband had already been executed, decides to stage *Un Caprice (Caprice)*, Alfred de Musset's charming and innocent comedy.[8] The first act of *Les Hommes* shows the women getting ready

---

6 Madeleine Chapsal, 'Rien que des femmes', in *L'Express*, 14–20 February 1966: 'I had been Jouvet's secretary. I knew entire plays by heart, including stage directions and lighting effects. I could recite plays and describe the acting, and this I did for the women who were gathered around me.'

7 *Qui rapportera ces paroles?*, p. 53, my translation: 'Straighten yourself up, Marie. If we can find a dry corner to sit while we eat our soup, we'll ask Françoise to take us to the theatre. What shall she perform tonight? She is so good at telling stories and she can do the voices too. One can almost hear the actors.'

8 See Alfred de Musset, *Musset: Five Plays* (London: Methuen World Classics, 1995).

to stage a performance in a manner which is far from amateurish. By a fortunate coincidence, most of the trades needed to put on a show happen to be found among the prisoners: Claire, who makes the costumes, used to work as seamstress for Lanvin; Louise is a hairdresser; Madeleine loves drawing; the first trade of 'Grandmother' Yvonne was that of *plumassière*, a maker of feathered ornaments; and, finally, there is Renée, a talented Jill-of-all-trades, who knows how to use a hammer and is not afraid to improvise a lighting system. They are all busy putting on a romantic play in order to try and forget the horror of the situation. Madeleine, the set designer, expresses superficial optimism when she justifies, to herself and her friends, the choice of play:

> Il faut une pièce qui rompe avec notre vie ici et notre vie avant; quand nous étions ces ombres fugitives qui auraient voulu être cloutées d'yeux perçants tout autour de la tête pour dépister les filatures, quand nous n'étions que tension et inquiétude, et résolution. Quelque chose de léger, 'd'ailleurs'. Des personnages comme il n'en existe plus de nos jours. Quelque chose de tellement différent, que nous plongions dans une autre vie, une autre époque.[9]

Madeleine's stage design incorporates cut-out birds, because, as she says, 'c'est toujours beau, les oiseaux, leurs ailes large ouvertes. C'est la liberté' (p. 16).[10] Does Madeleine want to remind us of the seagull which decorated the stage curtain in Stanislavsky's theatre? Perhaps not. But Charlotte Delbo undoubtedly manages to combine in a striking metaphor both the image of the enslavement of the prisoners to their Nazi captors and the image of the existential victim of Chekhov

---

[9] We need a play which will provide a complete contrast to our life here and our life before when we were fleeting shadows who wished to have their heads studded with piercing eyes so as to detect whoever was tailing us; when we were nothing but restlessness, worry and determination. We need something fluffy, something from 'elsewhere'. Characters the like of which you cannot find nowadays. Something so different that we shall lose ourselves in another life, in another time.

> (my translation, from original typescript)

[10] 'birds are always beautiful with their large open wings. They symbolize freedom.'

– which has become such a powerful symbol of art (and not only of theatre art).

Caprice is to be produced with painstaking attention to detail, since Françoise (like Charlotte Delbo, and like her mentor, Louis Jouvet) is a very meticulous director who has the greatest respect for the author and his text. To Cécile, who makes the costumes and who wants to change the text because she cannot find the fabric prescribed by Musset for Madame de Léry's costume, Françoise replies: 'On n'a pas droit de couper une réplique' (p. 29).[11] To make absolutely sure that everyone understands the lesson, she adds: 'Au théâtre, on est exigeant. On ne fait pas n'importe quoi' (p. 30).[12] Although she congratulates Mounette (who plays Mathilde) after the performance, she nevertheless points out to her that at one point she 'almost' made a mistake: 'Tu nous as presque mangé une réplique, mais tu t'es rattrapée à temps' (p. 49).[13]

The day of the performance arrives at last. Everything is ready. Everything, including the poster announcing the show. Everything, except the audience's enthusiasm. Everything, except that there are days when one does not feel at all like going to the theatre, and there are days when acting seems the most futile pastime in the world. Everything is ready: the actresses are all dressed and all made up; the show is about to start and the curtain is about to open to reveal '*un décor si merveilleux que l'assistance l'applaudira*' (p. 41).[14] The performance, however, starts by a dramatic turn of events which has nothing to do with Musset. A soldier (German, of course), the only man to appear on stage, enters followed by Claire, who assumes the role of camp leader, and he calls out a few names: Marguerite, Jeanne, Reine, Madeleine. These women are invited to go down to the yard to say their farewells to their men who are 'leaving' (p. 38). Nothing is said, but they all understand. Moving away from the group, Françoise whispers: 'L'après-midi. Moi, c'était le matin. Il faisait à peine jour' (p. 38).[15] Reine and Madeleine are not away for long, though. They were given no time at all

[11] 'No one has the right to cut out lines.'
[12] 'Theatre is very demanding. It does not allow for shoddy work.'
[13] 'You almost missed your cue, but you recovered just in time.'
[14] '*such a magnificent set that the audience will applaud*'.
[15] 'Afternoon. It was morning for me. The day had hardly broken.'

to say good-bye. When they return, *'droites, raides, elles vont à leur lit sans un mot'* (p. 40).[16] Reine quickly pulls herself together and urges them all to go on with the show.

> Camarades, il faut jouer la pièce. Se recroqueviller pour pleurer chacune dans son coin ne sert à rien. Les nuits seront toujours bien assez longues pour cela. Quand peut-on commencer?[17]

All enthusiasm has vanished and the spectators take their seats in silence. As in all traditional French theatre performances, Reine 'rolls' the nine short knocks and the three long knocks. She pulls the curtain open. Mounette/Mathilde is revealed busily embroidering a little red purse . . . and the performance begins with the applause of the audience. Not a single word of Musset's text will be spoken (what would be the point?). These are Charlotte Delbo's stage directions for the 'play-within-the-play':

> *Les actrices joueront sans parler. Elles mimeront* UN CAPRICE *sans émettre de son. Toutes sont enfermées en elles-mêmes. Cependant, on applaudira l'entrée de* GINA *[M. DE CHAVIGNY] et l'entrée d'*YVONNE *[MME DE LÉRY], seules interruptions aux monologues.* (p. 41)[18]

The first monologue is Madeleine's. She said good-bye to her eighteen-year-old brother and thinks of the distress her mother will feel when she learns of her son's death. Next comes Reine, who has just hugged her husband of twenty years and the father of her two sons for the last time. Finally there is Françoise, who painfully relives her own farewell scene: at the Santé prison, the day Paul was put to death.

The Men brilliantly illustrates the ambiguity of theatrical art in particular, and of the arts in general. In life's most difficult moments,

---

[16] *'upright and stiff, they go to their beds without a word'.*

[17] My friends, we must get on with the play. Now is not the time to hide in a corner and cry. That's what the long nights are for. How soon can we start?

[18] *The actresses act without uttering a word. They mime* A CAPRICE *without making a sound. They are withdrawn into themselves. But there is applause when* GINA [MONSIEUR DE CHAVIGNY] *and* YVONNE [MADAME DE LÉRY] *enter, the only interruptions to the monologues.*

nothing seems more pointless, more childish than playing a fictional character, decking oneself out in glad rags, and saying words which have nothing at all to do with the real situation. Mounette, who plays Mathilde, is outraged when she comes off stage to learn that Bob, her Resistance companion, is one of the hostages. 'Et pendant ce temps-là,' she says, 'pendant ce temps, je me fardais, je m'habillais, je jouais mon rôle de petite dinde. Reine, pourquoi ne l'as-tu pas dit tout de suite?'[19]

> REINE: Tu as perdu deux heures de chagrin. Tu as tout le temps de te rattraper.
> MOUNETTE: Pourquoi ne pas l'avoir dit tout de suite . . .
> REINE: J'ai fait ce que Bob voulait. Il a dit: 'J'aime mieux partir en sachant qu'au moment même où je pars, elle ne pleure pas. Mounette dans la jolie toilette rose, avec des anglaises et des petits nœuds dans ses beaux cheveux, des mules dorées à ses petits pieds, souriante, comme lorsque nous nous sommes connus. C'est la dernière image d'elle que j'emporterai. Son sourire.' (p. 51)[20]

At first the prisoners had not intended to put on a play from the classical repertory. Their aim was not to escape from reality, but to immerse themselves in it completely. *The Men* opens very abruptly, by a peremptory question:

> REINE: Alors, Françoise, ça y est? Tu as fini?
> FRANÇOISE: Je n'ai pas commencé.[21]

---

[19] 'All the while, all the while this was happening I was putting on make-up; I was getting dressed; I was playing the role of a stupid little goose. Reine, why didn't you let me know right away?'

[20] REINE: You have lost two hours of grief. You have got all the time to make up for it.
MOUNETTE: Why did you not tell me as soon as you knew . . .
REINE: I did what Bob wanted me to do. He told me: 'I'd rather leave knowing that as I'm going she's not crying. Mounette, in her pretty pink dress, ringlets and little ribbons in her beautiful hair, golden shoes on her tiny feet, smiling as she did when we first met. Her smile will be the last picture of her that I will take with me. Her smile.'

[21] REINE: Well then, Françoise, is it done? Have you finished?
FRANÇOISE: It's not even started.

What has Françoise not started? What has she not finished? She has not written the first line of the play that she had promised she would write and direct; the play that was to be the pretext of the show to be put on by the prisoners of the fortress. And yet, as Madeleine says, 'l'idée enthousiasmait tout le monde', and Françoise is such a good storyteller that Reine 'voyait déjà la pièce, les personnages qui entraient, parlaient, criaient, tombaient' (p. 1).[22] Yet, Françoise not only feels that she cannot write anything under these circumstances, but – in a bout of despair – she declares, 'Je ne pourrai plus jamais écrire. Plus jamais. Cela paraît si vain, si en dehors de la vérité. À côté, comme tout le reste, d'ailleurs' (p. 9).[23]

We learn from Cécile (the wardrobe mistress for *Un Caprice*) what the original idea was, because she does not like it at all and roundly criticizes it:

> Mettre en scène notre situation présente: des femmes qui
> sont enfermées dans un fort en attendant d'être déportées,
> des femmes qui inventent mille ruses pour passer le temps et
> tricher avec le destin comme si on pouvait l'esquiver, qui font
> des efforts surhumains pour ne pas penser à la menace de
> mort qui pèse sur elles, sur leurs maris ou leurs frères . . . Des
> femmes enfermées dans une aile de ce fort et qui sont toujours
> sur le qui-vive, qui font le guet par n'importe quelle fente
> dans l'espoir d'apercevoir les hommes qui sont enfermés dans
> l'aile voisine, qui griffonnent sans cesse des petits mots qu'elles
> essaient de leur faire passer . . . Des hommes qui se sont battus
> et qui maintenant attendent que leur vie soit tranchée . . .
> Non, cela ne faisait pas une pièce pour nous en ce moment,
> même en déplaçant l'action dans l'antiquité . . . Aucune
> n'aurait pu jouer son propre rôle. C'était trop dur.[24]

---

[22] 'everyone was so very enthusiastic', and Françoise is such a good storyteller that Reine 'could already see the play with the characters entering, speaking, screaming and falling.'

[23] 'Never again will I be able to write anything. Never again. It seems so vain, so far from the truth. It's all so false, like everything else.'

[24] To stage our predicament: women locked up in a fortress, waiting to be deported, women who invent hundreds of ways to pass the time, to cheat fate as if escape were possible, women who make superhuman

Françoise replies:

> C'est justement la raison pour laquelle je ne peux pas l'écrire. Le jouer, ç'aurait été prendre une conscience si aiguë de la réalité que personne ne l'aurait supporté. Ni les actrices, ni les spectatrices. (p. 5)[25]

The play that Françoise did not have the courage to write in Romainville was indeed written by Charlotte Delbo in Cyprus thirty-six years later, during the summer of 1978. She was able to write it because she survived, and she survived because of the seething rage inside her which gave her the will and the strength to come back and to testify. It was unthinkable that the last word should go to the barbarians.

Earlier I mentioned that I had no doubt about identifying Françoise with Charlotte Delbo, and I would like to return to this point. Charlotte Delbo admits that when she arrived at Auschwitz she had been tempted by the idea of taking her own life, and that she talked about suicide with her fellow prisoners. She changed her mind thanks to Josée Alonso.[26] One evening, a few days after their arrival, Josée

---

efforts to avoid thinking about the death threat they, or their husbands, or their brothers, are under . . . Women, locked up in a fortress, always on edge, spying through every possible opening in the hope of catching a glimpse of the men locked up in another wing. Women who forever try to send them scribbled notes . . . Men who have fought and who now wait for their life to be taken away . . . No, this was not a suitable scenario, not now, even if the action had been set in Antiquity . . . Not one of us could have played her own role. It was too hard.

[25] That's precisely why I can't write it. Playing our own roles would have made us so acutely aware of the terrible reality of our situation that no one could have endured it. Neither the actresses, nor the spectators.

[26] Born 20 August 1910, Maria Alonso (known as Josée) was a nurse at the Tenon hospital in Paris at the outbreak of war. She worked underground to look after wounded Resistance fighters. She was arrested a first time in October 1941, but got released; arrested a second time in November, she was sent to the fort de Romainville on 1 August 1942, where she became 'camp leader', like Claire in *Les Hommes*. In Auschwitz the kapos viciously assaulted her, and Josée died soon after arrival (on 14 or 15 February 1943). See *Le Convoi du 24 janvier* (Paris: Editions de Minuit, 1965), pp. 28–31.

called Charlotte over to her corner of the hut (Madame Delbo recounts the event to Madeleine Chapsal):

'– Viens un peu par ici, j'ai quelque chose à te dire.' Je la suis. '– Qu'est-ce que j'entends? Il paraît que tu veux te pendre?' C'était très facile à imaginer, il y avait les bois superposés et les poutres du toit, apparentes; on n'avait qu'à déchirer sa robe. '– Eh bien, oui, et quoi?' '– Tu n'as pas le droit.' '– Comment je n'ai pas le droit? C'est le dernier droit qui me reste!' '– Une communiste n'a pas le droit de se suicider!' '– Rengaine tes slogans, c'est bien le moment de sortir tes proverbes.' Je me disais: '– Qu'est-ce qu'elle me chante? On est là et voilà ce qu'elle vient me dire.'[27]

This exchange is repeated almost word for word in the opening dialogue between Françoise and Claire in *Qui rapportera ces paroles?*:

CLAIRE: Viens par ici, toi, j'ai à te parler. Qu'est-ce que j'ai entendu dire?
FRANÇOISE: Qu'est-ce que tu as entendu dire?
CLAIRE: Que tu voulais te suicider?
FRANÇOISE: Oui. Eh! bien?
CLAIRE: Eh! bien, tu n'en as pas le droit.
FRANÇOISE: Oh! assez, Claire. Laisse tes formules. Ici, elles n'ont plus cours. C'est le seul droit qui me reste, le seul choix. Le dernier acte libre. (p. 12)[28]

---

27 [J. A.] '– Come here a minute, I have something to tell you.' I follow her. [J. A.] '– What's this I hear? They tell me that you want to hang yourself?' This was not difficult to imagine. There were the bunk-beds and the beams of the roof; one only had to tear up one's dress. [C. D.] '– Well, yes. What about it?' [J. A.] '– You don't have the right.' [C. D.] '– What do you mean, I don't have the right? It's the only right I've left!' [J. A.] '– A Communist does not have the right to take her own life!' [C. D.] '– Don't bother, I don't want to hear this nonsense.' I told myself: 'What the hell is she going on about? Here we are, and that's what she's telling me!'

(*L'Express*, 14–20 February 1966)

28 CLAIRE: Come here, you. I want a word with you. What's this I've heard?
FRANÇOISE: What did you hear?
CLAIRE: That you wanted to kill yourself?

In Auschwitz, Josée found the right words to galvanize Charlotte and to
bring back her courage:

> Il y a des petites jeunes sur qui tu as de l'influence ([Mme Delbo
> adds:] celles à qui j'enseignais la littérature au fort de
> Romainville), qui te suivent, pour qui tu es un exemple, imagine
> qu'il n'y en ait qu'une seule qui doive rentrer et que, suivant ton
> exemple, elle se suicide? Tu n'en as pas le droit.[29]

And she concludes: 'Eh bien! j'ai trouvé ça convaincant! Je me suis dit:
"Bon, allons-y." Josée Alonso est morte peu après.'[30] As we know only
too well, very few came back from the death camps. Even rarer are those
who had within themselves the desire, the strength or the will to speak
about it, the heroic courage to relive their agony so that all this suffering might not be forgotten by the rest of the world. If some deportees are
of the opinion that all art forms inspired by the Holocaust are a form of
sacrilege, Charlotte Delbo was certainly not one of them:

> Certains ont dit que la déportation ne pouvait pas entrer dans la
> littérature, que c'était trop terrible, que l'on n'avait pas le droit
> d'y toucher . . . Dire ça, c'est diminuer la littérature, je crois
> qu'elle est assez grande pour tout englober. Un écrivain doit
> écrire sur ce qui le touche. J'y suis allée, pourquoi n'aurais-je pas
> le droit d'écrire là-dessus ce que j'ai envie d'écrire? Il n'y a pas de

---

FRANÇOISE: Yes. So what?
CLAIRE: Well, you don't have the right.
FRANÇOISE: Oh, stop it, Claire! Forget your slogans. They're no good
here. It's the only right, the only choice that's left. The last act of
freedom.

29 (*L'Express*, 14–20 February 1966) You have a great influence on the
younger prisoners (those to whom I taught literature at the
Romainville fortress), who follow your lead and for whom you are a
role model. Imagine that only one of them should go back and that she
takes her own life to follow your example? You cannot do it. You don't
have the right.

30 Ibid. 'Well, she convinced me! I said to myself: "All right, let's do it."
Josée Alonso died soon afterwards.'

mots pour le dire. Eh bien! vous n'avez qu'à en trouver – rien ne doit échapper au langage.[31]

'Rien ne doit échapper au langage.' Everything can and *must* be put into words. By her work Charlotte Delbo proves that language should never be surrendered to the enemy and that it can be the most effective means of survival.

In conclusion, I would like to quote a wonderful poem, a wonderful celebration of life: Charlotte Delbo learnt in Auschwitz that 'qu'il ne fallait pas laisser filer son être', 'that one should never let one's being escape', and she, certainly, never let it go:

Je vous en supplie	I beg of you
faites quelque chose	do something
apprenez un pas	learn a new step
une danse	a new dance
quelque chose qui vous justifie	something that justifies your existence
qui vous donne le droit	that gives you the right
d'être habillés de votre peau	to be clothed by your skin
de votre poil	by your hair
apprenez à marcher et à rire	learn to walk and laugh
parce que ce serait trop bête	because it would be too awful
à la fin	in the end
que tant soient morts	that so many should have died
et que vous viviez	and that you should live
sans rien faire de votre vie.	without doing anything with your life.[32]

[31] Some people have said that deportation has nothing to do with literature, because it was too awful, that no one had the right to touch it . . . This is to devalue literature, I believe it is strong enough to include everything. An author should write about things that move her. I was there, why shouldn't I be allowed to write what I feel like writing about it? There are no words to describe it? Well, let's invent them – nothing is beyond words. (Ibid.)

[32] Primo Levi's point of view is exactly the same as Charlotte Delbo's. See 'The Canto of Ulysses' in *If This Is A Man*, translated by Stuart Woolf (London: Abacus, 1996), pp. 115–21. See also chapter 14, by Helga Finter, in this book.

14 Primo Levi's stage version of
Se questo è un uomo

HELGA FINTER

Primo Levi's book on his Auschwitz experience – *Se questo è uomo*[1] – is not only one of the most widely read testimonies on the Shoah, it is also what Philip Roth called *'une œuvre d'art* about Auschwitz'.[2] Yet some critics regard the evident literary quality of the work as detracting from its value as testimony.[3] It will be readily admitted, however, that every type of narration is governed by structural constraints. The idea of non-mediated testimony, reduced to a naively faithful fiction, is similarly untenable.

Why is only art capable of conveying the experience of human limits? In his latest book, *L'Ecriture ou la vie*,[4] Jorge Semprun, a survivor from Buchenwald, provides some pertinent answers. Like many others before him,[5] and like Primo Levi himself, Semprun detects the crucial problem of Shoah testimony to lie not in the allegedly

---

[1] Primo Levi, *Se questo è un uomo* (Firenze: De Silva, 1947; Torino: Einaudi, 1958); also in *Opere*, vol. 1 (Torino: Einaudi Biblioteca dell' Orsa, 1987); translated by Stuart Woolf as *Survival in Auschwitz: The Nazi Assault on Humanity* (New York: Collier Books, 1961). Stage version, *Se questo è un uomo*. Versione drammatica di Pieralberto Marché e Primo Levi (Turin: Einaudi (collezione di teatro, 99), 13 October 1966).

[2] 'Philip Roth et Primo Levi', in *Lettre Internationale*, 15 (Winter 1987), pp. 25–31.

[3] See Lawrence L. Langer, 'Interpreting Survivor Testimony', in Berel Lang, ed., *Writing the Holocaust* (New York and London: Holmes and Meier, 1988), pp. 26–40.

[4] Jorge Semprun, *L'Ecriture ou la vie* (Paris: Gallimard, 1994).

[5] See Annette Wiervorka, 'Indicible ou inaudible? La déportation: premiers récits (1944–1947)', in *Parades*, 9–10 (1989), pp. 23–51.

unspeakable – *indicible* – nature of the event, but in the double barrier erected by the circumstances of reception: the primary obstacle is the 'inaudibility' of what is narrated. And this psychic deafness derives from the 'unlivable' – *invivable* – character of the experience. How are such barriers surmounted? This is not a problem of form, suggests Semprun, but a problem of articulation, of density – *densité* – of the *récit*. Only the artefact of a controlled narration will succeed in partially transmitting the truth of the testimony. Everything can be said, he affirms. The claim of the 'unspeakable' is only an alibi, or a sign of laziness. At the same time, he questions whether everything can really all be heard, can really all be imagined.[6] When a group of concentration camp prisoners discuss the possibility of communicating their experiences, they stress the necessity of art precisely for its power to overcome the deafness. Literary *écriture* is above all needed to transmit the essence of an experience which will not be exhausted in the description of the horror, but which aims to explore the human soul facing the horror of evil. One of the prisoners, a scholar from Strasbourg, remarks on the need for a new Dostoyevsky.[7]

Jorge Semprun raises a problem inherent in all verbal representation: the decoding of the signifier chain requires not only linguistic competence, but participation of the reader's cultural memory reinforced by his or her imaginary. This unconscious relationship between language and desire decides in fact what can be read or heard by each individual reader.[8]

The exploration of the human soul facing the horror of evil is what Levi's text shows us masterfully: the universe of concentration camps is analysed as the concretization, the acting out of an insane affect – which is in fact a *hate of desire*[9] – leading to the confinement of the *heterogeneous* – in Georges Bataille's terminology – to specific

---

[6] Semprun, *L'Ecriture*, pp. 23–4: 'seul l'artifice d'un récit maîtrisé parviendra à transmettre partiellement la vérité du témoignage'.

[7] Ibid., pp. 135–6.

[8] See Octave Mannoni, *Clefs pour l'imaginatire ou l'autre scène* (Paris: Editions du Seuil, 1969), pp. 34–74.

[9] See Daniel Sibony, 'L'affect ratial', in *Ecrits sur le racisme* (Paris: Christian Bourgois, 1988), pp. 22–72.

spaces: black holes in the homogeneity of an imaginary 'pure' nation. These places are ruled by a 'Law' of negativity usurping the name of law: its foundation and content is human *abjection*. Aiming to get rid of all heterogeneity and projecting it on to individual human subjects grouped according to imaginary pseudo-biological criteria, the social structures operative in this concentration camp universe tend to reduce its victims to embody what the so-called homogeneous group desires to eliminate, the *abject*.[10] In other words, a rigid difference is maintained between victimizers and victims and its price will be the violent indifferentiation process which leads to the elimination of what could threaten such an absurd fiction.

The difficulty of speaking and representing mechanisms of abjection and of hearing and receiving them lies in the fact that the abject and the heterogeneous play their own part in each psychogenesis. What we find abject may be an unconscious source not only of horror, but also of lust.[11] Literature and art, especially in the twentieth century, have always willingly explored this ambiguous territory where horror shades over into lust. But there is a decisive difference between the two kinds of exploration: in art and literature the artist or writer chooses to outline for himself or herself the ways of transgressing a recognized law, whereas the transgression is inflicted on concentration camp victims by a simulacrum of law, which is abjection itself and transforms civil and human law, operative in the civilized world, into the heterogeneous universe of the concentration camp. Reading or hearing its testimony in our civilized world creates a crucial problem of reception deriving from the fact that aspects are narrated which could appeal to the reader who may be unconsciously drawn to certain forms of abjection. All critique of the high violence level of television news can be understood as a recognition of this danger. In dealing with the Shoah and the problems of its representation, it will be necessary to

---

[10] See Helga Finter, '"E bello raccontare i guai passati": Primo Levi, Schriftsteller und Zeuge', in *Romanische Zeitschrift für Literaturgeschichte/Cahiers d'Histoire des Littératures Romanes*, 49 (1993), pp. 437–50.

[11] See the fundamental study on this problem by Julia Kristeva, *Pouvoirs de l'horreur. Essais sur l'abjection* (Paris: Editions du Seuil, 1980).

sider this aspect, because of its implications for the question of esentation.

Levi's *écriture* proposes an ethic of writing the Shoah crystallized in his style. The precise, non-metaphoric and clear language of his narration not only permits a quasi-ethnological analysis of the concentration camp universe, but also saves the memory of many of the men he met there from the indifferentiation into which the Nazis tried to thrust them, together with their death. This represents a counterpart to a narrative system of evaluation in keys of sympathy and antipathy which appeals to known values and affects. Primo Levi refuses complicity with evil as a basis of communication, which Georges Bataille detected in the literature of transgression,[12] and in this way he avoids the inherent possibility of a perverse voyeurism of suffering.

A similar function is performed by Levi's reference to the first part of Dante's *Divina commedia*, culminating in his *Canto di Ulisse*.[13] This chapter in Levi's work has been widely criticized for its literary nature. Yet the Dante intertext not only serves to recall a forgotten interpretation of the medieval Christian – Thomist – ethical system, on which Dante based his ideas; it also affords some insights into the logic of evil to which victims of Nazism were subjected. Recognizing, with Jean in the *Canto di Ulisse*, that the falsification of signs is the gravest of sins because it implies a falsification of the symbolic law, Levi points out that Nazi usurpation represents not merely a transgression but the negation of all Law. The specificity of the Shoah as a war machine against the people of the Law here finds an explanation.[14]

In the written text such a reading is the result of the combination of the narrator's voice with a sober presentation of episodes and scenes, guiding the imaginary staging of the reading act by raising an everyday memory to the level of the memory of a specific cultural representation of evil. But everything changes, if a book, giving place to an imaginary *mise en scène*, has to be represented on stage. The problem of overcom-

---

[12] Finter, '"E bello raccontare i guai passati"', pp. 441ff.

[13] See chapter 13, 'Charlotte Delbo: theatre as a means of survival'.

[14] Finter, '"E bello raccontare i guai passati"', pp. 444–9.

ing the psychic deafness noted earlier, while at the same time avoiding complicity with evil, changes into the question of what can be made audible and visible without giving into the perverse delectation of voyeurism. Can the experience of evil be fixed in audiovisual representations? What type of representation comes closest to communicating such experiences?

Here we risk losing ourselves in discussions on drama found in western thinking from the Bible to Plato, from Tertullian to St Augustine, from Calvin to Rousseau. Without entering into the vast field of what some may call anti-theatrical prejudice, we can nevertheless retain as pertinent some features of the psychological mechanism of theatre reception: its audiovisual reception implies the incantatory drive but also the scopic drive (Lacan), that is, the desire and the lust of audition and of gaze, implying an appeal to unconscious drives of destruction and indifferentiation, playing with the contradictions and the splitting of the subject activated in each spectator. In this way, cathartic, theatrical procedures help, under the protection of the representational frame, to discover the evil in oneself and to purify it by tears and sorrow. This idea may be unacceptable when it comes to the representation of the Shoah: there can be no relief here. On the other hand to claim unrepresentability for the Shoah comes dangerously close to rendering it sacred. Moreover, when confronted with traumatic events surpassing all imagination, human beings may need representation to soothe the unhealed wound, to affirm the will to live. If the written or oral testimony has to cope with the difficulty of being heard and imagined, which is also a way of *living* an imaginary event, how can the *unlivable* be shown on stage? What type of representation, what *ethic of representation*, can deal with what cannot have a repetition, what defies plausibility, the basis of all representation? Are there any theatrical forms appropriate for this task?[15]

The questions and problems outlined here are multiple and complex. Only partial answers can be given when we approach Primo Levi's stage version of his Auschwitz testimony. A paradigm of the problems posed by the investigation of the Shoah in dramatic form, this research

---

[15] All the chapters in this book offer varied and creative answers to these fundamental questions.

on the stage version of *Se questo è un uomo* will also give us the opportunity of presenting an almost unknown part of Primo Levi's work.

An unknown playwright

In the three-volume edition of Primo Levi's writings, the stage version of *Se questo è un uomo* is not included (although Ernesto Ferrero's chronology erroneously dates it from 1967, instead of 1966).[16] The stage version was preceded by two radio adaptations. The first, produced by Radio Canada in 1963, impressed Levi so favourably that he proposed his own version to the Italian Radio Broadcast (RAI).[17] This second adaptation, produced by Giorgio Bondini, was broadcast on 24 April 1964, on the occasion of the anniversary of Italy's liberation.[18] The stage version followed, written in collaboration with Pieralberto Marché, an actor who had taken part in the radio production. It was performed on 19 November 1966 by Turin's Teatro Stabile at the Teatro Carignano and received some months later the prize of the Instituto del Dramma Italiano for the most important new drama of the year.[19]

The context

To understand the importance of Primo Levi's production, it is useful to give a brief indication of how the Shoah was represented on stage in the early sixties and to sketch in the Italian theatrical context.

(1) In the early sixties several plays dealing with the Shoah and Nazism were written and staged: Max Frisch's *Andorra*, premièred at

---

[16] See Primo Levi, *Opere*, 3 vols. (Turin: Einaudi Biblioteca dell'Orsa, 1987, 1988, 1990), vol. 1, p. 51.

[17] Primo Levi, *If This Is A Man*, radio adaptation by John Wallet after the translation by Stuart Woolf, director John Reeves, CBC Radio-Network, 1962, 67 minutes. Primo Levi, *Se questo è un uomo. Racconto sceneggiato*, RAI, Turin, Sezione drammatica.

[18] See Gabriella Polli and Giorgio Calcagno, *Echi di una voce perduta. Incontri, interviste e conversazioni con Primo Levi* (Milan: Mursia 1992), pp. 26ff.

[19] Ibid., pp. 42–7. My special thanks go to Piero Ferrero and his collaborators of the Centro Studi Teatrali who generously helped me to find the material necessary to my research.

the Züricher Schauspielhaus (1961); Armand Gatti's, *La Deuxième Existence du camp de Tatenberg* (1962), directed in Lyon by Roger Planchon, and *Chroniques d'une planète provisoire* (1963), directed by Gatti himself in Toulon; Erwin Piscator directed *Der Stellvertreter* (*The Representative/The Deputy*) by Rolf Hochhuth, followed by Peter Brook in London (both 1963); in 1964 Peter Palitzsch directed Martin Walser's *Der schwarze Schwan* (*The Black Swan*) at Stuttgart and in 1965 different European theatres premièred simultaneously Peter Weiss's *Die Ermittlung* (*The Investigation*). For Piscator's production the Italian composer Luigi Nono wrote music which he synthesized a year later into *Ricorda che ti hanno fatto a Auschwitz* (*Remember What They Did To You In Auschwitz*), performed for the first time on 17 March 1967. With Nono we come to the musical and operatic representation of concentration camp experiences. In his opera *Intolleranza 1960*, first staged in Venice in 1961, the concentration camps in Algeria are evoked in the same pregnant way as the suffering and dignity of death candidates in the *Canto sospeso* of 1955–6. Together with Weiss's *Ermittlung*, subtitled *Oratorium in 11 Gesängen*, Nono's choir pieces provide a model for dealing with the representation of events and themes linked to the Shoah. The music speaks for the affects: a painful, viscerally felt music without driving rhythm, reaching the frontier of scream, sheer carnal sound, electronically transformed and the words, freed of any embodied warmth and timbre, represent what is unimaginable.

In Italy Weiss's *Oratorio* was directed by Virginio Puecher at Milan's Piccolo Theatre in early spring 1967; the Italian translation had been published, at the same time as Primo Levi's Turin stage production, in November 1966.

(Another generic, earlier model for the representation of concentration camp experience is Leo Janacek's posthumous opera, *Z mrtvého domu* (*From the House of the Dead*), Dostoyevsky's autobiographical account of his Siberian camp experience in Tsarist Russia. First staged in Brno in 1930, it had splendid productions at the Edinburgh Fringe Festival in 1964, at Sadler's Wells in 1965 and at La Scala in 1966/7.)

(2) Apart from the fact that Primo Levi lived in Turin, the production of his play in that city owes much to the special situation in which the local theatre found itself at the time. A few years prior to the congress of Ivrea in 1967, where a group of avant-garde artists outlined

the structures of a 'new' Italian theatre,[20] some members of the Teatri Stabili had tried to establish for themselves a renewed dramaturgy and a more imaginative programme. Among them was the director of the Teatro Carignano, Gianfranco De Bosio, well known for his student productions in Padova and his rediscovery of Ruzzante for the stage. As director in Turin since 1955, he welcomed new dramatists, among them Alberto Moravia and Natalia Ginzburg. In the official publication of the Stabile, the policy of foregrounding these authors was explained at length,[21] and in the part dedicated to *Se questo è un uomo*, De Bosio claimed that the staging of Levi's piece was the 'high point of a long evolution and also the beginning of a new theatre'.[22]

This context shows us, then, that the staging of Levi's and Marché's stage version had to satisfy a triple expectation: (a) to show the specificity of the Auschwitz experience without sentimentality, as Levi himself stated; (b) to live up to one or other of two dramatic models – secular oratorio or mimetic form of prisoner camp scenes; (c) to realize the innovation in Italian theatre asked for by De Bosio.

The performance at the Teatro Carignano, Turin, 19 November 1966

Although we lack the necessary documents which would enable us to reconstruct the staging of *Se questo è un uomo* with any degree of precision, sufficient material is available (photographs, audiotapes, director's notes, programmes, press comments) to allow us to discuss the *mise en scène*. Primo Levi and Pieralberto Marché's text of the stage version helps us primarily to establish the syntagmatic order of the staging.[23]

---

[20] See Franco Quadri, *L'avanguardia teatrale in Italia* (materiali 1960–76) (Turin: Einaudi, 1977), vol. I, pp. 133ff.; Helga Finter, 'Ein Raum für das Wort. Zum "Teatro di Parola" des neuen Theater in Italien', in *Zeitschrift für Literaturwissenschaft und Linguistik*, 21.81 (1991), pp. 53–69.

[21] See Gian Renzo Morteo, 'Gli autori italiani e il nostro teatro', in *I Quaderni del Teatro Stabile*, 8 (Turin, 1966), pp. 5–17.

[22] Gianfranco De Bosio, 'Note di regia', *I Quaderni*, p. 53.

[23] Pieralberto Marché's contribution to this text seems to have been that of a guide in dramatic and theatrical matters more than that of a co-writer. This hypothesis is suggested because for someone acquainted with Levi's *écriture* no stylistic gap can be detected between this text and Levi's

Levi's insistence on showing the specificity of the Auschwitz experience without sentimentality is responsible for a dramatic text which itself contributed to a decisively new *mise en scène*. Thus the explicit and implicit commentaries of the narrator in the original work are transformed in the following way: first, they are transferred to the author, who appears in a sort of prologue with a role, comparable to the *subscriptio* in emblematic theatre. Secondly, the commentaries are spoken by a chorus of six men and six women who frame the beginning and the end of the play with the poem with which the book opens. In addition, this chorus tells the facts four times, in each of the two parts of the play. Respecting the book's diegesis, Levi dramatizes scenes and introduces characters from eleven chapters (out of seventeen),[24] and adds other events and figures, as for instance the young Italian chemist Aldo. The list of *dramatis personae* mentions thirty-eight characters speaking in a multitude of languages and who are confronted with the anonymous German voices of the SS coming from the loudspeakers. Thus avoiding to give a face to evil, this method is the opposite of that chosen by Peter Weiss, who identifies neither criminals nor victims in the stage directions, but names the criminals in the dialogue. The type of representation chosen is also in contrast to Weiss. Stressing the loss of the symbolic common law, the Tower of Babel motif is not only omnipresent in two specific scenes in the first and second part, where a pile of wooden beams is heaped up and a wall constructed, but makes itself felt above all by the presence of a multitude of different languages in the text.[25]

other writings. Pieralberto Marché writes in an unpublished article which he had the kindness to show me (kindness for which I want to thank him) that he provided the main ideas for the stage adaptation: the absence of the SS from the stage, the new conception of the 'Levi' character and the choral structure.

[24] These are *Il viaggio* (The Journey), *Sul fondo* (On the Bottom), *Iniziazione* (Initiation), *Ka-Be*, *Le nostre notte* (Our Nights), *L'esame di chimica* (Chemical Examination), *Il canto di Ulisse* (The Canto of Ulysses), *Ottobre 1944* (October 1944), *Die drei Leute vom Labor*, *L'Ultimo* (The Last One), *Storia di dieci giorni* (The Story of Ten Days).

[25] The Canadian radio adaptation may have given Levi this dramaturgical idea, also a feature of his Italian radio version.

Detailed lighting instructions help to steer the production away from a mimetic or documentary style of representation: the various events are to emerge like apparitions from the dark to which they return by the fading of the light. This could give a quality of ambiguous reality to what is shown on stage: it could be a scene evoked by memory but also a dream. In this way, Levi stresses the dialectic of lost reality and bad dreams which is not only a motif of the book but also a lived experience of many survivors.[26] The stage directions for the set are less detailed, giving simple indications for the places of action like 'interior of a hut', '*Appellplatz*', and so on.

Summing up these textual characteristics, we can state that the text itself sets the representation midway between an oratorio and the quasi-cinematographic evocation of a dream or memory.

The production, directed by Gianfranco De Bosio in collaboration with Giovanni Bruno and Marta Egri, with sets designed by Gianni Polidori and sound by Paolo Ketoff and Gino Marinuzzi, followed many of these stage directions. Though the directors did not stage the author's prologue, they respected the multilinguism by engaging actors from France, Israel, Poland and Hungary. The SS were represented only by German voices coming from the loudspeakers, without the hysterical exaggerations commonly used in films. Judging by the numerous photographs, the principle behind the lighting instructions was likewise respected. As a result, light and sound (the column marching to the tune of the famous *Rosamunde*, the noise of sirens, explosions, rifle shots and water splattering) created an audiovisual impression which could have been that of filmic dream or memory sequences.

By comparing photos and photo-plates with the text, the following syntagmatic visual structure can be reconstructed with its corresponding actions:

The stage, entirely covered by a structure of movable wooden beams, was divided into two sections, one was fixed, the other movable. The

---

[26] Semprun, for instance, discusses this problem extensively in *L'Écriture ou la vie*.

Primo tempo *(first part)*

Coro, chorus of six men and six women

In darkness, on forestage: 'Voi che vivete . . .'

Il viaggio, the journey

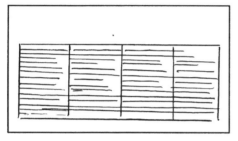

Coro, mixed choir, *kaddish*

The camp of Fossoli

Coro, mixed chorus

Il viaggio sul treno, the train journey.

Coro of six men

Arrival at Auschwitz: Selection in three groups

Sul fondo (On the bottom)

Alberto and Fleck
change into prisoner's
uniforms, tattoo, lack
of water

Coro, chorus of
prisoners in line

Prisoners' march:
Rosamunde
Dawn, snow

Al fondo (in the deepest
part of the camp) *Le
barrache* (the huts)

Iniziazione (Initiation)

Construction of the
Tower of Babel: Flesh,
Piotr, Aldo, Jean,
'Walze'

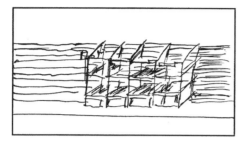

In the huts: eating
the soup

The beams:
transporting the beams;
Flesh, Piotr, Aldo, Jean,
Elias. The sack

Ka-be (The Infirmary) The hut full of sick prisoners

Hurting shoes, the line
of sick prisoners

Aldo on the forestage:
a group of Polish
prisoners

Le nostre notti (our nights)

Nel block (in the block): bunks with Henri, Walter, Aldo and the *cantastorie*, the singer: 'Wohin auch das Auge blicket.'

Coro of six men: Musical theme of the *sogno* (dream)

Il sogno (the dream): Aldo approaches his mother and sister

Selection: Nurses bring bread on a litter; the doctor carries out the selection. The precious spoon.

Secondo tempo *(second part)*

Inside a Block, two rows of three bunks: arrival of Elias, Alberto, Kuhn, Wachsmann and Aldo

Outside: stage in
darkness; Alex and Sigi
in the light on forestage,
Alex knocks Aldo down

L'esame di chimica (Chemistry examination)

Buna: Doctor
Pannwitz's desk, Alex's
arrival with Aldo,
chemistry exam

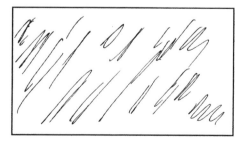

Bombardamento
(bombing). Alarm; Aldo
and Sonnino, sit on the
ground, against sacks,
eating, Goldner joins
them

Un muro in costruzione (building a wall): Aldo and Pietro

Destruction of the bridge, table and trestle taken away, Alex with Elias, Alberto, Jean, Flesh, Sonnino, Sigi *'digging the earth'*, with a shovel

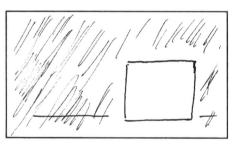

'a sun beam', *'in the background a stream dredger'*

The Bread Lesson: Flesh eats the bread, Alberto, Resnyk, Jean, Sonnino

Il canto di Ulisse (The Canto of Ulysses)

Jean and Aldo alone, '*essen holen*', a kapo on his bicycle

Back stage: the kitchen huts and vats of soup, 'Kohl und Rüben'. Aldo: '*Infin che il mar fu sopra noi rinchiuso*'

Il mercato (The market): inside the washroom; German inscriptions; Alberto and Sonnino, Henri, Elias, Aldo

Survival lesson: '*organizzazione, pietà, furto*' darkness

Coro of six men

'Winter'

Inside the washroom: Aldo, Adler, Alberto, Piotr, Resnyk

October 1944

'*Selektion*' with
a doctor in white
blouse; on his right a
functionary with green
triangle and military
jacket; files of prisoners

Inside a hut, two rows
of three bunks: Kuhn

The Double Ration:
Alex enters followed by
two prisoners with the
soup vat

Die drei Leute vom Labor (Three from the Laboratory)

*The chemistry
laboratory at Buna*:
Stawinga, Aldo,
Goldner

Enter three young ladies
Alex

L'ultimo (the last one)

Appelplatz: the hanging of a prisoner

Coro of six prisoners

'aveva preso parte alla rivolta di Birkenau'

Storia di dieci giorni (The Story of Ten Days)

The Hospital: Arturo, Charles, Aldo. Noises of the evacuation of the camp. Ashkenazi, Samuelidis Barbiere; noises of cars; absolute silence; bombing

Schenk, Arthur with filthy plaids to cover the windows

A stove arrives on a
little car; cauliflower;
Samogyni's death-rattle

Coro of six men

'*L'ultima traccia di
civilita*'

Outside the camp:
Aldo and Charles enter
at the back covered
with plaids and rags. It
snows. They disappear

The Kaddish

Coro

All characters in
prisoners uniform: '*Voi
che vivete sicuri . . .*'

beams had been oxidized by flame and darkened by carbon soot.[27] This
structure reminds one of Paolo Burri's reliefs, and it is also an evocation
of the iron structure that was the gate to Auschwitz.

Another movable structure of four wooden folding screens, also
grey, served as the exterior walls of the Fossoli camp or the train, as the
gate to Auschwitz, as the walls of the huts, as an office in Buna, and so
on. Wooden superposed bunks, a blockboard, a desk, gallows and other
precise accessories like a stove or a vat for soup were the only mimetic
objects in this abstract space. There was precision, too, in the signs
stitched on the clothes, by which the status of the prisoner was indicated. Levi insisted on this.

A visual dialectic between empty and filled space, open and
closed screens, sustained a cinematographic alternation between exterior and interior.[28] The dominating grey tones of the set found an echo
in the striped uniforms of the prisoners and also in those of the kapos,
an echo reinforced by expressionist make-up. The only spots of colour
were those of the secretaries' dresses at the Buna offices, contrasting
with the grey and sombre universe of the camp.

This is as much information as one can draw from the archive
documents. To get an idea of how the actors dealt with the text, an
audiotape of the production would have been useful. Lacking such a
recording, we have to content ourselves with press cuttings, but these

[27] I owe this information, which cannot be seen in the black and white
photographs, to Professor Carlo Giuliani, Turin, who supervised the
realization of the set.

[28] See plates 28–31.

28. **Primo Levi**, *Se questo è un uomo* (Teatro Stabile, Turin, 19 November 1966). 'On the bottom.'

29. *Se questo è un uomo.* 'At the gate of the camp.'

30. *Se questo è un uomo.* 'Selection.'

31. *Se questo è un uomo.* 'The bread lesson.'

are full of contradictions. Who can be trusted? Those who like Alberto Blandi found that 'all sounded false'?[29] Or Roberto Monicelli[30] and Guido Boursier[31] who perceived a 'reality stronger than all theatre'? Or should we believe the young Silvio Berutti, who was impressed by the mixture of voices, noises and terrible military music?[32] Who was right: those who praise the discreet acting,[33] or those who speak of a 'hesitant manner of playing'?[34] All shades of opinion are represented. There are those who saw 'una sacra rappresentazione profana, quasi un nuovo "autosacramental"';[35] others considered the play as 'visual evidence' or perceived 'a representation truly worthy of the text'.[36] All these critics reflect more the contextual horizon of expectation described earlier, than on the production itself. Further research – interviews with the director and the actors – may give us a clearer picture in the future.

To conclude provisionally: the theatrical version of Primo Levi's testimony on the Shoah provides, by its stage directions and form, a means of resolving the dichotomy between oratorio and an impossible realistic representation. Lighting, stylization of acting and stress on the musicality of the text complemented by the chorus, together with visual abstraction for the set but precision in the accessories, these are the aesthetic theatrical means which could give some idea of what this universe of the 'real' was like, a universe of abjection, from which hardly anyone returned. The real (i.e. the reality of the camps), the memory of which still threatens the survivors' sense of reality, cannot be staged, because the reality of such a death, the reality of such abjection has no signifier, no sign. The stench of burnt human flesh and the excretions of dying women and men are physically engraved in the memories of those who were there. They are engraved like wounds in their bodies and souls. Those who came back, when speaking of such

---

[29] *La Stampa*, 20 November 1966.
[30] *Epoca*, 4 December 1966.
[31] *Gazetta dello popolo*, 20 November 1966.
[32] 'Riflessione di un giovane' (source unidentified).
[33] Sinah Kessler, *Frankfurter Allgemeine Zeitung*, 17 December 1966.
[34] *Eco degli spettacoli* and *Cinema-Sport*, both 26 November 1966.
[35] Raoul Radice, *Corriere della sera*, 20 November 1966, and Carlo Maria Pensa, *Il Dramma*, November 1966.
[36] *L'Italia* and *Gazetta di Parma*, both 3 December 1966.

experiences, live them again; and this real, this abjection becomes for them once more a threatening present. Those who hear them speak, only hear the words and can only approach what is told by activating their memory of personal experiences of abjection. It is perhaps for this reason that the Shoah in representation comes closest when it hurts with words, when the dissonances between the materiality of the signifiers and their possible signification come to reach the skin, come to frighten the imaginary, because the body is disturbed.

For the Berlin *Investigation* at the Volksbühne, Luigi Nono not only surrounded the spectators with loudspeakers on the walls of the theatre; the sound came also from the ceiling and from under the floor.[37] This musically created affect is the opposite of the euphemistic technical language of the Nazi murderers and to the modest language of the witnesses. Primo Levi tried to inject a similar affect into the language of the victims by varying text types and enunciation types, by separating the noises of power and force from the noises of human suffering. To put such a dramaturgy to the test today remains a challenge. Given the contemporary background of new music which evokes the Shoah by a language of affect – from Schoenberg to Webern, from Nono to Berio and Bernd Alois Zimmermann – this likewise presents a challenge for a *teatro della parola*, for a theatre of the spoken word.

[37] See Mateo Taibon, *Luigi Nono und sein Musiktheater* (Vienna, Cologne and Weimar: Böhlau Verlag, 1993), pp. 131ff.

15 Heinar Kipphardt's *Brother Eichmann*

ALEXANDER STILLMARK

1984

In 1984 the Wall was still dividing Berlin. I was living and working in the East as a director at the Deutsches Theater. When we decided to put on Heinar Kipphardt's play, the first thing which confronted us was the title: *Bruder Eichmann* (*Brother Eichmann*). What a provocation! Fascism had long been defeated, its testimonies banished to the museums. History, clothed in the costume of the bipolar world order, seemed logical and controllable. Behind the Berlin Wall, our ideology was anti-Fascism. Fascists only existed in the world outside our borders, on the other side. How could a Fascist criminal be my brother?

Originally, the role of Eichmann was to have been performed by a fifty-year-old actor. This was Eichmann's age at the time of the trial in Jerusalem; the trial of the man in the glass box, the subject of our play. This actor approached his role with skill and he worked hard at using his personality to theatricalize the character. His aim was to achieve maximum impact in a 'big theatrical evening'. Using his creativity and stage presence, he worked relentlessly to overcome the Spartan documentary text and to portray a character with the charisma of a major criminal. However, 'Eichmann was not Iago and not Macbeth and nothing would have been further from his mind than to determine with Richard III "to prove a villain". Except for an extraordinary diligence in looking out for his personal advancement, he had no motives at all.'[1] The actor was unable to put a distance between his experience as a wartime child and the character. Perhaps he had not yet managed to

---

[1] Hannah Arendt, *Eichmann in Jerusalem* (New York: Viking Press, 1963; Harmondsworth: Penguin, 1977), p. 287.

32. **Heinar Kipphardt**, *Brother Eichmann* (Deutsches Theater, 1984). The setting represents the 'Eichmann museum'.

come to terms with the events of that period and it was all too painful for him. We had to part company and a younger actor was eventually cast in the title role.

On his working methods, Kipphardt writes:

> There is just as much subjectivity involved with documents as with other artistic forms. My technique has always been to include the reader or spectator in the process taking place within me because I have always wanted him to be relatively free . . . I considered the method of documentary evidence to be the correct one because we are subject to so much ideology, so much false awareness, so much prejudice, fear and suppression. That is why I work with materials which cannot be rejected by the spectator. He should have the feeling: 'I can trust the person who wrote this since he is inviting me to examine it. He can provide evidence for it.' My aim has always been to provide material with the character of documentary proof, to create something with the dignity of a document.[2]

For the première of *Brother Eichmann* in East Berlin the stage represented a fictional 'Eichmann museum'. The backdrop was cordoned off by a rope barrier. It consisted of a black, weathered architrave in a concentration camp with compartments, their half-open doors bulging with suitcases and clothing. In front of this was an SS uniform on a stand – faceless – and objects from Eichmann's prison cell in Israel: table, chair, broom, bucket, washing bowl, cardigan, handcuffs, slippers. A sofa from the theatre foyer provided a link with the reality of the audience. Kipphardt's playscript lay on a stool.

The actors were visitors to the museum and were guided around the exhibition by loudspeakers. At the beginning they heard a description of how prisoners were guarded in the high security prison. The group moved on. A young man remained behind, staring at the script.

The young actor, Thomas Neumann, then thirty years old, picked up the text concerning a 54-year-old defendant, and leafed through

---

[2] Heinar Kipphardt, 'Notizen zu Bruder Eichmann', a programme note for the 1984 Deutsches Theater production, 1984. Original translations by Roy Kift.

it. He was the same age as Adolf Eichmann had been in 1942, at the peak of his career, when 'his arm stretched over the whole of Europe'.[3] Neumann started back on the path leading to the unknown person. He read aloud what Eichmann said and did, what the prisoner did in his cell: counting, washing the floor, talking to himself in successive monologues. He tried on the handcuffs and slowly (and literally) slipped into Eichmann's jacket, and into his slippers. Suddenly a voice behind him called: 'Your breakfast, Herr Eichmann!' The young man turned round and found himself face to face with the prison governor. He stood to attention and uttered a submissive 'Jawohl', before sitting down upright, at a perfect right angle to the table, hands neatly placed on his thighs. The Israeli official asked routinely: 'Is there anything you would like, Herr Eichmann?' Hesitatingly the young man requests: 'If I could just talk to somebody.' The words are still unfamiliar, strange. The actor does not adopt Eichmann's speech patterns. On the contrary. He submits to them, he lets himself be infected by this alien language, this 'Eichmann language'.

Neumann made a point of eschewing any sign of charismatic presence. He achieved this by opening himself up to Eichmann; he tried as hard as possible to get behind the logic and thought processes of this person and, by doing so, he discovered the absence of conscience. He portrayed a man whose ego had been almost completely obliterated. The actor committed himself to the broken, fragmentary nature of this figure thereby making the logic of Eichmann's thoughts visible: a belief in the structure of command and authority. This process took hold of his whole body.

In the course of the evening his language became more fluid as he became more self-confident, but broke down into stammers and beseeching stutters when he felt cornered and in conflict with authority. He related differently to the female psychiatrist, seeing her primarily as a woman, and showed a different side (the old side) of his character to his defence lawyer. For him, Dr Servatius represented 'the law'. The law exonerated him by negating the competence of the Israeli court. And with the law on his side, Eichmann's fragile bond with the police officer,

---

[3] Gideon Hausner, attorney-general at the trial of Eichmann, Jerusalem 1961 (quoted in the Deustches Theater programme).

Leo Chass, which had led to some kind of rapport, snapped. Eichmann had only accepted the officer's presence in deference to his superior authority and had even tried to gain his approval. But now the young man suddenly revealed a presumptuous arrogance which gave the audience some inkling of what the historical Eichmann had been like at the height of his powers. The curtain was flung open for a moment.

With this self-infection with Eichmann's language, this experiment on ourselves, we were looking for historical answers to questions thrown up by our own situation in an authoritarian state. Many parallels were forced on us: the power pyramid; the idealistic manifestation of authoritarian rule which demanded a readiness to sacrifice and tolerated no critical questioning; the submission of the individual to the collective; the delegation of conscience to those giving the orders; and, above all, the unchanged German love for 'bureaucratic order'. This was revealed as the seedbed in which Eichmann's behaviour was nurtured. As such, it was part of the 'normal pattern of survival', not simply of 'bourgeois capitalists', but of modern man under any political system. The language of Eichmann in the mouth of a young person living in a contemporary socialist state resulted in an uncomfortable, artificial character and created a frightening proximity, almost too close for comfort.

> The play gives an account of how a rather average young man from Solingen, raised in Linz, a representative for Vacuum Oil, following a very normal path, became the monstrous figure Adolf Eichmann, the administrative authority responsible for the genocide of the European Jews, a 'cog in the wheel', as he called himself, a functionary of the 'war against the Jews', his conscience protected by orders and an oath of allegiance to the state . . . Looked at more closely it can be seen that Eichmann's behaviour has today become the norm in daily life, in politics and science, not to mention the macabre games of modern warfare which are conceived on a genocidal scale from the outset. That is why the play is called BROTHER EICHMANN.[4]

---

[4] Kipphardt, 'Notizen zu Bruder Eichmann' (Deutsches Theater programme).

1992

Eight years later, in 1992, as part of a large-scale exhibition in Berlin entitled 'Jewish Spheres of Life', we presented a different, shorter version of the play. Leaving out all the analogy scenes,[5] we concentrated on the theme of Eichmann and the Holocaust. Apart from the police captain Leo Chass, the female psychiatrist Schilch, the defence lawyer Dr Servatius and Adolf Eichmann, all other characters were dispensed with. This tightening up of the material proved to be very effective. Discussions after the performances revealed that the audience sought and found analogous associations to their present situation.

This time the play was not performed at the Deutsches Theater but in an alternative art centre, the 'Tacheles', next to the synagogue in Berlin's former Jewish quarter. The special occasion – it was the largest ever exhibition of Jewish culture in Berlin, the historical site of the building, the youthful audience, together with the news of neo-Fascist violence on the street outside, transformed not only our approach to the play, but the audience's reaction to it. Our relation to the historical phenomenon of an Adolf Eichmann had to be thought out afresh. As a reaction to the new audience situation, we abandoned the museum metaphor. Actors and audience were now together in one room, with nothing to separate them. As the audience entered the space, 'Eichmann' was standing in the background, waiting.

---

[5] Kipphardt's fascination with the Eichmann case was bound up with his fascination with the 'Eichmann-behaviour' ('Eichmann-Haltung') as he calls it: the behaviour of the modern, functional individual. To make his position clear, he included 'analogy scenes' using documentary material taken from seventies and early eighties events. He included episodes relating to psychological torture tactics used in the anti-terrorist warfare against the 'Rote Armee Faktion' and the Red Brigades, on NATO and US nuclear war games, scenes inspired by the massacres in the Palestinian refugee camps in the Lebanon during the Israeli occupation, by bio-genetics and the prospect of human clones, and by all kinds of nightmares.

As Kipphardt did not want his play to be used as anti-Communist propaganda, he restricted himself to examples taken from the western world. This one-sided approach attracted severe criticism and led to misunderstanding. Kipphardt died, in 1982, when the controversy over his play was at its fiercest.

33. *Brother Eichmann* (Deutsches Theater, 1984). Thomas Neumann as Eichmann.

Now, we were addressing a 'post-Wall' audience: young people who had begun to take responsibility for their own destiny in a period of revolutionary upheaval. Everywhere socialism was collapsing. We were living a 'timequake'. A time fissure was opening up, forcing us all to reassess state values.

34.   *Brother Eichmann* (Kammerspiele des Deutschen Theaters, 1992). Thomas Neumann as Eichmann, eight years later.

Once again we Germans were having to sweep up the broken pieces of a state – the fourth state this century since the collapse of the Wilhelmine Empire. Each successive state had been radically different from its predecessor. Although the socialist state had not been tainted with mass murder, great injustices had been carried out in its name, and blood had been spilt. Authoritarian socialism had been generally rejected in the German Democratic Republic, but social utopia was still accepted as an ideal by wide sections of the population east of the Wall. Many of us had hoped for a reformation of the system, a *'perestroika'*, as the way out. We were now facing the cold wind of the free-market economic system, experiencing, in Erich Fromm's words, the 'fear of freedom'.[6]

The 'Anschluss' with the Federal Republic was also – for us in the East – an 'Anschluss' with a National-Socialist past, with all its awkward concomitants. Many of Eichmann's comrades, former members of the SS, had escaped with light sentences and are now enjoying state pensions in the West. Yet behind Eichmann stood the 6,000,000 victims in a new form. In Communist Germany this question had been delegated to the West Germans. Now, it belonged to us, too. The question of our relationship to the victims and the dead was suddenly raised. We were surrounded by the dead: in front of us the dead from the Holocaust and the war; and behind us, ever more distinct, the dead of the Gulags and the Cultural Revolutions from Mao to Pol Pot, sacrificed in the name of the 'great doctrine'. Hitler wanted to wipe out Jewish culture, yet in his murderous way succeeded only in sealing the close relationship between German and Jewish cultures.

The name of the exhibition, 'Jewish Spheres of Life', was programmatic: 'life'. A sign of hope that fifty years after the Holocaust we can proclaim that German and Jewish cultures are inseparable. During the heady days of reunification, we were in the midst of confusion and contradictions. We had suddenly inherited a long-rejected past and were hit by the dialectics of history: in our case, the victims of dead Brother Eichmann announced their desire to speak.

---

[6] E. Fromm, *Escape from Freedom* (New York: Holt, Rinehart and Winston, 1941), published in German as *Die Furcht vor der Freiheit* (Vienna, 1983).

The original production of *Brother Eichmann* had been taken out of the Deutsches Theater repertory in 1988. The cast had not met for more than three years. However, the new rehearsals were breathtakingly fresh and up-to-date. The text took on a whole new dimension. By performing Kipphardt's text once more, we came to understand our own failure, our own disappointments, and the way we had functioned on our side of the Wall. The culprit–victim scenario, as questioned by Eichmann's behaviour, was thrown to the foreground. This was a profound experience for us; something we had only previously read about from our parents' generation.

Eichmann's disclosures, pauses, breaks and attempts at explanation took on a new meaning. His remark, 'It never occurred to me to sit in the nettles of my own decisions', acquired a different meaning. We could understand his attempts to conform, to fit in at all cost, to become the epitome of the functionless functionary.

Let me tell you an anecdote. The stage door was always open during rehearsals, and we were constantly aware of the noise of the street and life outside the theatre. During the dress rehearsal an Alsatian dog ambled in. He walked on to the stage and sniffed everyone as if he were searching for something. Then he sat down in front of Eichmann and stared at him for a long while. Nobody stopped the rehearsal. The dog walked away. We had understood.

Remembering and forgetting became suddenly tangible. We were in a time vortex. It was no longer theatre time. It was life time.

Following the successful production during the exhibition, the director of the Deutsches Theater decided to put this new compressed version back into repertory in the studio theatre, the Kammerspiele.[7] Here we had to return to the traditional division between audience and stage even though we played on a platform jutting out from the forestage in front of the safety curtain. We put more emphasis on the interplay between actors and audience and the questioning of Eichmann became a public event. Yet the production lost none of its concentrated power.

---

[7] I should like to thank the publishers Ute Nyssen and Bansemer of Cologne who enabled us, by means of a special agreement, to continue the work on the play.

1995

We are again performing *Brother Eichmann*. Our audience, like the public at the trial, sits in close intimacy to the action on the Studio stage of the Deutsches Theater. The walls of the playing area are stretched from side to side with sheets of shiny black plastic. An opening at the back gives on to a large mirrored surface in which the audience can see itself reflected. Eichmann stands in front of this mirror and looks back at the audience through it. As soon as he hears the steps of Leo Chass, the police captain, he turns round and comes downstage. The play begins. The confrontation is like a wrestling match: which of the two arguments will lay the opponent flat?

The fifty years which have elapsed since Auschwitz give the play a exemplary nature, almost the character of a model case. Its authenticity remains, the document is believable at all times and it continuously incites arguments and counter-arguments. The actor playing Eichmann has grown older: he has become a man who justifies himself with the weight of experience.

The audience has also changed in a radically changed world. The Cold War, to which the older generation had become accustomed, has not led to peace but war. Young people are now growing up in a Europe devastated by nationalist conflicts, a world full of hunger, where refugees and displaced people roam aimlessly. Worse: the aims of the warring parties are not to subjugate the enemy, but to expel or exterminate them as expeditiously as possible.

A diplomat from Bangladesh once said to me when he discovered that I was German: 'German very good. Hitler (raising his thumb to emphasize his admiration), we need a man like Hitler. We have only the typhoon and the floods. There are too many of us.'

In a gruesome way Auschwitz has turned out to be the discovery of the century, a discovery which finds its logical apotheosis at Hiroshima. In Kipphardt's play, we are shocked by Eichmann's lapidary answers, yet it is difficult to oppose his arguments. In today's world, every news broadcast confirms his cynical outlook.

Compared with the previous two productions, the actor's portrayal of the protagonist in 1995 has brought into sharper focus Eichmann's terrifying lack of feelings, not only towards his victims, but also towards himself. It is as if he is not really alive, as if a third person is observing everything from a distant watchtower or on a monitor. The world as fictional reality. Everything can be understood, everything can be explained. Eichmann himself plays no role in this. Unable to mourn, he exudes a frightening coldness. This, however, does not lessen his craving to function. He is caught up in the web of his own tissue of horrific information, which he carefully catalogues and files away. When, at the end, he gives the police captain the advice, 'it would be better if you got the timetable, Reichsbahnrat Stangl', he is simply referring him to the relevant authority. Such an attitude will survive.

Ominously, Eichmann's attitude and behaviour as analysed by Heinar Kipphardt become recognizable as those of so-called modern man. Eichmann's beliefs determine his relationship to the world, to life and death, and ultimately to himself. To the outside world Eichmann shows a belief in a God with whom he has an unproblematic relationship, the relationship of an obedient son to an authoritarian father. When he speaks about the mass killings he has witnessed, he faithfully describes his feelings: the pubescent feelings of a voyeur looking at something forbidden. But like an autistic child, he is incapable of any inner response, unable to draw any consequences from his deeds.

In *Brother Eichmann*, Kipphardt does not portray a terrifying criminal. What shocks us is how a 'normal man' deals with such inconceivable mass murders. Every soldier who has killed carries his dead within him. Every murderer does so too. But what about the millions of victims this century who never saw their murderers? What about the Jews killed by industrial means, who fell victim to a deadly, functional apparatus operating according to its own laws? What about the chief instigator of these unspeakable crimes?

The thought of these millions of 'unredeemed dead' is terrifying. It points directly towards the central question of our century: what is our attitude towards life when faced with technology which provides us with ever greater and more lethal powers? And all this in the face of an ethical awareness that cannot keep pace with our ceaseless striving for absolute supremacy.

We must learn to listen to Eichmann carefully, to descend deep into the lower reaches of his thoughts in order to understand the 'banality of evil' as his virulent truth.

The realization of this truth implies our complicity in it. Eichmann is not from another world. He is a product of our century like ourselves. The play is called *BROTHER* EICHMANN.[8]

---

[8] The première of *Bruder Eichmann* took place at the Deutsches Theater on 19 April 1984. It was directed by Alexander Stillmark. Design: Heinz Wenzel; costumes: Angelika Kemter. Adolf Eichmann: Thomas Neumann; Ofer: Dieter Mann; Chass: Klaus Piontek; Frieda Schilch: Christine Schorn; Servatius: Martin Trettau.

The English-language première of *Brother Eichmann* took place at the Library Theatre, Manchester, on 1 November 1990. It was directed by Chris Honer, with Alan Dobie playing the title role. The translation was by Roy Kift, and the rights are with John Rush, Sheil Land Associates, 43 Doughty Street, London WC1N 2LF.

16 George Tabori's mourning work in *Jubiläum*

ANAT FEINBERG

There are taboos that must be broken or they will continue
to choke us.[1]

'There are taboos that must be broken or they will continue to choke
us', wrote George Tabori in the late 1960s, and it was in that frame of
mind that he approached the writing and staging of *Jubiläum*:[2] he had
been invited by the city of Bochum, in the industrial region of the Ruhr,
to mark the fiftieth anniversary of the National-Socialists' rise to
power in Germany. The request had come from the subsidized municipal theatre to offer a theatrical vision solemnizing that fateful event:
their choice was an outsider. Tabori is a controversial figure: a Jew from
Budapest, with a British passport; a man who rejects any received
notion of 'Heimat' (homeland) in favour of an idiosyncratic definition,
'stage, bed and books'.[3] His father perished in Auschwitz like many of
his relatives; his mother survived thanks to her healthy cunning and
femininity.[4] Tabori himself escaped the net cast by the Nazis with a
great deal of luck, roaming through more than a dozen countries

[1] George Tabori, '*Die Kannibalen*: zur europäischen Erstaufführung',
Unterammergau oder die guten Deutschen (Frankfurt: Suhrkamp Verlag,
1981), p. 37.

[2] *Jubiläum* is available in George Tabori, *Theaterstücke* (Frankfurt-on-
Main: Fischer, 1994), vol. II, pp. 49–86.

[3] George Tabori, 'Budapest – Hollywood – Berlin', in *Tabori*, ed. Jörg W.
Gronius and Wend Kässens (Frankfurt: Athenäum Verlag, 1989), p. 122.

[4] Tabori based his play *Mutters Courage* (premièred in the Münchener
Kammerspiele, 17 May 1979) on the survival story of his mother,
Elsa Tabori.

through Europe and Asia.[5] In 1983 he was almost seventy years old, but theatrically speaking he was at the beginning of his career. He had been nearly unacknowledged in the United States, where he spent more than twenty years of his life, wrote screenplays for Hollywood, translated Brecht into English, participated as an observer in Lee Strasberg's 'Actors' Studio', founded and managed a travelling troupe of actors known as 'The Strolling Players'. Those few plays of his which saw the limelight were not particularly successful. Things began to change for the better when he staged *Kannibalen* in Berlin in 1969 – the story of concentration camp detainees who cook and eat one of their companions in order to survive.[6] While the critics were divided in their opinions,[7] the production gave rise to flurries of amazement, confusion, and rage. Heinz Galinski, an Auschwitz survivor and the leader of the re-emerging Jewish community in West Berlin, demanded the banning of the production.[8] But the audience seemed hypnotized – spectators maintained absolute silence at the end of the performance.

During the seventies Tabori attempted to actualize the principles of his stage theory in the framework of a theatre laboratory ('Theaterlabor'), an alternative theatre group working under the auspices

---

[5] For Tabori's account of his adventurous life, see Gronius and Kässens, eds., *Tabori*, pp. 105–22, and 'Zeuge des Jahrhunderts: Peter von Becker im Gespräch mit George Tabori', in *George Tabori: Dem Gedächtnis, der Trauer und dem Lachen gewidmet*, ed. Andrea Welker (Vienna and Linz: Bibliotek der Provinz, 1994), pp. 248–56.

[6] *Die Kannibalen* was premièred in English (*The Cannibals*) at the American Place Theatre, New York, 17 October 1968. The German première took place at the Schiller Theater, Berlin, 13 December 1969.

[7] See, for example, the critical reviews of Rolf Michaelis, 'Ein Alptraumspiel', *Frankfurter Allgemeine Zeitung*, 15 December 1969, or Christoph Müller, 'Darf man denn das?' *Die Zeit*, 9 January 1970. See also Jürgen Beckelmann, 'Widersinniger Nachruhm', *Frankfurter Rundschau*, 17 December 1969; Karena Niehoff, 'Der Mensch lebt nicht vom Mensch allein', *Süddeutsche Zeitung*, 18 December 1969; Friedrich Luft, 'Schwarze Messe mit einer Gruppe aus dem Tartarus', *Die Welt*, 15 December 1969; Ingvelde Geleng, 'Auschwitz als "Spiel"', *Giessener Allgemeine*, 16 December 1969. A descriptive review of the American production is available in Robert Breuer, 'Ein Tollhaus in der Kirche', *Der Bund* (Berne, Switzerland), 14 November 1968.

[8] See Tabori, *Unterammergau*, p. 23.

of the Bremen Municipal Theatre.[9] An enthusiastic group of actors performed under his direction texts by Kafka and Beckett, some of his own plays, and, in Munich, improvisations around the figure of Shylock.

Jubiläum (premièred on 30 January 1983) does not attempt to investigate the historical, political or social aspects of the Third Reich. Tabori's interest does not lie in presenting historical reality or factual truth. His theatre confronts the malaise of National-Socialism and the systematic murder of European Jewry in a way that is highly original and daring, even revolutionary. Tabori's so-called Holocaust theatre is far removed from the dramatic (and mostly melodramatic) attempts made in West Germany in the 1950s to lend the anonymous suffering a concrete shape in the figure of a single representative martyr, or to confront German collective guilt through the character of a Nazi who comes to acknowledge his mistake or make amends as an act of belated atonement. Tabori is equally distanced from the other current, that of the 1960s, which tried to confront Fascism and its roots in documentary drama, in which Jewish suffering was, more often than not, marginalized.[10] His pursuit of the past does not seek, as so many Germans have, to overcome the past ('die Vergangenheit zu bewältigen'), since such an approach is fundamentally erroneous. His interest lies neither in presenting a charge sheet nor in providing an outlet for feelings of revenge; neither in awakening spectators' pity nor in revering the perished and exalting them into martyrs; certainly not in evoking a sentimental response as did the dramatization of *Anne Frank's Diary* in the fifties or the American television soap-opera hit *Holocaust,* shown in Germany in the late seventies.

'It would be an insult to the dead, to beg for sympathy or to lament their crushed nakedness. The event is beyond tears', writes Tabori.[11] He tries to free the experience of confronting the past, to free

---

[9] For a detailed discussion of Tabori's Theater Labor, see my article, 'Taboris Bremen Theaterlabor. Projekte – Ehrfahrungen – Resultate', in Hans-Peter Bayerdörfer and Jörg Schönert, eds., *Theater gegen das Vergessen: Bühnenarbeit und Drama bei George Tabori* (Tübingen: Niemeyer, 1997), pp. 62–97.

[10] See my *Wiedergutmachung im Programm: Jüdisches Schicksal im deutschen Nachkriegsdrama* (Cologne: Prometh Verlag, 1988), pp. 15–64.

[11] Tabori, *Unterammergau,* p. 38.

the actors and the spectators from those conventions and taboos which burden and strain, distort and falsify it; from sentimental pity, sanctimonious judgement and from that hypocritical philo-Semitism which, to many, is the reverse side of anti-Semitism.[12]

The systematic murder of millions binds together Jews and Germans forever, claims Tabori, and he offers both sides a theatrical experience whose core I would term 'Erinnerungsarbeit', paraphrasing the notion of 'Trauerarbeit' coined by the Mitscherlichs.[13] Indeed, Tabori's understanding of the theatrical experience as a form of remembering is closely related to Freud's therapeutic approach – his 'Erinnerungsarbeit' – which is a threefold experience involving 'erinnern, wiederholen und durcharbeiten'.[14]

Tabori's theatre thus becomes a locus of remembrance ('Gedächtnisort'[15]). Yet this experience of remembrance is far from being a ritual, which might suggest automatism, a convention of conduct demanding no individual choice. It is underlined by its concrete, sensual and all-embracing manifestations: 'True remembrance is possible only through sensual remembrance: it is impossible to confront the past without sensing it again in one's skin, nose, tongue, buttocks, legs and stomach.'[16]

The theatrical experience of remembrance thus involves actors and spectators physically, intellectually and emotionally. It consciously obliterates the line dividing theatre and life. Moreover, Tabori's 'Erinnerungsarbeit' deliberately blurs the line demarcating past and present, life and death, thus expanding, as it were, the volume of time.

[12] See Rainer Werner Fassbinder, 'Philosemiten und Antisemiten', in *Die Zeit*, 9 April 1976.

[13] Alexander and Margarete Mitscherlich, *Die Unfähigkeit zu trauern* (Munich: Piper, 1967).

[14] Sigmund Freud, 'Erinnern, Wiederholen und Durcharbeiten', *Gesammelte Werke* (Frankfurt-on-Main: Fischer, 1973), vol. x, pp. 126–36.

[15] The term is used by Jochen Winter in his 'Hommage an Tabori', unpublished manuscript. Winter participated in several Tabori productions and wrote his article after the production of Beckett's *Der Verwaiser* (*The Lost Ones*) in 1981.

[16] Tabori, 'Es geht schon wieder los', *Unterammergau*, p. 202.

This is a highly intensive, concrete theatrical experience taking apart and rebuilding, chaining and liberating. For 'we can only forget what we remember'.[17]

The setting of *Jubiläum* is a cemetery on the banks of the Rhine. The ghosts of the dead, victims of the Third Reich, find no peace. They are disturbed by the hostile writings and the acts of desecration of neo-Nazis such as Jürgen, acts which suggest the continuation of past hostility and hatred. 'Thirty-four years of democracy and again the same old story', says Otto, and Lotte adds, 'Here we go again.'[18] Jürgen's anti-Semitism is not motivated by ideology. He hates the 'Other', the stranger whoever he or she may be, he bullies the weak and the victims of social stigmatization out of frustration, pleasure and, perhaps, driven by the desire to protest against a society he detests. The dead rise from their graves: Arnold the musician, his wife Lotte, her niece Mitzi, a spastic girl, Helmut the homosexual and his lover Otto the barber. Tabori deliberately presents non-Jewish as well as Jewish victims: Jews have no monopoly on suffering, although they were the main targets of mass annihilation. Lotte dies as the Nazis rise to power, drowning in a telephone booth while calling her friends and acquaintances. The others commit suicide – Helmut by hanging, Otto by drowning in the bath water, and Mitzi by shoving her head into the oven – three victims of the evil which did not end with that legendary 'Stunde Null'.

Jubiläum is not structured as a logical and orderly development of scenes conveying a conventional plot, but as a collage – a sequence of scenes which are essentially fragments of remembrance. The theatrical experience draws its force from the cumulative effect of one intense episode after another, while the episodes themselves have that anecdotal quality which is so typical of Tabori's writing.[19] There is no message and no truth which Tabori intends to transmit to his audience. The truth, or what we normally call the truth, is a stranger to Tabori. Instead there are specific, private instances, or anecdotes. 'The true, the

---

[17] Ibid., p. 201.   [18] Tabori, *Jubiläum*, pp. 59, 73.

[19] Claus Peymann, artistic director of the Vienna Burgtheater, writes about Tabori's inclination 'die Welt sofort in eine Anekdote umzumünzen' in 'Die Welt in eine Anekdote', *Profil*, 16 May 1994. See also Wend Kässens, 'Die Scherze der Verzweiflung: Zur Prosa von George Tabori', in *Tabori*, ed. Gronius and Kässens, pp. 79–88.

original is only within us, if we dare to discover it', he once said and spoke in the same context of 'several truths'.[20] Following Adorno, in a way, Tabori offers a theatrical experience which 'is liberated from the lie of being the truth',[21] an experience which is by definition fragmentary, like variations on a theme. Therefore it is possible – as has indeed been done – to rearrange the written scenes according to a different order. 'Every life has a beginning, a middle and an end, though not necessarily in that order', says Tabori in his introductory remarks to *Jubiläum*.[22] All levels of time are interwoven in the play, the past is freed of its 'historicity' and made contemporary.

The questioning of Truth and the collage structure are postmodern features. Tabori's text and staging also vibrate with echoes of other works. It is clear that the episode of 'The Jewish Woman' from Brecht's *Furcht und Elend des Dritten Reiches* underlies Lotte's moving farewell scene, although it stems also from a personal recollection: Tabori's aunt Piroschka committed suicide in a telephone booth.[23] The spirit of *Hamlet*'s gravediggers' scene lingers in the episode with Wumpf the gravedigger, and the spirit of Hamlet's dead father is evoked by the figure of Arnold's father, albeit the latter does not seek revenge. Kafka's world is echoed in the play's despair and dread. The grating bond between the murderer and the murdered – Tabori claims that 'criminals are wont to return to the scene of the crime; so are, occasionally, the victims'[24] – brings to mind Raskolnikov from Dostoyevsky's *Crime and Punishment*, an author whose work Tabori tried to bring on to the stage.[25] Also dear to Tabori's heart is Beckett, an author with whom he corresponded and whose works he staged, particularly during the period preceding and following *Jubiläum*. The vivid images of Lotte sitting up in her grave (scene 2) or being submerged in floods of water in a telephone booth which cannot be opened are characteristic of

[20] Tabori, 'Verrückte und Verliebte', in *Betractungen über das Feigenblatt: Ein Handbuch für Verrückte und Verliebte* (Frankfurt, 1993), p. 85.

[21] See C. Bernd Sucher, 'George Taboris Chuzpe', *Süddeutsche Zeitung*, 1 February 1983.

[22] Tabori, *Jubiläum*, p. 52.   [23] Tabori, *Unterammergau*, p. 34.

[24] Tabori, *Jubiläum*, p. 52.

[25] See '*Der Grossinquisitor*', premièred at the Residenztheater, Munich, on 29 January 1993.

35. **George Tabori**, *Jubiläum*, rehearsal in the Bochum Kammerspiel foyer, 1983. Beyond the defaced window, the 'Jewish cemetery'. Eleonore Zetzsche (Lotte) and Stanley Walden (Arnold, the Jewish musician).

Beckett. Beckett is also recalled in the arrested motion, the stagnation, the time of waiting – real time, Godotian time – of which Arnold speaks when he tells of his never-ending waiting for his father (scene 7).[26]

No less original than the text was Tabori's staging of *Jubiläum*. Seeking to expand memory space ('Erinnerungsraum'), coalescing past and present, Tabori shifted the production from the auditorium to the foyer. Fiction and reality, theatre and life, exterior and interior merged into each other. The foyer was covered with mounds of earth, tombstones and foliage – and looking through the big glass windows spectators could see the traffic flowing in the Königsallee.[27] The neo-Nazi Jürgen emerged out of a taxi in front of the theatre and wrote on the

[26] For Tabori's special relationship with Beckett and his various Beckett productions see my article 'The Task is not to Reproduce the External Form, but to Find the Subtext: George Tabori's Productions of Samuel Beckett's Texts', in *Journal of Beckett Studies*, 1.1–2 (1992), pp. 95–115.

[27] Stage and costumes were designed by Kazuko Watanabe.

glass window the anti-Semitic slogan '*Juda verreke*' ('To hell with Jews', with a spelling mistake!). On the opening night Tabori, in the role of the ghost of Arnold's father, left the foyer and walked along the pavement outside the theatre building. Under his woollen coat he wore the outfit of a concentration camp detainee, with number and yellow star. Snow was falling. Tabori knocked on the glass and later gave Stanley Walden – his son, Arnold – a chala covered with white cloth.

Eating is an important motif in Tabori's theatre, in *Kannibalen* (1968), *Mein Kampf* (1987) or *Die Ballade vom Wiener Schnitzel* (1996). In *Mein Kampf*, Schlomo Herzl's dear chicken Mizzi is slaughtered, dissected and fried by Himmlischst. Schlomo picks up the remains and as he utters the Kaddish over the dead chicken – reminiscent of the traditional expiatory sacrifice before the Day of Atonement[28] – his tears trickle down his cheeks and are mixed with the meat he is swallowing. In *Jubiläum* Arnold shares the Shabbat-bread his father gives him. Here too then is a Jewish ritual, though its meaning transcends the purely ritualistic – religious act or the symbolic reconciliation of father and son. It suggests the principle of hope ('Prinzip Hoffnung') which is crucial to Tabori's theatre.[29] For a moment Arnold is made to believe that the Auschwitz ovens were used to bake bread, not to gas human beings, a grotesque variation on the 'Auschwitzlüge'. The lie turns into a moment of truth or a momentary truth. A similar connotation arises from *Mein Kampf*: Lobkowitz, the godly cook, serves Schlomo the chicken saying 'eat, my son, not out of hunger but with the hope of drawing the strength you will need in the coming years'.[30]

Jubiläum is set in a cemetery on the banks of the Rhine. During both World Wars the Rhine was of major strategic significance. The river is overloaded with historical associations, and Tabori, an exceptionally erudite European, knows them all. He is well acquainted with the repertory of legends and myths connected with the Rhine, one of

---

[28] The holiest Jewish day, the Day of Atonement is mentioned also in *Jubiläum*, p. 53.
[29] See for example Tabori's Notes to *Sigmunds Freude* (James' Joys), unpublished manuscript, July 1975, p. 5. See also André Müller, 'Ich habe mein Lachen verloren', *Die Zeit*, 6 May 1994.
[30] Tabori, *Mein Kampf*, *Theaterstücke*, vol. II, p. 203.

the major arteries in German culture and folklore; from the Rhine-daughters who watch over the gold in the *Ring of the Nibelungen* and Heine's 'Lorelei' (quoted in the play)[31] to the romantic aura of ruined castles along the river.[32]

This wide range of associations – a manifold metaphor of Germanism – is deeply embedded in *Jubiläum*. Moreover, the river-bank, with its cemetery, is the domain of death. Tabori's preoccupation with death is obsessive; there is hardly a production or a play of his in which death has no dominion. In *Mein Kampf* he introduces us to Mrs Death (Frau Tod) in person. Schlomo Herzl believes that she is after Hitler and he tries to save his friend's life. Of course, he is wrong since Frau Tod comes to appoint Hitler as her chief emissary. Thus, on the one hand, lie putrefaction, extinction, nothingness (as Tabori suggests in his introductory remarks to *Jubiläum*[33]) and, on the other, there is the gravedigger's witty claim that 'only the dead have it good', since they enjoy eternal tranquillity.[34] For Tabori 'life is an incurable sickness and death perhaps the only end to misfortune'.[35] But is it really so? The dead in *Jubiläum* know no peace and quiet. The burden of private memories accompanies them in their state of non-being and quiescence, haunts them and becomes a nightmarish presence. Tabori's wise 'Shakespearian' gravedigger argues, moreover, that no two graves are alike.[36] But the Holocaust has taught us the lesson of anonymous death, laid bare a pit which is no grave, a pit meant to obliterate and blot out memory rather than commemorate as graves or tombstones do. Naming the dead endows them with the dignity reserved for human beings, while the systematic mass extermination was an unprecedented humiliation, an indignity which only memory, 'Erinnerungsarbeit', can redeem.

Tabori has chosen the cemetery on the banks of the Rhine also because death is a 'quiet return to the moist beginning; the wheel has

---

[31] Tabori, *Jubiläum*, p. 55.
[32] The symbolism of the Rhine often verges on the banal, and it is partly this quality which provoked the protest of post-1945 German artists such as Anselm Kiefer, painter of cycle 'Der Rhein', or of his teacher Joseph Beuys.
[33] Tabori, *Jubiläum*, p. 51. [34] Ibid., p. 63.
[35] Tabori, 'Vom Wesen des Glücks', in Welker, ed., *Tabori*, p. 80.
[36] Tabori, *Jubiläum*, p. 63.

36. *Jubiläum*. A young Nazi (Klaus Fischer) in a Gestapo leather coat screams at Arnold, while Lotte looks on.

come full circle'.[37] Tabori has often spoken of death as a form of birth. In his poem 'Was mich ärgert, was mich am meisten ärgert' he says: 'dying (is) like being born, only the other way round'.[38] Wumpf the gravedigger describes the grave as 'deep and moist as a mother'.[39] Dying is the return to the maternal womb, the uterus full of amniotic fluid, the source of life, *prima materia*. In *Jubiläum* Lotte and Otto die in water,[40] but there are those who die in the opposite element, fire: Mitzi, the spastic who sticks her head into her oven and the millions sent to the Nazi crematoria. The symbolic significance of water is emphasized by a key sentence of Tabori's alter ego, Arnold. What happens when a song is sung to its end, Arnold asks and answers himself: 'It remains.'[41]

---

[37] Ibid.
[38] Tabori, 'Was mich ärgert, was mich am meisten ärgert', in *Betrachtungen*, p. 274.
[39] Tabori, *Jubiläum*, p. 63.
[40] See also the case of the two prisoners killed in water, ibid., p. 67.
[41] Ibid., pp. 70–1.

Whatever has taken place – exists, lives on in memory. Helmut's reply to this sophisticated, philosophical argument is that he himself hears nothing, to which Arnold the musician – in the original production Stanley Walden with the clarinet – retorts: 'I am a white whale in a sea of music.'[42]

Water is the source of infinite potential, the origin and endpoint of all things in the universe. The whale's belly is a place of death and darkness as well as rebirth and resurrection, and Jonah, 'the retired prophet',[43] is Tabori's favourite biblical figure. This tension between death and regeneration is part and parcel of Tabori's experience of remembering. In the European tradition of symbolism water is also associated with unconsciousness and forgetfulness: the mythological Lethe, or the German Rhine in *Jubiläum* is the river of the underworld, the river of forgetfulness.[44] Tabori's 'Erinnerungsarbeit' is based on the dialectics of forgetfulness and remembrance, since 'we can only forget what we really remember'.

The hidden tensions latent in Tabori's 'Erinnerungsarbeit' also include the complex relationship between victim ('Opfer') and perpetrator ('Täter'). Tabori emphasizes the fact that the victims – not only the perpetrators – try to forget or suppress the gruesome past. The tension between the two seems to reach a climax in *Mein Kampf*, where the affinity between Schlomo and Hitler turns out to be a love–hate relationship. This is indeed an example of Tabori's revolutionary thinking: Schlomo loves Hitler, treats him like a loving (Jewish) mother, is concerned about him.[45] In *Jubiläum*, too, the victims and the

---

[42] Stanley Walden describes his part in *Jubiläum* in 'Das Jucken, das nicht nachlässt', in Welker, ed., *Tabori*, pp. 295–8. See also the discussion of music in the production in Gundula Ohngemach, 'George Taboris Theaterarbeit: Eine Analyse der Probenarbeit am beispiel von "*Jubiläum*"', unpublished M. A. dissertation, Munich 1983, pp. 94–101.

[43] Herlinde Koelbl, *Jüdische Portraits* (Frankfurt-on-Main: Fischer, 1989), p. 237. See also Tabori's version of the Jonah story in 'Berliner Betten', *Betrachtungen*, p. 255, and in 'Frühstück', *Betrachtungen*, p. 224, as well as the incorporation of the Jonah story in his play *Goldberg Variationen*.

[44] See Mitzi: 'Und der Rhein wältzt sich immer weiter'. *Jubiläum*, p. 56.

[45] See Arnold's remark about Hitler's loneliness, ibid., p. 76.

perpetrators are linked to each other: it is not only the murderer who returns to the scene of the crime, as in Dostoyevsky's model, but also the victim, as Arnold testifies.[46] In all his Holocaust plays, *Jubiläum* included, Tabori rejects the mythologization of Auschwitz: Auschwitz is not a remote and alien planet, the victims are not saints but flesh-and-blood men, women and children, with their virtues and their flaws, their dreams and their passions. Like all human beings they are flawed by envy, rage and baseness. Tabori makes his point very theatrically: the interchange of roles is of major significance in his collage. The dead, the victims, slip into the role of the vicious perpetrators while the neo-Nazi Jürgen, for instance, plays the prosecutor at a trial. Historical materials are mingled with fiction, and the victims are required to try and understand the motivations and state of mind of the Nazis they are made to play. This is typical of Tabori. The key sentence to the understanding of the tension between victim and perpetrator is to be found in Jürgen's monologue (scene 7). The 'Nazi' – or in the wider sense of the word, evil – is latent in all human beings. The difference between Jürgen and others is that he has let the evil spirit out: 'It's only because you do not have the courage to let the little Nazi in you loose', he explains.[47]

Belonging to one side or to the other is a matter of choice. It is always possible to choose between alternatives, even in extreme situations – 'Grenzsituationen' – and it is indeed the possibility of choice which makes humans human. This belief, shared by Primo Levi, is already expressed in *Kannibalen*, and underlies *Jubiläum* too. In *Jubiläum*, Arnold recounts the fate of his father, Cornelius (named after Tabori's own father). Cornelius, an inveterate humanist, had refused to go into hiding even when the Nazis were about to arrest him. He would not give up his faith in human justice. So, he turned himself into the Gestapo, dressed in the costume he had worn as an opera singer in Wagner's *Parsifal* – his German identity.[48]

The clear differentiation between victims and perpetrators is thus misconceived, based on an illusion or self-deception. It is the

---

[46] Ibid., p. 70.   [47] Ibid., p. 65.

[48] Modelled partly at least on Tabori's uncle Zoltan, the 'only lanky Wagner tenor in Europe', *Unterammergau*, p. 12.

choice which determines what one will be, in any given situation. The complexity of being a victim is manifest in the fate of Helmut the homosexual and of Mitzi the spastic. The figure of the physically handicapped, the invalid, has preoccupied Tabori time and again, in his own plays and in productions of plays by other authors. The best instances are his choice of the wheelchair invalid, Peter Radtke, for the leading male part in *M.* (1985), in *Happy Days* (1986), or in Kafka's *Bericht für eine Akademie* (1992),[49] and the moving figure of Ruth, the mongoloid handicapped in his own play, *Weisman und Rotgesicht* (1990). Mitzi is *the* victim in *Jubiläum*. Physical impairment – humanity in an extreme state – is in Tabori's vision the best symbol of resourceful inner energy, the fruitful dialectics of 'extreme physical handicap and an inner freedom no less extreme'.[50]

Tabori's theatre of mourning is so effective in its 'Erinnerungsarbeit' because it is empowered by his very special black humour, which is grotesque, biting, terrifying, macabre. The sources of Tabori's humour are a long Jewish tradition of bittersweet jokes and witty anecdotes, Hollywood slapstick (for example, Arnold throwing a cream cake at Jürgen in scene 7), as well as the vulgar and repulsive humour of virulent anti-Semitism (the awful joke about Jews in the ashtray of a Volkswagen).

Tabori's humour is mercilessly funny. It can be bitter as poison, as in the beautifully rhymed, mesmerizing song about the extermination, which is based on the popular German nursery rhyme 'Die Vogelhochzeit'. Often a joke and tears come together, 'Scherz und Schmerz', as for Tabori 'humour is no laughing matter'.[51] The Taborian joke, which gets stuck in the throat and, at the same time, liberates suppressed feelings, is a conscious attempt to break a taboo and is yet another manifestation of his 'Prinzip Hoffnung'. Directed against affected piousness and mawkish sympathy, his humour liberates the

---

[49] Peter Radtke provides an account of his theatre work with Tabori in *M – wie Tabori* (Zürich: Pendo-Verlag, 1987) and in 'Täter und Opfer', in Welker, ed., *Tabori*, pp. 118–20.

[50] Tabori, 'Warten auf Beckett', *Betrachtungen*, p. 60.

[51] Tabori, 'Notes to *Sigmunds Freude*', p. 5.

spectator from the conditioned consternation, or 'Betroffenheit'. It is this perspective of humour which affords us a more profound insight into the heart of darkness. It enables us to recognize the true dimensions of the tragedy and stimulates a sincere and valuable 'Erinnerungsarbeit'.

17 Thomas Bernhard, Jews, *Heldenplatz*

JEANETTE R. MALKIN

The year 1995 was fraught with commemorations. The fiftieth anniversary of the ending of World War Two, of the freeing of the concentration camps, of the bombings of Hiroshima and Nagasaki were all marked and remembered in a spectrum of official and cultural activities. The performance of memory took many shapes, but the most important theatre event connected with a 'fiftieth' commemoration had already been played out seven years earlier – in 1988, in Vienna. The event was the Burgtheater production of Thomas Bernhard's *Heldenplatz*; and the anniversary it 'commemorated' and probed was the Anschluss: Hitler's 1938 annexation of Austria into the Third Reich. More than that, the production placed at its centre the widely repressed memory of the destruction of Austria's Jews, in a play written by a non-Jew, for an audience whose major relation to the Shoah and to Nazism is one of denial and forgetting.

Thomas Bernhard is Austria's most important postwar writer and playwright, and was (until his death in 1989) its most notorious *Nestbeschmutzer*: one who defiles his 'nest', his homeland. 'In Austria you have to be either Catholic / or a National Socialist', he wrote in *Heldenplatz*, 'nothing else is tolerated / everything else is destroyed'.[1] Bernhard's implacable, some would say *ferocious*, memory

---

[1] All translations from *Heldenplatz* are my own, and refer to Thomas Bernhard, *Heldenplatz* (Frankfurt-on-Main: Suhrkamp Verlag, 1988), here, p. 63. Subsequent references to this edition will appear parenthetically within the text. An English translation of the play has yet to be published.

was permanently enraged against the collective amnesia of his Heimat, Austria. As famous for the scandals he created as for his thirty prose works, twenty plays, and numerous books of poetry, Bernhard's fight with Austria, with amnesia, with the cover-ups and euphemisms and hypocrisies of a German language inherited from a polluted past, was long-standing and deep. During that memorial year of 1988, his dramatic outrage hit a particularly sensitive public nerve, producing a theatrical and political uproar which became the focal point of Austria's commemorative activities.

Heldenplatz centres on a Jewish family in the Vienna of 1988. The main character, Professor Josef Schuster, commits suicide by jumping out of his apartment window on to the historic Heldenplatz before the play begins. The metaphoric centre, his wife Hedwig Schuster, falls dead into her bowl of soup at the end of the play. Both of these extravagant and unheroic deaths are directly related to what Bernhard shows to be Austria's willing acceptance of the Anschluss, and to its active role in the destruction of its Jews. Between these two framing and accusatory deaths, Bernhard managed to infuriate most of Austria – including its Jews. Unlike most other post-Shoah plays written in Germany or Austria, Bernhard produced a work in which the Jews are neither especially nice, nor especially Jewish; in fact, they are not much different from Bernhard's usual cast of complex, misanthropic, self-centred and slightly mad characters. Unlike most other post-Shoah plays written in Germany or Austria, anger, hatred and bile are here unmitigated by any moral agenda of forgiveness or reconciliation, or by any metaphysical appeal to higher meanings. Both of these provocative stances engendered one of Austria's most significant postwar theatre scandals, and one of its more revealing political fracases.

Heldenplatz premièred under tight police security on 4 November 1988, fifty years after the Anschluss (March 1938), fifty years almost to the day after Kristallnacht (9 November 1938), for which Vienna had a particularly despicable record: virtually all of Vienna's many synagogues were burnt down, over 4,000 Jewish shops were looted or destroyed, thousands of Jewish apartments were expropriated, Jews in their thousands were sent to Dachau concentration camp,

37. Vienna: Heldenplatz, situated behind the arched gateway, the Burgtor. To the left is the Volksgarten, with the Burgtheater further left, behind the columned Theseustempel.

and numerous murders and atrocities were committed.[2] Kristallnacht
and the Anschluss were, however, not the only anniversaries of that
officially titled 'memorial year': 1988 also marked the 100th anniversary of Vienna's famous Burgtheater building, and it was within those
centenary festivities that Bernhard's play was commissioned by Claus
Peymann – the politically controversial German director who had
worked closely with Bernhard for almost twenty years, directing most
of his plays, and who was then beginning his directorship of Austria's
National Theatre. Peymann had been expected to commemorate a century of Austrian culture. The fiftieth anniversary of the Anschluss
and the memory of Austria's Jews and their destruction were not
considered, by most, to be fitting subjects. *Heldenplatz* erupted in an
Austria still bruised by the campaign surrounding the election of the
Nazi collaborator (and two-time UN secretary general) Kurt Waldheim
to the presidency. Waldheim, in his victory, proved Austria's determination not to see itself as anything other than 'Hitler's first victim',
an epithet long cherished in Bernhard's homeland. With *Heldenplatz*,
Bernhard created a memory scandal within the deeply etched space of
Austrian repression and denial. *Heldenplatz*, like Bernhard's earlier
play on a continuing Nazi mentality in Germany, *Eve of Retirement*
(*Vor dem Ruhestand*; 1979), is a provocative dialogue with the knowledge and memory of his audience; and as was the case with *Eve of
Retirement*, the context of its performance, the concrete socio-political
situation within which it appeared, was very much part of the theatrical event.[3]

---

[2] See for example, Bruce F. Pauley, *From Prejudice to Persecution: A
History of Austrian Anti-Semitism* (Chapel Hill: University of North
Carolina Press, 1992), pp. 286–9, on 'The November Pogrom'.

[3] *Eve of Retirement*, which premièred in Stuttgart in 1979, was, in part,
an intervention in the scandal concerning the prominent conservative minister–president of Baden-Württemberg, Hans Karl Filbinger.
Filbinger, like the main character of *Eve of Retirement*, had long hidden
his past as a 'hanging' judge during the Nazi regime. The revelation of
that past is referred to in the play, just as the fiftieth anniversary of the
Anschluss is referred to in *Heldenplatz*. See my article 'Pulling the Pants
Off History: Politics and Postmodernism in Thomas Bernhard's *Eve of
Retirement*', in *Theatre Journal*, 47.1 (March 1995), pp. 105–19.

Heldenplatz is a square at the centre of historic Vienna. It is positioned close to the lovely Volksgarten (the garden where scene 2 of Bernhard's play takes place), and near the famous Burgtheater (where the play was originally performed). Two large museums, the National Library and the Hofburg (old Kaiser palace) are all situated around this central square. As many have noted, Heldenplatz embodies much of Austria's national identity.[4] Meaning 'Hero's Square', Heldenplatz figures in Bernhard's play as geography, history, and fable. During Austria's First Republic, Heldenplatz was the place for military parades and troop call-ups. Already in 1932, the first Nazi demonstration with Goebbels and Röhm took place there. It was at Heldenplatz that the crowds gathered in 1934 to mourn the assassination of their right-wing chancellor, Engelbert Dollfuss. And in 1938 – the important date for this play, and the most infamous event connected with that square – hundreds of thousands of cheering Austrians gathered at Heldenplatz to welcome Hitler and the Anschluss that ended the First Republic and made Austria part of the German Reich. Bernhard did not need to detail all this history within the play. As always, he wrote for a specific audience, at a specific place and time: he could thus assume the audience's knowledge of the history and centrality of Heldenplatz.

The public outcry against Bernhard's play preceded both its performance and its publication, and was based on passages 'leaked' to the press during rehearsals, passages attacking the Austrians, their government, their mendacity and vulgarity, and including historically accusatory sections such as: 'What they would really want / if they were honest / is to gas us again today / just as they did fifty years ago / it's in their nature' (p. 115).[5] Such provocations encouraged the outcry that followed. The media dedicated weeks of daily coverage to the reactions and debates surrounding the as yet unseen and unread play. Waldheim called the play an insult to all Austrians. He was joined by

---

[4] See for example, Egon Schwarz, '*Helden*platz?', in *German Politics and Society*, 21 (Fall 1990), p. 36.

[5] Most critics suspected Peymann and Bernhard of orchestrating the scandal by leaking the passages themselves, and of purposely postponing publication of the play text until the première in order to increase tension and interest.

ex-chancellor Bruno Kreisky, among others, in calling for the play's removal from the Burgtheater. Bernhard was vilified, and he was even attacked in the street by an angry citizen. 'What writers write / is nothing compared with reality' – one of the characters in Bernhard's play says; 'yes yes they write that everything is terrible / that everything is ruined and depraved / that it's all a catastrophe / that it's hopeless / but all of this / is nothing compared with the reality' (p. 115). Bernhard claimed that he had to keep revising and 'sharpening' his text during rehearsals in order, as he put it, 'not to be left behind by reality'[6] – that is, by the uproar raging in the press, in parliament, and on the streets. Egon Schwarz summarized it well: 'One could say that the play was already being performed in the country, while it was still in rehearsal at the Burgtheater.'[7] And indeed, on opening day, two groups of protesters – for and against Bernhard – chanted and marched in front of the theatre; and a group of rightists dumped horse manure on the theatre steps. This *furor austriacus*, as the critic Bernhard Sorg called these displays,[8] had as much to do with the public determination not to face their own history of Nazi collaboration, as with the determined provocations of Bernhard's play.

Heldenplatz begins in the Schusters' apartment, three floors above Heldenplatz. Schuster, a mathematics professor and a Jew, was driven from Vienna with his family by the Anschluss; he escaped to Oxford, where he lived and taught for many years. His brother Robert, a philosophy professor and the main speaker in the play, found work in Cambridge. Later, Schuster was invited back to teach at the University of Vienna, and he returned – so Robert tells us – because he missed the music of Vienna. 'He wanted his music / he wanted his childhood / again / But the Viennese were no longer / the way he remembered them.' The Austria to which the Schusters returned was the Austria of

---

[6] Quoted in the wide-ranging book published by Peymann and the Burgtheater, documenting the scandal, the play, and subsequent reactions, from 1 August to 31 December 1988. *Heldenplatz: Eine Dokumentation* (Vienna: Burgtheater, 1989), p. 220.

[7] Schwarz, '*Helden*platz?', p. 38.

[8] Bernhard Sorg, 'Die Zeichen des Zerfalls: Zu Thomas Bernhards *Auslöschung* und *Heldenplatz*', in *Thomas Bernhard*, ed. Heinz Ludwig Arnold, *Text+Kritik*, 43 (3rd expanded edition, 1991), p. 84.

denial and revisionism; everything about it seemed tainted, even the music. 'The Austrians after the war / had become much more hateful and even more Jew hating / than before the war / no one could have foreseen that' (p. 112), Robert says. 'The circumstances today are really / just as they were in thirty-eight', one of the Schuster daughters, Anna, declares; except that 'there are now more Nazis in Vienna / than in thirty-eight / . . . now they're again coming up / out of all their holes' (pp. 62–3). These perceptions finally convinced the Schusters to leave Austria again and return to Oxford. Before the play begins, all had been packed and made ready for the family's departure; a house had been bought in Oxford, the Heldenplatz apartment had been sold when, on the eve of the fiftieth anniversary of the Anschluss – Josef jumped out of his third-floor window. The play consists of a series of discussions in Bernhard's usual monologic form, in which the life and reasons for Josef's suicide are interrogated by the Schusters' housekeeper, their two daughters, and brother Robert. Characters evoke Austria's past – which drove the Schusters into exile – and the unchanged present – which finally led to Schuster's suicide.

Another vital strand concerns Schuster's wife Hedwig, who, since returning to Vienna, suffers constant auditory seizures in which she – and finally the audience too – relives the cheering of the crowds as they applaud Hitler's triumphant speech of 1938 on the square below. Hedwig has undergone treatments for her 'condition' at the Steinhof sanatorium, including shock therapy. But all to no avail. This is hardly surprising since disease (which is often a subject in Bernhard's works) is not the point here: memory, in Bernhard, like resentment, cannot be cured. It can only be overcome (if at all) through death. By the end of the play, the roaring choruses of '*Sieg Heil Sieg Heil*' will lead to Hedwig's final collapse. Through these two framing deaths, Bernhard performs the taboo evocation of the destruction of Austria's Jews, connecting it with the Austrian part in Nazism, with their willing acceptance of the Anschluss, and with their continued refusal to 'hear' the voices of a still present past.

Reflexive geography: place and complicity

Bernhard's tactics in this uncompromising play go beyond the litany of fierce verbal attacks anticipated by his audience. This outer layer is combined with a complex recreation of the geographic and historic 'space' within which Austria, and the audience, are defined. The audience is always the centre of Bernhard's plays, and here it is signified both through direct reference and, more interestingly, through the spatial reinscription of the Burgtheater (within which the audience was sitting) and the Heldenplatz (geographically so close) – on stage. Through this, the audience is imaged as contained within, and complicit with, the stage reality it is viewing. Bernhard conflated the play's *fabula* with the geography of the theatre and city where the performance was held; moreover, he evoked the past through the geography it shares with the present. Visual reinscription is one of Bernhard's central strategies for tying audience, city and history into what Mikhail Bakhtin calls a 'chronotope': that is, the unique space/time relationship that characterizes and underwrites every genre. *Heldenplatz* stresses the simultaneity of stage and world, of past and present, of Heldenplatz as diachronic and synchronic site of memory and identity.

Scene 1 takes place in Professor Schuster's large linen-room. It contains one high window from which Herta, the maid, constantly stares down on to the square below, directing the audience's attention to the spot where she had found Professor Schuster's broken body.[9] Scene 2 moves to the Volksgarten which adjoins Heldenplatz to the Burgtheater. For this scene, Peymann had his set designer, Karl-Ernst Herrmann, build a sidewall of the Burgtheater on stage, thus reflecting the outside of the building inside of which the audience watching this play was sitting.[10] The second scene is the key to this reconstructed geography. With the Burgtheater wall at one side, and Heldenplatz in the distance on the other, Josef's daughters and their uncle, Robert Schuster, sit on a bench in Vienna's famous park facing what would, if the on-stage geography were extended to the auditorium, be the parliament building. The conversation between the daughters and their

---

[9] This is dramatic licence on Bernhard's part, since no apartments border Heldenplatz, although some are within hearing distance.

[10] In the text, Bernhard writes that from the garden we can see the Burgtheater 'through a fog'. In production, Peymann and Bernhard placed the theatre wall right by the bench where the characters were sitting.

uncle, resting after Josef's funeral, also centres on geography. It moves between Oxford – 'in Oxford there is no Heldenplatz', Anna says; 'in Oxford Hitler never came / in Oxford there are no Viennese / in Oxford the masses never screamed' (p. 13); and Vienna – 'in Vienna you see and hear everything / and every day more clearly / the Jews are afraid in Vienna / they were always afraid in Vienna' (pp. 82–3). Like the French historian Pierre Nora, Bernhard and Peymann mapped out the central *lieux de mémoire* (sites of memory)[11] of Vienna, and thus of Austria: the central square, the most acclaimed and tradition-filled theatre, the garden at the heart of the capital city, the parliament to which Bernhard often refers – and they placed the audience at the centre of this reflexive geography. Scene 3 returns to the dining-room of the Schuster apartment. Against the back wall of the stage Bernhard placed *'Three large high windows which look out onto Heldenplatz'* (p. 117). This time, the audience can *see* the square which gives the play its title. The stage area in scene 3 is strategically centred between Heldenplatz, imaged through the three windows behind, and the audience sitting in front. This positioning becomes vital for the final effect of the performance.

Throughout the play we have heard numerous references to Mrs Schuster's unusual form of memory madness: her constant reliving of the screams of welcome that greeted Hitler's arrival at Heldenplatz in 1938. The housekeeper early on describes the symptoms: 'barely has she eaten a few spoons of soup / when her face turns white and she goes completely stiff' (p. 13) each time she hears the screams. This has been going on for at least ten years, 'all day continuously / continuously continuously' (p. 27). At the end of scene 3, Mrs Schuster enters the stage for the first time. She has come to join the family for a 'Last Supper' before leaving the apartment for good. As she begins to eat her soup, Mrs Schuster's affliction suddenly becomes a reality: the audience – together with her – hears the *'slowly swelling cheers of the masses at Hitler's arrival on Heldenplatz nineteen-thirty-eight'* (p. 159). These

---

[11] In the 1980s, Pierre Nora proposed an 'archaeological' method for studying (France's) past based on the objects and sites that codify and anchor a national memory. See Pierre Nora, 'Between Memory and History: *Les Lieux de mémoire*', trans. Marc Roudebush, in *Representations*, 26 (1989), pp. 7–25.

cheers, as though struggling to break through the barrier of collective repression, begin as barely audible background noise. Mrs Schuster goes stiff and pale in her chair. Meanwhile, as the screams from Heldenplatz are swelling, Robert, unaware, continues to discuss Vienna: 'In this most terrible of all cities', he says, 'an unbearable stink spreads itself out / from the Hofburg and the Ballhausplatz / and from the Parliament / over the entire wretched and despoiled land' – thus remapping a circle around the same Heldenplatz. 'This little city is one huge pile of garbage' (p. 164), Robert concludes, as *the shouts of the masses in Heldenplatz swell to the limits of the bearable* – and Mrs Schuster falls face forward into her soup bowl.[12] *'All react with fear / The end'* (p. 165).[13]

The unbearable shouts of the masses welcoming Hitler fifty years earlier, at a spot close enough to the theatre for the shouts to have been heard inside the theatre – those same shouts fill the theatre for the last long stretch of the play. Peymann, however, did not turn the horrible noise off with the play's end. Gitta Honegger, who was in the audience that night, describes how the first performance ended:

> The four-hour-long performance was followed by forty minutes of thundering applause, standing ovations, boos and whistles, with the Austrian flag and banners unfolding from the balcony

[12] In his short 'dramolette' *Der deutsche Mittagstisch* (*The German Lunch Table: A Tragedy to be Performed by the Burgtheater when Touring Germany*), which premièred in Bochum in 1981, Bernhard develops the connections between soup and ideology. A couple named Mr and Mrs Bernhard try to eat a lunch of hot soup with their great- and great-great-grandchildren, but keep on finding 'Nazis in the soup'. This dramatized verbal coinage – the equivalent of finding a Nazi under every bush – stands, in this short, mock-expressionist play, for the invasion of a still-open past into the most basic rituals of daily life.

[13] The theatrical ending of *Heldenplatz*, like that of *Eve of Retirement* (where the 'hero' also falls over dead), is obviously exaggerated and contrived – almost like a gestural summation of the play's major themes. In both plays, the final twist allows a performative device to supplement and give sensual emphasis to the rhetorics which are Bernhard's main tool. And in both plays, the audience – who is always the real subject of his plays – is reflected and implicated in the ironic ending. I discuss this below.

both in support of and against Peymann, who bowed next to
Bernhard . . . To some, the two men, their hands clasped and
held up high, appeared like a triumphant pair of conquerors as
the 'Sieg Heil' choruses on stage segued hauntingly into the
warring choruses in the auditorium.[14]

Thus, the unbearable shouts coming from backstage, from the stage's
(and history's?) hidden recesses, merged with the cheers and boos coming from the front, from the audience that was simultaneously acclaim-
ing and booing the performance of memory it had just participated in.
Together, these concrete gestures, and the dead Mrs Schuster on stage,
made an iconic – and ironic – statement about Austria's willing part in
Nazism, in the destruction of its Jews, and in the repression of its past.

The presentation of the Shoah
The question of how the Shoah is presented in this play is particularly
complex and interesting. Two things are clear: Bernhard avoids the
metaphysical discourse, the tendency to seek compensating 'meanings' and messages found, for example, in plays such as Rolf Hochhuth's *The Deputy (Der Stellvertreter;* 1963) – in which Mengele and
Auschwitz are finally depicted as the Devil and Hell incarnate; or
Erwin Sylvanus' 1957 Pirandellian play, *Dr Korczak and the Children –*
which ends with recitations from Ezekiel that prophesy redemption
and statehood for the Jewish people. Even Peter Weiss's acclaimed
quasi-documentary play *The Investigation (Die Ermittlung;* 1965), a
play based on the transcripts of the Frankfurt Auschwitz trials and
which rejects all representation, using only voices, 'speaking tubes', as
vocal witness to the reality of Auschwitz: even here, Weiss structured
his play as an oratorio in thirty-three songs, or *canti,* which parallels
the structure of Dante's *Inferno* while inverting its theological under-
pinnings. Dante's divine geography, his theologically ordered rings of
Hell, overlays and gives heightened significance to the profane sitings
of Weiss's play which moves (via vocal testimony) from the train platform, through the 'selection' point, the bunkers, torture cells and gas

---

[14] Gitta Honegger, 'Thomas Bernhard', in *Partisan Review,* 58.3 (1991),
p. 496.

chambers, to the last ring of Auschwitz's hell – the crematorium. By evoking Dante, the metaphysical invades the helpless impossibility of dramatizing the Shoah. It is here that Bernhard differs. Bernhard refused any framing context – aside from the specific political situation (the fiftieth anniversary of the Anschluss) within which the play appeared. And he refused any transcendent allusions. No classical text, neither biblical nor Dantesque, structures or heightens Bernhard's concrete positioning of Austrian history within the geography and memory of his concrete audience.

Thus Bernhard's theatre becomes a platform, and an instrument, for political intervention. Vienna was his extended stage, just as his theatre stage reflected the geography of Vienna. The concreteness of this reflexivity had everything to do with the type of memory Bernhard was calling forth: of a specific past (the willing acceptance of the Anschluss, Austria's active participation in the Third Reich and the Shoah) everywhere blurred and obfuscated in his country, for fifty years ignored or denied. It was this specific past that Bernhard insisted on recreating for his audience. But this 'concrete audience' contained not only Austria's Christians, but also its small community of Jews. And many were outraged. The prominent Jewish journalist Peter Sichrovsky wrote: 'I condemn this play, I'm afraid of it, I'm horrified and insulted. Again I feel used.'[15] Simon Wiesenthal also rejected the play, coming out against 'generalizations' and assigning 'collective guilt' to any people.[16] Many feared anti-Semitic reactions because Bernhard had turned the Jews into the mouthpieces of his deepest anti-Austrian sentiments. Other Jews, however, identified precisely with the anger and unforgiving forthrightness of Bernhard's characters. They saw this as one of the few examples of a 'mature' portrayal of Jews on the German/Austrian stage – the Jew not as *type*, not as innocent or protected by the guilt of the non-Jew; rather, the Jew as idiosyncratic, unforgiving, and filled with resentment.[17] Bernhard was in any case not

---

[15] From *Heldenplatz: Eine Dokumentation*, p. 187.   [16] Ibid., p. 24.

[17] Robert Singer, in the *Jüdischen Rundschau*, saw no problem with Bernhard's portrayal of Jews as both difficult and resentful towards Austria. Most Austrians, he writes, 'still prefer their Jews to be servile and bowing' (p. 264) – and thankful for being tolerated at all.

speaking for, or on behalf of the survivors' community. He was speaking in the name of concrete memory itself, as one who refused to accept historical amnesia and erasure – on principle.

Bernhard, Jean Améry and resentment

The need to confront the past and to give it public form clearly connects Bernhard, and his character Schuster – who, we are told, had for years been accumulating 'heaps of notes' (p. 163) which he planned, one day, to turn into a 'comprehensive study' of Austria[18] – with another Austrian whose story and voice is unmistakably echoed in Bernhard's play, namely Jean Améry. Josef Schuster was loosely based on the life and suicide of the Austrian writer, philosopher, and concentration camp survivor Hans Maier – better known under the anagram of Jean Améry. After the Anschluss, Maier, son of a Jewish father, escaped from Vienna to Belgium where he changed his name. He was captured in 1943, tortured by the Gestapo, and spent the rest of the war in concentration camps, including Auschwitz. He never returned to live in Austria (he made his home in Brussels). Améry – who retained his anagram as a sign of his radically rearranged post-torture identity – did however continue to write and lecture in his native German language, becoming one of Germany's most flagrant *Ruhestörer* ('disturbers of the peace'), as was Bernhard in Austria. Améry's uncompromising memory, his strict sense of resentment and his precise, dispassionate, repetition of how he had lost his 'name', strongly link him to the character of Schuster. Améry wrote and spoke relentlessly about the torture and destruction he had experienced. Like Schuster, and Bernhard, he retained permanent offence – and a keen memory – of what the Germans and Austrians had done. Améry's most famous book on the memory of his torture by the Gestapo, and the eternal torture of that memory, bears the clearly Nietzschean title *Jenseits von Schuld und Sühne* (1966, 'Beyond Guilt and Repentance' – translated into English as *At the Mind's Limits*). In a chapter of that book entitled

---

[18] This work, to be called 'The Sign of the Times', was never written; almost none of Bernhard's many writer-protagonists (in his novels and plays) ever write the books they so carefully plan.

'Resentments', Améry wrote of the 'antimoral natural process of healing that time brings'.[19] Only active memory, he believed, could prevent the industrial murder of millions by the Germans from being

> lumped with the bloody expulsion of the Armenians by the Turks or with the shameful acts of violence by the colonial French: as regrettable, but in no way unique. Everything will be submerged in a general 'Century of Barbarism'. *We*, the victims, will appear as the truly incorrigible, irreconcilable ones, as the anti-historical reactionaries in the exact sense of the word, and in the end it will seem like a technical mishap that some of us still survived.[20]

This view precisely fits Bernhard's portrayal of the Schusters: 'anti-historical reactionaries' who, fifty years later, still insist on hearing the roars that greeted the Anschluss fifty years before, and who throw themselves out of windows against the flow of history which decrees the 'natural process of healing'.

Améry, in his refusal to forget, represents the same type of morality as that of Bernhard: the morality of memory – and of 'resentment'. Resentment, Améry wrote, is the 'emotional source of every genuine morality, which was always a morality for the losers'.[21] Literally meaning to re-sense – to feel again, and again, the humiliation and pain experienced in the past – Améry's use of this word echoes, and subverts the writings of Nietzsche. *Ressentiment* (resentment), according to

---

[19] Jean Améry, *At the Mind's Limits: Contemplations by a Survivor on Auschwitz and its Realities*, trans. Sidney Rosenfeld and Stella P. Rosenfeld (Bloomington: Indiana University Press, 1980), p. 77. My reading here is influenced by Stephen D. Dowden's *Understanding Thomas Bernhard* (South Carolina: University of South Carolina Press, 1991). Dowden writes with great insight on the connections between Améry and Bernhard (pp. 80–2).

[20] Améry, *At the Mind's Limits*, p. 80.

[21] Ibid., p. 81. For an essay on Améry and the morality of 'witnessing', see Alvin Rosenfeld, 'Jean Améry as Witness', in *Holocaust Remembrance: The Shapes of Memory*, ed. Geoffrey H. Hartman (Oxford: Blackwell, 1994), pp. 59–69.

Nietzsche, is characteristic of 'natures that are denied the true reaction, that of deeds, and compensate themselves with an imaginary revenge'.[22] For Nietzsche, the impotence of resentment characterizes the slave, the *Untermensch*, such as Dostoyevsky's 'underground man'. The Master is always a man of action and of the future, who refuses to internalize his enemies and injuries and can thus, as Nietzsche writes in *The Genealogy of Morals*, 'shake off with one shrug' resentments from the past.[23] Michael André Bernstein rephrases Nietzsche's *ressentiment* into three components: the 'inability to forget, to rise above, or to avenge an injury'.[24] But how, we might ask, does one 'rise above' or 'avenge' an 'injury' like the Shoah? What remains of this list – is to forget: and it is this that people like Josef Schuster, Thomas Bernhard, and Jean Améry absolutely refuse to do. Their resentment takes the form of a 'daemonically obsessive total recall' – on principle; a form of recall that Bernstein terms 'reminiscence-as-suffering',[25] and which prefers the self-abuse of memory to the 'antimoral natural process of healing'. Bernhard, like Améry (and quite *contra* Nietzsche) made of resentment a creed. This comes fully to the fore in the dramatic, theatrical, political, event of *Heldenplatz*. Here, through concrete and unforgiving remembrance – through *resentful* remembrance of the Anschluss and of Austria's determined distortion of its memory, and by theatrically 'placing' the audience at the centre of their own blighted past, Bernhard affirmed the power of recall, and performed the disgust he felt with his own people. He also forced those same people – his audience and compatriots, the object and subject of all of his plays – to participate in the performance of their own denial and complicity, both in the public and in the theatrical realms.

For Améry, like Bernhard's character Schuster, only death could still memory and resentment. 'We victims must finish with our retroactive rancour,' Améry wrote, 'in the sense that the KZ [concentration

---

22 Friedrich Nietzsche, *On the Genealogy of Morals*, in *Basic Writings of Nietzsche*, trans. Walter Kaufmann (New York: Modern Library, 1966), p. 472.

23 Ibid., p. 475.

24 Michael André Bernstein, *Bitter Carnival*: Ressentiment *and the Abject Hero* (Princeton: Princeton University Press, 1992), p. 102.

25 Ibid.

camp] argot once gave to the word "finish"; it meant as much as "to kill". Soon we must and will be finished. Until that time has come, we request of those whose peace is disturbed by our grudge that they be patient.'[26] And indeed, Améry, like Schuster, finished off his 'retroactive rancour' by finishing off his life. In 1978 he returned to Austria, to Bernhard's city of Salzburg, rented a room and hanged himself. Like Schuster – or Paul Celan, or Primo Levi – he did not leave a note of explanation: his life and writings would serve as witnesses to the reasons for his death.[27]

The connection between memory, resentment, and performance has one final link in this context: a link which again ties theatre and performance to politics and memory. This link is Bernhard's own death, which came suddenly, three months after the première of *Heldenplatz*. He died during its run, some say as a result of the enormous scandal caused by this most provocative of his plays. Bernhard's death created an additional scandal. Like Josef Schuster, Bernhard too left a will that specified he was to be buried privately, and that his death was to remain unannounced until after the burial. But most stunningly, his will states that nothing he has ever written, neither book nor essay nor play, is to be published or performed 'within the borders of the Austrian state, however that state describes itself . . . for all time to come'[28] – or at least for the duration of his copyright (seventy years). Bernhard also forbade his own commemoration by Austria in any form, or by any

---

[26] Améry, *At the Mind's Limits*, p. 81.

[27] Although he does not refer to him directly, it is clear that Bernhard was acquainted with this famous intellectual whose temperament was so similar to his own. Moreover, Améry published an appreciative review of Bernhard's memoirs *The Cause* and of his novel *Correction* entitled 'Morbus Austriacus', in *Merkur*, 30 (1976), pp. 91–6; and another just before his death in 1978, 'Atemnot', in *Merkur*, 32 (1978), pp. 947–9.
   Like Bernhard, Améry was preoccupied with ageing and death. A few years before his suicide he published a book on the subject: *Hand an sich legen. Diskurs über den Freitod* (Stuttgart: E. Klett, 1976).

[28] Quoted from Heinrich Wille, 'Wunsch oder Bedingung? Zum Rechtsstreit über Thomas Bernhards letztwillige Verfügung', *Der Standard*, 7 March 1989, p. 19.

country supported by Austrian money or institutions. Thus, in a sense, he outdid both Schuster and Améry. His rancour and resentment live on after him in an act which continues to express his will to remember and, in a typical Bernhardian paradox, his refusal to *be* remembered in a country whose betrayals he could not forget.

18 Select bibliography of Holocaust plays, 1933–1997

ALVIN GOLDFARB

In 1986 I prepared a selected bibliography of Holocaust plays for Elinor Fuchs' *Plays of the Holocaust* (New York: Theatre Communications Group, 1987). In the decade since the appearance of that anthology, a number of other works have come to my attention. The following is the original listing of works merged with those new ones I have discovered since 1986.

As I indicated in the earlier bibliography, these are dramas which are set during the Holocaust, deal with survivors of the Holocaust, depict Jews and non-Jews who were involved in the Holocaust, and/or use the image of the Holocaust as a significant dramatic metaphor. I have been as expansive as possible and, if I have erred, it is in being more inclusive.

Works are listed according to the author's current country of citizenship. The titles are either in the original language or in English, if there is a translation or a title frequently used in critical writings. The dates are either initial publication or performance dates. I have included publication information where available, to help researchers locate a play more easily, although in many instances works are as yet unpublished. When a date does not follow the publisher this indicates that the date in parenthesis is also the year of publication. Again, the listing is clearly not exhaustive.

AUSTRALIA

Elisha, Ron. *Two* (1985). Sydney, Australia: Currency Press.

An encounter between a rabbi and a woman wishing to learn Hebrew leads to the exploration of Holocaust issues in postwar Germany.

298

AUSTRIA

Bernhard, Thomas. *Eve of Retirement* (1979). Trans. Gitta Honegger. In Thomas Bernhard, *The President and Eve of Retirement*. New York: Performing Arts Journal Publications, 1982.

A family of contemporary Nazis, including a father who is a former SS officer and now a chief justice, celebrate Himmler's birthday and confront their beliefs in the Third Reich's ideals.

Bernhard, Thomas. *Heldenplatz* (1988). Frankfurt-on-Main: Suhrkamp Verlag.

The play takes place following the suicide – on the site where Hitler celebrated the Austrian Anschluss – of a Jewish professor, who was a survivor. The play focuses on those who survive him, family members and acquaintances, and reflects an unrepentant Austrian world.

Csokor, Franz Theodor. *Das Zeichen an der Wand* (*The Writing on the Wall*; 1962). Hamburg: P. Zsolnay.

An Adolf Eichmann-like character, who has been hiding in South America, is entrapped through a fictitious business deal set up by a concentration camp survivor. The survivor is saved by the Nazi's daughter, who herself prosecutes war criminals.

Kien, Peter (libretto) and Viktor Ullman (composer). *The Emperor of Atlantis* (n.d.). Trans. Aaron Kramer. English language libretto can be found in the programme for the production staged at the Brooklyn Academy of Music, 19–22 May 1977.

This opera, written in Theresienstadt by prisoners, is an allegorical representation of life in the concentration camp.

Zwillinger Frank, *Between Death and Life* (1967). Trans. Roger Clement. *Modern International Drama*, 13.1 (Fall 1979), pp. 49–87.

In a ghetto hospital in Lemberg (Lvov), Jewish doctors decide to commit suicide so that their soon-to-be-deported patients can escape. The play compares this act to the heroic suicide at Massada.

BELGIUM

Kalisky, René. *Jim the Lionhearted* (1972). In David Willinger and Luc Denevlin (trans. and eds.), *An Anthology of Contemporary Belgian Plays: 1970–1982*. Troy, NY: Whitston Publishing Company, 1984.

A survivor, who escaped deportation, exiles himself to his bed and creates a world populated by Hitler, Himmler, etc.

CANADA

Czierniecki, Marion Andre. *The Aching Heart of Samuel Kleinerman* (1984). In Marion Andre Czierniecki, *The Gates: Three Stories and a Play*. Cincinnati, OH: Mosaic Press.

Kleinerman, a moralistic Jewish jeweller, has to decide whether or not to use money, given to him for safekeeping by his hospital-ridden aunt, for passports for him and his family so they can flee Berlin in 1936. After deciding to do so, he is faced with the sudden arrival of the aunt's son, who has escaped from a concentration camp.

Emanuel, Gabriel. *Children of the Night* (1978). In Gabriel Emanuel, *Einstein and Childen of Night: Two Plays*. Toronto: Playwright's Canada, 1985.

Dramatization of Dr Korczak and his children at the orphanage in Warsaw in 1942; in act 2 the children put on a Passover play as an act of resistance just prior to the final deportation.

Rosenfield, David. *Hasid* (1978). Toronto: Playwright's Canada.

A poetic drama in which a survivor recalls his Holocaust past.

Roskies, David G. *Night Words: A Midrash on the Holocaust* (1971). New York: Bnai Brith.

A participatory performance piece in which thirty-six roles are distributed to audience members and biblical tales and prayers are rewritten using Holocaust accounts and images.

Wade, Bryan. *Blitzkrieg* (1973). Toronto: Playwrights Group.

A camp representation of Adolf Hitler and Eva Braun's sadomasochistic sexual relationship.

FRANCE

Atlan, Liliane. *Les Messies ou le mal de terre* (*The Messiahs*; 1969). Paris: Editions du Seuil.

The play centres on eight *dei absconditi*: the author and her cortege; and the dead people on the raft (Jews refused safe harbour during World War Two). It mixes medieval pageantry with modern technology

– masks with radios, chasubles and prayer shawls with telescopes and mobile galaxies.

Atlan, Liliane. *Monsieur Fugue, ou le mal de terre (Mister Fugue, or The Earth Sickness;* 1967). Trans. Marguerite Feitlowitz. In Elinor Fuchs (ed.), *Plays of the Holocaust.* New York: Theatre Communications Group, 1987.
    A runaway German soldier accompanies Jewish children on a truck to their deaths.

Atlan, Liliane. *Un opéra pour Terezin* (1986). In *L'Avant-Scène,* 1007–8 (April 1997).
    A four-overture, full-night multimedia opera about children, from a world in which there is no emotion, who relive the experiences of Terezin.

Billetdoux, François. *Comme va le monde, mossieu? Il tourne, mossieu! (How Goes the World, Mister? It Turns, Mister!;* 1964). In Billetdoux. *Theatre,* vol. II. Paris: La Table Ronde.
    The journey of a Frenchman and an American who escape a concentration camp.

Chartreux, Bernard. *Violences à Vichy* (1995). Paris: Editions Théâtrales.
    A bunch of excited speakers pore over the violent past of collaborationist Vichy in the light of contemporary events. A tragicomic buffoonery.

Delbo, Charlotte. *Et toi, comment as-tu fait? (Crawling from the Wreckage;* 1978), Unpublished English translation by Brian Singleton.
    A semi-documentary montage of interviews with camps survivors. 'How did you, how did we, how did I survive?' asks Françoise.

Delbo, Charlotte. *Kalavrita des mille Antigone* (1979). Paris: Berg International. (*Kalavrita's One Thousand Antigones.* Unpublished English translation by Karen Alexander.)
    The women of a small village in the Peloponnese remember the days the retreating SS massacred all their menfolk in 1943.

Delbo, Charlotte. *Les Hommes (The Men;* 1978). Unpublished and unperformed.

In a transit camp in Romainville, waiting to be deported to an unknown destination (Auschwitz), French women perform Musset's *Caprice* while some of their men are being shot as hostages.

Delbo, Charlotte. *Scene in Memory* (1967). Unpublished English translation by Claude Schumacher.

The protagonist remembers her last meeting with her Resistance fighter husband before he is executed by the Nazis.

Delbo, Charlotte. *Qui rapportera ces paroles? (Who Will Carry the Word?*; 1966). In Robert Skloot (ed.), *The Theatre of the Holocaust: Four Plays*. Madison: University of Wisconsin Press, 1982.

The lives of French concentration camp prisoners, expressionistically recounted by two survivors.

Deutsch, Michel. *Convoi* (1967). Paris: Stock.

Performed as 'Vichy-Fictions' with Chartreux's *Violences à Vichy*. The everyday lives and struggles of Anne and Marthe, of Jean and Pierre, under the German Occupation.

Eydoux, Emmanuel. *Ghetto à Varsovie* (1960). Marseille: Editions LeConte.

A fictional dramatization of the history of the Warsaw Ghetto and outside reactions to its circumstances.

Fossier, Joëlle. *Les Spécialités d'Albertine* (1996). First performed at Théâtre du Lucemaire, Paris.

The encounter between a French judge, son of a Vichy magistrate, and a young woman whose family was deported during the war. The action is set at the present time.

Gatti, Armand. *Le Chant d'amour des alphabets d'Auschwitz* (1989). In Armand Gatti, *Œuvres théâtrales*. Paris: Verdier, 1991.

A multimedia pageant, performed in Marseille in 1995.

Gatti, Armand. *Chroniques d'une planète provisoire (Chronicles of a Provisional Planet*; 1963, 1967). In Armand Gatti, *Œuvres théâtrales*. Paris: Verdier, 1991.

Astronauts discover a planet on which Jews are being murdered and which is governed by characters who parallel Hitler, Himmler, Eichmann, etc.

Gatti, Armand. *Le Cinécadre de l'Esplanade Loreto* (1990). In Armand Gatti, *Œuvres théâtrales*. Paris: Verdier, 1991.

An avant-garde drama which takes place in Milan at the time Mussolini is hanged, in Marseille where fifteen French hostages were executed by the Nazis, and contains many other historic moments, some connected to World War Two.

Gatti, Armand. *La Deuxième Existence du camp de Tatenberg* (*The Second Existence of the Tatenberg Camp*; 1962). In Armand Gatti, *Œuvres théâtrales*. Paris: Verdier, 1991.

The continued impact of the camps on the lives of a fairground troupe.

Gatti, Armand. *L'Enfant-Rat* (*The Infant Rat*; 1960). In Armand Gatti, *Œuvres théâtrales*. Paris: Verdier, 1991.

Guilt for inhuman acts in the camp haunts survivors.

Gatti, Armand. *Opéra avec titre long* (1986). In Armand Gatti, *Œuvres théâtrales*. Paris: Verdier, 1991.

Gatti, Armand. *Les 7 Possibilités du Train 713 en partance d'Auschwitz* (1988). In Armand Gatti, *Œuvres théâtrales*. Paris: Verdier, 1991. Trans. Teresa L. Jillson. Los Angeles: Sun and Moon Press, 1996.

An avant-garde theatre piece based on the fact that Auschwitz survivors were placed on a train following the camp's liberation by the Soviets and travelled through the ruins of Europe for nine months.

Grumberg, Jean-Claude. *The Free Zone* (1990). Trans. Catherine Temerson, in *The Free Zone* and *The Workroom*. New York: Ubu Repertory Theatre Publications, 1993.

The chronicle of a Jewish family hidden by a peasant in non-occupied France during World War Two and their ultimate liberation.

Grumberg, Jean-Claude. *The Workroom* (1979). Trans. Catherine Temerson, in *The Free Zone* and *The Workroom*. New York: Ubu Repertory Theatre Publications, 1993.

Four Jewish survivors and four French employees of a postwar French clothing workroom attempt to throw off the grip of the Holocaust and World War Two.

Mnouchkine, Ariane. *Mephisto* (1979). Paris: Solin.

    An adaptation of the novel by Klaus Mann about the actor Gustav Gründgens, who collaborated during the Third Reich.

Sartre, Jean-Paul. *The Condemned of Altona* (1959). Trans. Sylvia and George Leeson. New York: Knopf, 1961.

    A German family confronts its war guilt.

Segal, Gilles. *All the Tricks But One* (1992). Trans. Sara O'Connor. New York: Samuel French, 1993.

    The play focuses on Little Slam, a Jewish vaudevillian mime who conceals his background from the Nazis in occupied France. The mime never speaks, to hide his accent.

Segal, Gilles. *The Puppetmaster of Lodz* (1988). Trans. Sara O'Connor. New York: Samuel French, 1989.

    A Jew, who was a master puppeteer and death camp escapee, refuses to believe that World War Two is over and continues to hide in his room in Berlin in 1950, rehearsing a new puppet show which is the story of his camp life.

GERMANY

Borchert, Wolfgang. *The Outsider* (1946). Trans. David Porter. London: Calder and Boyars, 1966.

    A home-coming play about a German soldier.

Brecht, Bertolt. *The Informer* (1939). In Stephen Moore (ed.), *Six Anti-Nazi One-Act Plays*. New York: Contemporary Play Publications.

    A German couple is terrified that their young son has left the house to inform on them for having expressed minimal anti-Nazi sentiments.

Brecht, Bertolt. *The Private Life of the Master Race* (1935–8). Trans. Eric Bentley. New York: New Directions, 1944.

    Short scenes depicting civilian life during the early years of the Third Reich.

Brecht, Bertolt. *Roundheads and Peakheads* (1934). Trans. N. Goold-Verschoyle. In Bertolt Brecht, *Jungle of Cities and Other Plays*. New York: Grove Press, 1966.

Brecht's adaptation of *Measure for Measure*, which presents Hitler's racial policy in Marxist terms.

Bruckner, Ferdinand. *Races* (1934). Trans. Ruth Langner. New York: Alfred A. Knopf.

Set in Germany in 1933, the play dramatizes the effect of the Nazis' early racial laws on a group of young German medical students.

Eich, Günter. *Dreams* (1953). In Everett Frost and Margaret Herzfeld-Sander (eds.), *German Radio Plays*. New York: Continuum, 1991.

A radio play in which the first dream of a series reminds audiences of the train transports to the camps and seems to suggest that this is the recurrent nightmare of contemporary Germany.

Eine Synagoge in Wassenberg: Historische Revue (1988). Typescript available at Yad Vashem.

A theatre piece created by the Theatergruppe der Evangelischen Kirchengemeinde in Wassenberg, which deals with the destruction of the synagogue in Wassenberg.

Goetz, Rainald. *Festung* (1992). Frankfurt-on-Main: Suhrkamp, 1993.

A fictitious dramatized talk show with sixty-six scenes and sub-scenes, with clear referents to the Wannsee Conference, Third Reich leaders, Auschwitz, and the postwar Nazi crime trials.

Hochhuth, Rolf. *Der Stellvertreter* (*The Representative/The Deputy*; 1963). Trans. Richard and Clara Winston. New York: Grove Press, 1964.

A historical play that depicts the attempt by a priest and a rebellious SS officer to persuade the Pope to speak out against the extermination of the Jews.

Kipphardt, Heinar. *Bruder Eichmann* (1983). Reinbek bei Hamburg: Rowohlt.

Eichmann's Israeli captivity, interspersed with twenty-one 'analogy scenes' which draw parallels to the Holocaust in documentary drama fashion.

Kipphardt, Heinar. *Joel Brand* (1964). Frankfurt-on-Main: Suhrkamp, 1965.

The Hungarian Jewish leader Joel Brand's attempt to buy the lives of 1,000,000 Jews from the Germans with the help of the Allies.

Lotar, Peter. *Das Bild des Menschen* (1952). Bonn: Schlimmelbusch, 1954.

A dramatic depiction of the assassination attempt on Hitler in July 1944.

Michelsen, Hans Günter. *Helm* (1965). Frankfurt-on-Main: Suhrkamp.

Five former Nazi soldiers share responsibility for having had their cook assigned to a punishment battalion. Following a reunion in the woods, four are shot, possibly, but not definitively, by Helm, the former cook.

Müller, Heiner. *The Slaughter* (1976).

A grotesque representation of common Germans, including an 'SS-man'.

Sachs, Nelly. *Eli: A Mystery Play of the Sufferings of Israel* (1940). Trans. Christopher Holme. In Elinor Fuchs (ed.), *Plays of the Holocaust.* New York: Theatre Communications Group, 1987.

A surreal, ritualistic, poetic search by Michael, one of God's thirty-six chosen, for the murderer of Eli, an innocent child, slain as his parents were being led to their deaths.

Schneider, Rolf. *Prozess in Nuremberg* (1968). Hamburg: Fischer-Bucherei.

East German documentary drama of the Nuremberg trial.

Schneider, Rolf. *The Story of Moischele* (1965). In Rolf Schneider, *Stücke.* Berlin: Henschelverlag, 1970.

The play depicts, in twelve scenes, the life of a poor Polish villager from ghetto to concentration camp, to postwar profiteering, to a re-education camp in East Germany.

Sperr, Martin. *Koralle Meier* (1970). Frankfurt-on-Main: Verlag der Autoren.

The depiction of the life of a 'beloved whore' in a town bordering on a concentration camp.

Sperr, Martin. *Tales from Landshut* (1967). Trans. Anthony Vivis. London: Methuen, 1969.

Two builders compete in postwar Germany, even though their children wish to marry. The first wife of one of the builders was a Jew killed in a concentration camp and he subsequently changed his daughter's name and religion to shield her from the racial laws. The other builder and his family continue to speak positively of the Third Reich.

Strittmatter, Thomas. *Kaiserwalzer* (1986). In *Viehjud Levi und andere Stücke*. Zurich: Diogenes, 1992.

   A crippled old man suffering from syphilis is associated with Nazi ideology.

Strittmatter, Thomas. *Polenweiher* (1984). In *Viehjud Levi und andere Stücke*. Zurich: Diogenes, 1992.

   Deals with the death of a young Polish girl who does forced labour on a farm.

Strittmatter, Thomas. *Viehjud Levi* (1982). In *Viehjud Levi und andere Stücke*. Zurich: Diogenes, 1992.

   Soon after Hitler's rise to power, Hirsch Levi, a Jewish livestock dealer in a Black Forest village, is shot to death. The case is never solved and the town wishes it to be forgotten.

Sylvanus, Erwin. *Dr Korczak and the Children* (1957). In Michael Benedikt and George Wellwarth (eds.), *Postwar German Theatre*. New York: E. P. Dutton, 1967.

   A Pirandellian presentation of the life of the protector of the orphans in the Warsaw Ghetto.

Theatergruppe der Evangelischen Kirchengemeinde Wassenberg. *Eine Synagoge in Wassenberg* (1988). Typescript can be found in the archives at Yad Vashem.

   An historical revue which commemorates the destruction of the Wassenberg synagogue and the Nazi pogrom of 1938.

Walser, Martin. *Eiche und Angora* (1962). In Martin Walser, *Gesammelte Werke*. Frankfurt-on-Main: Suhrkamp Verlag, 1971. An adaptation by Robert Duncan, entitled *Rabbit Race*, can be found in Martin Walser, *Plays*. London: J. Calder, 1963.

   Scenes from 1945 to the present day detailing the absurd existence of the castrated German survivor Alois.

Walser, Martin. *Der schwarze Schwan* (*The Black Swan*; 1964). In Martin Walser, *Gesammelte Werke*. Frankfurt-on-Main: Suhrkamp Verlag, 1971.

   A Hamlet-like tale in which a son discovers his father's SS past.

Weiss, Peter. *Die Ermittlung* (*The Investigation*; 1965). Trans. Jon Swan and Ulu Grosbard. New York: Atheneum, 1966.

A documentary drama based on the Frankfurt Auschwitz trials of 1963–4.

Wolf, Friedrich. *Professor Mamlock* (1934). Trans. Anne Bromberger. New York: Universum Publishers and Distributors, 1935.
   The Third Reich's racial laws destroy a German Jewish doctor.

Zinner, Hedda. *Ravensbrücker Ballade* (1961). Berlin: Henschel.
   A melodramatic play set in the female internment centre.

Zuckmayer, Carl. *Des Teufels General* (*The Devil's General*; 1946). In Carl Zuckmayer, *Gesammelte Werke*. Berlin: S. Fischer, 1960.
   A general, who loves to fly, secretly opposes the Nazi racial policy, smuggling Jews out of the Reich. Arrested for sabotage, he refuses to reveal the true saboteur and commits suicide.

Zuckmayer, Carl. *Der Gesang im Feuerofen* (*Song of the Furnace*; 1950). In Carl Zuckmayer, *Gesammelte Werke*. Berlin: S. Fischer, 1960.
   The circumstances surrounding the burning to death of twenty French Resistance fighters on Christmas Eve, 1943, are dramatized. German soldiers and French police are given the same names and are to be played by the same actors.

GREAT BRITAIN

Allen, Jim. *Perdition* (1987). Atlantic Highlands, NJ: Ithaca Press.
   A trial in London in 1967 supposedly reveals how some Zionist leaders collaborated with the Nazis prior to and during World War Two. This controversial play's production at the Royal Court Theatre Upstairs was cancelled.

Antrobus, John. *Hitler in Liverpool* (1983). London: J. Calder.
   A pre-World War Two Hitler is depicted absorbing his Fascist and racist ideas from Britain's German population in Liverpool.

Barnes, Peter. *Auschwitz* (1978). In Elinor Fuchs (ed.), *Plays of the Holocaust*. New York: Theatre Communications Group, 1987.
   The one-act play takes place in the bureaucratic office which operates the death camps and has a highly theatrical final scene set in the gas chambers of Auschwitz.

Bond, Edward. *Summer* (1982). London: Methuen.

Set in an Eastern Europe resort island, the play focuses on a present-day encounter between two women, one of whom, a servant to the other's family, had been sentenced to death by the Nazis but was saved by her employer, whom she later testified against for collaborating. Another island tourist is a former German soldier who has returned to what had been the site of a concentration camp.

Burrell, Michael. *Hess* (1980). Ashover, Derby: Amber Lane Press.

A monologue in which Rudolf Hess rationalizes his actions based on England's colonial history and the United States' involvement in Vietnam.

Garner, Julian. *The Flight Into Egypt* (1997). London: Nick Hern Books.

Poland, 1939. Beile, fourteen, Jewish, and already a recognized artist, flees her village's pogrom. In Cracow an ordinary man, a non-Jew, keeps her concealed for four years at enormous personal risk. A remarkable bond develops between them.

Hampton, Christopher. *The Portage to San Cristobal of A. H.* (1982). London: Faber and Faber, 1983.

Adolf Hitler is captured by Israeli Nazi hunters in this stage adaptation of George Steiner's novel.

Harwood, Ronald. *Taking Sides* (1995). In Ronald Harwood, *Plays, Two*. London: Faber and Faber.

Following World War Two, the renowned conductor Wilhelm Furtwängler, who remained in Nazi Germany, is interrogated by an American soldier, who is haunted by the camp he liberated. 'Was Furtwängler a Nazi' is the question at the heart of the play.

Holman, David. *No Pasaran* (1979). In Pam Schweitzer (ed.), *Theatre-in-Education*. London: Eyre Methuen.

A play for young audiences, which details the struggles of a German-Jewish fighter who leaves the Third Reich for England, but is persecuted there by Brownshirts.

Kift, Roy. *Dreams of Beating Time* (1986). Unpublished manuscript, Shiel Land Associates, London.

Classical musicians, prisoners in Theresienstadt, reflect on their lives and careers in Germany, London and New York between 1917 and 1944.

Kift, Roy. *Camp Comedy* (1996). Unpublished manuscript, Shiel Land Associates, London.

In Theresienstadt, Kurt Gerron performs songs and sketches in his cabaret before being forced to collaborate in directing the Nazi propaganda film *Der Führer schenkt den Juden eine Stadt*.

Leer, van Wim . *The Final Solution (D. R. P. 861731)* (1964).

A baking equipment factory is used to build the crematoria for the death camps. While the head engineer exhibits moral qualms – allowing a Jewish prisoner provided for experiments to escape – he is coerced by Nazi terror to continue developing the mechanism for mass cremation.

Leer, van Wim. *Pavane for a Pile of Junk* (1966). Typescript can be found in the archives at Yad Vashem.

A play which takes place in a large loft in a middle-class row of apartments in Frankfurt-on-Main just after World War Two has begun on 2 and 3 September 1939.

Norton-Taylor, Richard. *Nuremberg* (1997). London: Nick Hern Books.

A reconstruction of the trial of the surviving Nazi High Command for crimes against humanity, using only the words spoken at the time.

Pip Simmons Group. *An die Musik* (1975).

A performance piece that presents the dilemma of musicians forced to entertain in a Nazi concentration camp.

Reed, Douglas. *Downfall* (1942).

An imaginary dramatization of the downfall of Hitler in a play that treats that eventuality three years before it occurred.

Samuels, Diane. *Kindertransport* (1993). New York: Plume, 1995.

An Englishwoman, who had been transported to safety, at first refuses to reunite with her mother, who survived the concentration camps, and to admit her past to her daughter. The play concludes with the revelation of the past.

Scanlon, Bob. *What Does Peace Mean?* (1991). Cheshire: New Playwrights' Network.

A play for young audiences in which surviving Jewish teenage inmates of a concentration camp must decide what action to take against the commandant's teenage son.

Shaw, Robert. *The Man in the Glass Booth* (1967). New York: Grove Press, 1968.

A fictionalized treatment of the Eichmann trial.

Taylor, C. P. *Good* (1981). London: Methuen.

A 'good' German professor capitulates to Nazism during the Third Reich.

Wincelberg, Shimon. *Resort 76* (1964). In Robert Skloot (ed.), *The Theatre of the Holocaust: Four Plays*. Madison: University of Wisconsin Press, 1982.

Depiction of the life in the Lodz Ghetto.

HOLLAND

Hartog, Jan de. *Skipper Next to God* (1949). New York: Dramatists Play Service.

A Dutch captain, with 136 Jewish refugees on his ship, attempts unsuccessfully to find safe haven.

HUNGARY

Déry, Tibor. *The Witnesses* (1945). In Tibor Déry, *Felelet: Regeny*. Budapest: Szepirodalmi Konyvkiado, 1981.

The life of a Jewish doctor and his family in Budapest during the Nazi occupation.

Heimler, Eugene. *The Storm* (*The Tragedy of Sinai*; 1976). Trans. Anthony Rudolf. London: Menard Press, 1976.

A play set in Massada, during Roman times, the Middle Ages, and the Holocaust, in order to draw parallels to historic anti-Semitism.

Wenckheim, Nicholas. *Image and Likeness* (1979). Trans. Wanda Grabia. Hicksville, New York: Exposition Press.

A play about Raoul Wallenberg, who saved 50,000 Hungarian Jews.

Wenckheim, Nicholas. *The Wallenberg Mission* (1995).
　　A later version of the story of Raoul Wallenberg, as told in
39 scenes, with 6 actors playing 30 roles.

IRELAND

Forristal, Desmond. *Kolbe* (1982).
　　Dramatization of the Auschwitz imprisonment of the Franciscan
priest who volunteered to die in place of a Jewish prisoner. The Jewish prisoner, the camp commandant Rudolph Hess, and Himmler are characters.

Kilroy, Thomas. *Double Cross* (1986). London: Faber and Faber.
　　A play about Brendan Bracken, Churchill's Minister of Informa-
tion, and William Joyce, an Irishman who broadcast virulent anti-
Semitic Nazi propaganda.

ISRAEL

Adam's Purim Party (1981).
　　A stage adaptation of Yoram Kaniuk's 1971 novel, *Adam, Son of a
Dog*, dealing with a Holocaust survivor. A collective work created by the
Neve Zedek Theatre Centre and directed by Nora Chilton.

Adam Son of a Dog (1993).
　　Another stage adaptation of Yoram Kaniuk's novel. Adam
survived the Holocaust by playing the circus dog for the Nazis and is now
in a mental hospital, reliving his experiences. It was adapted and staged
in 1993 by the Russian immigrant theatre, Gesher.

Amichai, Yehuda. *Bells and Trains* (1966). In *Midstream*, 12 (October
1966), pp. 55–66.
　　An Israeli visits a relative in a German old-people's home, all of
whose inhabitants are survivors of the Nazi concentration camps.

Dagan, Gabriel. *The Reunion* (1972). In *Midstream*, 19 (April 1973),
pp. 4–32.
　　Survivor-playwright Peter Stone, along with other survivors,
stages a replay of the Nazi occupation in order to reveal Third Reich
inhumanity to his uncle, who spent the war years in America.

Eliach, Yaffa and Yuri Assaf. *The Last Jew* (1977). Trans. Yaffa Eliach. Israel: Alef-Alef Theatre Publications.

Vladimir, psychiatrist, converted Jew and Israeli immigrant, is the son of a Nazi collaborator who murdered the Jews in a small conquered town in the Soviet Union. His wife, Bluma, also a psychiatrist, is the daughter of the last Jew of the town, Schneidermann, who remained in the village for thirty years following the war and is now Vladimir's father's business partner. Vladimir and Bluma have two patients, Nachummadman and Maphtir-Yonah, who are lunatic survivors, who force all parties to confront the past.

Eliraz, Israel and Anna Sokolow. *Kenatayim* (1979).

A theatre dance piece which deals with the story of Hannah Senesh and was staged at the Haifa Municipal Theatre.

Goldberg, Leah. *The Lady of the Castle* (1955). Trans. T. Carmi. Tel Aviv: Institute for the Translation of Hebrew Literature, 1974. Also in Michael Taub (ed.), *Israeli Holocaust Drama* (Syracuse, NY: Syracuse University Press, 1996).

Two Israelis, charged with bringing back children who survived the Holocaust, encounter an Eastern European aristocrat who continues to keep a Jewish girl in hiding after the war has ended.

Hameiri, Avigdor. *Blessed be the Match* (1958).

An epic play, in which biographical information about Hannah Senesh is juxtaposed with other Jewish stories of martyrdom.

Hasfain, Shmuel. *Hametz* (1995). Rehearsal manuscript, Tel Aviv: Beth-Lessin Theatre.

Horowitz, Danny. *Tscherly KaTscherly* (1977).

A cabaret-like drama in which a series of pictures are presented by individual speakers. Many of the early 'pictures' deal with images from the Holocaust.

Horowitz, Danny. *Uncle Artur* (1981).

A play based on *The Reunion* by Gabriel Dagan (see above).

Lerner, Motti. *Kastner* (1985). Tel Aviv: Or Am. Also in Michael Taub (ed.), *Israeli Holocaust Drama* (Syracuse, NY: Syracuse University Press, 1996).

Deals with the Hungarian Jewish leader Kastner, who was accused of collaborating with the Nazis but was also responsible for saving hundreds of Jews.

Levin, Hanoch. *The Boy Dreams* (1993). Unpublished translation by Barbara Harshav.

The life of a sleeping boy is disrupted when his home is invaded and his father is brutally murdered. He and his mother become fleeing refugees. In the final scene of the drama, the boy arrives in the land of dead children. While the play is not specifically set during the Holocaust, its imagery is clearly connected to its horrors.

Mayaan, David and Smadar Yaaron. *Arbeit Macht Frei From Toitland Europa* (1991).

A performance piece in which the audience moves through spaces in which they see grotesque imagery connected to the Holocaust and which is contrasted to scenes depicting contemporary sensibilities about the Shoah in Germany and Israel.

Megged, Aharon. *Hanna Senesh* (1958). Jerusalem: World Zionist Organization Department for Education and Culture in the Diaspora, 1974, and Tel Aviv: Or Am, 1989. Also in Michael Taub (ed.), *Israeli Holocaust Drama* (Syracuse, NY: Syracuse University Press, 1996).

The true story of the Jewish girl the Allies sent to Nazi-occupied Hungary in an attempt to save the country's Jewish population.

Megged, Aharon. *Haona Habboret* (*The Burning Season*; 1967). Tel Aviv: Amikam.

A retelling of the story of Job, with Job representing the Jewish survivors of the Holocaust.

Milstein, Avishai. *Piwnica* (1994). Tel Aviv: National Theatre Habima.

The play deals with the making of an American film whose subject matter is Jews in hiding. The father of the author of the screenplay is a Holocaust Survivor.

Mittelpunkt, Hillel, Omry Nitzan, and Avraham Oz. *The Poison Mushroom* (1984).

A documentary drama composed of fictional and non-fictional German writings and speeches dealing with daily, social, or political issues from 1933 to 1939.

Orlev, Uri. *Janusz Korczak* (1985).
Dramatization of the life of the Jewish teacher in the Warsaw Ghetto who died with the orphans he protected.

Porat, Yoram. *The Last Golem Show* (1989).
Inmates in a concentration camp form a theatre company to present a command performance of *The Golem* for the commandant and his entourage.

Sadeh, Yitzhak. *Hannah's Road* (1947).
A dramatization of the Hannah Senesh story.

Shaham, Nathan. *Hesbon Hadas* (*A New Reckoning*; 1954). In *Masach*, 1 (1954), pp. 5–37.
A refugee attempts to start a new life in Israel but is haunted by his having been a kapo.

Shamir, Moshe. *Hayyores* (*The Heir*; 1963). In *Teatron*, 9 (1963), pp. 27–47.
An Israeli poses as a wealthy German Holocaust victim in order to claim the dead man's reparation payments.

Sobol, Joshua. *Adam* (1989). Tel Aviv: Or Am. Also in Michael Taub (ed.), *Israeli Holocaust Drama* (Syracuse, NY: Syracuse University Press, 1996). Translated into German by Jürgen Fischer. Wuppertal: Wuppertaler Bühnen, 1989.
The second in Sobol's Vilna trilogy, this play deals with the resistance in the ghetto. The play focuses on Yitzak Wittenberg, the head of the Vilna resistance, and the Nazis' ultimatum that either the ghetto *Judenrat* turns him over or hundreds will be executed.

Sobol, Joshua. *Ghetto* (1983). In Elinor Fuchs (ed.), *Plays of the Holocaust*. New York: Theatre Communications Group, 1987.
The play takes place in the mind of Srulik, the artistic director of the Vilna Ghetto theatre, and theatrically reconstructs the world of the ghetto and its theatre.

Sobol, Joshua. *The Underground* (1991). Translated and adapted by Ron Jenkins for the première at the Yale Repertory Theatre. Tel Aviv: Or Am.
The last in Sobol's Vilna trilogy, the play opens in the present, with a survivor arriving at a Jerusalem hospital following an Iraqi missile

attack. He has a doctor's diary from Vilna, which leads to flashbacks drama-tizing how the ghetto physicians hid a typhus epidemic from the Nazis.

Strassberg, Sara. *El Rescoldo* (1979). Manuscript available at Yad Vashem.
A Spanish-language play dealing with the Warsaw Ghetto.

Tomer, Ben-Zion. *Children of the Shadows* (1963). Trans. Hillel Halkin.
Tel Aviv: Institute for the Translation of Hebrew Literature, 1982. Also
in Michael Taub (ed.), *Israeli Holocaust Drama* (Syracuse, NY: Syracuse
University Press, 1996).
The effects of the Holocaust on a young survivor who tries to
forget his past but is unable to do so.

ITALY

Franchi, Eva. *La Ragazza di Dachau* (1965). In *Ridotto* (July–August
1965), pp. 59–73.
A tribunal hears of the horrors of Dachau.

Levi, Primo and Pieralberto Marche. *Se questo è un uomo: versionne
drammatica* (1966). Turin: Einaudi.
Stage adaptation of Levi's Auschwitz memoir, *If This Is A Man*.

Moravia, Alberto. *Il dio Kurt* (*The God Kurt*; 1968). Milan: Bompiani.
Kurt, the commandant of a concentration camp, has an imprisoned Jewish family act out the Oedipus myth.

Perotti, Berto. *Kristallnacht* (1961). Available in German translation.
Darmstadt: Progress-Verlag Johann Fladung.
Fictional account of the effects of Kristallnacht on a German
village.

NEW ZEALAND

Fuller, Deb and Alison Summers. *Punch Me in the Stomach* (1991).
The child of an Auschwitz survivor discusses growing up with the
imagined experiences of her survivor father, alternating his story with
stories of her youth.

POLAND

Adamsk, Jerzy. *The World of Stone* (1966).
An adaptation of Tadeusz Borowski's short story.

Bobkowski, Andrzej. *Black Sand* (1959). *Kultura* 145. Unpublished
English translation by Ben Conrad.
    An elderly Polish Jewish survivor kills his daughter's black lover.
In the sub-plot, a Polish woman is married to the Latvian SS officer who
saved her and her mother.

Brandstaetter, Roman. *The Day of Wrath* (1965). Warsaw: Pax, 1962.
Unpublished English translation by Ben Conrad.
    An SS man, a one-time student at a seminary, visits a schoolmate
who is now responsible for the seminary in an occupied country. The
SS officer discovers that a Jew is hidden in the monastery and decides to
capture him.

Fink, Ida. *The Table* (1987). In Ida Fink, *A Scrap of Time and Other Stories.*
Trans. Madeline Levine and Francine Prose. New York: Pantheon Books.
    Jewish Holocaust survivors testify against a man in Poland who is
accused of wartime atrocities.

Grotowski, Jerzy and Jozef Szajna. *Akropolis* (1962).
    A metaphoric representation of the camps, loosely based on
Wyspianski's classic drama, in which the inmates act out their fantasies
until at the end they go to their death.

Hanuszkiewicz, Adam. *Kolmbowie-rocznik 20* (*The Columbus Boys:
Warsaw 44–46*; 1965).
    An adaptation of Roman Bratny's novel of 1957 about the lives of
Polish underground fighters during and immediately following the war.

Heler, Bine. *A House in the Ghetto* (1953).
    A ghetto drama, written in Yiddish, and staged by the Jewish State
Theatre of Poland.

Holuj, Tadeusz. *Puste Pole* (*The Empty Field*; 1963). *Dialog*, 4 (1963),
pp. 4–33.
    A survivor continues to work in a camp that has become a
museum for martyrs.

Iredynski, Ireneusz. *The Modern Nativity Play* (1962). *Dialog*, 7 (November 1962), pp. 15–36. Unpublished English translation by A. M. Furdyna.
    Internees stage a Christmas play written and controlled by the
commandant.

Karren, Tamara. *Who Was This Man?* (n.d.). Unpublished English translation by Jacek Laskowski.

The last days of Janusz Korczak, as he prepares for the deportation of the orphans of the Warsaw Ghetto.

Krall, Hanna. *To Steal a March on God* (1980). Trans. Jadwiga Kosicka. Amsterdam: Harwood Academic Publishers, 1996.

A present-day Marek Edelman, an actual leader of the Warsaw Ghetto Uprising, discusses the reality of the revolt with the 1943 Marek Edelman, with frequent interruptions by his dead comrades.

Mirsky, Mikhl. *Der Kheshbn* (*The Bill*; 1963).

A Communist representation of the Warsaw Ghetto Uprising, in which Communists – Jewish and non-Jewish – are presented as heroes and Zionists as villains.

Moczarski, Kazimierz and Zygmunt Hubner. *Conversations with the Executioner* (1977). Trans. Earl Ostroff and Daniel Gerould. New York: CASTA Publications, 1983.

Imprisoned in the same cell at the close of the war, the non-Communist Polish Resistance leader, Moczarski, confronts Lieutenant-General Jürgen von Stroop, the SS officer responsible for the liquidation of the Warsaw Ghetto.

Nowak, Alina. *Auschwitz Oratorio* (n.d.). Unpublished English translation by A. M. Furdyna.

The verse drama details the horrors of the maternity barracks in Auschwitz.

Prorok, Leszek. *Freya – the Golden Goddess of Love* (1976). Zaklad Narodowy im. Ossolinskich, 1977. Unpublished English translation by Marcus Wheeler.

A German doctor questions the Ravensbrück survivor Agnes Sielska, a Pole who also spent two years at a Nazi-controlled villa at which girls with Nordic features were used to breed 'perfect' human beings.

Szajna, Jozef. *Replika* (1972). Trans. E. J. Czerwinski. In Elinor Fuchs (ed.), *Plays of the Holocaust*, 1987.

Shvinshiniski, Anna. *Janfire in Dulga Street* (1948).
A Yiddish drama dealing with the Holocaust staged by the Jewish State Theatre of Poland.

Sloves, Khayim. *Haman's Defeat* (1950).
A Yiddish drama that uses parallels to the Purim story.

Taborski, Boleslaw. *Guilt* (n.d.). Unpublished English translation by the author.
Present-day encounters of Holocaust victims, victimizers, and the children of both.

Terlecki, Wladyslaw Lech. *Archeologia* (*Archeology*; n.d.).
A radio play in which a journalist investigates a concentration camp survivor who was forced to use his medical training to castrate prisoners.

Wazacz, Mieczyslaw. *Prize-Winner* (n.d.). Unpublished English translation by Jacek Laskowski.
A female director, who won a prize for her film on the Nazi concentration camps, explores Poland's relationships with Germany and Russia.

Wiernik, Bronislaw. *Gwiazdy na Nitce* (*A Star on a String*; n.d.).
A radio play in which a woman, who survived the ghetto by removing her loose star of David, retells her story.

Zawieyski, Jerzy. *The Deliverance of Jacob* (1947). Warsaw: Sztuka. Unpublished English translation by Boleslaw Taborski and Lance Wright.
A husband returns from a concentration camp to discover his wife with a fellow prisoner whom he betrayed.

SCOTLAND

Eveling, Harry Stanley. *The Strange Case of Martin Richter* (1967). In Harry Stanley Eveling, *The Balachites* and *The Strange Case of Martin Richter*. London: Calder and Boyars, 1970.
A fictional/allegorical representation of the rise of Fascism in the home of an industrialist.

MacDonald, Robert. *Summit Conference* (1983). New York: Broadway Play Publishers.

In 1941, Eva Braun meets with Clara Petacci in the Berlin chancellery while Hitler and Mussolini confer.

MacDonald, Robert. *In Quest of Conscience* (1994). First performed at Citizens' Theatre, Glasgow.

Dramatization of Gitta Sereny's *Into That Darkness*, her account of conversations with Franz Strangl, commandant at Sobibor and Treblinka, as well as with his family members and colleagues.

SOVIET UNION

Galitzky, Y. *The Cave* (1944). In M. G. Mayorga (ed.), *Plays of Democracy*. New York: Dodd, Mead, 1944.

A German Jewish doctor refuses the Nazis' offer to allow him to treat soldiers at his old hospital and to leave the ghetto.

SWITZERLAND

Frisch, Max. *Andorra* (1961). In Max Frisch, *Three Plays*. London: Methuen Drama, 1992.

A supposed Jewish boy is murdered because of political pressure from a neighbouring state.

Frisch, Max. *Nun singen sie wieder* (*Now They Are Singing Again*; 1945). In Max Frisch, *Gesammelte Werke*. Frankfurt-on-Main: Suhrkamp, 1976.

The destruction of humanism is illustrated in the story of a Nazi soldier who executes hostages.

UNITED STATES

Ackerman, Michael F. *Goldberg's Kaddish* (1995).

The husband of a survivor kills a former Nazi, who has received minimal punishment for his crimes and has been elected mayor of a German town.

Adler, Esther. *The Brothers* (1983). New York: Board of Jewish Education.

A play for young audiences which portrays the difficulties of a Jewish boy, Dov, who emigrates to Israel from Nazi-occupied Poland, without his family. At the close, he is reunited with his younger brother.

Adler, Esther. *Lech Lecha – Go Forth* (1983). New York: Board of Jewish Education.

A play for young audiences which dramatizes, in flashbacks, the friendship of two Jewish girls living in Third Reich Germany. One chooses to leave for Israel, the other remains.

Adler, Esther. *Me-afelah le'or Gadol* (1983). New York: Board of Jewish Education.
    A sequel to *Lech Lecha – Go Forth*.

American Jewish Ensemble. *The Theatre of Peretz* (1976).
    An adaptation in which concentration camp inmates present the Peretz stories.

Allen, John. *The Other Man* (1967). New York: Samuel French, 1970.
    Israeli agents track down a former Nazi now living in Buenos Aires.

Anderson, Maxwell. *Candle in the Wind* (1941). Washington, DC: Anderson House.
    An American actress, in love with a French Resistance fighter who is imprisoned in a Nazi concentration camp, lends strength to his cause.

Baitz, Jon Robin. *The Substance of Fire* (1991). New York: Samuel French, 1992.
    A survivor book publisher fights to keep his business from his children.

Benet, Stephen Vincent. *They Burned the Books* (1942). New York: Farrar and Rinehart.
    A radio play which details the book-burning policy of the Nazis and brings to life those authors whose works were outlawed, with a particular focus on Heine.

Bernard, Kenneth. *How We Danced While We Burned* (1973). In Kenneth Bernard, *Two Plays*. Santa Maria, CA: Asylum Arts, 1990.
    A cabaret/quiz show theatrical representation of Nazi brutality. The MC is a Nazi victimizer.

Bernt, Peter. *The Pretext* (1939). In Stephen Moore (ed.), *Six Anti-Nazi One Acts Plays*. New York: Contemporary Play Publications.
    A one-act play in which an exiled German Jew accidentally kills a Nazi diplomat in Paris, providing the Nazis with a pretext for a pogrom to strip the Jews of their property and wealth in Germany.

Bianchi, Dan. *Night and Fog* (1978).

A stranger forces an ex-SS officer, now living secretly in the United States, to confront his past.

Boothe, Clare (Luce). *Margin for Error* (1939). New York: Random House, 1940.

A mystery in which a Jewish–American policeman is sent to protect a Nazi German consul. When the consul is murdered, the policeman uncovers the killer to protect international Jewry from further propagandistic attacks.

Bowie, Tom. *The Pit* (1991). In Tom Bowie, *Three Plays for Reading.* St Charles, IL: Seven Oaks Press.

A US army platoon liberates a Nazi death camp.

Brady, Michael. *Korczak's Children* (1983).

The drama deals with Korczak's attempt to save his orphanage and children in the Warsaw Ghetto. Emmanuel Ringelblum, the Ghetto chronicler, is a secondary character in the play.

Caisley, Robert. LETTERS TO AN ALIEN (Woodstock, IL: Dramatic Publishing Company, 1996).

A young Jewish girl learns about the Holocaust and the concept of hate while visiting her grandfather, who is a camp survivor. Her lessons are further reinforced when she is transported back to Poland during the war by space aliens.

Citron, Samuel J. *The Little People* (1945). New York: Jewish Education Committee.

A French couple hides Jewish children as well as French and surviving Jewish Resistance fighters on the eve of the Normandy invasion. The children aid the invading forces by preventing the Nazis from blowing up a bridge.

Cooperman, Melvin I. *Dispatches from Hell* (1985). In Melvin I. Cooperman, *Off-Off Broadway Festival Plays*, 10th series. New York: Samuel French.

An exploration of the role the German railroads played in the extermination of the Jews.

Coopersmith, Jerome. (libretto); William Goldstein (music); Joe Derion (lyrics). *Oswego* (1993). Typescript can be found in the archives at the US Holocaust Memorial Museum, Washington, DC.

Based on *The Haven* by Ruth Gruber, this musical dramatizes the plight of 1,000 refugee survivors who were allowed to emigrate temporarily to Oswego, New York. Imprisoned in a military fortress, a female State Department official, who falls in love with one of the survivors, tries to gain permanent residence for them.

Cornish, Roger. *Offshore Signals* (1989).

Dramatization of the failure of American leaders to save 70,000 Jews in Rumania in 1943. Mixes historical figures (FDR, Rabbi Stephen Wise, Cordell Hull, Breckenridge Long) with fictional characters, such as a Jew who escaped from Poland and who details Holocaust horrors.

Cowan, Sada. *Auf Wiedersehn* (1937). In Rachel France (ed.), *A Century of Plays by American Women*. New York: Richards Rosen Press, 1979.

A Jewish woman, who has raised her dead Christian friend's children, commits suicide in order to protect them from the Nazi racial policies.

Craft, H. S. *The Bishop of Münster* (1939). In Stephen Moore (ed.), *Six Anti-Nazi One Acts Plays*. New York: Contemporary Play Publications.

A monologue by a bishop in which he protests against the Nazis' policy of incarcerating Jews and others in concentration camps. The play closes with the sounds of Nazis entering the church and a woman's scream.

Cristofer, Michael. *The Black Angel* (1982). New York: Dramatists Play Service, 1984.

A former SS officer, now living in France, is confronted by his past.

Deutsch, Henri Zvi. *The Eternal Light* (1986). Typescript can be found in the archives at Yad Vashem.

A radio play set in the Lodz Ghetto in September 1944.

Dimondstein, Boris. *Hitler's Victims* (1957). In Boris Dimondstein, *Short Plays and One-Act Plays*. Tujunge, CA: Literarishe Helfn, 1957.

A one-act play, in which the adopted parents of a surviving German Jewish child help him cope with the terrors of his past.

Ehrlich, Max. *Der Führer (and the Great Lie He Borrowed)* (1944). Typescript available in the Theatre Research Division of the Lincoln Center Library for the Performing Arts.

A radio play which outlines the history of the *Protocols of the Elders of Zion* and how this work influenced the Nazis' racial policy.

Etlinger, Nini. *The Promised Land* (n.d.)

A play based on Brecht's ballad about children who travelled across war-torn Poland, unsuccessfully searching for a land of peace.

Fox, Susan (libretto) and Joel Mandelbaum (composer). *The Village* (1995).

An opera about Houdan, a French village which hid two Jewish brothers from the occupying Nazis.

Freed, Morris. *The Survivors: Six One-Acts* (1956). Trans. A. D. Mankoff. Cambridge, MA: Sci-Art Publishers.

A series of Yiddish one-act dramas depicting survivors immediately following the war. Some are realistically set in DP camps, others surrealistically represent the Holocaust. For example, in one, soap speaks of the horrors perpetrated on the Jews; in another, voices of liquidated Jews call for a judgement.

Friedman, Leah K. *Before She Is Even Born* (1982).

Raisel, who escaped pre-Nazi Europe using her sister's passport, is confronted in memory by her mother, who died before the war, and her sister and her sister's daughter, who perished in the Holocaust.

Giron, Arthur. *Edith Stein* (1988). New York: Samuel French, 1991.

The play opens in the convent outside the gates of Auschwitz and then presents continuous scenes depicting the life of the nun – and convert from Judaism – Edith Stein, from just after World War One to her death in Auschwitz.

Goodrich, Frances and Albert Hackett. *The Diary of Anne Frank* (1956). New York: Harcourt Brace Jovanovich, 1993; New York: Dramatists Play Service, 1986; New York: Random House, 1956.

A stage adaptation of the world-famous diary.

Green, Phoebe. *Blessed is the Match* (1981).

Dramatization of Hannah Szenes' heroism.

Greenspan, Hank. *Remnants* (1992). First performed, Michigan Radio Theatre, WUOM-FM.

Both a radio and a stage play in which six Holocaust survivors reflect on the destruction and on what it may mean to live after.

Harbach, Otto. *Hitler Has a Vision* (1943). Typescript available in the Theatre Research Division of the Lincoln Center Library for the Performing Arts.

An outdoor pageant in which Hitler is visited by Satan and the Spirit of Decency; Hitler is forced to view his horrific deeds and his eventual defeat.

Harvey, Dorcas. *The Refugee* (1944). In M. G. Mayorga (ed.), *Plays of Democracy*. New York: Dodd, Mead.

An anti-Semitic naturalized German American objects to an apartment building allowing a Jewish refugee to move in after leaving Europe. The refugee, when he arrives, brings miracles with him and is almost Christ-like in image.

Hashisha, Jacob Weinberger. *Justice, Justice Shall You Pursue* (1989). Typescript can be found in the archives at the US Holocaust Memorial Museum, Washington, DC.

The final judgement of Nazi leaders in the presence of God, the prophets, and the matriarchs.

Hecht, Ben. *A Flag Is Born.* (1946). New York: American League for a Free Palestine.

A pageant arguing for the establishment of the state of Israel, using Holocaust survivors as protagonists.

Hecht, Ben. *We Will Never Die* (1943). New York: Committee for a Jewish Army of Stateless and Palestinian Jews.

A theatrical pageant presented at Madison Square Garden to call attention to the mass murder of Europe's Jews.

Hellman, Lillian. *Watch on the Rhine* (1941). New York: Dramatists Play Service, 1971.

An anti-Nazi German Resistance fighter is forced to kill a Rumanian Nazi sympathizer while both are visiting their German in-laws in the United States. The sympathizer threatens to blackmail the Resistance supporter and prevent him from returning to Germany to aid imprisoned colleagues.

Herstand, Theodore. *The Emigration of Adam Kurtzik* (1987).
Tragicomic representation of the bungling head of a Jewish Council in a small ghetto.

Kader, Boris M. *Dervakhung: A Drame in Tray Aktn fun dem Idishen Leben in Natsi-Daytshland* (1939). Chicago: Arbeiter Velt.
A Yiddish melodramatic family drama about Jews in Germany in 1932 and 1933, during the beginnings of the Third Reich's racial policies.

Karo, Inge Heilman. *The Library* (1993). Typescript can be found in the archives at the US Holocaust Memorial Museum, Washington, DC.
A seven-minute children's play about a young girl who must give up her library card following the enactment of the Reich's early racial laws. In the opening scene, the girl is living in the United States and is a children's librarian.

Katz, Morris. *The Nazi's Jewish Daughter* (1947). London: Nerod Press.
A Yiddish play in which a German, who later becomes a Nazi, adopts a Jewish child prior to the rise of Nazism. The play takes place between 1923 and 1945, concluding in America following the war.

Katz, Susan B. *Courage Untold* (1986; revised 1991). Typescript can be found in the archives at the US Holocaust Memorial Museum, Washington, DC.
Jewish women working in the ammunition factory in Auschwitz assist the underground with its plot to blow up the crematorium. After the explosion the women smugglers are caught but do not reveal the membership of the underground, even after they are beaten and sentenced to death.

Kesselman, Wendy. *I Love You, I Love You Not* (1983). New York: Samuel French.
A granddaughter who is struggling with adolescence and her Jewish identity visits her survivor grandmother.

Kozlenko, William. *Jacob Comes Home* (1939). In Stephen Moore (ed.), *Six Anti-Nazi One-Act Plays*. New York: Contemporary Play Publications.

A one-act in which a German Jewish family awaits the return of their father from an early concentration camp. The irony is that his ashes are returned to the family at the play's close.

Krakow, Michael. *The False Witness* (1995).
Hitler is judged in front of the ultimate tribunal.

Kraus, Joanna Halpert. *Remember My Name* (1989). New York: Samuel French.
An eleven-year-old Jewish child hides in an isolated French mountain village. The child reunites with her survivor father in 1945.

Lampell, Mildred. *The Wall* (1960). New York: Samuel French, 1964.
An adaptation of John Hersey's novel.

Larche, Douglas W. *Number the Stars*. Woodstock, IL: Dramatic Publishing, 1996.
During the German occupation of Denmark two young non-Jews try to help their Jewish friend escape to Sweden. The play is an adaptation of Lois Lowry's award-winning book.

Lebow, Barbara. *A Shayna Maidel* (1984). New York: Dramatists Play Service, 1988.
Two sisters, separated before the war, are reunited in New York City after World War Two; one has grown up in America, the other is a camp survivor.

Leitner, Isabella. *Fragments of Isabella* (1984).
Dramatic readings of segments of Leitner's Auschwitz memoir.

Leivick, H. *Miracle of the Warsaw Ghetto* (1944).
A Yiddish fictional dramatization of the uprising in the Warsaw Ghetto.

Levitt, H. N. *The Beasts* (1970). Typescript available in the Theatre Research Division of the Lincoln Center Library for the Performing Arts.
The incarceration of a fictional last member of Hitler's inner circle becomes an obsession for the Allies. In visions, the prisoner sees Hitler, Goebbels, and Goering.

Lieberman, Harold and Edith. *Throne of Straw* (1973). In Robert Skloot (ed.), *The Theatre of the Holocaust: Four Plays*. Madison: University of Wisconsin Press, 1982.

An epic play about Mordechai Chaim Rumkowski, the chairman of the *Judenrat* (Jewish Council) in the Lodz Ghetto.

Lieberman, Susan and Stephen J. Morewitz. *Steamship Quanza* (1991).

Based on the true story of two married US maritime lawyers who fought to have eighty-two Jewish refugees admitted at the port in Hampton Roads, Virginia, and who were assisted in their battle by Eleanor Roosevelt.

Linney, Romulus. 2 (1993). New York: Dramatists Play Service.

Depicts the interrogation of Hermann Goering at the Nuremberg trial.

Mann, Emily. *Annulla: An Autobiography* (1978; revised 1985). New York: Theatre Communications Group, 1985.

A young American searching for her family in Europe spends an afternoon with an elderly woman who recounts the true story of how she passed for Aryan, got her husband out of Dachau, and escaped to England.

Marans, Jon. *Old Wicked Songs* (1996). Garden City, NY: Fireside Theatre, 1996.

An American pianist, unable to play for emotional reasons, studies in Vienna with a teacher he believes to be a Nazi sympathizer. After a visit to Dachan and the revelation that his teacher is a camp survivor, the pianist rediscovers his Jewish past and the ability to play.

Margulies, Donald. *The Model Apartment* (1988). New York: Dramatists Play Service, 1990.

Set in a model apartment in a condominium development in Florida, two survivors and their mentally unstable daughter – named after the father's first child who was murdered by the Nazis – struggle with memories of the Holocaust. There are also references to the Holocaust in Margulies' *The Loman Family Picnic* (1989) and *Sight Unseen* (1992).

Miller, Arthur. *Broken Glass* (1994). New York: Penguin.

After seeing photos of Kristallnacht, a once-healthy American wife suffers from a mysterious paralysis. Her husband and doctor do not understand the significance of the event in the same way she does.

Miller, Arthur. *Incident at Vichy* (1964). New York: Viking, 1965.

Set in a detention centre in France, the play contrasts the fate of a group of Jews who are soon to be sent to a death camp with a 'mistakenly' detained non-Jewish character.

Miller, Arthur. *Playing for Time* (1985). Woodstock, IL: Dramatic Publishing Company. First shown as a screenplay in 1980, later presented in a stage version.

After her arrest in Paris, Fania Fénelon, a singer, is sent to Auschwitz where she is forced to join the female orchestra founded to entertain the camp commandant. As long as the musicians find favour, they are spared the gas chamber: they are 'playing for time'.

Miller, Boruch. *Here Is Your Jew!* (1934). Trans. Herman Eichenthal and the author. In Boruch Miller, *The Wet King*. Verlag, 1979.

A Yiddish play in which a Jewish farmer, his non-Jewish wife, and their daughter all suffer under the Nazis' early racial laws. The farmer, a war hero, goes to the Nazi official whose life he saved in World War One to ask that he stop the persecution of his family. Instead, he is brought back dead to his family.

McDonagh, Richard P. *War Criminals and Punishment* (1944). Typescript available in the Theatre Research Division of the Lincoln Center Library for the Performing Arts.

A radio play which presents a fictional trial of Hitler, in which his atrocities are outlined. Jews bear witness. Argues that Hitler and his hierarchy must be held accountable.

Nanus, Susan. *The Survivor* (1981).

Seven children survive as smugglers in the Warsaw Ghetto. Based on the memoir of Jack Eisner.

Nelson, Tim Blake. *The Grey Zone* (1996).

Drama focusing on the life of the twelfth Sonderkommando at Auschwitz, a Jew who struggled to survive and save his family by collaborating with the Nazis.

Newman, Louis I. *The Pangs of the Messiah* (1944). *Menorah Journal*, 32.4 (Autumn 1944), pp. 186–201.

    A one-act set in a little synagogue in the Eastern zone. Jews resist and stave off a massacre.

Ozick, Cynthia. *Blue Light (The Shawl*; 1994).

    Two Holocaust survivors, Rosa and her niece Stella, confront their past differently in Miami in 1979: the elder never escaping, frequently seeing her dead daughter Magda in her mind, while the younger wishing to forget. Based on Ozick's two pieces of fiction, *The Shawl* and *Rosa*.

Page, Alex. *The Cancelled Sky* (1989). In: Susan Vick (ed.), *From Valley Playwrights Theatre*. Amherst, MA: Playwrights Press.

    An expanded version of an earlier radio play which dramatizes the transport of Jewish women from Czechoslovakia in 1944 to a concentration camp.

Pearson, Sybille. *Unfinished Stories* (1992). New York: Dramatists Play Service, 1993.

    Three generations of a Jewish family confront the revelation that the survivor grandfather escaped at the cost of the life of a radical German Jewish intellectual friend.

Perry, Ruth. *The Great Hope* (1974). Woodstock, IL: Dramatic Publishing Company.

    In Nazi-occupied Vienna, a young woman with Jewish ancestry wears the star of David to show solidarity with her Jewish friends.

Raspanti, Celeste. *I Never Saw Another Butterfly* (1971). Woodstock, IL: Dramatic Publishing Company.

    Dramatic adaptation of poems and drawings by children in Theresienstadt.

Raspanti, Celeste. *No Fading Star* (1979). Chicago: Dramatic Publishing Company.

    In 1943, German Jewish children are taken to the border for escape by an underground network functioning out of a convent.

Robinson, Marvin W. *Exodus* (1949). In M. G. Mayorga (ed.), *Best One-Act Plays, 1949–50*. New York: Dodd, Mead, 1950.

Jewish refugees are returned to Europe after being denied admission elsewhere.

Roth, Ari. *Born Guilty* (1991). New York: Samuel French, 1994.

Based on the book by Peter Sichrovsky, a journalist and child of survivors, explores the past through interviews with former Nazis, average German citizens, and their children.

Ruffini, Gene. *The Choice* (1979). New York: Center for Holocaust Studies.

A former Nazi SS officer, responsible for the deaths of 2,300 Jews in a small Polish ghetto, is now a repentant priest who oversees a New York City mission for wayward teenagers. Should a hunter of Nazi war criminals bring him to trial?

Sack, Leeny. *The Survivor and the Translator* (1980). In Lenora Champagne (ed.), *Out from Under: Texts by Women Performance Artists*. New York: Theatre Communications Group, 1990.

According to the creator, 'a solo theatre work about not having experienced the Holocaust by a daughter of concentration camp survivors'. This highly physical performance piece includes testimony from the performer's maternal grandmother.

Schechter, David. *Hannah Senesh* (1984).

A one-woman drama detailing the life of the young Hungarian girl used by the Allies in an attempt to save the Jews of Hungary.

Schenkar, Joan. *The Last of Hitler* (1982).

A radio show in which Hitler is presented in a dreamlike landscape of personalities and places, including a Hasidic Jew who turns on the radio, Hitler and Braun who are hiding in a Miami retirement home, and a Dr Reich who does a Charlie McCarthy/Edgar Bergen routine with the skeleton of a six-year-old child and who has Goebbels and Goering hidden in his laboratory.

Schevill, James. *Cathedral of Ice* (1975). In Elinor Fuchs (ed.), *Plays of the Holocaust*. New York: Theatre Communications Group, 1987.

Set in Hitler's cathedral, the play is a musical revue in which despots from many ages appear. Among the characters are 'Night and Fog', representative of those who suffered in the Holocaust.

Schwartz, Jerome L. *Laugh God!* (1939). In Stephen Moore (ed.), *Six Anti-Nazi One-Act Plays*. New York: Contemporary Play Publications.

A one-act which opens and closes with the Nazis burning books by Jews, while the rest of the play dramatizes the great nationalistic fervour of the nineteenth-century German Jewish author Heine, who was forced to live in France for reasons of health.

Sherman, Martin. *Bent* (1979). New York: Avon, 1980.

A depiction of the Nazi oppression of homosexuals in the concentration camps.

Steinhorn, Harriet. *Shadows of the Holocaust* (1983). Rockville, MD: Kar-Ben Copiers.

A series of one-acts for children, detailing life, usually from the perspective of the young, in ghettos and concentration camps.

Swados, Elizabeth. *The Secret Window* (1997).

A musical for young audiences which deals with children hiding in Nazi-conquered Poland. The play was created in collaboration with the Dutch theatre company, Het Waterhuis.

George, Tabori. *Jubiläum* (1983). In George Tabori, *Theaterstücke*, vol. II., Frankfurt-on-Main: Fischer, 1994.

In a cemetery on the banks of the Rhine, victims of the Third Reich, disturbed by neo-Nazi acts of desecration, rise from their graves. Victims and perpetrators, sometimes interchanging roles, replay their tragedies.

Tabori, George. *Die Kannibalen* (*The Cannibals*; 1968). In Robert Skloot (ed.), *The Theatre of the Holocaust: Four Plays*. Madison: University of Wisconsin Press, 1982.

Two survivors and sons of camp inmates relive an act of cannibalism that occurred in the camp.

Tabori, George. *Mein Kampf* (1986). In Carl Weber (ed.), *Drama Contemporary: Germany*. Baltimore: Johns Hopkins University Press, 1996.

Trans. into German by Ursula Tabori-Grützmacher.[1] Munich: Hanser. Also in *Theaterstücke*. (See Tabori, *Mutters Courage*, below.)

    A farce set in a pre-World War Two flophouse; Hitler is befriended and protected by the Jewish Bible salesman, Herzl.

Tabori, George. *Mutters Courage (My Mother's Courage*; 1979). In George Tabori, *Theaterstücke*, vol. II. Foreword by Peter von Becker. Trans. into German by Ursula Tabori-Grützmacher, Peter Hirche and Peter Sandberg. Frankfurt-on-Main: Fischer, 1994.

    Dramatization of the deportation of the playwright's mother to Auschwitz.

Tabori, George. *Weisman and Copperface* (1990). Wien: Burgtheater Wien. Also in *Theaterstücke*. (See Tabori, *Mutters Courage*, above.)

    A spoof on westerns with Weisman, a Holocaust survivor, in the desert with his daughter and a bag of his wife's ashes. They encounter an Indian with whom Weisman has a high-noon confrontation, duelling over who suffered more.

Taylor, Will. *At the Wire's Edge* (1989).

    Five women are working voluntary service for the German army outside a Polish concentration camp. One is a scientist who experiments on inmates.

Toll, Nellie and William Kushner. *Behind A Closed Window* (1981).

    Dramatization of a diary of a nine-year-old Jewish girl in German-occupied Poland during World War Two.

Volkas, Armand. *Survivors* (1978).

    A play based on the author's parents' experiences as Resistance fighters and Auschwitz prisoners. Recreates the progression of events, from ghettoization to the transports.

Weill, Gus. *Rosenfeld's War* (1988).

    Documentary drama of the failed Congressional hearings that would have allowed 20,000 refugee children from Germany to enter the United States.

---

[1] George Tabori writes in English. However, his plays have been published in German translations and produced primarily in Vienna and other German-language theatres.

Wiesel, Elie. *A Black Canopy, A Black Sky* (1968).

A one-act drama, written in commemoration of the twenty-fifth anniversary of the Warsaw Ghetto Uprising, set in an underground bunker in an unnamed ghetto. A husband and wife are in hiding, joined by an itinerant Jewish preacher. The husband is mad because he mistakenly believes his wife has been killed by the Nazis. He has created a fantasy fiancée – a make-believe sister to his real wife – whose return he awaits.

Wishengrad, Morton. *The Battle of the Warsaw Ghetto* (1943). In Erik Bartow (ed.), *Radio Drama in Action*. New York: Farrar and Rinehart, 1945.

A radio play which details the daily life in the ghetto and the eventual uprising.

URUGUAY

Terrara, Louis Novas (Newlander). *Yom Kippur* (1973).

Three Jews in a death camp (an assimilated banker, a beggar, and a rabbi) are forced to put on an amusing play on Yom Kippur in order to save their lives. The entertainment, which uses the belongings of murdered Jews as props and scenery, fails to amuse their captors and they are condemned to die.

Select bibliography

Adler, H. G., *Die verheimlichte Wahrheit, Theresienstädter Dokumente* (Tübingen: Mohr, 1958).

Theresienstadt, 1941–1945. Das Antlitz einer Zwangsgemeinschaft, Geschichte, Soziologie, Psychologie (Tübingen: Mohr, 1960).

Améry, Jean, *At the Mind's Limits: Contemplations by a Survivor on Auschwitz and its Realities*, translation by Sydney Rosenfeld and Stella P. Rosenfeld (Bloomington: Indiana University Press, 1980).

Amichai, Yehuda, 'Bells and Trains', in *Midstream*, 2 (October 1966), pp. 55–66.

Antelme, Robert, *L'Espèce humaine* (Paris: Gallimard, 1996; first published 1957).

Appelfeld, Aharon, *For Every Sin*, translation by Jeffrey M. Green (New York: Weidenfeld and Nicolson, 1989).

Arendt, Hannah, *Eichmann in Jerusalem: A Report on the Banality of Evil* (New York: Viking Press, 1964; Harmondsworth: Penguin, 1977).

Atlan, Liliane, *Les Mains coupeuses de mémoire* (Paris: P. J. Oswald, 1961).

Le Maître-mur (Paris: Action poétique, 1962).

Monsieur Fugue ou le mal de terre (Paris: Le Seuil, 1967).

La petite voiture de flammes et de voix (Paris: Le Seuil, 1968).

Lapsus (Paris: Le Seuil, 1971).

Rêve des animaux rongeurs (Paris: L'Ether vague, 1980).

Les Passants (Paris: Payot, 1980; translated into English as *The Passers-by*, New York: Henry Holt and Company, 1993).

Les Musiciens, les émigrants (Paris: Editions des Quatre-vents, 1993).

Un opéra pour Terezin. In *L'Avant-Scène*, 1007–8 (1–15 April 1997).

Avisar, Ilan, 'The Evolution of the Israeli Attitude Toward the Holocaust as Reflected in Modern Hebrew Drama' in *Hebrew Annual Review*, 9 (1985), pp. 31–52.

Screening the Holocaust: Cinema's Images of the Unimaginable (Bloomington and Indianapolis: Indiana University Press, 1988).

Barzel, Hilel, *Drama of Extreme Situations: War and Holocaust* (Tel Aviv: Sifriat Poalim, 1995).

Bauer, Yehuda, *Fight and Rescue: Bricha* (New York: Random House, 1970).

American Jewry and the Holocaust (Detroit: Wayne State University Press, 1981).

'The Place of the Holocaust in Contemporary History', in *Holocaust: Religious and Philosophical Implications*, edited by John K. Roth and Michael Berenbaum (New York: Paragon House, 1989).

'Kasztner, Reszso' in *The Encyclopedia of the Holocaust* (London, 1990), vol. II, pp. 787–90.

Baumel, Judith Tydor, 'The Heroism of Hannah Senesz: An Exercise in Creating Collective National Memory in the State of Israel', in *Journal of Contemporary History*, 31.3 (1996), pp. 521–46.

Bayerdörfer, Hans-Peter, ed., *German–Israeli Theatre Relations After the Second World War* (Tübingen: Niemeyer Verlag, 1996).

Bayerdörfer, Hans-Peter and Schönert, Jorg, eds., *Theater gegen das Vergessen: Bühnenarbeit und drama bei George Tabori* (Tübingen: Niemeyer Verlag, 1997).

Ben-Ami, Yitshaq, *Years of Wrath Days of Glory* (New York: Robert Speller and Sons, 1982).

Benedikt, Michael and Wellworth, George, *Postwar German Theatre* (London, 1968).

Bernhard, Thomas, *Eve of Retirement*, in *The President* and *Eve of Retirement: Plays and Other Writings*, translation by Gitta Honegger (New York: Performing Arts Journal Publications, 1982).

Heldenplatz (Frankfurt-on-Main: Suhrkamp Verlag, 1988).

Bernstein, Michael André, *Bitter Carnival: Ressentiment and the Abject Hero* (Princeton: Princeton University Press, 1992).

Foregone Conclusions: Against Apocalyptic History (Berkeley and Los Angeles: University of California Press, 1994).

Blau, Herbert, 25 *yor yidisher melukhe-teater in folks-poyln* (Warsaw: Arkady, 1975).

Take up the Bodies: Theater at the Vanishing Point (Urbana: University of Illinois Press, 1982).

Bondy, Ruth, *Elder of the Jews: Jaerb Edelstein of Theresienstadt*, translated by Grdyn Adel (New York: Grove Press, 1989).

Bosmajian, Hamida, *Metaphors of Evil: Contemporary German Literature and the Shadow of Nazism* (Iowa City: University of Iowa Press, 1979).

Broder, Henrik, 'Das richtige Stück für das falsche Publikum', in Joshua Sobol, *Ghetto* (Berlin: Quadriga, 1984), pp. 215–26.

Brown-Naveh, Edith, 'Dramaturgical Problems in Plays with the Theme of the Holocaust', Ph.D. thesis, University of Pittsburgh, 1977.

Champagne, Leonora, 'Armand Gatti: Toward Spectacle Without Spectators', in *Theater*, 13.1 (1982), pp. 26–42.

Coe, Richard, 'Armand Gatti's Carnival of Compassion: *La Deuxième Existence du camp de Tatenberg*', in *Yale French Studies*, 46 (1971), pp. 60–7.

'The Theatre of the Last Chance: Catastrophe Theory in the Plays of Armand Gatti', in *Australian Journal of French Studies*, 20.1 (1983), pp. 71–92.

Créer pour survivre, (Paris: Fédération Nationale des Déportés et Internés Résistants et Patriotes, 1996).

Czerniakow, Adam, *Carnets du ghetto de Varsovie: 6 septembre 1939–23 juillet 1942* (Paris: Editions la Découverte, 1996).

Daviau, Donald G., 'Thomas Bernhard's *Heldenplatz*', in *Monatshefte* 83.1 (Spring 1991), pp. 29–44.

Davis, Colin, *Elie Wiesel's Secretive Texts* (Gainsville: University of Florida Press, 1994).

Delbo, Charlotte, *Le Convoi du 24 janvier*, written in 1946, published in 1965 (Paris: Editions de Minuit).

Aucun de nous ne reviendra (Genève: Editions Gonthier, 1965; Paris: Editions de Minuit, 1970).

La Sentence (Paris: P. J. Oswald, 1969).

Une connaissance inutile (Paris: Editions de Minuit, 1970).

Mesure de nos jours (Paris: Editions de Minuit, 1971).

Qui rapportera ces paroles? (Paris: P. J. Oswald, 1974; *Who Will Carry the Word?*, translated by Cynthia Haft, in *The Theatre of the Holocaust*, edited by Robert Skloot (University of Wisconsin Press, 1982)).

Kalavrita des mille Antigone (Paris: Editions LMP, 1977, 1979).

Spectres, mes compagnons (Lausanne: Maurice Bridel, 1977; translated by Rosette Lamont, *Massachusetts Review*, 1971).

La mémoire et les jours (Paris: Berg International, 1985; English translation, London: Marlboro Press, 1990).

Auschwitz and After, translation by Rosette C. Lamont with an introduction by Lawrence L. Langer (New Haven: Yale University Press, 1995).

Diner, Dan, 'Negative Symbioses: Germans and Jews after Auschwitz', in *Reworking the Past: Hitler, the Holocaust, and the Historians' Debate*, edited by Peter Baldwin (Boston: Beacon Press, 1990), pp. 251–61.

Douglas, Lawrence, 'Film as Witness: Screening *Nazi Concentration Camps* Before the Nuremberg Trial', in *Yale Law Journal*, 105 (1995).

'The Memory of Judgment: The Law, the Holocaust and Denial', in *History and Memory*, 7.2 (Fall/Winter 1996).

Dowden, Stephen D., *Understanding Thomas Bernhard* (South Carolina: University of South Carolina Press, 1991).

Heldenplatz: Eine Dokumentation (Vienna: Burgtheater, 1989).

Drein, Peter, *'Holocaust': Anatomie eines Medienereignisses* (Wien: n.p., 1979).

Dror, *Matsbi-hayer shel Yitshak Sadeh 'ha-zaken'* (Tel Aviv: Hotsaat ha-kibuts hameuhad, 1996).

Du Plessix Gray, Francine, 'When Memory Goes: The Rise and Fall of Klaus Barbie', in *Adam and Eve in the City* (New York: Simon and Schuster, 1987).

Ellul, Jacques, *Propaganda. The Formation of Men's Attitudes* (New York: Vintage Books, 1973).

Encyclopaedia of the Holocaust, edited by Israel Gutman (New York: Macmillan, 1995).

Federico, Joseph A., 'Millenarianism, Legitimation, and the National Socialist Universe in Thomas Bernhard's *Vor dem Ruhestand*', in *Germanic Review*, 59.4 (1984), pp. 142–8.

Feinberg, Anat, 'The Appeal of the Executive: Adolf Eichmann on the Stage', in *Monatshefte*, 78 (1986), pp. 203–14.

Wiedergutmachung im Programm: Jüdisches Schicksal im deutschen Nachkriegsdrama (Cologne: Prometh Verlag, 1988).

Feingold, Ben-Ami, *The Theme of the Holocaust in Hebrew Drama* (Tel Aviv: Hakkibutz Hameuchad, 1989).

'Hebrew Holocaust Drama as a Modern Morality Play', in *Theatre in Israel* (Ann Arbor: University of Michigan Press, 1996), pp. 269–83.

Feldman, Yael, ' "Identification with the Aggressor" or the "Victim's Complex", Holocaust Ideology in Israel: Theatre Ghetto by Joschua Sobol', *Modern Judaism*, 5 (Baltimore: Johns Hopkins University Press), pp. 165–78.

Felman, Shoshana and Laub, Dori, *Testimony: Crises of Witnessing in Literature, Psychoanalysis and History* (New York: Routledge, 1992).

Felsmann, B. and Prümm, K., *Kurt Gerron – Gefeiert und Gejagt* (Berlin: Hendrichs Verlag, 1992).

Fetherling, Doug, *The Five Lives of Ben Hecht* (Toronto: Lester and Orpen, 1977).

Finkielkraut, Alain, *The Defeat of the Mind*, translation by Judith Friedlander (New York: Columbia University Press, 1995; first published 1987).

Remembering in Vain: The Klaus Barbie Trial and Crimes Against Humanity, introduction by Alice Y. Kaplan, translation by Roxanne Lapidus and Sima Godfrey (New York: Columbia University Press, 1992).

Finter, Helga, ' "E bello raccontare i guai passati": Primo Levi, Schriftsteller und Zeuge', in *Romanische Zeitschrift für Literaturgeschichte/ Cahiers d'Histoire des Littératures Romanes*, 49 (1993), pp. 437–50.

Frank, Margit, *Das Bild des Juden in der deutschen Literatur im Wandel der Zeitgeschichte. Studien zu jüdischen Gestalten und Namen in deutschsprachigen Romanen und Erzählungen 1918–1945* (Freiburg: HochschulVerlag, 1987).

Frenzel, Elisabeth, *Judendarstellung auf der deutschen Bühne* (Munich, 1940).

Friedlander, Saul, *Reflections of Nazism: An Essay on Kitsch and Death*, translation by Thomas Weyr (New York: Harper and Row, 1982; Avon Discus Books, 1986).

'The Shoah Between Memory and History', in *Jerusalem Quarterly*, 53 (Winter 1990), pp. 116–25.

Friedlander, Saul, ed., *Heldenplatz: Eine Dokumentation* (Vienna: Burgtheater, 1989).

Probing the Limits of Representation: Nazism and the 'Final Solution' (Cambridge, MA: Harvard University Press, 1992).

Frenzel, Elisabeth, *Judendarstellung auf der deutschen Bühne* (Munich: Volksverlag, 1940).

Fromm, Erich, *Die Furcht vor der Freiheit* (Frankfurt-on-Main: Europäische Verlagsanstalt, 1973).

Fuchs, Elinor, ed., *Plays of the Holocaust: An International Anthology* (New York: Theatre Communications Group, 1987).

Gatti, Armand, *Les Analogues du réel* (Toulouse: L'Ether vague, 1988).

Œuvres théâtrales, 3 volumes, with introduction and presentations by Michel Séonnet (Paris: Verdier, 1991).

Gatti, Stéphane and Séonnet, Michel, *Gatti: Journal illustré d'une écriture* (Paris: Artefact, 1987).

Glassberg, David, *American Historical Pageantry* (Chapel Hill: University of North Carolina Press, 1990).

Goldfarb, Alvin, 'Theatre and Drama and Nazi Concentration Camps', Ph.D. thesis (University of New York City, 1978).

'A Selected Bibliography of Plays of the Holocaust', in Fuchs, ed., *Plays of the Holocaust*, pp. 303–10.

Goldwasser, Lee, 'Literature of the Holocaust: An Analysis', Ph.D. thesis, California State University, 1981.

Goslan, Richard J., ed., *Memory, The Holocaust, and French Justice* (Hanover, NH: University Press of New England, 1996).

Gozlan, Gérard and Pays, Jean-Louis, *Gatti Aujourd'hui* (Paris: Le Seuil, 1970).

Green, Gerald, *The Artists of Terezin* (New York: Hamthom Books, 1969).

Greenspan, Hank, 'Who Can Retell?: On the Recounting of Life History by Holocaust Survivors', Ph.D. thesis (Brandeis University, 1985).

Remnants, 1991. First produced for radio in 1992 by the Michigan Radio Theatre, WUOM-FM; Ann Arbor, Michigan.

'Lives as Texts: Symptoms as Modes of Recounting in the Life Histories of Holocaust Survivors', in George Rosenwald and Richard

Ochberg, eds., *Storied Lives: The Cultural Politics of Self-understanding* (New Haven: Yale University Press, 1992).

'Making a Story From What is Not a Story: The Oral Narratives of Holocaust Survivors', in Joachim Knuf, ed., *Texts and Identities: Studies on Language and Narrative* (Lexington: University of Kentucky, College of Communications and Information Studies, 1995).

On Listening to Holocaust Survivors: Recounting and Life History (Westport, CT: Praeger Publishers, 1998).

Grimm, Reinhold and Hermand, Jost, eds., *Geschichte im Gegenwartsdrama* (Stuttgart and Berlin: W. Kohlhammer, 1976).

Gronius, Jürg W. and Kässens, Wend, eds., *Theatermacher* (Frankfurt: Athenäum Verlag, 1987), pp. 157–74.

Tabori (Frankfurt: Athenäum Verlag, 1989).

Gudberry, Glen, *Theatre in the Third Reich* (Westport, CT: Greenwood Press, 1995).

Gutman, Israel, ed., *Encyclopaedia of the Holocaust* (New York: Macmillan, 1995).

Gutman, Israel and Michael Berenbaum, eds., *Anatomy of the Auschwitz Death Camp* (Bloomington: Indiana University Press, 1994).

Halperin, Samuel, *The Political World of American Zionism* (Detroit: Wayne State University Press, 1961).

Hampton, Christopher, *George Steiner's Portage to San Cristobal of A. H.* (London: Faber and Faber, 1983).

Hasfari, Shmuel, *Hametz* (Tel Aviv: Beth-Lessin Theatre, 1995).

Hartman, Geoffrey H., ed., *Holocaust Remembrance: The Shapes of Memory* (Oxford: Blackwell, 1994).

Hass, Aaron, *The Aftermath: Living with the Holocaust* (Cambridge: Cambridge University Press, 1995).

Hecht, Ben, *The Book of Miracles* (New York: Scribner and Sons, 1939).

Hecht, Ben and MacArthur, Charles, *It's Fun to be Free* (New York: Fight for Freedom, 1941).

'Remember Us', *American Mercury* (February 1943).

We Will Never Die (New York: Committee to Save the Jewish People of Europe, 1943).

A Guide for the Bedevilled (New York: Garden City, 1945).

A Flag Is Born (New York: American League for a Free Palestine, 1946).

A Child of the Century (New York: Simon and Schuster, 1954).

Herf, Jeffrey, 'The "Holocaust" Reception in West Germany: Right, Center and Left', in *New German Critique*, 19 (1980), pp. 30–52.

Hersh, Amy, 'A Survivor's Voice', in *American Theatre*, 5.8 (November 1988), pp. 8–9.

Hilberg, Raul, *The Destruction of the European Jews*, 3 volumes (Chicago: Quadrangle Books, 1961; revised edition, New York and London: Holmes and Meier, 1985).

    Perpetrators, Victims, Bystanders: The Jewish Catastrophe, 1933–1945 (London: Lime Tree Press, 1993).

    The Politics of Memory: The Journey of a Holocaust Historian (Chicago: Ivan R. Dee, 1996).

Hirsch, David H., *The Deconstruction of Literature: Criticism After Auschwitz* (Hanover, NH: Brown University Press, 1991).

Hirt-Manheimer, Aron, 'The Long Road to Liberation', in *Reform Judaism*, 24.1 (Fall 1995), pp. 10–19.

Honegger, Gitta, 'Thomas Bernhard', in *Partisan Review*, 58.3 (1991), pp. 493–505.

Huyssen, Andreas: 'The Politics of Identification: "Holocaust" and West German Drama', in *New German Critique*, 19 (1980), pp. 117–36.

Innes, Christopher D., *Modern German Drama: A Study in Form* (Cambridge: Cambridge University Press, 1979).

Ireland, John, 'Armand Gatti, Subject to History: The Problem of Representation', in *Modern Drama*, 25.3 (1982), pp. 374–86.

Isser, E. R., 'Toward a Feminist Perspective in American Holocaust Drama', in *Studies in the Humanities*, 17 (December 1990), pp. 139–48.

Kaminska, Ida, *My Life, My Theater*, edited and translated by Curt Leviant (New York: Macmillan, 1973).

Kaplan, Alice Y., *Reproductions of Banality: Fascism, Literature and French Intellectual Life* (Minneapolis: University of Minnesota Press, 1986).

Karas, Joseph, *Music in Terezin, 1941–1945* (New York: Leo Baeck Institute, 1985).

Kaynar, Gad, ' "Get Out of the Picture, Kid in a Cap": On the Interaction of the Israeli Drama and Reality Convention', in *Theatre in Israel* (1996), pp. 285–301.

    ' "What's Wrong with the Usual Description of the Extermination?!" National Socialism and the Holocaust as a Self-Image Metaphor in

Israeli Drama: The Aesthetic Conversion of a National Tragedy into Reality-Convention', in Bayerdörfer, ed., *German–Israeli Theatre Relations*, pp. 200–16.

Kift, Roy, *Camp Comedy* (unpublished playscript, 1996).

Kluger, Ruth, *Weiter leben* (Gottingen: Wallstein, 1992).

Knapp, Bettina, *Liliane Atlan* (Amsterdam: Rodopi, 1988).

Knowles, Dorothy, *Armand Gatti in the Theatre: Wild Duck Against the Wind* (London: Athlone Press, 1989).

Kramer, Richard, 'Annulla', in *Studies in American Drama, 1945-Present*, 4 (1989), p. 286.

Kravetz, Marc, *L'Aventure de la parole errante* (Toulouse: l'Ether vague, 1987).

Krakow, Robert M., *The False Witness* (unpublished playscript).

Kristeva, Julia, *Pouvoirs de l'horreur. Essais sur l'abjection* (Paris: Le Seuil, 1980).

Kubiak, Anthony, *Lexicon fun der nayer yidisher literatur* (New York: fun altveltlikhn yidishn kultur-kongres and Tsiko, 1963).

Stages of Terror: Terrorism, Ideology, and Coercion as Theater History (Bloomington: Indiana University Press, 1991).

Langer, Lawrence L., *The Holocaust and the Literary Imagination* (New Haven: Yale University Press, 1975).

'Interpreting Survivor Testimony', in Berel Lang, ed., *Writing the Holocaust* (New York and London: Holmes and Meier, 1988), pp. 26–40.

Versions of Survival: The Holocaust and the Human Spirit (Albany: State University of New York Press, 1982).

Holocaust Testimonies: The Ruins of Memory (New Haven: Yale University Press, 1991).

Admitting the Holocaust: Collected Essays (New York: Oxford University Press, 1995).

Laurence, Jerome, *Actor: The Life and Times of Paul Muni* (New York: Samuel French, 1974).

Lea, Charlene A., *Emancipation, Assimilation and Stereotype: The Image of the Jew in German and Austrian Drama, 1800–1850* (Bonn: Bouvier Verlag, H. Grundmann, 1972).

Lederer, Zdenek, *Ghetto Theresienstadt* (London: Goldston, 1953; New York: Fertig, 1983).

Lerner, Motti, *Kastner*, translation by Emre Goldstein, in *Modern International Drama*, 27.1 (1993).

Levi, Primo, *Se questo è un uomo* (Florence: De Silva, 1947; Turin: Einaudi, 1958); also in *Opere*, vol. 1 (Turin: Einaudi, Biblioteca dell'Orsa, 1987); translated by Stuart Woolf as *Survival in Auschwitz: The Nazi Assault on Humanity* (New York: Collier Books, 1961).

Se questo è un uomo. Versione drammatica di Pieralberto Marché Primo Levi (Turin: Einaudi, Collezione di Teatro, 99), 13 October 1966.

Opere, 3 volumes (Turin: Einaudi, Bibliotheca dell'Orsa, 1987, 1988, 1990).

The Drowned and the Saved, translated by Raymond Rosenthal (New York: Summit Books, 1988; London: Abacus, 1989).

If This Is A Man and *The Truce*, translated by Stuart Woolf (London: Abacus, 1996).

Levin, Hanoch, 'The Child Dreams', in *Plays (4)* (Tel Aviv: Siman Kriah–Hakkibutz Hameuchad, 1991), pp. 261–331.

Lewis, Helen, *A Time to Speak* (Belfast: Blackstaff Press, 1992).

Lichtenstein, Heiner, ed., *Die Fassbinder-Kontroverse oder das Ende der Schonzeit* (Königstein: Athenäum–Verlag, 1986).

Lindenberger, Herbert, *The History in Literature: On Value, Genre, Institutions* (New York: Columbia University Press, 1990).

Lookstein, Haskel, *Were We Our Brothers' Keepers? The Public Response of American Jews to the Holocaust, 1938–1944* (New York: Vintage Books, 1988).

MacAdams, William, *Ben Hecht: The Man Behind the Legend* (New York: Scribner's Sons, 1990).

Malkin, Jeanette R., 'Pulling the Pants off History: Politics and Postmodernism in Thomas Bernhard's *Eve of Retirement*', in *Theatre Journal*, 47.1 (March 1995), pp. 105–19.

Mannoni, Octave, *Clefs pour l'imaginaire ou l'autre scène* (Paris: Le Seuil, 1969).

Mark, Ber, *Der Oyfshtand in Varshever geto* (Moscow, 1947).

Märthesheimer, Peter and Frenzel, Ivo, eds., *Im Kreuzfeuer: Der Fernsehfilm 'Holocaust'. Eine Nation ist betroffen* (Frankfurt-on-Main: Fischer Taschenbuch, 1979).

Masters, A., *The Summer that Bled: The Biography of Hannah Senesh* (London: Mitchell and Valentine, 1974).

Megged, Aharon, 'Hannah Szenes', translation by Michael Taub, in *Modern and International Drama*, 27.1 (1993).

Migdal, Ulrike, *Und die Musik spielt dazu, Chansons und Satiren aus dem KZ Theresienstadt* (Munich, 1986).

Milstein, Avishai, *Piwnica* (Tel Aviv: National Theatre Habima, 1994).

Mirski, Mikhl, *Der Kheshbn*, Number 138, Archive of Panstwowy Teatr Zydowski Im. E. R. Kaminskiej (Warsaw, 1963).

Morgan, Ted, *An Uncertain Hour: The French, the Germans, the Jews, the Klaus Barbie Trial, and the City of Lyon, 1940–1945* (New York: Morrow, 1990).

Morteo, Gian Renzo, 'Gli autori italiani e il nostro teatro', in *I Quaderni del Teatro Stabile*, 8 (Torino, 1966), pp. 5–17.

Nehring, Wolfgang, 'Die Bühne als Tribunal. Das Dritte Reich und der Zweiten Weltkrieg im Spiegel des dokumentarischen Theaters', in *Gegenwartliteratur und Drittes Reich*, edited by Hans Wagener (Stuttgart: P. Reclam, 1977), pp. 69–94.

Neumann-Riegner, Heinz, *Das Prinzip Leben, Macht, Widerstand and Erinnerung im Werk Armand Gattis* (Bonn: Romanistischer Verlag, 1993).

Nora, Pierre, 'Between Memory and History: *Les Lieux de mémoire*', translated by Marc Roudebush, in *Representations*, 26 (1989), pp. 7–29.

Ohngemach, Gundula, 'George Taboris Theaterabeit. Eine Analyse der Probenarbeit am Beispiel von "*Jubiläum*"', M. A. dissertation (Munich, 1983).

George Tabori (Frankfurt: Fischer Verlag, 1989).

Patraka, Vivian M., 'Fascist Ideology and Theatricalization', in *Critical Theory and Performance*, eds., Janelle G. Reinelt and Joseph R. Roach (Ann Arbor: University of Michigan Press, 1992), 336–49.

Patterson, Michael, 'The Final Chapter: Theatre in the Concentration Camps of Nazi Germany', in Glen W. Gudberry, ed., *Theatre in the Third Reich – Essays in Theatre in Nazi Germany*, (Connecticut: University of Connecticut Press, 1995), pp. 157–65.

Pauley, Bruce F., *From Prejudice to Persecution: A History of Austrian Anti-Semitism* (Chapel Hill: University of North Carolina Press, 1992).

Pazdro, Michel, 'L'Œuvre à l'affiche', in *Avant-Scène Opéra*, 107 (March 1988).

Polli, Gabriella and Calcagno, Giorgio, *Echi di una voce perduta. Incontri, interviste e conversazioni con Primo Levi* (Milan: Mursia, 1992).

Porat, Dina, 'Hannah Szenes', in *The Encyclopedia of the Holocaust* (London, 1990), vol. IV, pp. 1447–8.

Pres, Terrence Des, *The Survivor: An Anatomy of Life in the Death Camps* (New York: Oxford University Press, 1976).

Ringelblum, Emmanuel, *Notes for the Warsaw Ghetto: The Journal of Emmanuel Ringelblum*, translated and edited by Jacob Sloan (New York: Schocken Books, 1974).

Rokem, Freddie, 'Cultural Transformations of Evil and Pain: Some Recent Changes in the Israeli Perception of the Holocaust', in Bayerdörfer, ed., *German–Israeli Theatre Relations*, pp. 217–38.

Ronzier, Rolf, 'Theater als Prozess, Die Theaterarbeit George Taboris', M.A. dissertation (Berlin University, 1988).

Rosenfeld, Alvin, 'Jean Améry as Witness', in *Holocaust Remembrance: The Shapes of Memory*, ed. Geoffrey H. Hartman (Oxford: Blackwell, 1994), pp. 59–69.

Roskis, David G., *Against the Apocalypse: Response to Catastrophe*, in *Modern Jewish Culture* (Cambridge, MA: Harvard University Press, 1985).

Roth, Philip, 'Philip Roth et Primo Levi', in *Lettre Internationale*, 15 (Winter 1987), pp. 25–31.

Rothchild, Sylvia, *Voices from the Holocaust* (New York: New American Library, 1981).

Sadeh, Yitzak, *Lohamin: arbaah mahozot* (Tel Aviv: Hotsaat ha-kibuts hameuhad, 1952).

Sanders, Ronald, *The Days Grow Short: The Life and Music of Kurt Weill* (New York: Holt, Reinhart and Winston, 1980).

Sandrow, Nahma, *Vagabond Stars. A World History of Yiddish Theater* (New York: Harper and Row, 1977).

Schatz, Jeff, *The Generation: The Rise and Fall of the Jewish Communists of Poland* (Berkeley: University of California Press, 1991).

Schiff, Ellen, *From Stereotype to Metaphor: The Jew in Contemporary Drama* (Albany: State University of New York Press, 1982).

Schmelzkopf, Christiane, *Zur Gestaltung jüdischer Figuren in der deutsch-sprachigen Literatur nach 1945* (Hildesheim, Zürich, New York: Olms, 1983).

Schwarz, Egon. *'Helden*platz?' in *German Politics and Society*, 21 (Fall 1990), pp. 33–47.

Schwertfeger, Ruth, *Women of Theresienstadt – Voices from a Concentration Camp* (Oxford, New York and Hamburg: Berg, 1989).

Segev, Tom, *The Seventh Million: The Israelis and the Holocaust*, translation by Hiam Watzman (New York: Hill and Wang, 1993; originally published 1991).

Semprun, Jorge, *L'Ecriture ou la vie* (Paris: Gallimard, 1994).

Semprun, Jorge and Elie Wiesel, *Se taire est impossible* (Paris: Arte, 1995).

Senesh, Hanna, *Her Life and Diary*, introduced by Abba Eban (New York: Schocken Books, 1972).

Shacham, Nathan, *A New Account* (Tel Aviv: Or Am, 1989).

Shapira, Arie, *The Kastner Trial*, electronic opera in thirteen scenes (1991–4), compact disk published by the Society of Authors, Composers and Music Publishers in Israel, catalogue number AS-001.

Shmeruk, Chone, *Sholem Aleikhem. His Life and Literary Work* (Tel Aviv: Publications of the Porter Institute for Poetics and Semiotics, Tel Aviv University, 1980).

Shoham, Chaim, *The Drama of the 'Native Born' Generation in Israel (Challenge and Reality in Israeli Drama)* (Tel Aviv: Or Am, 1989), pp. 255–62.

Sibony, Daniel, 'L'affect racial', in *Ecrits sur le racisme* (Paris: Christian Bourgeois, 1988), pp. 22–72.

Skloot, Robert, *The Theater of the Holocaust: Four Plays* (Madison: University of Wisconsin Press, 1982).

The Darkness We Carry: The Drama of the Holocaust (Madison: University of Wisconsin Press, 1988).

'Stage Nazis: The Politics and Aesthetics of Memory', in *History and Memory*, 6.2 (Fall/Winter 1994).

Sorg, Bernhard, 'Die Zeichen des Zerfalls: Zu Thomas Bernhards *Auslöschung* und *Heldenplatz'*, in *Thomas Bernhard*, ed. Heinz Ludwig Arnold, *Text + Kritik*, 43 (1991), pp. 75–87.

Thomas Bernhard (Munich: Verlag C. H. Beck, 1992).

Spies, Gerty, *Drei Jahre Theresienstadt* (Munich: C. Kaiser, 1984). English translation: *My Years in Theresienstadt* (Amherst, NY: Prometheus Books, 1997).

Starke, Käthe, *Der Führer schenkt den Juden eine Stadt. Bilder – Impressionen – Reportagen – Dokumente* (Berlin: Hande und Spenersche Verlagsbuchhandlung, 1975).

Szanto, George S. *Theatre & Propaganda* (Austin and London: University of Texas Press, 1978).

Tabori, George, 'Hamlet in Blue', in *Theatre Quarterly*, 5.20 (December 1975–February 1976), pp. 116–32.

Unterammergau oder die guten Deutschen (Frankfurt: Suhrkamp Verlag, 1981).

Jubiläum, in *Theater Heute*, 2 and 3 (1983).

Betrachtungen über das Feigenblatt (Frankfurt: Hanser Verlag, 1991).

Theaterstücke, translated by Ursula Grützmacher-Tabori, Peter Hirche and Peter Sandberg, 2 volumes (Munich and Vienna: Hanser Verlag, 1994).

Tancelin, Philippe, ed., *Théâtre sur paroles* (Toulouse: l'Ether vague, 1989) [Published papers of the international 'Salut Armand Gatti' Conference, 22–3 April 1988, Université de Paris VIII].

Temple, Emanu-El, *And So We Must Remember: Holocaust Remembrances* (Oak Park, MI: Temple Emanu-El, 1992).

Todorov, Tzvetan, *The Fantastic: A Structural Approach to a Literary Genre* (Ithaca, NY: Cornell University Press, 1975).

Tomer, Ben-Zion, *Children of the Shadow* (Tel Aviv: Amikam, 1963).

Tory, Avraham, *Surviving the Holocaust: The Kovno Ghetto Diary*, translation by Jerzy Michalowicz (Cambridge, MA: Harvard University Press, 1990).

Trunk, Isaiah, *Judenrat: the Jewish Councils in Eastern Europe Under Nazi Occupation* (New York: 1972).

Urian, Dan and Yaari, Nurit, 'Ghetto – From Play to Performance', in *Bama*, 98–9, pp. 116–36.

Welker, Andrea, ed., *George Tabori: Dem Gedächtnis, der Trauer und dem Lachen gewidmet* (Vienna and Linz: Bibliothek der Provinz, 1994).

Wiesel, Elie, *A Jew Today*, translated by Marion Wiesel (New York: Random House, 1978).

Wiervorka, Annette, 'Indicible ou inaudible? La déportation: premiers récits (1944–1947)', in *Parades*, 9–10 (Paris, 1989), pp. 23–51.

Witz, Yehiam, *The Man Who Was Murdered Twice* (Jerusalem: Keter Publishing, 1995) [Hebrew].

Wyman, David, *The Abandonment of the Jews. America and the Holocaust 1941–1945* (New York: Pantheon Books, 1984).

Yachil-Wachs, Miriam, 'Circus as a Madhouse', in *Yediot Achronot*, 22 October 1993.

Zuckerman, Yitshak, *A Surplus of Memory: Chronicles of the Warsaw Ghetto Uprising* (Berkeley: University of California Press, 1993).

Index

compiled by Luc Schumacher

Index

Index